Seapower
and
Strategy

SEAPOWER
and
STRATEGY

Colin S. Gray
Roger W. Barnett

Editors

NAVAL INSTITUTE PRESS
Annapolis, Maryland

Library of Congress Cataloging-in-Publication Data
Seapower and strategy / Colin S. Gray, Roger W. Barnett, editors.
p. cm.
Includes bibliographies and index.
ISBN 0-87021-579-5
1. Sea-power. 2. Naval strategy. 3. Naval art and science—
History. 4. Naval history. I. Gray, Colin S. II. Barnett, Roger W.
V25.S424 1989
359'.03—dc20 89-33233
CIP

This edition is authorized for sale only in the United States,
its territories and possessions, and Canada.

Printed in the United States of America
9 8 7 6 5 4 3 2
First printing

Contents

Contents

vi

Foreword

As president of the Naval Institute, I am pleased that we are able to offer to students of maritime affairs a single volume that masterfully presents a wide range of thinking on seapower and its uses. In addition to chapters by scholars and practitioners of naval warfare that deal in depth with the theory and history of seapower, Colin Gray and Roger Barnett have succeeded in presenting some enduring principles of conflict in the maritime environment.

Seapower and Strategy captures the richness of maritime strategies and operations, seeking to draw from them important constants of interest to professional and student alike. This book will fill an important place as a resource for all those who think about the employment of naval forces in time of conflict. In an era when conflict is never very far away, such thinking is not optional—it is a necessity. Equally important, *Seapower and Strategy* will contribute to an informed dialogue on the principles of the use of naval forces in support of national policy that will go far toward the development of a well-read population that understands the principles of maritime strategy. Such an understanding, supported by a nation that believes in the need to maintain the freedom of the seas upon which its survival ultimately rests, will ensure that freedom endures.

C. Trost

ADMIRAL CARLISLE A. H. TROST, USN
Chief of Naval Operations

Introduction

First and foremost, one should remember that *there is an enduring geopolitical difference between land and sea that affects importantly how man thinks about his natural habitat, the land, and an environment that is fundamentally hostile to him, the sea. The natural condition of the land is to be politically controlled.* With unimportant exceptions, all of the landmasses of the world today are politically organized by sovereign states. While one might argue about relative differences in the amount of sovereignty actually exercised by various countries, the world has evolved into a large system of nation-states, and only one state "rules" a unique piece of territory at one time. Joint ownership of land areas must be placed in the column that is marked "rare," and history indicates that such a condition is artificial and does not last long.

The natural condition of the sea, in sharp contrast, is to be uncontrolled. In modern times, for reasons of national security, the interface between land and sea was not at the geographic shoreline, but a short distance at sea in order to provide a buffer zone for the littoral state. As the ability of states to control sea areas adjacent to their shorelines has improved over time, and as the ability to claim the ocean's resources has become greater, there has been pressure to move those boundaries farther and farther seaward. Yet, the "rule of law" in the open oceans differs significantly and fundamentally from the control over land by a sovereign power (territorial state), which has the sole power to make and impose the laws within its borders.

Wars, for the most part, have been fought to gain control of the land. States have also joined in combat to gain control of sea areas. Sea control, however, is not permanent. It is employed for a discrete purpose, over a finite period of time. These observations lead to the second theme of the book: *States seek to control the open seas in order to affect or influence what is happening on the land.* In this way, the impact of seapower is primarily strategical. As a general rule, seapower is not capable of direct, decisive action to secure territorial objectives in war. It is able, however, to contribute to efforts ashore and "influence the course and the outcome" of war, as the Soviets might put it. But it is unable to act decisively in the determination of sovereign control over the land. That must be accomplished by land forces. Incorrectly or improperly employed, on the other hand, seapower is fully capable of being instrumental in losses so serious that the objectives of war become unattainable.

There is a corollary to this line of thought, which is also important to note. In its traditional modes, seapower cannot easily threaten vital or core national interests. Maritime warfare erodes strength and vitality (trade, overseas investments, and political influence), but it does not destroy industry or territory at a stroke.

It should be understood that seapower and landpower are not abstractions, endowed conclusively with some mystical quantity and quality. Recognition of this gives rise to the third theme: Conflicts between great sea powers and great land powers are always between particular states that have particular strengths and weaknesses. Before conclusions are drawn about the meaning of a given incident, practice, or outcome in which seapower was involved, one must ask whether it was British or U.S., or Roman, or Dutch, or another brand of seapower in a specific historical context that is the true subject, rather than seapower per se. In this way, seapower and its exercise must always be concretely linked to a historical context.

The principles of war, the lessons of strategy, and the manner of combat as they have been developed in the context of land warfare should not uncritically be carried over into maritime strategy or warfare. This constitutes the fourth general theme. Activities at sea take place outside the view of the ordinary citizen. Most people have never been to sea on a ship, or outside the sight of land, and therefore they have no direct experience about things maritime to which to relate. Because there are no topographical features at sea (except other ships), the familiar signposts that regularly orient and guide man's life are unavailable. Unless they are traveling in company, or sailing along a major trade route, ships at sea are generally not in sight of one another.

The lack of firsthand knowledge about the sea results in a broad ignorance in the general populace about seafaring. This helps also to explain much of the mystery and superstition that accompanies folklore about the sea. It indicates why most prominent strategists knew and wrote only about land warfare, and, for the most part, were completely unaware of the difference. The world has witnessed far fewer giants when it comes to strategizing about seapower than about landpower.

The offensive is the stronger form of combat at sea. This will continue to be the case because the defense lacks most of the attributes that make it so strong on land. According to an acknowledged naval expert of some forty years ago:

> At sea . . . all the conditions that on land tend to strengthen the defense *vis-à-vis* the attack are absent. No common frontier enables the defender to establish and maintain contact; no accidents of ground help to canalise his opponent's advance into predictable lines, nor to support him in making his stand. On the contrary, once on the open sea an attacker . . . enjoys practically unlimited possibilities for evading the defender's forces and falling by surprise upon some part of his far-flung commitments. Incertitude as to the opponent's dispositions and movements is thus the normal and characteristic condition of naval warfare.*

The offensive form of combat is attractive also because the inventory of capital ships—even in large, world-class navies—is relatively small, rendering them lucrative targets. Because of the small number and signal importance of capital ships, sinking one tends to be an event of strategic significance. Destruction or capture of land or air units, even large ones, only infrequently carries strategic meaning. Thus, it is common to see a strategic defensive mixed with a tactical offensive at sea. The offense in such a case might not attempt to take command of the sea, but would seek either to whittle the enemy down to size or to dispute control—while avoiding major fleet action.

The sixth theme recognizes that *landpower must contend with more "friction" than must seapower.* Geography, both physical and political, impedes the extension, consolidation, and exploitation of landpower

---

*Herbert Rosinski, "Mahan and World War II: A commentary from the United States," in B. Mitchell Simpson III, *The Development of Naval Thought: Essays by Herbert Rosinski* (Newport, RI: Naval War College Press, 1977), 23–24. This particular essay dates from 1941.

in ways that have no approximate parallels at sea. The balance of advantage tends to shift to seapower in protracted conflict because dominant landpower generates countervailing opposition. That is, the fact of very powerful land armies causes other states to amass their own armies in self-defense. These states—ones that seek to resist preponderant land powers—can be enlisted in a common anti-hegemonic cause by preeminent seapower. Stated directly: continental superstates perennially overreach themselves even in their own preferred environment of combat. (This is not to deny that a great maritime power also can overreach itself—as the chapter on Athens and Sparta makes abundantly plain.)

The next theme recognizes that *sea powers and land powers throughout history often have had great difficulty in reaching the enemy's center of strategic gravity for the purpose of forcing a favorable decision.* If total defeat of the enemy is the objective, sea powers and land powers have to find strategies for engagement with the strength of their adversary, otherwise limited objectives may be sought and secured by either power, and the other be incapable of preventing success. Still, in modern times no country has succeeded in achieving preponderance both on land and at sea. Strategic geography mandates that every country has a principal environmental focus for its system of deterrence and war. Great land powers have constructed powerful navies, and great sea powers have built powerful armies, but *in extremis* every country is obliged to be more attentive either to landward or to seaward threats.

As number eight on the list of themes, note that *sea powers and land powers focus strategic confidence in their traditional military instrument of excellence.* An essentially maritime or continental tradition (habit of mind, orientation, strategic culture, etc.) more often than not leads to the *misuse* of the traditionally *non-preferred* military instrument. Sea powers often fail to appreciate the damage that can be done them on land, and vice-versa for land powers. This underappreciation translates into less deterrent leverage than there should be for seapower against a continental-minded enemy, and less leverage for landpower *vis-à-vis* a maritime enemy.

Theme number nine draws an historical generalization and applies it to the present situation of the United States: *Over the course of history many countries have maintained large armies, but those that have built and provided for large navies number ten or fewer.* On the assumption that the United States will not shrink from maintaining its *strategic* forces at levels and capabilities sufficient to deter Soviet strategic use or coercion, the greatest danger to U.S. national security—and by extension to peace and stability in the world—is the possibility of a great land power (read the Soviet Union) becoming also a great sea power. History offers few data points to draw firm conclusions on this, but they are all most ominous.

Finally, it is important to recognize that *The United States is, in retrospect, a highly unusual case of a continental-size, effectively strategically insular, sea power.* For reasons of geography, American strategic culture has been shaped very significantly by what may be termed the logistical as contrasted with the operational needs of war. The "American way in warfare" is not classically maritime. Rather, U.S. military "style" is characterized by:

(a) a logistical focus—the need to conquer great distances for the projection of combat power;

(b) an enduring love affair with technology;

(c) a preference for direct approaches to the enemy's strength;

(d) sensitivity to American casualties and prisoners of war.

Because the United States must enjoy naval-air mastery in order to wage war in Eurasia, excellence in maritime conflict must have logical priority over excellence on land. Nevertheless, the inarguable success of U.S. seapower in war in the twentieth century to date should not obscure the major differences in strategic culture between the more "natural" sea powers of medieval Venice, and modern Holland and Britain, and the great naval power of contemporary *continental* America.

These, then, constitute the ten themes around which this book is organized. In some historical settings or other situations they will stand out prominently; in others, they will appear subordinate or perhaps even contradictory. They do, however, provide the contours that help explain—in a long view—the importance and value of maritime power.

The book is organized functionally into three parts, which are labeled "The Basics," "Strategy and History," and "Contemporary Maritime Strategy." Part I has three essays, one that sets forth the important distinctions between landpower and seapower, one that surveys the subject of maritime command from the point of view of the masters, Corbett and Mahan; prominent in the book's themes; and a third that provides perspective by placing the currents of strategy in the contexts of tactics and technology.

Part II contains seven chapters on maritime strategy in historical perspective. They deal, *seriatim*, with Athens and Sparta, Rome and Carthage, England and Spain, England and France, World War I, World War II—Atlantic Theater, and World War II—Pacific Theater.

The last part, Part III, centers its attention on contemporary matters of importance on the subject: Seapower and Geopolitics, Soviet Sea Power, the Current U.S. Maritime Strategy and Its Roots, and the Debate over Continental or Maritime Strategic Emphasis. The "Reflections" chapter endeavors to look back from the end and render a final assessment.

Colin S. Gray
Roger W. Barnett

Seapower
and
Strategy

I

THE BASICS

1

Seapower and Landpower

BY COLIN S. GRAY

THE COMPLEMENTARY RELATIONSHIP

This chapter seeks to clarify the strategic relationship between sea-power and landpower. These grand concepts are as inescapable as they can be confusing if employed carelessly. Without striving for un-reasonable and unhelpful precision, it is important that some com-mon-sense points be registered at the outset.

First, all power—sea, air, space, or whatever—ultimately is gener-ated by territorially organized countries or coalitions. Power may be sea-based, but it is the expression of countries in possession of par-ticular territories.

Second, with the exception of a few landlocked states, all countries maintain some power at sea. Similarly, there are very few countries that totally lack organized military power on land (Costa Rica and Iceland are rare examples of such a lack). This chapter, however, fo-cuses on sea powers and land powers that are unusually strong mil-itarily on the sea or on the land.

Third, as employed by Mahan, seapower was more than a little ambiguous. It could refer narrowly to the naval fighting instrument of a country, or more broadly to the sea-oriented assets of a country, including the navy. Classically, the broad view of seapower embraced the interconnected themes of maritime commerce, colonies (and other important trading partners), and the navy.

Fourth, there are "gray zones" between seapower and landpower, as there are between airpower and both the others. Definitions of—for example—what is seapower as contrasted with landpower, can only be arbitrary. Time should not be wasted on semantics, but it is worth remembering that command relationships in amphibious operations frequently have hinged on arbitrary decisions concerning the point when sea combat becomes land combat (e.g., who commands on the beach?).

Fifth, and finally, to cite a dictum of central importance in this book, man lives on the land, not on the sea, and conflict at sea has strategic meaning only with reference to what its outcome enables, or implies, for the course of events on land.

Circumstances of national geography typically mandate emphasis upon either the landward or the maritime elements of military power. All of the case studies in this book, up to and including the treatment of contemporary U.S.-Soviet strategic relations, involve conflicts between states or coalitions that have been asymmetrical in their dependence upon seapower or landpower. Of necessity, the history of conflict between great sea powers and great land powers has taken the form of the one kind of power striving to acquire sufficient of the other kind of power so that a favorable decision could be forced. Although this book emphasizes the interdependence of seapower and landpower, readers should not be misled by generic criticisms of "naval strategy." In his recent book on *Strategy*, Edward N. Luttwak argues that:

> There can be only valid justification for conceptualizing an autonomous strategy, confined to just one form of military power: that it is decisive in itself.[1]

It happens that seapower can be "decisive in itself" when it is applied against a great sea power or a maritime dependent coalition. Seapower, on the other hand, can never be decisive against a great continental power or coalition, which is why sea powers throughout history have sought continental allies. Clearly, great land powers can be beaten only on land and great sea powers can be beaten only at sea. It is in the structure of this historical and common-sense truth that, in the reach for decision in war, both sea powers and land powers have been obliged to provide or to ally with (and possibly to subsidize) the type of power that has not been their traditional instrument of excellence.

THEORY AND HISTORY

Navalist and anti-navalist writings over the centuries have been prone to discuss seapower and landpower as great abstractions, imbued with certain properties of a quasi-permanent character. Furthermore, the relations of net strategic advantage between seapower and landpower have been assessed with reference to general trends in technology, economic development, and political organization. For example, the British geographer, Sir Halford Mackinder, wrote in 1919 that:

> We have defeated the danger [from German landpower to British seapower] on this occasion [1914–1918], but the facts of geography remain, and offer ever-increasing strategical opportunities to landpower as against seapower.[2]

It was Mackinder's thesis, first, in argument advanced initially in public in 1904, and then refined at intervals until his death in 1947, that seapower had enjoyed an historically very unusual period of ascendancy over landpower in what he termed the "Columbian epoch" from 1500 to 1900 (approximately). Second, as suggested in the 1919 quotation above, that Columbian epoch allegedly was passing or already had passed, and the future appeared to belong to the great continental states. The basic reason lay in the field of relative advantage in transportation economics as between sea and land mobility. In sharp contrast, the bedrock of Alfred Thayer Mahan's theory of seapower lay in the plausible claim that:

> Notwithstanding all the familiar and unfamiliar dangers of the sea, both travel and traffic by water have always been easier and cheaper than by land.[3]

The new technologies of the seagoing sailing ship and ancillary (but essential) navigation aids had opened the shorelines of the entire world—aside from the unnavigable polar regions—to penetration by the trading and fighting sail of the ocean-facing states of Western Europe. In technical terms, sailing ships had a truly global mobility that was not enjoyed by the coal- and oil-fueled ships of the second half of the nineteenth and the first half of the twentieth centuries. Only with nuclear power has the maritime instrument (or, at least, some elements of it) regained the autonomy at sea enjoyed by the sailing ship. For the first three centuries of Mackinder's Columbian epoch, by far the most serious practical limitation upon the commercial and strategic reach of the sailing ship was the health of the crew.

It was Mackinder's thesis that the industrial revolution—from which Britain had been the first to benefit—particularly in its ramifications in the area of land transportation, had effected a radical shift in the terms of advantage as between seapower and landpower. In 1904 he wrote as follows:

> A generation ago steam and the Suez Canal appeared to have increased the mobility of seapower relatively to landpower. Railways acted chiefly as feeders to ocean-going commerce. But trans-continental rail-ways are now transmuting the conditions of land-power, and nowhere can they have such effect as in the closed heartland of Euro-Asia. . .[4]

Mackinder was predicting that the railroad (and later the internal combustion engine) would permit the effective economic and political unification of great landmasses. In Mackinder's world view, the most important landmass was that very large portion of Eurasia inaccessible from the readily navigable sea, which he termed the Heartland. The Heartland was defined and redefined in 1904, 1919, and finally in 1943. By that last date, Mackinder had come to equate the Heartland with the USSR and with those contiguous areas that the Heartland power strategically could dominate and therefore close to penetration from the sea (e.g., much of the Baltic and the Black seas).

Both Mackinder and Mahan have been very considerably misunderstood, both by people who were motivated to misunderstand them and by those who have not read sufficiently widely in their writings. While there is no substitute for reading Mahan's founding work, *The Influence of Sea Power upon History, 1660–1783* (1890), there is probably more nutritious food for contemporary thought in his brilliant collection of essays, *The Problem of Asia and Its Effect upon International Policies* (1900),[5] and in his analysis of "Considerations Governing the Disposition of Navies" (in his *Retrospect and Prospect: Studies in International Relations, Naval and Political,* 1902).[6] As frequently is the case with Clausewitz's writings also, Mackinder's geopolitical theory—with its opposed landpower-seapower centerpiece—can be misinterpreted all too easily if it is wrenched out of its historical and national-cultural context. Just as Clausewitz wrote as a Prussian of his time, knowing little and caring less about sea warfare, so Mackinder had the security of Britain and its very scattered empire very much in mind in his theoretical writings.

A very good deal of the apprehension, even pessimism, that one can discern in Mackinder's writings, is an apprehension and pessimism very specific indeed to his British orientation. Mahan's U.S.-continental frame of personal reference for the world, notwithstanding his anglophilia and the focus on the Royal Navy in his *magna opera*, in important ways made for a sounder comprehension of trends in the balance of power than was expounded by Mackinder. As the chapter in this book by John Gooch makes abundantly plain, there are good reasons to be critical of Mahan's scholarship.[7] Yet, criticism of Mahan, particularly with reference to his (real and alleged) exaggeration of the influence of seapower on the course and outcome of wars in the "Columbian epoch," has been excessive on the part of many scholars who do not themselves appear to have considered very carefully the strategic relationship between seapower and landpower. A reconsideration of Mahan is overdue.

Belatedly, Mackinder came to appreciate what the United States could mean for the protection of the human values that mattered to him the most. Mackinder's theoretical framework, organized around the enduring opposition between whichever power or coalition controlled the Eurasian continental Heartland and the ocean-facing states, essentially was correct. The persisting pattern of conflict over four centuries between continental powers striving to achieve hegemony on land, and coalitions organized by offshore sea powers for the purpose of thwarting those repeated bids for hegemony, has been too steady to be dismissed as a passing phase or an accident of particular circumstances. Where Mackinder and his Heartland theory can mislead, is in the exaggeration of the power of the Heartland states in coalition relative to the power both of what the Dutch-American geopolitician Nicholas Spykman was to call the Eurasian Rimland, and to the power of the extra-Eurasian world.[8] These seemingly abstruse points are critically important for current and future U.S./NATO decisions on defense strategy.

In fact, the historical record of British, later Anglo-American, sea-based power, in contest with aspiring continental-hegemonic landpower, shows that much less has altered in the twentieth century than many people have claimed.

First, critics of the naval dimension to U.S. military strategy in the 1980s argue with an air of revelation that the Soviet Union, a distinctively continental land power if ever there was one, cannot be defeated by action on, or directly from, the sea (setting aside the option of sea-based nuclear bombardment). This is true, but it is a very longstanding truth: it is not a truth unique to this century, expressive of some cumulatively radical shift in the terms of engagement between seapower and landpower. Even in the eighteenth century, when economic conditions rendered France, the greatest continental power of the period, distinctly vulnerable to (financial) pressure from action at sea, there were strict limits to what seapower could accomplish stra-tegically. In historical succession, the continental superstates of France, Germany, and the USSR could be overthrown only as a consequence of ruinous defeat on land.

The important and interesting question for East-West strategic relations today, as also with regard to the anti-hegemonic coalitions that thwarted the France of Louis XIV and Napoleon I, and the Germany of Kaiser Wilhelm II and Adolf Hitler, is not foolishly to attempt to pick the "winner" as between seapower and landpower (and air and missile power today) in the downfall of continental tyrants. Instead, the salient issue, and the real challenge to history-based, but forward-looking, strategic understanding, is the strategic relationship between seapower and landpower.

Second, the decline and generally fairly graceful fall of the worldwide British sea-based empire in the twentieth century, points to the truth in Mackinder's 1904 (and after) prediction that weight in the balance (or imbalance) of power increasingly will accrue to the larger territorially contiguous states. Through improvements in internal (landward) communications, those states are able to realize their economic potential. The British Empire vanished in a generation for two reasons, neither of which has anything to do with the strategic value of seapower vis-à-vis landpower. First, Europe—including Britain itself—exported the concept of nationalism to its colonies. Second, compelled to wage two Europe-focused wars of national survival, Britain lacked the economic strength to continue to enforce imperial control.

It is almost certainly true to claim that Hitler's Germany could not have been beaten by Anglo-American sea-based power without the massive assistance of Soviet landpower. However, it is no less plausible to argue that Soviet landpower alone could not have defeated Germany. The lack of historical novelty in the complementarity of Soviet and Anglo-American power in coalition is quite striking. Alone, Britain could not possibly have brought down the continental empire of Napoleon, notwithstanding the excellence of the Royal Navy in that period. Yet, the British political, financial, and military contribution was literally critical to the complex of factors that eventually brought about the destruction of that empire.

Certainly it is the case that global economic development and political modernization have meant a "closed world"—there are no more open and politically ineffectively organized (if organized at all) frontier shorelines for seapower to penetrate at will. But the threat to the balance of power that Mackinder foresaw, correctly, in the modernization of the Eurasian Heartland, has been more than offset by the expansion of the domestic base of Western seapower in the form of the United States. Furthermore, the political and economic modernization of the world that is beyond the easy reach of Heartland ground forces, has diminished greatly the potential value of achievement even of a true hegemony over Eurasia. In addition, the modernization of the Rimland state of China is a growing strategic complication for any Soviet leadership seriously interested in securing freedom from local continental distraction in order to challenge the U.S. superpower in its oceanic realm.

SOLDIERS AND SAILORS, OR FOXHOLES AND WIDE HORIZONS

The geophysical character of an environment for conflict has profound implications for the nature and purposes of such conflict, for the military means suitable for combat, for tactics, and—fundamentally—for the perspectives of combatants. Some of the differences between war at sea and war on land are so obvious that they have a way of functioning as a barrier to achieving a deeper comprehension of the individuality of the two environments. Strategically speaking, more often than not navies and armies have represented two reasonably distinct "cultures," whose mutual comprehension has left much to be desired. When great powers go to war, they are not usually at liberty to go to war strictly at sea, on land, or in the air (or looking to the future, in space). Instead they are, or may be, obliged to wage war as a whole. At the level of general description in peacetime, the degree to which the landward and seaward (with their tactical airpower adjuncts) instruments of military power may be planning for quite different wars, usually can be concealed—or even simply pass unnoticed. Because of their professional specializations, soldiers and sailors tend to see the world of conflict in considerably different terms.

J. H. Parry began his masterful study of *The Discovery of the Sea* with the simple, but strategically profound, observation that "[a]ll the seas of the world are one."[9] With only minor exceptions, there are no barriers of terrain or political frontiers to maritime transport. The horizon for the unaided senses of the sailor is the horizon provided by the curvature of the earth. The horizon for the soldier may be a hedgerow, or a wall, or a hill; it is vastly restricted compared with that for the sailor. The open space for maneuver that is fundamental to war at sea, can have a psychologically debilitating effect upon soldiers when they are confronted with the need to campaign in country that bears some resemblance to the open sea (for example, the desert or the steppes of Southern Russia). Writing of "the foreignness of it all" in his *War on the Eastern Front, 1941–1945: The German Soldier in Russia,* James Lucas observes:

> The same thought occurred to many; that extending from the German front line and reaching to as far as Vladivostok there existed a vast area of enemy territory wherein they, their regiments, indeed the whole German Army, could vanish without a trace.[10]

On their mental world maps, soldiers tend, understandably, to see more or less extensive lakes surrounded by land (the dominant feature). By way of contrast, sailors tend to see islands, more or less extensive in scale, surrounded by water (the dominant feature). Geopoliticians with a landward orientation have argued that the effective shrinkage in the size of the world (real travel and communication time and not mere distance) effected by modern technology, has rendered the oceans more lakelike in this century. The seaward tactical reach of landpower, and the landward tactical reach of seapower, plainly have grown exponentially since modern international law settled upon three miles as the proper extent for territorial waters—a distance safely exceeding the extreme range of cannon shot in the age of fighting sail. Although an ICBM can span an ocean in half an hour, and a jet aircraft in less than half a day, the air and missile age has not obliterated the strategic significance of distance, of the difference between continental and maritime environments, or the relevance for coherence in national and coalition military strategy of the distinctiveness of the particular, environmentally conditioned, world views of the sailor and the soldier.

In his now-classic work, *Military Strategy,* Rear Admiral J. C. Wylie wrote:

> Where the sailor or airman thinks in terms of an entire world, the soldier at work thinks in terms of theaters, in terms of campaigns, or in terms of battles. And the three concepts are not too markedly different from each other.
> Where the sailor and the airman are almost forced, by the nature of the sea and the air, to think in terms of a total world or, at the least, to look outside the physical limits of their immediate concerns, the soldier is almost hemmed in by his terrain.[11]

Because of the geographical constraints upon their agility, it is natural for soldiers to think in terms of campaign strategy for a theater— the "operational level of war," as it is known. Equally, it is natural for the thinking of sailors to encompass the levels of grand strategy and national or coalition military strategy, embracing many actual and potential theaters for campaigning, because of the inherent maneuverability of maritime power. Seapower and landpower tend to be able to accomplish different kinds of objectives; they wage different, if complementary, forms of war and, as a consequence, as often as not their practitioners have different perspectives on the conduct of war.

The differences between war at sea and war on land can be exaggerated, but it is true to claim that armies most often have occupation (or possession) goals, while navies have use or denial-of-use goals. In both cases the goals are instrumental (though they can be more than that for armies). Armies seek to occupy enemy territory in order to put pressure on the foe directly—either eventually to accomplish his overthrow, or to persuade him to accept a compromise peace. Secure military possession, or repossession, of national or allied territory, is both instrumental for victory and is an absolute value in its own right. Unlike the ocean, effective ownership of territory has value in and of itself. German occupation of nearly all of Belgium and of a part of Northern France throughout the First World War, had the consequence of compelling the Western alliance to assume the tactical offensive in that region, virtually regardless of broader strategic considerations.

In contrast to the land, the sea is a medium for movement. It cannot be occupied and fortified. Navies cannot "dig in" at sea, or seize and hold ocean areas that have great intrinsic value. By definition, since man lives on the land, the effect of seapower on the course and outcome of a war can only be indirect. However, indirect does not necessarily mean secondary or indecisive. *The* intended instrument of decision in war for Germany in 1917 and again in late 1942 and early 1943, was the U-boat. The relative importance of a kind of military power is a function of the particular vulnerability of the enemy of the day; it is not a function of the technical (or any other) character of the military instrument itself.

Readers of this book who are in the Anglo-American strategic tradition, understandably are reared in the strategic perspective of a great sea power (repeatedly) confronting continental (European or Eurasian) hegemonic/territorial imperialism. Every strategic culture and tradition is inclined to erect what purport to be general theories on the basis of national historical experience and circumstances. So, writing as an Englishman, Charles E. Callwell was correct in his assertion in 1897 that:

The effect of seapower upon land campaigns is in the main strategical. Its influence over the progress of military operations, however decisive this may be, is often only very indirect.[12]

For a great sea power waging war against a great land power, success at sea, in all its forms, really can have only "enabling" consequences. The landpower enemy may be brought down by the eventual consequences of poor performance at sea, but that poor performance cannot itself produce his defeat because he has nothing of a survival character at stake at sea. Plainly, contrasting argument applies to the sea power. Defeat at sea, the inability to move assets as needed on the oceans, would not have a "strategical"—in the particular sense of important but long-term and indirect—impact on a Britain or a Japan (or a United States *vis à vis* its ability to fight beyond North and Central America). Instead, the effect of such defeat at sea would have more or less immediate and devastating consequences for the conduct and hence outcome of war.

The point of importance here is to note that the inherent, direct, potential significance of seapower or of landpower cannot be assessed according to their distinctive characters, but only with reference to who is using them, and against whom. Although there is a four-hundred-year-long pattern of antagonism between the greatest land power and the greatest sea power (with only the identities of the players changing), landpower and seapower are strictly complementary forms and sources of strength. In the words of Mahan:

> . . . it must equally be recognized that each race [the Teutonic, which he equated with seapower, and the Slavic, which he equated with landpower] absolutely requires some foothold, though an inferior one, on the field which is not primarily its own . . .[13]

Just as generals and admirals can have difficulty sufficiently appreciating each other's problems, so sea powers and land powers at the highest level of national policy can have difficulty appreciating the extent of damage that can be wrought by the successful exercise of the enemy's military instrument of excellence. Furthermore, as a corollary, a sea power is prone to misuse its landpower and a land power is prone to misuse its seapower. One should hesitate before generalizing across historical periods, but the evidence of success and failure in conflict in modern times (which is to say, arbitrarily, after 1500), comprising some very different national casts of characters, suggests strongly that the wide horizon of the maritime world view, *on balance*, makes for sounder decisions on the conduct of war as a whole, than does the view from the foxhole of the more narrowly continentally minded.

Lest there be any misunderstanding, the claim registered immediately above bears not at all upon any alleged superiority of seapower *per se* over landpower. To reintroduce an earlier point, the issue is not, indeed cannot be, that of soldier *versus* sailor, landpower *versus* seapower. Rather, the issue is, and long has been, that of sea-based, encouraged, and organized landpower versus land-based, encouraged, and organized sea (or more narrowly, naval) power. In short, throughout modern times Britain and later the United States have been more able to generate a decisive (coalition-wide) quantity and quality of landpower to bring down continental enemies, than those continental enemies have been able to generate a decisive quantity and quality of seapower. It is no accident that this has been so—to employ a favorite Soviet turn of phrase.

Time and again in modern history, great continental states have been unable or unwilling to craft and execute effectively either grand or national military strategies, by way of contrast to their proficiency at the tactical and operational levels of war. But, such are the differences between the occupied land and the empty sea that—thus far at least—preponderant landpower is far more likely, in effect, to wreak its own destruction than is preponderant seapower. To date, the operational-level potency of the best army of the day (Spanish, French, German) repeatedly has proved incapable of offsetting the *eventual* operational-level consequences of conflict with an enemy whose center of strategic gravity is unreachably offshore. There is a very long historical pattern of sea powers being able to make better grand and military-strategic use of their superiority at sea for the generation and regeneration of landward fighting strength, than landpower could turn advantage on the continent into power of decision at and from the sea.

OCEAN AND CONTINENT IN GRAND STRATEGY

In a lecture in 1958, Britain's foremost soldier, Field Marshal Sir Bernard Montgomery, delivered a very mature professional judgment on the relationship between the land and the sea in war, which merits quotation at some length.

> We must confine Russia to a land strategy. *From the days when we humans first began to use the seas, the great lesson of history is that the enemy who is confined to a land strategy is in the end defeated.* This has been true since the days of Carthage. In more recent times, there is the

example of the French in the Napoleonic wars and the Germans in the Kaiser's war and Hitler's war. Another example can be found in the Russo-Japanese War in 1904. Japan had sea control; she fought Russia at the end of long communications with her own short; and won.

The second world war was, fundamentally, a struggle for the control of the major oceans and seas—the control of sea communications—and until we had won that struggle we could not proceed with our plans to win the war.

Today, our strategy must be based on confining Russia to a land strategy, by retaining control of the seas in our hands and by preventing Russia interfering with our use of the air flank. Any other strategy is useless.[14]

It is important to note that the field marshal did not claim that sea powers eventually always succeed in wars against land powers. Rather did he argue that powers "confined to a land strategy" eventually lose. If those powers happen to be critically dependent upon maritime communications, they will lose sooner rather than later. Generally, in modern times it has proved easier for a sea power coalition leader to acquire complementary landpower of the first rank, than it has been for a continental hegemon or coalition leader to acquire a truly superior fighting instrument for war at sea.

The military constraints in particular contemporary circumstances can mislead statesmen into believing that fairly pure forms of the principal pillar of their country's preferred "way in warfare" alone can secure success. The leaders of great land powers repeatedly have succumbed to the temptation to believe that their army can defeat the grand strategy of a sea-power enemy. Similarly, the leaders of great sea powers have been known to endorse the fallacy that sea-based action alone can bring intolerable pressure to bear upon continental enemies. These parallel errors—when truly they are errors and are not simply examples of politicians making a virtue of necessity—reflect a common phenomenon. Statesmen at war require a theory of victory (they cannot admit that they do not know how to win), and there are always projects that a superior army or navy can attempt in its own environment that, by more or less tenuous logic, just might bring the enemy down.

It is not unduly cynical to observe that a war can be regarded as a contest in which each side competes to set the stage most effectively for the other to commit fatal errors in grand strategy. Errors in grand strategy tend to have the consequence of posing problems of a severity beyond favorable resolution by excellence in military strategy or in operational art and tactics. For example, mistakes in statecraft at the highest level can have the effect of generating an enemy coalition of such strength that sufficiently definitive military victory is very close to impossible—this was the situation of France in 1813–14, and of Germany in 1918 and again in the period 1942–45.

When frustrated by an inability to bring a conflict to an immediate satisfactory conclusion, a land power or a sea power typically will attempt what it can with the limited military reach of its preferred and available instrument of excellence. The continental power will consider how it can use its thus-far victorious landward assets to defeat the strategy of the sea-power enemy, while the sea power will cast around for ways in which maritime supremacy can bring pressure to bear on the continental foe. The years 1801, 1806, and 1940 were all cases of the situation just outlined. In those years, as naval historian Geoffrey Marcus has written (of 1801):

> The strategical stalemate between Landpower and Seapower was complete. The French Army could no more overcome the British Navy than the British Navy could overcome the French Army.[15]

Given the obvious difficulty, not to say impracticality, of direct engagement for a definitive military decision between the battle fleet of a sea power and the principal field army of a land power (respectively the military "crown jewels" of seapower and landpower, prior to the nuclear-missile age), what were the rival grand-strategic solutions to the engagement problem? Nuclear facts simply complicate, they do not invalidate, analyses of landpower-seapower relations that rest heavily on the historical record prior to 1945—a topic addressed briefly towards the close of this chapter.

In modern times, with only the rarest of arguable exceptions (1690,1779), no great continental power has built, rented, or otherwise acquired a naval fighting instrument capable of challenging the British (later the U.S.) Navy in a stand-up fleet battle, with some reasonable prospect of success. At different times, French and then German leaders have aspired eventually to enjoy the services of a first-class fighting (surface) fleet. But, the exigencies of continental distractions always have obliged those French and German leaders to seek short-cuts to success at sea via naval strategies appropriate to the weaker side. Specifically, the French, the German—and possibly one day, the Soviets in their historical turn—have had to resort to a raiding strategy of dispersed assault upon the maritime communications of the sea-power enemy while endeavoring to avoid the concentrated strength of his naval forces.

War on seaborne trade is a strategy of weakness chosen because a strategy of strength (aiming at the achievement of some facsimile of "command") is impracticable. If, as near-universally has been the case, a continental power lacks the naval assets early in a conflict necessary for an assault upon the strategic center of gravity of a sea-power enemy, it can wage such maritime war as it is able (i.e., the *guerre de course*, or commerce raiding), while it seeks to set the continental stage for a stronger form of naval war or of strategy more broadly. This aspiration was stated very explicitly by Napoleon on 6 December 1806, when he wrote to his brother Louis, King of Holland:

> Je veux conquerir la mer par la puissance de terre [I intend to conquer the sea by the power of the land].[16]

In practice, Napoleon endeavored to bring financial ruin upon Britain through the imposition of a landward continental blockade against British commerce. Also, Napoleon sought to intimidate or bribe continental allies and other security dependents into contributing ships and sailors towards a great continental fleet for the smashing of British naval power. For reasons that, in detail, need not detain this discussion, not only did Napoleon fail to impose an effective continental blockade against Britain, but the effort to achieve a sufficiently impermeable system of economic pressure led him into catastrophic military overextension on land. The "Spanish ulcer" of 1808–14, and the Great Russian adventure of 1812, were both motivated non-trivially by the determination to close all of the continental littoral to British commerce. (Czar Alexander's defection in 1810 from Napoleon's "continental system" was a critical milestone on the path to the resumption of Franco-Russian hostilities.)

Aside from the options for economic warfare, a hardy perennial feature in the grand-strategic calculations of continental statesmen has been the belief that once bereft of a "continental sword" (the armies of continental allies), the sea-power enemy will be unable to wage war on land and, indeed, will be so thoroughly deprived of a plausible theory of eventual victory that it would choose to come to terms. Vice Admiral Sir Peter Gretton has reminded anybody in need of reminding that: "A maritime strategy assists and supports a continental strategy."[17]

Sea powers such as Britain or the United States could not, indeed still cannot, have a continental strategy in the absence of continental allies. It follows, or should follow, that if a France, a Germany, or a Soviet Union can eliminate the actual or potential continental allies of Britain and/or the United States, there can be no theory of victory in war for the sea powers, because the center of strategic gravity of the continental enemy is on land. A sea power that enjoys, or can ᶴ enforce at will, "working control" of maritime lines of communication, can exploit the agility of its naval assets so as carefully and very selectively to raid the coasts of an enemy-dominated landmass. But, those operations will have the character of raids for the purposes of local "ravage and destruction,"[18] or for the making of a political gesture; they cannot prudently aspire to "conquest and occupation" from a beachhead or an enclave from which a major land campaign could be launched. Britain could wage continuous war in the Iberian Peninsula from 1809 to 1814 only because Napoleon was massively distracted in Central and Eastern Europe, and because Spanish guerrillas obliged the French greatly to weaken their field armies in order to secure their exceedingly vulnerable (landward) lines of communication. Similarly, the Anglo-American amphibious expeditionary ventures against Hitler's *Festung Europa* from 1942 to 1944 were militarily feasible only because the German Armed Forces were very heavily preoccupied by the war on the Eastern Front.

As a grand strategy for hegemonic landpower, the idea of knocking the "continental sword" from the hands of a sea-power enemy *in principle* is entirely sound. When Hitler informed his military advisers on 31 July 1940 that he intended to invade the Soviet Union by no later than May 1941, and to defeat that country in a five-month campaign, certainly he was following his long-established personal agenda for expansion of the Reich. But, in addition, Hitler was advancing explicitly a theory of how Britain could be deprived of all reasonable hope of success in the war. The rapid defeat of Soviet landpower was to remove British hopes for re-creation of an anti-German coalition with an active continental fighting front. Also, the effective removal of the Soviet Union from the scales of the balance of power in Eurasia would render Japan so menacing in East Asia and the Pacific in U.S. perception that British hopes for American entry into the war in Europe (and the Atlantic) would be dashed.

If further illustration of the argument is needed, readers are invited to enquire as to British grand-strategic options had the Schlieffen Plan of Imperial Germany succeeded in August-September 1914. The plan was designed, first, to effect the annihilation of the French Army in a campaign of forty-two days in the West. Second, prompt success in the West was intended to permit Germany to transfer to the East the bulk of its victorious army, there to join the forces of Austria-Hungary in an offensive to break the back of (a then isolated) Russian military power. Had the Schlieffen Plan succeeded, Britain would have lost both its Franco-Russian "continental sword(s)" and its own small, but superbly trained, field army (the six-division British

Expeditionary Force [B.E.F.]). In such circumstances, with no major allies still fighting on the continent, with neutrals very naturally disinclined to take up arms against the victorious Central Powers, and with a very potent German Navy comprehensively intact, how and with what prospect of success could Britain have continued the war?

It may be worth mentioning that in circumstances somewhat similar to the above, Britain decided in 1802 to sign on for a very disadvantageous peace settlement with France (the Treaty of Amiens). But, in the summer of 1940, when British grand-strategic options again appeared to be distinctly unpromising, the character of the Nazi regime was such that London decided, in effect, to wait for "something" (i.e., the United States and just possibly the Soviet Union) to "turn up." The danger to Britain in 1802, as in the alternative history cited above for 1914, again in 1940, and possibly for the United States at some time in the future, was explained as follows by Halford Mackinder:

> What if the Great Continent, the whole World-Island [Europe, Asia, and Africa] or a large part of it, were at some future time to become a single and united base of sea power? Would not the other insular bases be outbuilt as regards ships and outmanned as regards seamen?
> . . . must we not still reckon with the possibility that a large part of the Great Continent might some day be united under a single sway, and that an invincible sea-power might be based upon it?[19]

In principle, through conquest and intimidation, the greatest land power of the day could use its army to acquire the production base and the ocean-facing geostrategic positions necessary for the development of really first-class seapower. However, no land-oriented state, empire, or coalition in *modern times* has translated preeminence on land into preeminence at sea. In ancient history, Republican Rome did exactly that; but the closed sea of the Mediterranean in the age of galley warfare geostrategically was very different from the open oceans today, notwithstanding the technological evolution that has reduced some of the significance of mere distance. A global scale of geography denies to Soviet legions the policy option noted by Mackinder as the preference of Rome.

> . . . landpower terminated a cycle of competition upon the water by depriving seapower of its bases.
> . . . that command [over all the sea] was not afterwards maintained upon the sea, but upon the land by holding the coasts.[20]

The United States has been very well advised in organizing, subsidizing, and directly supporting an anti-continental-hegemonic coalition around the periphery of Eurasia—lest Mackinder's nightmare of a politically consolidated continent, reflecting centuries-long British fears, should become a reality. However, the relevant contemporary trends look distinctly unpromising for Soviet prospects of freeing its hands of major Eurasian continental distractions, as a precondition for organizing and effecting a global maritime challenge to the United States. To secure their base in Eurasia, the Soviets require a grand strategy which, by whatever mix of means, would deny continental access to the United States. Even if one can write plausible scenarios for Soviet *Blitzkrieg* success in a non-nuclear war in Europe, how could the Soviets, prudently and reliably, deny the United States continental access, or reentry, via the "backdoor" of a mainland China? As China modernizes, and Japan slowly realizes at least a modest fraction of its defense potential, the problem of bi-continental perimeter defense for an endemically ailing Soviet defense economy assumes absurdly impractical dimensions.

Frequently in modern times, a hegemonic land power has toyed more or less seriously with the idea of assaulting an insular sea-power enemy directly by invasion. However, as Julian Corbett explained in 1911 with unsurpassed clarity, invasion over an uncommanded sea is not a practical operation of war.[21] Moreover, invasion would not be necessary if the navy of the land power could wrest maritime command from the sea power. A sea power effectively defenseless at sea could not continue a war.

A grand-strategic option for landpower eminently more feasible than the invasion of the sea power's home territory, is the seizure of continental "hostages." An important function of Britain's continental allies in the wars with France after 1689 (from the perspective of London) was so to limit French hostage-taking on land in Europe that Britain would not be obliged to hand back to France and her allies all of the colonial conquests that the Royal Navy managed to secure in the course of hostilities. Since the 1790s, however, no continental European power has possessed colonies or had other security wards at risk to wartime isolation and seizure by preponderant, insular sea-power, of such value that their conquest could balance the gains achievable by landpower in Europe. French, German, and now Soviet conquests (and possible conquests) in Europe were, and remain, beyond capability of offset through British and American seizure of "sugar islands" and the like.

For the United States today, as for Britain in the 1790s and 1800s, the only practicable policy solution to an overmighty hegemon in Eurasia lies in the provision of a "continental sword" capable of limiting the gains of the aspiring hegemon on land. The hostage problem under discussion here could take the form in the future of a Soviet Union successful on land throughout Western Europe, then inviting the United States to negotiate a peace treaty.

The great sea powers of history have all had in common a geostrategic insularity bequeathed by nature or by engineering artifice. Maritime excellence can be developed and sustained only if there is an absence of intense competition for scarce resources with the army. Mahan claimed that:

> History has conclusively demonstrated the inability of a state with even a single continental frontier to compete in naval development with one that is insular, although of smaller population and resources.[22]

Imperial Athens contrived its insularity by the construction of city fortifications and of the Long Walls to the port of Piraeus (between 461 and 456 B.C.)—thereby depriving its continentalist foes of an effective system of war; the Byzantine Empire had a pivot or center of gravity in a superbly sited capital, Constantinople, which was protected by the most formidable system of fortification in medieval Europe; Venice was established on offshore islands (mud banks, at least); the Dutch Republic was protected by major rivers and estuaries, by a network of fortress towns, and by very low-lying land that could be flooded at will; Britain, of course, is an island; and the United States effectively is insular, albeit on a continental scale, courtesy of the military weakness of its landward neighbors.

The great sea powers of different periods cited above, whatever their many and profound differences, have had in common the Janus-like strategic consequences of insularity. Specifically, to each of them the sea could be a protective moat or a highway for foreign threat, depending upon the balance of naval strength. In its grand strategy, a sea power competent in statecraft does not repose its security simply in the fact of a national geography that lends itself to maritime exploitation. The *final line* of national defense is provided by those military assets that directly protect the more or less insular homeland. But, the *first line* of defense for a well-governed sea power is the "continental sword" provided by land-oriented allies. Those allies distract the hegemony-intending enemy of the period from concentrating his potentially very formidable resources upon construction of a truly first-class naval fighting instrument.

Bearing in mind the strategic fact that seapower and landpower are natural complements and allies, not enemies, the history of the past several centuries reveals the grand strategy of a sea power (Britain, the United States) persistently to have the following key elements:

- Organization and partial subsidization of continental allies in a mixed maritime-continental coalition;
- A modest but noticeable continental commitment of soldiers on the ground, intended to fight alongside continental allies in the main theater of operations;
- Maritime blockade/economic warfare to isolate continental enemies from overseas supply (an activity much enhanced in effectiveness when continental allies close landward frontiers to the enemy);
- A peripheral raiding strategy on the continental flanks of the enemy (reflecting the limited merit in B. H. Liddell Hart's advice that: "[a]mphibious flexibility is the greatest strategic asset that a sea-based power possesses");[23]
- the isolation or conquest of the overseas assets of the land-power enemy.

Preponderance at sea—with, today, the backstop of a very robust nuclear deterrent—means that the strategic center of gravity of a sea-power-led coalition (the coalitions against Louis XIV, Napoleon, Germany [twice], and the USSR) cannot be reached, grasped, and conquered by the army of a continental enemy, *no matter how victorious he is on land.* Furthermore, superiority at sea, unlike superiority on land, tends to be general and complete. Even if there is no readily accessible continental ally to succor, maritime superiority positions the strategic frontier on the enemy's coastline. As the major wars of modern history all have illustrated, the power or coalition preponderant at sea has enjoyed—time and again—a critical advantage in grand-strategic flexibility. Whatever the flashy triumphs of continental operational art in success in battle and even in campaigns, the sea power has been able to outlast the land-power hegemon and to set the stage thereby for his self-destruction through imprudent over-extension. British military historian C. R. M. F. Cruttwell penetrated to the heart of the matter when he wrote:

> Still, generally speaking, it is true that British influence over continental wars has not been to determine their strategy in the narrow sense, but rather their general course and character. And this is so just because in naval as opposed to military strategy we have maintained our choice and control practically unfettered.[24]

Seapower is not about the direct military effect of fighting ships, which is the realm of tactics; it is rather about the use of maritime lines of communication for the effective interconnection, organization, and purposeful application of the war-making potential of many lands. Because of the unity of the oceans, the coalition superior at sea is able, uniquely, to wage a global war. Notwithstanding the advances in transportation technologies registered in this century, Mackinder's World-Island of Eurasia-Africa remains very far from comprising a strategically easily unifiable landmass. Geostrategically, much of Eurasia-Africa continues to constitute a great "promontory" or salient (with a base in the relatively inaccessible Arctic), far more easy of access from the sea than controllable from the Heartland by the Soviet continental empire.

Intentionally, little has been said about nuclear weapons in this chapter. This purposeful neglect expresses the author's belief that in war weapons would be subject to "the strategy principle." Specifically, states at war would not employ military means incompatible with the political ends that were being sought. There is no question but that much of the discussion in this chapter, indeed in this book, would be utterly irrelevant were the superpowers to escalate to a full-scale exchange of central strategic nuclear systems after a very brief passage of arms in Central Europe (or anywhere else). Should the United States and the Soviet Union launch 5,000–10,000 nuclear warheads at each other, not only would the relative and strategic effects of seapower and landpower upon the course of the war be blasted into irrelevance, but the very concepts of war, strategy, and weapons would be negated by that monstrous passage of arms. Of course, a very large nuclear war could occur, notwithstanding the common interest of all participants (and bystanders!) in preventing such a happening. But it is as certain as anything can be in the realm of statecraft that political and military leaders will try very hard indeed to avoid taking actions judged likely to have very negative, let alone suicidal, consequences.

Nuclear war at sea is no more autonomous a subject for consideration than is war at sea. Everything written in this book about the essential unity of war on land and war at sea, about the complementarity of landpower and seapower, applies with doubled emphasis to the connections between the use of nuclear weapons in the two environments.

The potential tactical benefits that could accrue to very hard-pressed Soviet naval and naval-air forces as a result of nuclear use at sea are as obvious as they lend themselves to exaggeration. However, those benefits—no matter how real and urgently needed by the Soviet Navy—are most unlikely to be judged by Soviet political and (non-naval) military leaders to be so important as to warrant transformation of the weapon terms of the conflict. Soviet leaders may decide to wage nuclear war, but they can be trusted to understand that they cannot decide to wage nuclear war discretely at sea. They would, or should, be deterred from using nuclear weapons at sea, for the excellent strategic reason that they must anticipate NATO responding with nuclear use against Soviet land targets. NATO's nuclear use on land should negate whatever benefit might have flowed to the Soviets from any tactical nuclear success at sea.

There are no grounds for complacency about nuclear dangers, but there is a very powerful argument that points to the active operational—as contrasted with deterrent—irrelevance of nuclear weapons. The kernel of this argument is that a country that is winning a conventional war can have no motive to employ nuclear weapons, while a country that is losing will recognize that nuclear use would make a bad situation very much worse.

Because the use of nuclear weapons is more likely to prove to be self-defeating than prospectively decisive in a classical military sense, and because both historical experience and common sense inform us that conflicts between great states and very powerful coalitions are extended in time and geography, this discussion of grand strategy should close with a judgment proffered by Herbert Rosinski in 1944: "In global war, merchant shipping is the ultimate key to strategy."[25]

CONCLUSIONS

Wars are deterred or waged by all of the armed services. In modern times, the leading Western sea power of the day has won (or at worst drawn) all of its major conflicts with the leading land power. However, although that fact certainly attests persuasively, even conclusively, to the enduring strategic influence of seapower upon the course and outcome of war, it does *not* attest to the unilateral influence of seapower. British seapower set the stage for the coalition endeavors that finally ruined Napoleonic France *on land*, and Imperial and Nazi Germany *on land*. Looking to a future where deterrence could fail, U.S. (and U.S.-allied) seapower alone could not bring down the Soviet continental empire. But, that seapower would knit together the war economies of several continents for the more or less agile and flexible global application of force. Seapower is about the transfer of the power of the production base on land at times and to places of strategic choice. Naval warfare is about the security of that process of transfer.

At best, these familiar words of Francis Bacon should be regarded as a half-truth:

> But this much is certain, that he that commands the sea is at great liberty, and may take as much or as little of the war as he will.

British, and later American, policy and strategy, frequently have taken practical operational advantage of the truth in Bacon's claim. The effective insularity of the homeland of the sea power does allow for a flexibility in military plans and operations typically not accorded a continental state obliged to defend its territory against actual or imminent landward invasion. Nonetheless, British and American statesmen, with tolerable—though certainly not absolute—consistency, have recognized a force of geopolitical prudence that Bacon's words could incline one to miss. Specifically, disdain for, or unreliability in, continental commitments could have the result of the insular sea power being confronted by a continent-wide hegemony. Continental allies active in the field drain enemy resources from concentration upon the building of maritime, air, and missile instruments that could challenge the sea power in the areas of its traditional strengths, very much closer to home.

NOTES

1. Edward N. Luttwak, *Strategy: The Logic of War and Peace* (Cambridge, MA: Harvard University Press, 1987), p. 161.

2. Halford J. Mackinder, *Democratic Ideals and Reality* (New York: W. W. Norton and Company, 1962; first pub. 1942), p. 111.

3. Alfred Thayer Mahan, *The Influence of Sea Power upon History, 1660–1783* (London: Methuen, 1965; first pub. 1890), p. 25.

4. Mackinder, *Democratic Ideals and Reality*, p. 259.

5. (Boston: Little, Brown & Co., 1905; first pub. 1900).

6. (London: Sampson Low, Marston and Company, 1902), pp. 139–205.

7. Chapter 2, "Maritime Command: Mahan and Corbett."

8. Nicholas John Spykman, *The Geography of the Peace* (New York: Harcourt, Brace, 1944).

9. J. H. Parry, *The Discovery of the Sea* (Berkeley, CA: University of California Press, 1981; first pub. 1976), p. xi.

10. (London: Jane's Publishing Company, 1979), p. 33.

11. (Westport, CT: Greenwood Press, 1980; first pub. 1967), p. 49.

12. Charles E. Callwell, *The Effects of Maritime Command on Land Campaigns Since Waterloo* (Edinburgh: William Blackwood and Sons, 1897), p. 29.

13. Mahan, *The Problem of Asia*, p. 117.

14. Quoted in Sir Peter Gretton, *Maritime Strategy: A Study of Defense Problems* (New York: Praeger, 1965), p. 43. Emphasis added.

15. G. J. Marcus, *The Age of Nelson: The Royal Navy, 1793–1815* (New York: Viking Press, 1971), p. 213.

16. Quoted in J. Holland Rose, *Man and the Sea: Stages in Maritime and Human Progress* (Cambridge: W. Heffer and Sons, 1935), p. 219.

17. Gretton, *Maritime Strategy*, p. 3.

18. P. H. Colomb, *Naval Warfare: Its Ruling Principles and Practice Historically Treated* (London: W. H. Allen and Company, 1891), pp. 216–17.

19. Mackinder, *Democratic Ideals and Reality*, p. 70.

20. *Ibid.*, p. 39.

21. Julian S. Corbett, *Some Principles of Maritime Strategy* (Annapolis, MD: Naval Institute Press, 1972; first pub. 1911), pp. 235–63.

22. Mahan, *Retrospect and Prospect*, p. 169.

23. B. H. Liddell Hart, "Marines and Strategy," *Marine Corps Gazette*, vol. 64, no. 1 (January 1980), p. 31.

24. C. R. M. F. Cruttwell, *The Role of British Strategy in the Great War* (Cambridge: Cambridge University Press, 1936), p. 3.

25. B. Mitchell Simpson III, *The Development of Naval Thought: Essays by Herbert Rosinski* (Newport, RI: Naval War College Press, 1977), p. 45.

BIBLIOGRAPHIC NOTE

For reasons that are obscure, there is very little readily available literature on the subject of the strategic relationship between seapower and landpower. Unsurprisingly, the book that is closest to the concerns and spirit of this chapter is the author's *Seapower and War* (New York: Free Press, forthcoming). The classics in the field are Alfred Thayer Mahan, *The Problem of Asia*, and Halford J. Mackinder, *Democratic Ideals and Reality*—both cited in full in the references above. Unfortunately, both of these works can be difficult to find. Probably the book that best combines quality of relevant analysis with availability, is J. C. Wylie, *Military Strategy: A General Theory of Power Control* (cited above), particularly chapters 5 and 6. Far too much of the popular and supposedly scholarly literature that addresses aspects of the strategic relationship between seapower and landpower suffers from the predetermined conclusion that one or the other really was the decisive factor in a particular war or campaign. The thrust of this chapter, as indeed of this book, is to emphasize the necessary complementarity of seapower and landpower.

ADDITIONAL SOURCES

In addition to the references cited above and in the endnotes (some of which, admittedly, can be difficult to locate), the following will be found useful:

Ambrose, Stephen E. "Seapower in World Wars I and II," in *To Use the Sea: Readings in Seapower and Maritime Affairs*. Annapolis, MD: Naval Institute Press, 1977, 2nd ed., pp. 16–24.

Coutau-Bégarie, Hervé. *La puissance maritime: Castex et la stratégie navale*. Paris: Fayard, 1985.

Daniel, Donald C. F. "The Soviet Navy and Tactical Nuclear War at Sea," *Survival*, vol. 29, no. 4 (July/August 1987), pp. 318–35.

Kennedy, Paul. "Mahan versus Mackinder: Two Interpretations of British Sea Power," in Kennedy, *Strategy and Diplomacy, 1870–1945: Eight Studies.* London: George Allen and Unwin, 1983, pp. 41–85.

Reynolds, Clark G. "The Maritime Strategy of World War II: Some Implications?" *Naval War College Review,* vol. 39, no. 3 (May/June 1986), pp. 43–50.

Rose, J. Holland. "Napoleon and Sea Power," in Rose, *The Indecisiveness of Modern War and Other Essays.* Port Washington, NY: Kennikat Press, 1968; first pub. 1927, pp. 98–124.

Syrett, David. "The Role of the Royal Navy in the Napoleonic Wars after Trafalgar, 1805–1814." *Naval War College Review,* vol. 32, no. 5 (September-October 1979), pp. 71–84.

2

Maritime Command: Mahan and Corbett

BY JOHN GOOCH

For most of the nineteenth century, maritime strategy was not much more than practical seamanship wedded to local circumstances and shaped by immediate demands. No general theories of war at sea existed; no body of evidence had been amassed upon which to base such theories; and no analytical techniques had been devised to sift everyday maritime facts and shape them into broad principles that any seagoing great power might adopt, regardless of its own unique circumstances and individual peculiarities. By the eve of the First World War this situation had been totally transformed. Alfred Thayer Mahan's *The Influence of Sea Power upon History, 1660–1783*, published in 1890, enjoyed immediate and spectacular worldwide success and was rapidly translated into Russian, German, Japanese, French, Spanish, and Swedish. It provided statesmen and sailors alike with the first general theory of seapower in modern times. Two decades later Julian Corbett's *Some Principles of Maritime Strategy* (1911) propounded an alternative thesis, based on a similar methodology but reaching quite different conclusions. Over the years Mahan's theories have worn less well than Corbett's, though that is partly due to Corbett's greater accessibility. But together the two men stand as the founding partners—as well as rivals—of modern maritime strategic thought.

Until a very few years before Mahan's great work appeared, naval officers had little concept of tactics, and none at all of strategy. The Royal Navy cherished its picture of the Nelsonic battle as a kind of naval free-for-all and stuck enthusiastically to the maxim coined in 1816 by Lord Dundonald: "never mind manoeuvre: always go at them." The perception that war at sea was a political act, whose occurrence, shape, and rhythm should be determined by broad general considerations of national policy and not by the location and size of an enemy fleet, was almost unheard of until Mahan's day. Admiral Bradley Fiske, arriving at the Naval War College in 1903, thought that war was "merely a situation in which great numbers of men or of ships fought one another."

Mahan introduced his students (among them Admiral Fiske) and his readers to the idea that war at sea was always part of a broader conflict of purpose and ideas, and taught them to regard fighting as merely an instrument to achieve a particular purpose. Corbett opened the eyes of his audience to the fact that Nelson was something more than a tactical genius and had perceived that the broad object of all naval warfare was to control seaborne communications. Both men related naval activity to political purpose—which is the fundamental requirement of all strategic theories. In this much they agreed, but when it came to detailed analysis and prescription, they differed profoundly.

THE ROOTS OF MARITIME STRATEGY

In the 1850s and 1860s, when the French and British navies were both converting to steam power, theories of naval warfare were no more than borrowings from land warfare, uneasily blended with a range of immediate problems that differed so much that no general strategic theory could accommodate them all. Some theorists saw fleets—"like well-trained armies in the field"—sailing in columns and trying to turn an enemy's flank; others regarded steamships as no more than troop transporters and imagined that naval war in the future would comprise a series of individual boarding attacks by marines; and others again expected that a key feature of sea warfare would be attacks on the fortified dockyards to which steam-powered fleets would frequently have to withdraw for repair. At a more down-to-earth level, naval attacks on the fortresses of Sevastopol and Sweaborg during the Crimean war (1854–56) pointed to the importance of flotillas of mortar-carrying vessels, while the valuable work of gunboats on the rivers of China—and later Africa—bred a separate group of enthusiasts for "fluvial warfare."

Before 1890 the only school of strategic thought worth the name was to be found in France. There Anglo-French rivalry—a traditional feature of the foreign policy of both countries, and one that did not begin to disappear until 1904—was overshadowed by Franco-German rivalry. France could not afford both a large army and a large navy, and since a large army was essential if she was to face the might of Germany, she was condemned to operate with a weak fleet. During the 1880s, however, under the guiding hand of Admiral Theophile Aube, the French Navy made the best of a bad job and elaborated on a theory of commerce warfare: a *guerre de course.*

Aube correctly ascertained that Great Britain's vulnerability lay in her heavy dependence on imported food and raw materials to feed her population and fuel her industry. By attacking British commerce, rather than seeking to destroy her naval power, France could raise British insurance rates, thereby producing economic panic and annihilating Britain's financial power. Technical developments put into Aube's hands the torpedo boat and the submarine—weapons relatively cheap to build and which, when deployed in this way against a power such as Great Britain, promised to be highly effective. Aube's theory, which had some influence in Russia and the United States and which could be supported by a variety of historical examples, suffered from two fundamental difficulties. It depended upon a capability to strike the enemy fleet effectively with offensive weapons, and it applied only to specific cases. Also, it was seen as the weapon of the avowedly weaker power.

Aube's ideas were no more than a practical prescription to meet particular national circumstances, and general theories of seapower and maritime strategy remained virtually unknown until 1890, so that the very novelty of Mahan's—and later Corbett's—ideas might alone have gained them a wide audience. But two other general trends worked to stimulate that audience and prepared the ground for their theories. One was the pace of development of naval technology. The first steam-powered vessel, the *Demologos,* had been built in 1814 by Robert Fulton to defend New York harbor; and from the 1840s, with the invention of the screw propellor, a period of some thirty years of naval innovation set in. Armor and ordnance improved rapidly; sail power was gradually discarded, and the introduction in 1859 of the compound engine with its relatively modest coal consumption greatly extended the range of roaming fleets. With the completion of the *Devastation* in 1873, the modern warship had arrived on the scene: iron-hulled, screw-driven, armor-plated, her four rifled guns mounted in turrets fore-and-aft, her mast used only for signaling, she was essentially much like the capital ship of the early twentieth century and very much unlike the three-decker ship-of-the-line that had been the primary weapon at sea only half a century earlier. Experimentations and refinements followed—most notably the quick-firing gun and the gyroscopically controlled torpedo—but by 1890 the age of radical alteration in ship design was at an end. New instruments of seapower were at hand. Mahan provided a strategic formula for their use.

The second factor affecting the market for strategic ideas was the state of mounting international rivalry that characterized the late-nineteenth-century world. During the first half of that century no significant challenge was mounted to unseat Great Britain from her position as naval top dog. This changed in the second half of the century. Britain's lead as the first industrialized nation was steadily eroded with the rise of major industrial competitors: Germany, France, and Russia within Europe, Japan and the United States beyond it. The world depression, which lasted from 1875 until 1896, and the adoption by most nations of protective tariffs in order to protect home markets and nurture infant industries served only to heighten growing international rivalry.

This rivalry found expression outside Europe in a race to seize uncolonized areas and a re-division of territories belonging to powers too weak to hold on to them. Thus Britain, France, Italy, and Germany collided in the scramble for Africa after 1882; the Spanish and Portuguese empires were carved up anew; and the great powers scrabbled for spheres of influence in China. This global rivalry made seapower a vital arm for every modern state that aspired to great power status—necessary for the protection of its coasts and its commerce and necessary also for the projection of power if it was to exercise influence in far corners of the globe. The time was ripe for the ideas that Mahan was developing at the Naval War College, which were to burst upon the world in 1890.

What marked out both Mahan and Corbett from their predecessors was their concern to establish a body of scientific knowledge and their belief that general principles of naval strategy existed, merely awaiting discovery. Unlike previous thinkers, both men set out to develop a systematic study of war at sea in its broadest sense—that is, to identify by analysis permanent and general strategic principles that were universally applicable. They sought these principles through the study of history. Mahan talked of "those permanent strategic lessons which lie close to the surface of naval history." Embedded in the past like fossils, such principles merely awaited excavation. But while historical study was the backbone of the new strategic theories, it alone could not yield the truth. The past had to be fitted into a conceptual framework, and both men turned to earlier theorists to help them: Mahan to Antoine Jomini, the Swiss writer on land warfare, and Corbett to Karl von Clausewitz. By this means each man produced a "big picture," and together they provided the terminology, the definitions, and the concepts that are the foundation of all subsequent discussion of seapower and maritime strategy.

MAHAN

When he came to the Naval War College in 1886, Mahan was a forty-five-year-old naval officer of no great note, "drifting," as he later put it, "on lines of simple respectability." He had been born at West Point on 27 September 1840, the son of Dennis Hart Mahan, dean of the faculty there. He entered Annapolis in 1856 and left three years later, graduating second in his class. At that time the United States Navy still lived under sail, and Mahan always felt more at home there than in the age of coal-fired armor-plated warships to which he addressed his theories. After an undistinguished part in the Civil War, about which he published a book in 1883, he languished until called to Newport to lecture on naval history, tactics, and strategy.

Although his immediate task was to educate naval officers, Mahan's work was from the first addressed to a wider audience. *The Influence of Sea Power upon History* (1890), the most celebrated work in a stream of 20 books, 161 articles, and numerous letters, pamphlets, and essays, had a practical object as well as a pedagogical one: "to draw from the lessons of history inferences applicable to one's own country . . ." Mahan's message to Americans was that they must now play an international role upon the world scene. To do this, the United States must cease to be an insular continental power and instead become a global force by building up her maritime power. The first step in this process had already been taken: a naval appropriations bill in 1883 had authorized the construction of four steel battleships in American yards, and they had been completed four years later. Mahan's ideas gave this policy a new impetus. Six weeks after the publication of his book, Congress agreed to the construction of three "sea-going, coast-line battleships." With this decision the United States set out on the path to seapower as Mahan understood, explained, and preached it.

Mahan never clearly defined the term "seapower," though in 1897 he remarked—unhelpfully—that it was "at once an abstraction and a concrete fact." Nor did he clearly distinguish it from the ideas of "command of the sea"—the concept for which he is best known—

and "sea control." Indeed, from time to time he used the three terms as if they were synonymous, thereby making it difficult to work out his exact meaning. However, by separating out his ideas in ways he did not himself undertake, it is possible to understand what he thought and to identify a hierarchy of interrelated concepts. This helps us to see that *The Influence of Sea Power upon History*, although it is ostensibly a narrative history, is in fact about three different ideas and that history is merely a means of explaining and illustrating them.

At the top of the Mahanian hierarchy stands the concept of seapower. This was very much more than merely the size and strength of a fleet of warships, or even of the combined size of a state's commercial and naval resources. Seapower consisted of a series of interlocking factors. Possession of a powerful navy permitted a country to acquire colonies and overseas possessions, which in turn strengthened and expanded its commerce, thus increasing its wealth. This, in turn, increased its strength and therefore its capacity—to quote the eighteenth-century French statesman Choiseul—to "maintain numerous armies, to increase its population and to make possible the most glorious and most useful enterprises." Thus, on the basis of the example of Britain in the seventeenth and eighteenth centuries, Mahan concluded that being a great power meant being a sea power and that seapower meant commercial and naval strength.

MAHAN'S ELEMENTS OF SEAPOWER

To explain what made a country into a sea power—rather than just how seapower worked—Mahan identified six critical elements. The first was *geographical position.* The ideal was England, an island power with no land frontiers to defend, so situated as to have easy access to the major trade routes of the North Sea and the Atlantic. By contrast France and the United States were both powers that sat astride two bodies of water, forcing them to disperse their attentions and their efforts instead of being able to concentrate them. Next came *physical conformation,* by which Mahan meant the seaboard. Good ports were an obvious advantage, and a poor hinterland could force a country outward into world trade since its own resources were not rich enough to support its people. *Extent of territory* Mahan explained not as sheer numbers of people, but as the proportion of the population to the length of the coastline; and in identifying the *number of the population* as a fourth element of seapower he meant the percentage of a nation's inhabitants who followed the sea for a living.

Very much a child of his age, Mahan believed in the idea of *national character* and selected this as the fifth element of seapower.

Some countries, such as England and Holland, had an open attitude toward commerce and a creative vision of colonies; others, such as Spain and Portugal, were merely acquisitive and rapacious, seeing colonies as targets for plunder; and others again, notably the French, despised commerce and lauded thrift, making them a race of hoarders. Finally Mahan highlighted the *character of government* as a vital element of seapower. In Louis XIV's France, Colbert had guided government so that it actively stimulated shipping, markets, and colonies, and in eighteenth-century England Mahan perceived a government that had paid careful attention to creating, equipping, and maintaining the nation's navy and securing for it bases of operation. A watchful government, prepared to intervene wherever necessary to build up and sustain the navy, was Mahan's ideal.

This part of Mahan's work does not offer prescriptions for action, but this should not necessarily be viewed as a criticism. For, as we have seen, in defining the six elements of seapower Mahan was moving towards a general theory of power politics. Even here Mahan was engaged in a form of strategic analysis, for it is an essential part of the strategist's task to identify the basic components of power. Without doing so, he is incapable of arriving at any valid calculus as to his own and the enemy's resources, upon the basis of which strength can be maximized and deficiencies minimized.

Next in importance to *seapower* came *naval* power. All the elements of seapower contributed indirectly to naval power. For example, a population that included a high proportion of seafaring folk could be expected to produce a better-manned navy than one whose people were landlubbers. But three particular factors came together to make up naval power, which can best be seen as fighting power at sea. The first was position: the accidents of geography put some nations in a more advantageous position to use and contest the ocean seaways than others. Second came bases, essential for extended naval reach around the globe and never more so than in the age of coal. Third came the fleet itself: ships of the line, numerous but not overlarge, manned by capable and well-trained crews.

Superior naval power conferred upon the nation that possessed it the ability to exercise command of the sea. Mahan defined this as "the possession of that overpowering power on the sea which drives the enemy's flag from it, or allows it to appear only as a fugitive; and which by controlling the great common, closes the highway by which commerce moves to and from the enemy's shores." Naval strategy, the third element in the Mahanian hierarchy, determined how naval power must be used in order to secure the goal of command of the sea.

Fundamental to Mahan's thinking was the belief that wars were won by the economic strangulation of the enemy from the sea. His study of English history between 1688 and 1814 (the closing date of his last great historical study, *Sea Power in its Relations to the War of 1812*, published in 1905) convinced him that in every phase of prolonged war between England and France command of the sea by naval domination—or the lack of it—had determined the outcome. The fundamental aim of strategy was the destruction of commerce, which to Mahan was the same thing as breaking the enemy's economic strength and therefore depriving him of his power to continue resistance. However, unlike Admiral Aube and the theorists of the *guerre de course* who had preceded him, Mahan did not believe that this could—or should—be done by commerce raiding. Cruiser warfare was a valuable weapon of naval strategy, but it was not the only, or even the chief, weapon.

For insight into how to wield the weapon of naval power, Mahan turned to Jomini and the well-tried principles of land warfare. His guide was Jomini's dictum that "the organized forces of the enemy are ever the chief objective"; in Mahan's hands this became the proposition that "the enemy's ships and fleets are the true objects to be assailed on all occasions." Jomini's rules of land strategy shaped and determined Mahan's precepts for strategy at sea. From Jomini he learned the importance of using preponderant force at the decisive point in battle, and armed with this insight he then scanned the past to locate examples that confirmed it.

The first strategic proposition Mahan presented to his readers was the notion that the fleet was an offensive weapon. As such it should be used offensively wherever possible: "the assumption of simple defensive in war is ruin," he wrote. "War, once declared, must be waged offensively, aggressively. The enemy must not be fended off, but smitten down." From this it followed that battle was the central act of war at sea, at once the most effective and the most necessary of all strategies. Because the possession of a superior fleet gave command of the sea, Mahan held that the enemy's fleet, if it could be reached, was the paramount objective. Thus, naval strategy could be reduced to a matter of fighting a single cataclysmic and decisive battle in which victory would confer command of the sea on one side or the other. This at any rate was the picture of Mahan's thought that was painted later by popularizers and disciples. So it is important to note that Mahan himself qualified his strategic recommendations.

First, he recognized that fighting a decisive battle was *not essential* for the destruction of an opponent. The prospect of defeat, if ever he ventured to sea, could force an enemy to adopt ineffective strategies, thereby bringing about his own exhaustion and strangulation. Secondly, Mahan realized that seapower was not a shock weapon alone. In an interesting but often neglected passage in *The Influence of Sea Power Upon History*, he spoke of the "noiseless, steady, exhausting pressure with which seapower acts, cutting off the resources of the enemy while maintaining its own, supporting war in scenes where it does not appear itself, or appears only in the background, and striking open blows at rare intervals . . ." But perhaps most significant was Mahan's change of heart over blockade and commerce warfare.

In 1890 Mahan saw a place for blockade as a minor but contributory element of naval strategy. Destroying commerce he relegated to the status of a secondary operation of war if it involved the independent action of cruisers; only if it involved the control of a "strategic center" by a great fleet was he prepared to see it as a primary operation. However, within two years he had begun to change his mind, and in an article written in 1895 he argued for the importance of "offensive blockade," which aimed at preventing incoming supplies from reaching an enemy, and "defensive blockade," which sought to stop an enemy fleet from leaving port "because such freedom of issue to an enemy means danger to certain national interests!" In *The Influence of Sea Power Upon the French Revolution and Empire, 1793–1812* (1892) and subsequent articles, he suggested that war against trade was a primary and not a secondary strategy. Navies existed for the protection of commerce, and therefore in war they ought to aim at depriving their enemy of it. By 1905 he was emphasizing the importance of blockade and the capture of commerce as important constituents in a strategy aimed at commerce prevention or commerce destruction. But in *Naval Strategy*, his unsatisfactory attempt to sum up his own theories published in 1911, he completely omitted any reference to blockade.

The final principle of Mahanian strategy was the importance of concentration. This was unavoidable—indeed essential—if, as Jomini dictated, the mass of one's own fleet was to be directed against fractions of the enemy's at the decisive point. Here the importance of one of Mahan's six elements of seapower—geographical position—came into play as an agent that might confer a natural advantage or disadvantage. But beyond the happenstances of nature there were decisions to be made. Concentration had both a tactical and a strategical dimension, and if command of the sea was first to be attained and then maintained, it was necessary to decide on a scale of defensive priorities. Failure to make the necessary hard choices, Mahan believed, was what had brought Britain to defeat in 1780–1781 when she tried to fight France and America simultaneously.

Mahan's ideas won a worldwide audience and made him one of the most celebrated figures of the age. Command of the sea was at one level a straightforward and attractive idea that was easily assimilable. At another level it explained how to use the new warships of the industrial age, ever growing in size and power. And beyond this, seapower, as preached by Mahan, seemed to be the formula for great power status and world influence. What made the new ideas all the more acceptable was that they seemed to be hallowed by history: not invented, but quarried from the true past. Yet almost as soon as the ink had dried upon the page, Mahan's theories began to appear suspect. The deepest flaws in the theory of command of the sea are the consequence of the deficiencies in his intellectual method. His historical evidence was based on few sources and sifted according to preconceptions that dictated what he wanted to find. And his reasoning was often faulty; for example, where Mahan claimed that Britain was a predominant naval power because she possessed colonies and reaped the rewards of overseas commerce, the relationship is probably more near the truth if put the other way around. But over the years two major grounds for criticism of Mahan's views on seapower have come to predominate.

The first questions Mahan's assumptions about the nature and source of economic power. Mahan's analysis was rooted in the history of pre-industrial Europe and applied to an era of exploration and commercial exploitation in which maritime transport created trade and trade created wealth. By 1890 this age had already passed, and the conditions he regarded as fixed no longer applied. The roots of national power were now to be found in manufacturing and heavy industry, and political developments such as the unification of Germany between 1864 and 1871 and the emancipation of Russian serfs in 1861 stimulated the rise of other industrial powers to challenge and overhaul Great Britain.

The main challenge to the framework upon which all Mahan's ideas hung came from the British geopolitician, Sir Halford Mackinder. In a lecture published in 1904 entitled "The Geographical Pivot of History," Mackinder argued that the Columbian age of overseas exploration and conquest, which had lasted for 400 years, had come to an end. The future lay with large, continental land powers who, thanks to modern science, were now beginning to realize their innate potential. Their large populations provided reservoirs for factory labor; new metallurgical, mining, and manufacturing techniques allowed them to create wealth at a rate hitherto unseen; and railways linked them together, freeing them from dependence on the sea. The future, Mackinder prophesied, belonged to the "greatest natural fortress on earth," the Heartland as he called it. By 1943 Mackinder explicitly equated his Heartland with the Soviet Union, and expressed his conviction that the greatest danger for the democratic states was that the dominant land power in the Heartland would become strong in the maritime arena and challenge the sea powers *at sea*.

The sheer pace of technological change, and its expression in the arms race that took place in the years up to 1914, also challenged the universal validity of Mahan's theories. He believed—and said—that the general principles of maritime warfare were essentially unaffected by technological change; but even as he wrote, developments were taking place that made it doubtful whether command of the sea, as he conceived it, could ever be won. Mines and torpedoes exposed the vulnerability of expensive capital ships, diminishing their power to exercise control over the seas and—no less importantly—affecting a commander's will to press home attacks on the enemy. The airplane exposed the surface warship yet further, forcing some wrenching readjustments in thinking and operations during World War II. If command of the sea was the essence of naval strategy, then that essence was no sooner identified than it evaporated. As one critic put it, "Mahan's dictum had lost its validity within two decades of its pronouncement."

CORBETT

Although the possible effects that such new weapons as the torpedo and the submarine were likely to have on war at sea were a little easier to discern at the opening of the twentieth century than they had been fifteen years earlier, it is not because of any greater technological perceptiveness that Sir Julian Corbett's work came to rival that of Admiral Mahan. Unlike Mahan, Corbett offered no general theory of seapower; instead he focused his thoughts on the nature of maritime strategy and the purposes of naval warfare. His ideas were less grand in their sweep, but more sophisticated in their expression. In Corbett's writings, ideas were carefully thought through and plainly stated. As a result, his thought is easier to understand and assimilate—not least because, unlike Mahan's, it is not woven into extensive forays into naval history. Yet despite their many differences, the two great theorists of maritime command are alike in one important respect: both sought to persuade their audience that there was a "correct" way in which to make use of seapower.

A brief glance at his background reveals that Julian Stafford Corbett lacked everything in the way of practical experience of the sea that Mahan enjoyed. He was born in England on 12 November 1854 and educated as a lawyer, a profession that he practiced until 1882. A deep interest in naval history, starting with the Tudor age, led him to publish a series of historical studies from 1898, and these brought him to the attention of the British Admiralty. In August 1902 he was invited to give a course of lectures at the Royal Naval College, Greenwich, and urged by the course director to use this opportunity to demonstrate the influence of politics on strategy. Corbett did not find the task an easy one; writing to a friend three years later he said, "I had no idea when I undertook it how difficult it was to present theory in a digestible form to the unused organs of naval officers." In November 1906 he wrote up his "Notes on Strategy," and after undergoing some revision they were published in 1911 as *Some Principles of Maritime Strategy*. Thereafter Corbett worked closely with the Admiralty, first drawing up war plans and then writing the early volumes of the official naval history of the First World War, until his death on 22 September 1922. It is worth noting that the Admiralty was by no means overjoyed by Corbett's official histories, even going so far as to issue a formal disclaimer of official responsibility for the texts.

Where Mahan learned from Jomini, Corbett drew upon Clausewitz. The briefest excursion into *Some Principles of Maritime Strategy* immediately reveals this: on the second page Corbett quotes Clausewitz—who remains unnamed—on the value of theory as a guide to self-education. Clausewitz's influence on Corbett is apparent at various points in the work, particularly in discussions of the nature of friction at sea and of limited warfare—what Clausewitz called "war limited by contingent." Clausewitz's central proposition—that war is a political act—underpins the whole of the work; but here Clausewitz probably only reinforced what Corbett had already perceived. His early historical work, carried out before he had read *On War*, shows a clear awareness of the interrelationship of war and policy. However, the theme that in war the determining factor is the political object is very much sharper in Corbett's work after 1907, when he had read Clausewitz, than in 1904 when he had not.

Like Mahan, Corbett believed that pursuing the minutiae of naval activity without constant reference to the main purpose that generated such activity distorted the historical perspective. Unlike Mahan, he had reservations about the value of adopting other people's theories wholesale, or even quarrying them for analogies. First, and more generally, he thought that the interest and requirements of a sea power differed in fundamental ways from those of a land power: "where a maritime empire is concerned caution is required in applying the simple formulae of continental strategists." Secondly he believed that land warfare was unlike sea warfare in several fundamental respects.

In war on land it was always theoretically possible to strike at the enemy; in sea warfare it was not. The enemy might not be located, or might simply stay out of reach. This meant that concentration of force was not a golden rule in naval warfare. The maxim that lines of communication must be protected was much more difficult to follow at sea than on land, since at sea those lines were not fixed. And where destroying an enemy's army was the highest objective of land war, destroying his battle fleet was not the highest objective at sea. Protecting commerce was more important. In other words, Corbett analyzed sea warfare as a thing in itself, essentially unlike any other and having its own unique characteristics. In doing so, he was deeply influenced by his interpretation of British history, as was Mahan.

Corbett drew a clear distinction between maritime strategy and naval strategy. By maritime strategy he meant the principles governing a war in which the sea is a substantial factor. Naval strategy was what determined the movement of the fleet after maritime strategy had determined what part the fleet should play in relation to land forces. Here, as we shall see, Corbett's thought was unfinished and even perhaps contradictory, for within this distinction there lurked two different views about the primary task of sea warfare. Corbett divided strategy into two kinds: "major strategy," worked out with reference to the purpose of the war as a whole and embracing diplomatic and trade considerations, and "minor strategy," or the planning of specific operations. The nature of the object determined the nature of the strategy: a negative object required a defensive strategy (denial), while a positive object demanded an offensive strategy (acquisition). Conceptually very sophisticated in their day, Corbett's ideas were a distinct advance on Mahan's loose terminology.

Like Mahan, Corbett saw command of the sea as the central issue in naval warfare. Thereafter he disputed everything Mahan had said about it. About its importance he was uncompromising: "The object of naval warfare," he wrote, "must always be directly or indirectly either to secure the command of the sea or to prevent the enemy from securing it." However, to Corbett command of the sea was a relative and not an absolute: it could be either general or local, temporary or permanent. Where Mahan suggested that command of the seas was possessed either by one side or the other, Corbett proposed that this state of affairs was highly unusual; normally, the seas were uncommanded. What mattered was not conquering the sea but securing for oneself the right of passage upon it.

Corbett believed that the prime object of naval warfare, and therefore the first task of the fleet, was to secure communications. This was achieved by sea control, not command of the sea. Getting what he called "working control of the sea" did not necessitate concentrating all one's efforts on fighting and winning a decisive naval battle. Winning battles at sea was "the supreme function of a fleet," but since all that was necessary to achieve one's objects was local or temporary control, naval powers had a range of options at their disposal. These included fighting a partially successful defensive action; forcing the enemy to concentrate elsewhere; and marking or containing the enemy's sea forces bearing on a particular area. Corbett's most important contribution to theories of maritime command was to demonstrate that what mattered was not the enemy's fleet but the right of passage on the sea. Only if an enemy fleet was in a position to render this unsafe must it be put out of action.

This emphasis on use of the sea brings in its train the question: what is the right of passage to be used for? Here Corbett was of two minds. On the one hand—and thinking in very broad terms—he believed that war was fundamentally a matter of exerting overwhelming economic pressure on an opponent. "Wars," he suggested, "are not decided exclusively by military and naval force. Finance is scarcely less important. When other things are equal, it is the longest purse that wins." (Here Corbett was quoting Choiseul who originally made this remark.) Following this line of thought, Corbett suggested that victory at sea, or preponderance upon it, should be used primarily to capture or destroy enemy property. Crippling an enemy's finance was a direct step towards his overthrow, and therefore any operations that aimed to do this should be considered as primary strategic operations. However, Corbett also believed that it was almost impossible that a war could be decided by naval action alone. This led him to propound a theory of naval and maritime strategy that has proved over the years to have been very seductive.

Corbett's early historical work had led him to conclude that naval action undertaken by ships alone was not likely to produce decisive results. "The real importance of maritime power," he wrote in *The Successors of Drake*, published in 1900, "is its influence on military operations." England's failure during the reign of Queen Elizabeth I to gain a decisive success on the continent was due, he believed, not to the stupidity of her policy or the manner in which seapower had been deployed, but to the lack of a proper army with which to exploit naval opportunities. A subsequent study of *The Campaign of Trafalgar* (1910) convinced him that, great as it was, Nelson's victory had been overshadowed in importance by the battle of Austerlitz. British seapower had been insufficient to defeat Napoleon. Without a supporting army, imaginatively led, a navy was not a decisively effective weapon. It was the task of maritime strategy to determine the mutual relations of army and navy in a plan of war.

Analytical study based on the Clausewitzian dictum that war is an act of policy, and has as its object a settlement of disputes that is politically more favorable to oneself, confirmed Corbett's thinking on the close relationship between sea warfare and land warfare. "Since men live upon land and not upon the sea," he pointed out, "great issues between nations at war have always been decided—except in the rarest cases—either by what your army can do against your enemy's territory and national life, or else by the fear of what the fleet makes it possible for your army to do." Corbett rested his case chiefly, however, on British experience during the Napoleonic wars. Then, the effects of her intervention by amphibious operations had always been out of proportion to their intrinsic strength—or so he believed.

The nub of Corbett's thinking was pithily summed up by Admiral Sir Jackie Fisher, British First Sea Lord from 1904 until 1910, when he remarked, "The army is a projectile to be fired by the navy." But this brief and accurate summary of the core of Corbett's thought about naval power and maritime strategy conceals more than mere straightforward observation of the lessons of history. Corbett heartily disliked the total war which—as Clausewitz taught—Napoleon had introduced into European history and which had as its aim the annihilation of an opponent's armed might and will to resist. For him, limited war was the ideal. Britain's tradition of using her strength at sea to assist powerful land allies whenever the balance of power in Europe threatened to succumb to hegemonic control had been effective without being unduly costly. Thus, as long as she was secure against direct invasion Britain could safely—and successfully—adopt a policy of limited war by committing only a portion of her strength directly to the fray.

Corbett recognized that strategic operations of this kind were possible only for a maritime power, and that the same reasoning did not apply to land powers. But he left his readers in no doubt as to the place of limited war and amphibious operations in the hierarchy of maritime and naval strategies: it was, he said, the true meaning and highest military value of what was called command of the sea. To back up his assertion he quoted Francis Bacon's famous remark that "He that commandeth the sea is at great liberty and may take as much or as little of the war as he will." He also called in his support Clausewitz's contention that the defensive was inherently the stronger form of warfare and his proposition that, in certain circumstances, war might be limited "by contingent." To demonstrate that by adopting this strategy it was possible to maintain the initiative and yet take advantage of the inherent power of the defense, Corbett sketched a scenario in which a sea power could take the initiative by selecting a territorial objective on the edge of a land mass and land troops to seize it, thereby forcing the enemy to take the offensive in order to dislodge the landing party.

From what has been said so far it will be obvious that battle—interpreted as the clash of capital fleets in a single decisive encounter—played only an ancillary role in Corbett's scheme of things. This was partly because Corbett saw war at sea as presenting a range of problems and options, where Mahan saw it in more black-and-white terms. Indeed, in a sideswipe aimed at his American predecessor and rival, he criticized "the firm faith in the decisive action as the key of all strategical problems." If an enemy fleet held back from battle, then it was neither necessary nor wise to try to bring about a decisive encounter. War at sea consisted of very much more than long interludes of inactivity punctuated by brief and violent clashes; as he pointed out in *England in the Seven Years' War*, published in 1907, moments when the destruction of an enemy's main fleet and securing the command "of a certain sea" were of prime importance were rare. If such great moments were to occur, they had to be worked for. But he made it explicitly and implicitly clear that since the object of naval warfare was not command of the sea but sea control or sea denial, battle was not the be-all and end-all. The mere presence of a major naval force on the margin of an ocean area—a "fleet in being"—might alone be enough to prevent the enemy from putting to sea to disrupt or deny use of it.

Corbett regarded concentration of the fleet as both undesirable and unnecessary—at least in the way that Mahan interpreted it. Massing the fleet meant that concealment of dispositions and of intentions was at an end; "The further, therefore, from the formation of the ultimate mass we can stop the process of concentration, the better designed it will be." True concentration involved elasticity of distribution and control from a common center. Ships would best be used when spread out to cover a wide area and yet able to combine when and where necessary. If concentration as Corbett perceived it—

which could be called "controlled dispersion"—were done effectively, then the enemy would have to disperse also. It therefore followed that proper (i.e., Corbettian) concentration of one's own fleet would never result in the massing of the hostile fleet—"the almost necessary preliminary to securing one of those crushing victories at which we must always aim, but which so seldom are obtained."

From Corbett's proposition that war was at rock bottom an issue of competing economic strengths, it followed that the destruction of an opponent's seaborne trade and protection of one's own were important tasks that should affect naval strategy. At first Corbett was inclined to underplay this fact. In an early study of *Drake and the Tudor Navy* (1898), he condemned Hawkins for attacking commerce and thereby adopting a wasteful and inefficient form of warfare. But by 1911 he was prepared to acknowledge a place for attacks on trade in the panoply of sea warfare. However, his preference was for blockade as one means by which a stronger fleet might secure command of the sea. Such a blockade might be either "open"—that is, conducted at a distance—or "close," when it aimed at sealing shut specific enemy ports and harbors by a combination of mines and patrolling ships.

Corbett paid rather more attention to commerce protection than to commerce destruction, and he took a very positive view about the prospects of being able successfully to defend commerce against enemy attack in time of war. In place of the Mahanian commandment to attack the enemy's fleet, he suggested that merchant shipping could be protected in three different ways: by staking out defended areas, by establishing terminal defense systems about the points of departure and arrival, and by the use of convoys and escorts in between. He did not believe that Britain's greater dependence on overseas trade made her more vulnerable than ever before; the greater the volume of trade, he suggested, the less effective the impression an enemy could make upon it. Attack was more difficult because routes could be varied with steamships in a way that had been impossible in the age of sail and because an increase in the number of ports had divided up trade, and defense was easier. To justify the latter proposition Corbett quoted the old adage "Where the carcass is, there will the eagles be gathered together"—which proved to be the downfall of the German U-boat campaign in World War II.

Corbett was writing for and about a maritime power, and although his prescriptions were uncompromisingly plain, he was aware that circumstances alter cases: "a system of operations which suits one form [of war]," he warned his readers, "may not be that best suited to another." Nevertheless, his ideas were no more flawless than Mahan's. For one thing, he too failed to discern the likely effects of technological developments. He explicitly discounted the possibility that the torpedo might nullify the idea of defended areas for commerce protection. He also very much underestimated the damage the submarines could do to maritime trade by assuming that the aim of commerce raiding would be to capture rather than to destroy enemy ships—which would require them to be manned by prize crews—or that if it were otherwise, the laws of war at sea, which required that warnings be given to merchantmen under attack and provision made to remove passengers and crew safely before sinking them, would be adhered to. This was not to be the case.

More fundamentally, Corbett's preference for limited war over absolute war led him to allot to amphibious operations a significance and value that were probably greater than they deserved. His historical studies underemphasized the importance to Britain of powerful continental allies and of the direct support she gave them by contributing large forces to the fray. And at bottom they were a negation of the most fundamental aspect of Clausewitz's thought. If war is shaped by the political object, it follows that greater objects require larger injections of force if they are to be achieved. Eventually there comes a point when amphibious operations are simply not enough— as Britain discovered in both the world wars.

REFLECTION

The theories of maritime command expounded by Mahan and Corbett were rooted in their study of an age when command—or control—of the sea was a matter of mastering a medium that had only a surface dimension. By the time of Mahan's death the advent of the submarine had added a second dimension to the problem. And by the time of Corbett's demise the airplane pointed to a third. Moreover, although the dreadnoughts of the early twentieth century packed much more power than the *Victory* or the *Temeraire*, their role in war at sea did not differ very greatly from that of the "wooden walls" of Nelson's age. The power of seaborne ordnance to strike deep into continental land masses, the contribution naval air could make to land battles, and the operation of a nuclear deterrent at sea had yet to exert their full force on naval and maritime strategy. These considerations might appear to render irrelevant ideas that are now more than three-quarters of a century old. But to carry out any and all naval tasks it is first necessary to have unrestricted use of a portion of the world's seas. Together, Mahan and Corbett identified a fundamental problem of sea warfare to which every age must find its own solutions.

BIBLIOGRAPHIC NOTE

Mahan has been much written about, and there are several good brief introductions to his thought. The most recent is Philip A. Crowl, "Alfred Thayer Mahan: The Naval Historian," in Peter Paret, ed., *Makers of Modern Strategy from Machiavelli to the Nuclear Age* (Princeton: Princeton University Press, 1986). Margaret Tuttle Sprout, "Mahan: Evangelist of Seapower," in Edward Mead Earle, ed., *Makers of Modern Strategy: Military Thought from Machiavelli to Hitler* (Princeton: Princeton University Press, 1971), pp. 415–45 is still worth reading. Much the best short introduction to Julian Corbett is to be found in Geoffrey Till and others, *Maritime Strategy and the Nuclear Age* (New York: St. Martin's Press, 1982), pp. 39–43.

Quarrying Mahan's writings for a few representative extracts summarizing the main elements of his thought is well-nigh impossible, as his ideas were widely scattered through a large number of books and articles. It is possible, however, to get a useful insight into his thought from Alfred Thayer Mahan, *The Influence of Sea Power upon History 1660–1783* (London: Methuen, 1965), pp. 1–24 (Introduction), 25–89 (chapter 1) and 505–41 (chapter 14). Corbett is much more accessible; see in particular Julian S. Corbett, *Some Principles of Maritime Strategy* (London: Longmans Green, 1911), pp. 1–9 (Introduction), 13–27 (part I, chapter I), 49–56 (part I, chapter 4), 157–68 (part 2, chapter 1).

ADDITIONAL SOURCES

Field, James A., Jr. "Alfred Thayer Mahan Speaks for Himself." *Naval War College Review.* (Fall 1976), pp. 47–60.

Graham, Gerald S. *The Politics of Naval Supremacy, Studies in British Maritime Ascendancy.* Cambridge: Cambridge University Press, 1965.

Kennedy, Paul M. *The Rise and Fall of British Naval Mastery.* New York. Crane, Russak & Co., 1983, chapters 6–8.

———. *The Rise of Anglo-German Antagonism, 1860–1914.* London: George Allen & Unwin, 1979.

———. "Mahan versus Mackinder: Two Interpretations of British Seapower." *Strategy and Diplomacy 1870–1945.* London: Fontana, 1984, pp. 43–85.

Kennedy, Paul M., ed. *The War Plans of the Great Powers 1880–1914.* London: George Allen & Unwin, 1979.

Livezy, William E. *Mahan on Seapower.* Norman, OK: University of Oklahoma Press, 1981.

Marder, Arthur J. *From the Dreadnought to Scapa Flow. I: The Road to War 1901–1914.* London: Oxford University Press, 1961.

McNeill, William H. *The Pursuit of Power: Technology, Armed Force, and Society Since A.D. 1000.* Oxford: Basil Blackwell, 1983, pp. 224–41, 262–306.

Nelson, Jean Ware. *The Seapower Doctrine of Alfred Thayer Mahan.* Stanford: Naval Warfare Research Center, 1960.

Schurman, Donald M. *The Education of a Navy: The Development of British*

Naval Strategic Thought, 1867–1914. Chicago: University of Chicago Press, 1965.

———. *Julian S. Corbett, 1854–1922: Historian of British Maritime Policy from Drake to Jellicoe.* London: Royal Historical Society, 1981.

Seager, Robert, II. *Alfred Thayer Mahan: The Man and His Letters.* Annapolis: Naval Institute Press, 1977.

Semmel, Bernard. *Liberalism and Naval Strategy: Ideology, Interest, and Seapower During the Pax Britannica.* London: George Allen &. Unwin, 1986, pp. 134–51.

3

The Strategy-Tactics Relationship

BY WAYNE P. HUGHES, JR.

At the most fundamental level, it is accepted that the strategist directs the tactician. The mission of every battle plan is passed from the higher commander to the lower. There is no more basic precept than that, and no principle of war is given greater status than the primacy of the objective.

This is not the same as saying that strategy determines tactics and the course of battle. Strategy and tactics are best thought of as hand-maidens, but if one must choose, it is probably more correct to say that tactics come first, because they dictate the limits of strategy. Strategy must be conceived with battle in mind—or, as Soviet doctrine requires, with due regard for the correlation of forces and means of the two opponents.

Strategy is paramount in determining the aims of the tactician. But strategy is limited by means. An assessment of means—the combat power available and its utility to achieve strategic objectives—starts with an adequate understanding of the tactical employment of forces in battle. In the golden age of naval thought before World War I, *war-fare* was the subject, and strategy, tactics, and technology were debated all together.

Tactics are the activities of forces in battle. A tactical commander directs these activities. One should be careful to distinguish between *forces* on one hand and the concept of *Force* on the other hand.

Force describes *forces* united in action under the direction of a commander, and which embody combat power.

Force, F, is a function of *forces, m,* of a certain quality and quantity, and their combat activities of a certain rate and coordination of effort. If Force, or fighting power, is directly proportional to the product of these quantities, then the useful assertion becomes:

$$F = ma$$

Whether this is merely an analogy with physics, or contains the grains of truth, the distinction to retain is the difference between forces *m*, which is a quantity the strategist provides, and Force, *F*, which the tactical commander generates by *the manner in which he activates—employs—his assigned forces.*[1]

Recall what Clausewitz has written. He should be quoted at length in full context, because like the Bible, Clausewitz can be cited to make contradistinctive points:

> What actually halts the aggressor's action is the fear of defeat by the defender's forces, [even though] he is not likely to concede this, at least not openly.
>
> One may admit that even where the decision has been bloodless, it was determined in the last analysis by engagements that did not take place but had merely been offered. . .where the tactical results of the engagement are assumed to be the *basis* of all strategic plans, it is always possible, and a serious risk, that the attacker will proceed on that basis. He will endeavor above all to be tactically superior, in order to upset the enemy's strategic planning. The latter [strategic planning], therefore, can never be considered *as something* independent: it can only become valid when one has reason to be confident of tactical success. . .it is useful to emphasize that all strategic planning rests on tactical success alone, and that—whether the solution is arrived at in battle or not—this is in all cases the actual fundamental basis for the decision. Only when one has no need to fear the outcome—because of the enemy's character or situation or because the two armies are unevenly matched physically and psychologically or indeed because one's own side is the stronger—only then can one expect results from strategic combinations alone.[2]

Clausewitz dealt with ground warfare. The passage above is found in his discussion of defense, which he and other analysts believe is the stronger tactical posture on land. As will be seen, the tactical nature of ground-war force often differs from sea-war force. Specifically there has been no corresponding tactical advantage for the defense in naval combat. Nevertheless, in this instance, what Clausewitz thought to be the link between tactics and strategy on the ground applies even more strongly at sea, if that is possible.

The reason, therefore, that a discussion of tactics is appropriate in a book on strategy is because strategy must rest on combat power. One builds decisions from the bottom up: tactics affect the efficacy of forces, the correlation of forces reveals what strategy those forces can support, and a supportable military strategy governs national aims and ambitions.

This is the opposite of an approach that starts with national goals and policies, that in due course defines military strategy, and that all the time takes largely for granted that the forces will be able to execute it. The top-down approach is proper for deriving force requirements to guide procurement policies; but force requirements, if they exceed existing force levels, can only be built for the future. If one is concerned with present strategy, he must know current capabilities and design his strategy accordingly. If forces are inadequate, then a strategy that is part bluff may be necessary, but it is important for the bluffing state to understand that the strategy is in fact unexecutable and may lead to self-delusion. Many will remember the days when the U.S. defense department proclaimed a 2 1/2 war strategy, which, in fact, was not a strategy at all but a method of sizing general-purpose military forces. The notion of maintaining sufficient general-purpose forces to fight two full-scale wars and simultaneously to deal with a lesser contingency lingered on long after it was beyond U.S. capabilities to accomplish.

Of course, a current maritime strategy is not really so simple that it can be built from bottom up. The process is dialectical, with policy and strategy goals juxtaposed against combat capabilities. But current strategy must derive from realistic force comparisons.

Perhaps the pivotal nature of tactical considerations will be made more concrete by starting with this: It is demonstrable both by history and theory that not only has a small net advantage in Force (not, remember, the same as forces) often been decisive in naval battles, but also that the slightly inferior force tends to lose with very little to show for its destruction in damage to the enemy.

At sea, there has been no counterpart to prepared positions and the effects of terrain, nor anything corresponding to the land warfare rule-of-thumb 3-to-1 attackers-to-defender ratio. There are no mountains nor swamps to guard flanks, no rivers to cross or defend, and no high ground—except perhaps the high ground of space, which is common to both land and sea warfare. A fleet tactical commander keeps no force in tactical reserve, and all his energy is devoted to attacking the enemy effectively before the enemy can attack him. At sea, offense dominates in a way foreign to ground commanders. When a strategist's force is not competitive, he would be well advised to stand clear, because he will have little to show for the loss of his forces.

In peacetime, every strategist must estimate the true worth of his navy vis-à-vis the enemy in combat or he risks deep humiliation with or without bloodshed. That, above all, was the lesson for Argentina in the Falklands War, which found its armed forces outclassed by those of the United Kingdom. In wartime, every strategist must know the relative fighting value of his navy, so carefully nurtured and expensive to build and maintain in peacetime. When committed in battle, the heart of a fleet can be cut out in an afternoon.

If sea battles are so quick and decisive when they occur, then why is it that the consequences of seapower are so slow-acting? There are two reasons. One is that the inferior force, recognizing its inferiority and the probable consequences of battle, declines to fight until pressed by some prospective overriding consequence on land. Instead, the inferior navy seeks to nibble away at the enemy's control of the sea. The other is that the fruits of satisfactory command at sea ripen slowly. An abiding theme of this book is that seapower is not an end, but one means to the end, which is to affect events on the land. A quick tactical decision often entails a prolonged strategic result.

THE TECHNOLOGY-TACTICS RELATIONSHIP: TWO SIDES OF ONE COIN

Historically the inferior navy has usually been well aware of its strategic inferiority. Today such knowledge is not so certain. Determining the relative capabilities of modern U.S. and Soviet forces is particularly challenging. In part, this is because the two fleets are so asymmetrical in composition. We cannot compare battle lines and their supporting cruisers, destroyers, and submarines. Much of Soviet seapower is represented in land-based bombers, still more in the Soviet submarine fleet. Much of the weight of U.S. antisubmarine forces are P-3s, likewise based on land. Many countries have the capability to launch not only an air strike but also a missile attack from the land. Modern "coast artillery" represents a new breed of cat, reaching out into what used to be the exclusive domain of ships.

The second major reason it is difficult to correlate force today is that there has been no major fleet action since 1945. Without battle we can only infer the influence of technology on tactics. It is certain that missile propulsion, guidance systems, satellites in the sky, nuclear power, computers, and a host of other developments will dramatically change war at sea if and when it occurs. We have only a handful of clues in the public domain, however, like the damage to the USS *Liberty* by an Israeli attack, the capture of the USS *Pueblo* by the North Koreans (which was an indication of the importance of signals warfare and the responsibilities of command and control—C^2), and the "old fashioned" way an unopposed navy supports operations both coastal and inshore, exhibited by the Korean and Vietnam wars.

For fleet actions, there are only two data points—the Israeli missile-ship battle against the Syrian and Egyptian forces in 1973, and the Falkland Islands War in 1982. It is not much on which to base far-reaching decisions regarding present tactics and future procurement of ships, aircraft, sensors, and C^2 systems.

Technological change in the absence of battle testing is not new, however. There are remarkable parallels between the current period, 1945 to the present, and another era of vast technological progress from the middle of the nineteenth century to the beginning of World War I. That earlier period saw only the Battle of Lissa in 1866, the Battle of the Yalu in the Sino-Japanese War in 1894, and the Battle of Tsushima in 1905 as major fleet actions.

That technology would revolutionize tactics was seen by naval officers of all great powers. The implications of steam propulsion and its dramatic effect on tactical maneuver, the countervailing advances in armament and armor, the role of the ram, advances in mines and torpedoes, and towards the end of the period the wireless, the submarine, and the aircraft, all were subjects of a great tactical debate. These and lesser devices wrought by technological progress were then, as now, imagined to carry the most extravagant implications.

The period was also a golden age of tactical study, analysis, and writing, without parallel before or since. The remarkable result was that by the outbreak of World War I the debate, in the main conducted in public, had arrived at an accurate consensus of how battleships, cruisers, destroyers, and—insofar as fleet actions were concerned—submarines would be fought. Tactical study, combined with intensive fleet exercises, paid off. At sea, there were a few, but only a few, tactical surprises in World War I.

TECHNOLOGY AND STRATEGY: THE OVERLOOKED CONNECTION

On the other hand, the influence of technology on maritime *strategy* was not only sweeping in World War I but also largely unforeseen. The end of the close blockade, the effect of the mine and submarine on amphibious and other inshore operations, and the end of the surface raider as a major player in maritime warfare were anticipated by a few farsighted strategists, but the full impact in World War I had to be discovered by trial and error and amended by fire. Even before the war, the shift from sail to steam had changed the nature of tactics enormously. But its strategic consequences were no less dramatic. So much were ships tied to coaling stations that it was often hard to say whether the fleets deployed to protect colonies or colonies were established to support the fleets and the movement of trade in the new steamships. In the North Sea, the cockpit of the naval war, all fleet movements were short runs governed by the limited endurance of the participants. Wireless affected the deployment of the fleets throughout the world, and code breaking by both the British and Germans repeatedly brought about or frustrated the efforts of both sides to entrap the other. Finally, neither the Germans who conceived the first U-boat campaign, nor the British who were victimized by it, had manifested an inkling of understanding of the submarine's potential before war broke out in 1914. Fleet action was the full basis of strategy in the major navies of the world. While much brooding took place over the torpedo threat and the submarine as instruments that threatened battleships, the strategic surprise was that the submarine could serve as the replacement of the surface raider as a massive new threat to shipping—in the end so formidable that the traditional and virtually discarded means of protecting trade, the venerable convoy, had to be revived after a sharp and lengthy debate.

Mahan, for all his wisdom, had contributed to the mistaken belief in the durability of strategy and its relative immunity to technological change. His oft quoted "from time to time the structure of tactics has to be wholly torn down, but the foundations of strategy so far remain as though laid upon a rock" went astray because it failed to distinguish principles from practice.[3] Whether in the realm of strategy or tactics, there is a difference between principles and the actions that derive from them. Even though tactics are changed by new technology, that does not preclude the search for tactical principles nor a recognition that some ways of combat abide. And if there are strategic principles, that does not mean the strategies will be unaffected by new technology. Strategies as well as tactics are influenced by "the weapons made by man . . . in the change and progress of the race."

In fact, strategy, standing as it does above tactics, is twice vulnerable to technological change. It is affected directly: consider, for example, new forms of mines, first magnetic, then acoustic and pressure actuated, and now deep ocean mines and how they have altered the ways that surface warships, submarines, and merchant ships may safely be employed around the world in war. Strategic weapons—ICBMs, SLBMs, and long-range bombers—by their very name belie the possibility that strategy can escape basic change caused by technology.

In addition, strategy is affected indirectly through changes in the form of battle tactics. Some naval examples will be revealed in due course. Here one might note briefly how the machine gun, a modest little weapon, so enhanced the power of the tactical defense on the ground that it led to a shocking end to maneuver warfare on the Western Front in World War I. The primacy of the defense having been a lesson too well learned, it was implemented by new static fortifications, the most noteworthy of which was the Maginot Line. Then in 1940 tanks and tactical aircraft were married in a new concept that punched holes in the defense, restored the vigor of initiative and the power of the offense, and resulted in the gravest strategic consequences with "lightning war," the aptly named *Blitzkrieg*.

It is well to consider what revolutionary strategic consequences new technology might have wrought since 1945, nuclear weapons apart. If the defense on the ground has regained much of its potency, the strategic implications are nearly boundless. If the potency of maneuver with deep penetrations by helicopter-borne forces augmented by long-range missiles is ascendant, then technology may have reshaped not only the battlefield but also the very nature of war with equal drama, accompanied by a potential strategic finality as sweeping as the rapid capitulations of Poland, Belgium, the Netherlands, and France to the *Wehrmacht*.

THE FOUNDATIONS OF TACTICS:
TRENDS, CONSTANTS, AND CONTEXTS

Trends. Nearly always the effect of technology is to enhance a trend already manifest. This may be, in the end, a better reason to study naval history than the search for principles or constants. To see trends and evaluate the pace of change is the closest thing that military men will ever have in peacetime to foreseeing the nature of the next war, whether it starts tomorrow or a long time hence. These trends can be exposed only in an abbreviated way here. A fuller accounting may be found in *Fleet Tactics: Theory and Practice*.[4] Evidently the most basic trend is the increasing range and lethality of weapons. From these flow the expansion of the battlefield, the dispersal of forces over greater distances, the need for sensors compatible with weapons' ranges, the importance of sensor countermeasures and exploitation, and the ability to command forces over great distances without giving away fatal information to the enemy.

Constants. Yet, not everything at sea is in flux. There *are* constants—sturdy guides that have held so far. One, of course, is the importance of combat leadership and its special relationship to strategic leadership. Strategists *plan*, tacticians *do*. A strategy is an ambition, a tactic is an activity. The strategist may expose himself and his country to consequences of the deepest and most far-reaching kind, but the arena of the tactician is one of mortal danger, of exposure to physical violence and morally debilitating chaos for himself and his comrades. No one should assert that the future sea battle will be more destructive than, say, those of the seventeenth century Anglo-Dutch Wars, but equally no one should believe that there were ever heavier demands on tactical commanders and their men for sustained moral and physical courage than will be seen on the vast future battlefield at sea. We may expect a combat environment like that at Okinawa, when the danger of kamikaze attacks had to be endured for weeks on end. Or we may see a blow as sudden as that felt by the Syrian and Egyptian naval forces from the Israeli missile boats in 1973.

The tactician knows he must prepare his men for rapid collective action. To do so in a very large organization requires continuity in doctrine and training. A major revision of established methods is not a step lightly undertaken. Looking at a lower level, battle plans cannot be modified very many times without creating hopeless confusion. The best battle plan looks almost too simple and obvious after the fact, but its essence is a distillation of considerations without end. The best strategy may be labyrinthine in its interlocking, multifaceted, ingenious, ambiguous intricacy. The best tactics will rest on elegant simplicity and clarity, achieving control, unity, and order in the face of the ominous potential for fear, panic, and chaos that lurks beneath the surface of the staunchest warrior.

The best known of all constants is the principle of concentration. Its discovery as a principle of action comes at about the time two boys learn to pick on one. It is embodied in the unethical but practical twist, "In war, never pick on somebody your own size." Broadly and carefully expressed it says (as Soviet doctrine does), "concentrate the main effort and create superiority in forces and means over the enemy at the decisive place and time." At sea there is a simpler maxim, and one that happens to hold up even better: *attack effectively first.* The latter will be demonstrated to be a more satisfactory central and unifying principle than concentration when modern missile warfare is discussed later in the chapter.

Contexts. This is a book that examines the fundamentals of maritime strategy. In this chapter some relationships between tactics and strategy are assessed. In such a book, one has to deal with general truths couched as trends and constants. This means that the treatment is constrained to remain, by and large, in the domain of theory. *Contexts* determine the particulars of a battle plan and the forms and patterns of specific tactics. The two orders of battle, the opposing missions in their larger strategic contexts, the ocean environment, and the proximity and influence of land—these are the great variables that cannot come into sharp focus until the eve of battle. A smooth transition from tactical theory to peacetime preparation to wartime practice depends on sound combat doctrine.

DOCTRINE: THE GLUE OF TACTICS

As much as can be foreseen in peacetime must be imbedded in doctrine, and training must be assiduously keyed to it. Doctrine integrates and institutionalizes the right combination of tactics so that a nation's forces will fight as a coordinated unit, with minimum signals and extemporizations during battle. When a navy's possible wartime tasks are as sweeping as those of the U.S. Navy, the structure of combat doctrine is acutely difficult to formulate.

Combat activities that cannot be doctrinally preordained and practiced in peacetime must be inserted into the wartime operation order, which is close enough to battle to remove most of the peacetime uncertainties. In fact, an operation order, fleet fighting instructions, or a battle plan are all properly thought of as case-specific doctrine, applicable to an arena of war and a set of forces with tasks to accomplish. All these written instruments, along with the signal book and team training, are the means by which a commander builds tactical unity into his force in advance, the way a coach unites his team by practice with specific plays. They are the *foremost* ways a commander exercises command and control.

Doctrine is one of the subtle concepts of command. Its implementation varies from country to country and service to service. In the United States it is best thought of as a set of policies and procedures followed by forces to assist in collective action. At the tactical level procedures dominate policies as to content. Tactical doctrine must never be interpreted as dogma, to be followed heedlessly. But doctrine must not be abandoned without justification. There is always a tension in the sound formulation and implementation of doctrine. Too tightly phrased and enforced, it stultifies initiative; too loosely phrased it is a collection of useless platitudes, and when too loosely practiced it loses its unifying power.

Naval history's most famous example of a departure from doctrine to good purpose was Nelson's at the Battle of Cape St. Vincent on 14 February 1797. The British had a chance to split the French and Spanish, but if they maneuvered as a unit as required by doctrine—the Fighting Instructions—the opportunity would be lost. Nelson, close to the rear of the fighting column, wore his ship out of line (thus turning *away* momentarily from the enemy) as the quickest way to get at the enemy and, supported by one other ship captain who saw what Nelson was about, independently headed off the enemy, in that way precipitating a victory. In those days the Fighting Instructions *were* tantamount to dogma, and Nelson's superior was John Jervis, notorious as a remorseless disciplinarian. Nelson had no assurance that Jervis would concede the primacy of tactical brilliance over good order and discipline in the fleet. But in this instance Nelson's move was so decisive and his physical courage and combat skill so manifest in the outcome that Jervis—later Earl St. Vincent—was quick not only to forgive but to praise Nelson's boldness.

THREE TACTICS-STRATEGY INTERRELATIONSHIPS

We have seen that military forces are transformed into force, or combat power, by being put in action by command. That is why tacticians emphasize not forces but the tactics those forces employ. Before the essence of naval tactics is examined, it is worth pausing to investigate three examples of the tactical-strategical relationship. The first example is in the realm of force planning, the Washington arena. The second deals with naval operations, the battle arena. The third illustrates the danger when either the strategist or the tactician lays his plans without due regard for the risks he may impose on his counterpart.

First, in U.S. and NATO studies of the military reinforcement and resupply of Europe in the 1960s and early 1970s, classical convoy tactics were used. The escorts formed a ring around the merchant ships, but the ASW screens so configured could not prevent the penetration of many torpedo-firing submarines. The navy's strategists drew the conclusion that more ASW protection should be acquired. Other strategists who toted up the navy's hardware bill said there must be a better strategy—better meaning less expensive. One solution was to preposition army divisional combat equipment in Europe and then fly the troops over to marry up with it. No one questioned the soundness of the convoy tactics on which the gloomy losses were based until the early 1970s when some work done concurrently by the Center for Naval Analyses, the Commander Antisubmarine Warfare Atlantic Fleet staff, and a small NATO study group at the headquarters of the Supreme Allied Commander, Atlantic, concluded that if you opened out the merchant ship formation and imbedded the protection *inside* the convoys, then the losses to merchant ships would be reduced by a factor of two or three. Sound tactics and strategy had been interwoven. Suppression of submarine effectiveness at the convoys would reduce the rate of shipping losses, giving time for other ASW forces remote from the sea lanes to kill the submarines.

The same studies of the tactical details of the convoy engagements revealed that the submarines ought to be able to find enough targets to unload all of their torpedoes on every patrol, unlike the experience of World War II when the average U-boat fired less than one-sixth of its torpedoes on a patrol. The number of torpedoes carried to sea, therefore, became a number of extreme importance, because estimates of shipping losses over the entire campaign were in direct proportion to torpedoes carried. When that fact was appreciated, intelligence analysts took a more careful look at the torpedo load of enemy submarines and decided they had probably overestimated it, and in so doing overestimated the damage the submarines could do over their lifetimes.

With the estimates of probable losses of merchant ships reduced dramatically, did convoying re-emerge as the preferred strategy? Not exactly, because there were too many other considerations—political, budgetary, and strategic—affecting the decision. The present attitude toward the desirability of convoying is: in some circumstances yes, in others, no. Here the interrelationship with strategy again enters the picture. If a U.S. ASW policy that emphasizes forward antisubmarine operations and barriers to prevent Soviet submarines from reaching oceanic sea lanes in significant numbers is executable, then that will have a powerful and positive effect to reduce the need for convoying. If the United States is surprised, however, as the Allies were in World Wars I and II, then the strategist has some assurance that the tactics are in hand to convoy the most vital shipping if that becomes necessary.

Secondly, consider a radically different example of the integration of strategy and tactics. It shows up at the interface between land and sea, in what felicitously has been called "littoral warfare." Navies are built and supported in order to influence events on land. Almost impossible to find is an instance of two fleets going out to fight like boxers in a ring, may the best ships win, and to the victor go the spoils and command of the sea. Seldom has the inferior fleet failed to appreciate its inferiority, and so it has been only some matter of the gravest consequence that drew the weaker fleet into battle.

One tactical implication is that the larger fleet in case after case has been burdened with the forbidden sin of split objectives. Consider the 1942–45 Pacific War. Japan or the U.S., whichever was superior and on the offensive, almost always entered into battle with prioritized, but nevertheless dual, missions: to shield the movement of some vital force and to destroy the enemy fleet. The whole Pacific strategy-tactics interface can be studied and understood in that context. The maxim that a fleet should first gain control of the sea before risking an amphibious assault turned out to be impossible to follow, because short of the overwhelming strategic consequences of homeland invasion, the smaller fleet would not fight.

Now look at the sea battles in World War I—in particular, those in the North Sea. In this case the battles came about by some subterfuge, a strategic entrapment, the British hoping to lure the German High Seas Fleet into a death trap, and the Germans hoping to snare some detachments of the Royal Navy and whittle the larger fleet down to equality. Since neither Britain nor Germany had strategic motivation to come to battle at a disadvantage, and since the German Admiral, Scheer, knew his fleet was decisively inferior, there was never a fight to the finish, as strategists had anticipated before the war. The German High Seas Fleet ended its days not with a bang, but with a whimper.

As the range of weapons and sensors increased, so did the direct, tactical interaction between land-based and sea-based forces. There is no finer example than the Solomon Islands Campaign of 1942–43 of ground, sea, and air forces all acting in unison—not coincidentally or serendipitously, but necessarily and vitally. A subject worthy of more study is the way these tactical interactions on a wider, deeper future battlefield will carry over into the realm of strategy and policy. Land-based aircraft and missiles already reach well out to sea. Sea-based aircraft have had an influence that is well known, and now missiles from the sea will also play a role. One of the tactical lessons of the Solomons is this: do not plan to put a Marine Brigade into northern Norway merely to hold the land flank, but also to hold the maritime flank. The Marines and their accompanying air power fight from a vital piece of real estate that will support operations at sea as well as on the ground. It is hard to find a more apt example of littoral warfare in the making.

Thirdly, ponder the problem of the U.S. Sixth Fleet Commander in the Mediterranean. He is very conscious of the need to attack effectively first, but he knows American policy is unlikely to give him the freedom to do so. He also appreciates that policy has often required a forward and exposed presence in the Eastern Mediterranean. His survival at the onset of war rests on two hopes to offset these two liabilities. The first is that he will be given the freedom of movement in sufficient time to take a geographical position that will make a major attack on him difficult. The second is that his Rules of Engagement will allow him to act with measured force when certain circumstances demand it. Since the steps he must take are in the nature of denying the enemy tracking and targeting information—"anti-scouting" as the term will be defined later—both the location he must take and actions he must be authorized to take have to be understood and accepted at the policy level.

The *modus vivendi* in effect must be satisfactory both with regard to tactics (battlefield risks) and to strategy (political risks). It is important to see the conflict between the statesman's political objectives and the naval commander's tactical operations in a crisis. The tactician at the scene usually understands the primacy of diplomatic and political objectives. But an optimum political stance, such as a highly visible naval presence, can require a vulnerable and risky battlefield posture. The tactician and strategist both need agreement that to contain a crisis, the nation must position itself to win twice, both politically and on the field of battle.

HOW TACTICIANS THINK: THE PROCESSES OF NAVAL BATTLE

The essence of naval tactical theory is simple. It reduces to four statements, each describing a process.

1. Naval warfare is attrition-centered. Attrition comes from the successful delivery of firepower.
2. Scouting (to be defined momentarily) is a crucial and integral part of the tactical process.
3. Command and control transform firepower and scouting potential into delivered force upon the enemy.
4. Naval combat is a force-on-force process involving, in the threat or realization, the simultaneous attrition of both sides. To achieve tactical victory, one must attack effectively first.

Firepower, scouting, and C^2 are the three elements of naval forces—the means—and attrition is the great end. That is all there is to it, but that will prove to be enough to challenge the wiliest tactician. Napoleon himself knew how simple naval warfare was. Of his 115 maxims of war, only the last three refer to naval matters. "The art of land warfare is an art of genius, of inspiration," he wrote in his final maxim.

On the sea, nothing is genius or inspiration, everything is positive or em-
piric. The admiral needs only one science, that of navigation. The general
needs all of the sciences, or a talent which is equivalent to all; that of
profiting by all experience and all knowledge.[5]

Every navy reader will detect the irony in Bonaparte's final thrust,
as he vented his frustration over French admirals who never seemed
able to beat the British at sea. Yet Bonaparte was right. He saw that
naval warfare is simpler in tactical essence and that the complexity
arises in the execution, even as he said, "The qualities required to
command an army are born in one, but those to command a fleet
are obtained only by experience." It is a venerable truth that seamanship was the first essential of success at sea, and in addition that "on
the land men fight with machines, but at sea machines are fought by
men."

Of course, the four elements of naval combat are permuted in many
ways, rather like physicists and engineers elaborate on and apply Sir
Isaac Newton's laws of motion. A few of these formulations will be
explored in order to establish the basis for richer discussions of tactics-strategy interrelationships.

TACTICIANS WIN BY ATTACKING EFFECTIVELY FIRST: FIREPOWER AND DEFENSIVE FORCE

Let us shift from viewing firepower delivery, scouting, and C^2 as
processes and treat them as elements of naval force. Evidently there
is an antithesis to each.

The antithesis of firepower is the ability to destroy the attacker's
aircraft, missiles, or torpedoes. Call it "defensive force." Offensive and
defensive power could be substituted as well, but it is a useful cue
to retain the asymmetry of defensive force as the defender's response
to firepower. Navies historically (less evidently today) responded to
enemy firepower by building survivability into the hulls of warships,
which was called "staying power" in the days of 16-inch guns and
12-inch armor belts.

SCOUTING AND ANTISCOUTING

In order to discuss the antithesis of *scouting*, termed simply *anti-
scouting*, it is time to define the term. Scouting is information gathering by any and all means: reconnaissance, surveillance, cryptanalysis, or any other type of what some call information warfare. But the
scouting process is not complete until the information is delivered
to the tactical commander. The correct image of a scout is
J. E. B. Stuart riding up to Robert E. Lee and saying, "I have seen Joe
Hooker starting to cross the Rappahannock at Germanna Ford and

he will not be across for three more hours." Scouting is delivered tactical information about the enemy's position, movement, vulnerabilities, strengths, and (in the best of worlds) intentions.

Naval scouting consumes a lot of resources. A quarter, no less, of the British Grand Fleet and German High Seas Fleet at Jutland (measured in major-caliber guns) were in the two scouting formations. If Beatty had thought more of his role as scout and screen for the Grand Fleet and less of his own firepower, he would have saved Jellicoe a great deal of tension later when the High Seas Fleet hove into view.

Tactical scouting consists of four elements: detection, tracking, targeting, and post-attack damage assessment. The first three—detection, tracking, and targeting—form a chain, with as much redundancy built into the chain as possible. Anti-scouting is activity to break the chain, or more commonly, to retard the enemy's rate of accumulating targeting information. Anti-scouting is like a handful of sand in the eyes. Smoke screens were an old measure used; search-radar jamming is a major modern method. We could call this interference "screening," except that screening has come to be used ambiguously, both as anti-scouting and as a counterforce term (*viz* antisubmarine or anti-air warfare screens).

C^2 AND C^2 CM

Command decides what is wanted from the forces, and control transforms the want into realization. Communications (as signals) is embodied in control, indeed it is the principal instrument of on-the-scene control. C^2 operates on its forces to scout, and to position and deliver firepower.

Command and control *countermeasures* are the steps to limit the enemy's ability to decide (command) and disseminate decisions (control). For some naval officers that is an unusually narrow definition. It is not anything that needs to be explored here. What is important is to think of each tactical commander allocating his forces among four functions,

Firepower	Defensive force
Scouting	Anti-scouting

Meanwhile, the enemy commander is doing the same thing. Some (perhaps most) weapon systems from a fleet commander's point of view can be used for more than one purpose, and so an allocation of forces among these four roles is one of his major decisions. Among the fascinating stories of these allocations is the evolution of U.S. and Japanese carrier deck loads among fighters, scouts, and bombers through World War II, and how the tactical commanders split their assets among reconnaissance, attack, fighter escort, and combat air patrol.

As the two opposing commanders make their allocations and deploy for battle, they are simultaneously making positioning and timing decisions. A naval battle "starts" well before the first weapons are fired. Both are taking a series of steps building toward a climactic decision, in which the winner will be the force that attacks effectively first.

MANEUVER, POSITION, FIREPOWER, AND SCOUTS

Already the simplicity of three tactical activities—shooting, scouting, and commanding—begins to seem ominously not so simple. Setting aside C^2 as activity (however complicated) that merely directs, four interrelated activities remain for C^2 to orchestrate. Considering that the enemy commander is doing the same thing, each commander has eight variables to integrate into his thinking, four that he normally controls and four that he will attempt to influence but that he cannot control. If a tactical commander's analysis admitted only two possible states of each variable, that is already 64 sets of circumstances.

Maneuver ranked first in classical naval tactics. In fact, some have defined fleet tactics as maneuvers. On the ground, tactical maneuver must be retained as one of the indispensable elements of tactical thought. In modern naval combat, speed of the weapon has so come to dominate speed of the platform, that for the sake of simplicity and clarity relative position is emphasized instead. Advantageous position, usually in terms of weapon range and sensor reach, is the correct frame of reference. Motion over time is the means, but *position* is the end. Start the tactical estimate with desired positional relationships as the goal, and work back to see whether sensors and weapons can be maneuvered to achieve them.

A BRIEF EXAMINATION OF SOME TRENDS IN TACTICS

Four things have been established. First, the strategist must know something about force, which is the tactician's province, as well as forces, which is his own. Second, future strategic decisions are affected by technology just as are tactical decisions. Third, the probable effects of new technology on future war are best seen through the contrast between trends and constants of battle. Fourth, a structure for analysis, describing the processes (or activities) of combat will provide direction as we next examine history to discern some of the essential changes wrought by technology.

Four historical periods will be discussed, with explicit emphasis on the trends of the attrition process but with some salient conclusions regarding the emerging importance of the scouting process as well. The ways and means of concentrating force will be the principal theme, with tempering provided by the appearance of missiles and modern naval tactics. The example should illuminate why "attack effectively first" is a stronger expression of the tactical aim of naval action than merely concentrating force.

THE AGE OF FIGHTING SAIL, 1550–1810

Because the effective range of naval gunnery was under half a mile, it was impossible to concentrate more than two sailing ships on one of the enemy. Even that was rare against a well-organized, tightly spaced enemy column. So concentration of firepower was built into the ship-of-the-line herself, by adding more decks of guns. Moreover, it was well understood that when both ships were handled competently, a three-decker would not only destroy a two-decker, but the latter would lose without having done much damage to the former. A 3:2 advantage in firepower was overwhelming.

THE BIG GUN ERA, 1890–1930

By contrast, when the effective range of guns opened to about eight or ten miles early in the twentieth century, it was possible to concentrate the firepower of the entire battle line. The focus of the tactician of the period was on ways to concentrate the fire of his whole line on a portion of the enemy's line. "Crossing-the-T" of the enemy battle line was the dream of every battleship admiral. Moreover, the advantage did not have to last for very long. Under conditions of good visibility, a ten-minute initial advantage could be decisive. It was further observed that a force advantage even as small as 4:3 would be equally decisive. An American naval officer, Bradley A. Fiske, and a Frenchman named Ambroise Baudry showed how this worked with successive salvos. A small advantage rapidly became greater as the weaker force sustained damage at an increasingly greater relative rate. They called this the N-square effect. Lanchester transformed their laborious salvo calculations into simple, coupled differential equations. He did so merely to illustrate the principle of cumulative advantage in a more elegant way, using his square-law equations. Almost simultaneously, the Russian M. Osipov[6] discovered the Lanchester form, apparently on his own, and wrote sixty pages of analysis, including the comparison of theory with historical battles.

Baudry and Fiske illustrated the square-law with tables such as

TABLE 1.

End of Minute	Units of Residual Firepower and Staying Power	
	Side A	Side B
0	10	10
2	10	9
4	10	8
6	9.2	7
8	8.5	6.08
10	7.89	5.23
12	7.37	4.44
14	6.93	3.70
16	6.56	3.01
18	6.26	2.35
20	6.00	1.72
22	5.83	1.12
24	5.72	0.54
26	5.67	0

the one below. Sides A and B are two identical forces, each with the firepower to reduce the enemy at the rate of 10 percent every two minutes. The tables show that if you give side A a mere four-minute advantage in opening fire, side B will be destroyed while side A retains more than half (57 percent) of its fighting power.

Baudry and Fiske built similarly simple tables to show the cumulative effect of preponderant force. Let A now have two warships to concentrate on one of B. Under the same conditions as before of firepower and staying power, the table of surviving fighting power looks like this:

TABLE 2.

End of Minute	Superior Side A			Side B
	Ship A_1	Ship A_2	$A_1 + A_2$ Force	B Ship
0	10	10	20	10
2	9.5	9.5	19	8
4	9.1	9.1	18.20	6.1
6	8.79	8.79	17.58	4.40
8	8.57	8.57	17.14	2.70
10	8.43	8.43	16.86	1.00
11.19	8.38	8.38	16.70	0

A "firepower kill" on Side B is achieved in only 11.2 minutes (un-opposed it would take Side A 10 minutes). Moreover, Side A has 16.7 or 83 percent of its fighting power remaining. If the Lanchester "continuous fire" form is used, side A's surviving fighting power is slightly greater, 17.3 instead of 16.7. The reason is similar to the reason that compounding interest daily yields slightly more return than compounding annually.

The Lanchester equations derive the results much more compactly than Fiske's laborious salvo computations. The latter has one great advantage: it leads easily to a discussion of World War II. Say that one ship's salvo destroyed not 10 percent but 50 percent of an enemy ship's fighting strength. If A has a 2:1 advantage, B is eliminated after the first salvo, of course, but he is actually more effective, taking out 25 percent of A's fighting strength (as against 19 percent). That is because the effect of B's first—and only—salvo is greater. What if the possibility that B gets in an *unanswered* salvo first should be allowed? That came to be the frightening possibility of carrier warfare in World War II, and with even greater firepower packed in a single strike by a carrier air wing.

THE AGE OF THE AIRCRAFT CARRIER

In World War II, an attack by a carrier's air wing of dive-bombers and torpedo bombers had the effect of one great salvo of the whole of a carrier's firepower arriving at the enemy in a mighty pulse of destructive force. As a result, whichever carrier fleet commander attacked first did great damage. So for damage assessment it was either

A strikes B first, or

B strikes A first, or

A and B strike simultaneously.

The crucial question was, how much damage could an air wing do? No matter how lacking the consensus before the war about battleship survivability, by the late 1930s there was common accord that a CV was a vulnerable target. For the moment, we will assume that one carrier's air wing had the net delivered firepower to sink one carrier in one attack. The theoretical results are displayed in table 3:

TABLE 3.

	INITIAL NUMBER OF CARRIERS (A/B)				
	2/2	4/3	3/2	2/1	3/1
A STRIKES FIRST	2/0	4/0	3/0	2/0	3/0
B STRIKES FIRST	0/2	1/3	1/2	1/1	2/1

TABLE 3. (*cont.*)

	INITIAL NUMBER OF CARRIERS (A/B)				
	2/2	4/3	3/2	2/1	3/1
A AND B STRIKE SIMULTANEOUSLY	0/0	1/0	1/0	1/0	2/0
LANCHESTER	0/0	2.6/0	2.2/0	1.7/0	2.8/0

When the stronger force, A, attacks first, the consequences are obvious and devastating. However, when the weaker force, B, succeeds in attacking first, then the row "B STRIKES FIRST" demonstrates that the inferior force can be outnumbered by as much as 2:3, accept the disadvantage, and win. In effect, B achieves tactical advantage, neither by superior firepower, nor maneuver as with crossing the T, but by superior scouting.

In the Pacific Ocean carrier battles in World War II, more frequently than not both sides located the other and launched their strikes before the enemy attack arrived. Under the as yet uncorroborated effectiveness assumption of one-for-one, the outcome should be as shown in the row, "A AND B STRIKE SIMULTANEOUSLY." If we inspect the A/B = 3/2 column, we may readily see the dramatic way the outcomes change under the "Pulsed Power" model from the Lanchester (continuous fire) model of naval battle. In the carrier paradigm, A and B both lose two carriers and the outcome leaves A with one carrier and B with none. If both sides had been firing continuously, then the square law would have taken effect for the superior force, and A would have destroyed B while suffering little damage, expecting over two-thirds of his forces to survive (in the "LANCHESTER" row, see, "2.2/0").

What happens when force A is able to counterattack after first sustaining a surprise attack by B? The theoretical results (again under our one-for-one hypothesis) are shown in the next table. B, even when outnumbered 3:2 by A—a disadvantage that is overwhelming under continuous fire—will emerge from the battle with the same number of survivors ("1/1"). But, *only if B was able to attack effectively first*.

Thus far the pulsed power model has been described as pure theory. What are the facts? To calibrate the carrier effectiveness model,

TABLE 4.

RESULTS AFTER A COUNTERATTACKS				
INITIAL FORCE (A/B)	4/3	3/2	2/1	3/1
SURVIVORS (A/B)	1/2	1/1	1/0	2/0

TABLE 5.
THE BATTLE OF MIDWAY
(JUNE 1942) BATTLE SYNOPSIS

	INITIAL FORCES		ACTUAL SURVIVORS	
	CVs	Aircraft	CVs	Aircraft
A JAPAN	4	272	0	0
B U.S.	3	233	2	124

review the five great carrier battles in the Pacific War: Coral Sea, Midway, Eastern Solomons, Santa Cruz Islands, and Philippine Sea. (The Battle for Leyte Gulf was not carrier vs. carrier, but a series of surface actions, sprinkled liberally with land-based and sea-based air attacks on gun-ships.) None works out more handsomely than the Battle of Midway. Table 5 shows the initial forces and final results, with air craft survivors thrown in for detail. (Carrier aircraft losses were brutal in all these battles.) The Japanese started with four carriers, and ended with zero, because American skill, courage, and luck produced the first effective attack. The U.S. Navy started with three carriers and ended with two.

The results are the same as theory would have predicted when calibrated at the one-for-one level of effectiveness. This is shown in table 6. The example lets the Battle of Midway evolve as it did, in three steps: inferior force B (the U.S.) attacked superior A (the Japanese) first and sank three carriers. After absorbing the attack, the remaining carrier of A counterattacked B and sank one carrier. Then in one final re-attack, B attacked A and sank its last carrier.

The four other Pacific carrier battle results are similar. The pulsed power model, for all its simplicity, is an accurate description of the carrier battles in 1942, under the assumption that the net destructive firepower of a carrier wing had the capacity to sink one carrier in one attack. It may surprise some that as the war progressed, it took more than one air wing's attack to sink a carrier. In a mere two years, between December 1941 and the end of 1943, warships had built up their staying power and expanded their anti-air "counterforce" by 100-fold.

TABLE 6.
THEORETICAL SURVIVORS

	After U.S. Strike	After Japanese Counterattack	After U.S. Mop Up
A. JAPAN (4 CV)	1	1	0
B. U.S. (3 CV)	3	2	2

Finally, the point needs to be emphasized again that *superior scouting* was what unleashed the power of attacking first. As a demonstrable trend, commanders at sea in the future will need to devote more and more of their time and energy to the scouting process as opposed to firepower delivery.

MODERN MISSILE WARFARE

One thing plausible, if not probable, about modern naval combat is that some of today's warcraft carry "more than their weight" of deliverable firepower. Hypothesize a missile ship that has the net offensive capability to achieve a firepower kill on three identical enemy ships. Draw up a chart similar to the one-for-one kill capability of carrier air wings that were used to describe the big Pacific battles in World War II.

Table 7 illustrates:

1. What U.S. and Japanese carrier air proponents *believed* would be the effectiveness of an air strike in 1941.
2. The often-held image of modern missile effectiveness with conventional warheads at sea.
3. The universally agreed image of modern nuclear warfare on land and at sea, in the absence of much improved (and some would say scarcely imagined) defensive force.

A major conclusion is that when such a multiple kill capability exists, there are strong reasons to disperse forces and no reasons to mass them. The commander's goal is to concentrate firepower through greater weapon range and modern communications, while operating in a dispersed disposition.

TACTICS AND MODERN CONVENTIONAL NAVAL COMBAT

When the naval war is non-nuclear, the case for dispersal can be overstated. There is insufficient space to develop the model with its

TABLE 7.

	INITIAL NUMBER OF SHIPS (A/B)		
	3/3	3/1	N/1
A STRIKES FIRST	3/0	3/0	N/0
B STRIKES FIRST	0/3	0/1	(N-3)/1
A AND B STRIKE SIMULTANEOUSLY	0/0	0/0	(N-3)/0

extensive treatment of scouting on both sides, but it can be shown that two things continue to have a centripetal effect on naval formations in conventional war, the bread-and-butter environment of the great bulk of the world's warships.

One is scouting. Aggregate scouting capacity of the force may prove decisive in finding the enemy first, leading to the first effective attack. In this instance, the aggregation of forces under a united command aims for superior scouting rather than superior firepower.

The other is defense. It may be the best tactic to mass defensive potential—enough to beat off any attack under the local circumstances in space and time. Oftentimes, the modern decision to mass naval components is not for the purpose of aggregating firepower, but to aggregate defensive force.

As far as the U.S. Navy is concerned, its firepower is concentrated in very large ships. To offset the "modern missile effect," the fleet must have either a better firepower-scouting combination to reach out and strike first, or adequate defenses to stop the enemy's first strike with residual firepower sufficient to let a counterstrike be decisive. Evidently, the modern U.S. battle fleet with its large hunks of firepower and strong anti-air and anti-submarine defenses has implicitly adopted the second method, adequate defensive force. Here are four implications:

1. The massing of battle groups in mutual support is a tactic used primarily for defensive reasons, or sometimes to marshal sufficient surveillance and reconnaissance capability.
2. Navy carrier battle force attacks will be overt, but will employ anti-targeting tactics. Usually the presence of the force cannot be concealed, and for defensive warning and firepower effectiveness, some radiations will be made. But the tactical disposition will be masked by shrewd emission-control planning, cover, and deception.
3. To see whether a carrier battle force should attempt an operation, it is necessary to correlate the force on both sides with competent analysis of all eight elements: comparing one's own firepower, defensive force, scouting, and anti-scouting capacities against those of the enemy.
4. When the carrier battle force is not strong enough to fight its way in, it should not attempt the operation.

CONCLUSION: ATTACK EFFECTIVELY FIRST

When principles are put into practice, changes in the modes of warfare brought about by new technology are as apt to alter strategic possibilities and constraints as those of tactics. The best way to anticipate the changes is to look for trends and constants in the history of warfare.

The result of one's best estimate of the way war will be fought is imbedded in peacetime doctrine, principally as policy at the strategic level and as procedures at the tactical level. The contexts of battle, which can only become manifest when the battle becomes imminent, are reflected in battle plans by whatever names they are called.

Because war is two-sided, a battle plan must be flexible enough to accept tactical changes in action. The plan concerts action, but allows latitude for initiative to exploit opportunity and respond to unanticipated threats.

Modern tactics can be studied and battle plans formulated in the context of the activation and allocation of firepower and scouting assets by a tactical commander, who transforms forces into Force. Maneuver is a means to the end of establishing favorable positions relative to the enemy. Through C^2 a tactical commander scouts and shoots and attempts to reduce the timeliness and effectiveness of the enemy's efforts.

The trends generated by technology indicate that in future naval battles properly handled forces may be able to defeat more than their weight of enemy forces. As a result, sound scouting has been elevated in importance, and detection, tracking, and targeting must be treated by the commander as a major and integral part of the operation. Also as a result, classical concepts of massing firepower at sea have had to be reevaluated.

It is fitting to close with reference to an article from that time when naval tactics and strategy were ably debated in the world's naval journals. In 1905 (then) Commander Bradley A. Fiske was awarded the Naval Institute's Prize for his essay *American Naval Policy*. In it, Fiske devoted no less than 24 of 80 pages to tactics, including the aforementioned rich mathematical illustration of the cumulative effects of firepower. Fiske was an archetypal modern naval leader in four respects:

- He knew technology. For instance he patented plans for an aerial torpedo before aircraft engines were powerful enough to carry it aloft.
- He espoused tactical computations in a form that today is called operations analysis.
- He argued that technology and calculations together were what improved tactics, and better tactics won battles.
- He insisted that in the end the capacity to win battles determined a successful national strategy and policy.

Fiske wrote: "No naval policy can be wise unless it takes into very careful account the tactics that ought to be used in war; in order that the proper ships may be built and the proper kinds of organizations, drills and discipline be devised to carry those tactics into good effect."[7]

The navy has, in the last few years, revitalized interest by its officer corps in modern tactics, and when this interest is reduced to writing and transformed into better tactics, then there will be important effects on American military strategy, organization, and operations in peace and war. Strategy in any war rests on genuine battlefield capability, and the knowledge of who should win if battles at sea take place. New weapons and winning tactics are to fit like hand in glove, and all the military panoply of organization and training in peacetime in the last analysis should be designed to win battles, big or small, fought or declined by the enemy.

Because of the need to establish greater common ground and mutual influence between tactical and strategic planning, we have examined the structure of tactics, both as to historical trends and as to modern practice. We have seen that the strategist supplies *forces* and *aims* and the tactician generates *Force* and *results*. But there are strategists and tacticians on both sides of a conflict. Each opposing tactical commander attempts to deploy his forces at sea in a coherent, integrated way, each with the objective of attacking effectively first.

NOTES

1. This simple point leads down many paths, most of which there is insufficient space to explore here. The seminal work by Dr. Joel S. Lawson (1980) conjectures a useful dynamic model in terms of pressure. The Military Conflict Institute (1987) casts the relationship such that military momentum is the basic quantity of military power, proportionate to forces and their activity. If that is more realistic, then Force varies with the rate of change of activity.

2. Karl Von Clausewitz, *On War* (Princeton, NJ: Princeton University Press, 1976), p. 386.

3. Alfred Thayer Mahan, *The Influence of Sea Power Upon History, 1660–1783* (Boston, MA: Little, Brown & Co., 1890), p. 8.

4. Wayne P. Hughes, Jr., *Fleet Tactics: Theory and Practice.* (Annapolis, MD: Naval Institute Press, 1986), pp. 140–74.

5. Maxim CXV. Reprinted in William A. Mitchell, *Outlines of the World's Military History* (Harrisburg, PA: Military Service Pub. Co., 1940), p. 739.

6. Citations for Fiske's, Baudry's, Lanchester, and Osipov's writings may be found in the section on Additional Sources at the end of the chapter.

7. Bradley A. Fiske, "American Naval Policy," in U.S. Naval Institute *Proceedings*, January 1905.

BIBLIOGRAPHIC NOTE

Wayne P. Hughes, Jr.'s, *Fleet Tactics: Theory and Practice*. (Annapolis, MD: Naval Institute Press, 1986). Chapter three is in many respects a précis of *Fleet Tactics*. Especially pertinent amplification can be found in: "The Seat of Purpose Is On The Land," pages 33–34; "Summary of [Naval] Tactical Trends and Constants," pages 196–99; Chapter 8: "The Trends and Constants of Technology," pages 200–215; and Chapter 10: "Modern Fleet Tactics," pages 240–68. Because battlefield contexts are given scanty treatment here, Chapter 9: "The Great Variables" may also be read profitably.

Giuseppi Fioravanzo, Admiral, Italian Navy. *A History of Naval Tactical Thought*. Translated by Arthur W. Holst. (Annapolis, MD: Naval Institute Press, 1979). Anyone accepting the study of trends, constants, and contexts as the proper basis of sound naval tactics should read this little book in its entirety. He should start with part I, Strategy and Tactics, and if not put off by Fioravanzo's continuing citation of his own earlier tactical writings, will want to read straight through. Either way, part V, The Age of Naval Aviation, should be read.

J. S. Lawson, "The State Variables of a Command Control System" in J. Hwang, D. Schutzer, K. Shere, and P. Vena, eds. *Selected Analytical Concepts in Command and Control*. (New York: Gordon and Breach, 1982). One of the best brief introductions to command and control as a discipline. Lawson, who is the former Chief Scientist of NAVELEX, recognized the need for underlying theory of C^2 to assist him in the practical procurement of better electronic systems for the navy. This reading summarizes many of the best ideas and their applicability.

Charles D. Allen, Captain, USN (Retired). "Forecasting Future Forces." U.S. Naval Institute *Proceedings* (November 1982). In the past half-dozen years there has been a resurgence of interest in tactics in our journals. Allen's article is representative of the best. It is a stimulating blend of strategy, technology, and fleet tactics.

ADDITIONAL SOURCES

Baudry, Ambroise, Lieutenant, French Navy. *The Naval Battle: Studies of Tactical Factors*. London: Hughes Rees, Ltd., 1914.

Bernotti, Romeo, Lieutenant, Italian Navy. *The Fundamentals of Naval Tactics*. Annapolis, MD: U.S. Naval Institute, 1912.

Brodie, Bernard. *Seapower In The Machine Age*. Princeton, NJ: Princeton University Press, 1943.

Clausewitz, Karl Von. *On War*. Edited and translated by Michael Howard and Peter Paret. Princeton, NJ: Princeton University Press, 1976.

Creveld, Martin van. *Command in War*. Cambridge, MA: Harvard University Press, 1985.

Dupuy, Trevor N., Colonel, U.S. Army (Ret,). *Understanding War: History and Theory of Combat*. New York: Paragon House, 1987.

Fiske, Bradley A., Commander, U.S. Navy. "American Naval Policy." U.S. Naval Institute *Proceedings*, Jan. 1905.

Kelsey, Robert J., Commander, U.S. Navy. "Maneuver Warfare At Sea." U.S. Naval Institute *Proceedings*, Sept. 1982.

Lanchester, Frederick W. "Mathematics In Warfare." In *The World of Mathematics*, edited by J.R. Newman. New York: Simon and Schuster, 1956.

Lanza, Conrad H. *Napoleon and Modern War: His Military Maxims*. Harrisburg, PA: Military Service Pub. Co., 1943.

Lewin, Ronald. *The American Magic: Codes, Ciphers, and the Defeat of Japan*. London: Hutchinson & Co., Ltd., 1982; New York: Penguin Books, 1983.

Mahan, Alfred Thayer. *The Influence of Sea Power Upon History, 1660–1783*. Boston, MA: Little, Brown & Co., 1890.

Makaroff, S.O., Vice Admiral, Russian Navy. *Discussion of Questions In Naval Tactics*. Translated by Lt. John B. Bernadou, USN. ONI, Part 2, General Information Series, No. 17. Washington, DC: Government Printing Office, 1898.

Melhorn, Charles M. *Two-Block Fox: The Rise of the Aircraft Carrier, 1911–1929*. Annapolis, MD: Naval Institute Press, 1974.

Morison, E. E. *Admiral Sims and the Modern American Navy*. Boston, MA: Houghton-Mifflin, 1942.

Military Conflict Institute, The. *A Theory of Military Combat and Its Practical Application*. Unpublished draft, Berkeley, CA: TMCI, 1987.

Osipov, M. "The Influence of the Numerical Strength of Engaged Sides On Their Losses," *Voenniz Sbornik* (No. 6, June 1915; no. 7, July 1915; no. 8, August 1915; no. 9, Sept. 1915; no. 10, Oct. 1915). Draft translation by J. J. Schneider, U.S.A., C & GSC, Ft. Leavenworth, 1986.

Reynolds, Clark G. *Command of the Sea: The History and Strategy of Maritime Empires*. New York: William Morrow, 1974.

Richten, Eberhardt. "The Technology of Command." *Naval War College Review*, March-April, 1984.

Robison, Samuel S. Rear Admiral, USN, and Mary L. Robison. *A History of Naval Tactics from 1530 to 1930*. Annapolis, MD: U.S. Naval Institute, 1942.

Uhlig, Frank, Jr. "Naval Tactics: Examples and Analogies." *Naval War College Review*, March-April 1981.

Whaley, Barton. *Stratagem: Deception and Surprise In War*. Cambridge, MA: MIT Center for International Studies, 1969.

II

STRATEGY
AND
HISTORY

4

Athens
and
Sparta

BY BARRY S. STRAUSS

The conflict between Athens and Sparta that came to a head in the Peloponnesian War of 431–404 B.C. is perhaps the classic case of a war between a great land power and a great sea power.[1] In the Peloponnesian War, the fleet of Athens and its allies controlled the seas, while the armies of Sparta and its allies dominated the land. The inability of either side to reach the enemy's center of gravity, and the determination of the combatants—not to mention the limited destructive capabilities of ancient technology—led to a lengthy war of twenty-seven years and to the involvement of virtually all of the Greek world (which included, at that time, the coastal cities of Asia Minor, southern Italy, and Sicily) as well as of the Persian Empire.

These factors also inspired the deposed Athenian commander Thucydides to write his great history of the war. His book is important not only because it is our main account of what happened, but because it is a brilliant, enduring analysis of the nature of war and politics—a "possession for all time," as Thucydides predicted, proudly but justly. A chapter on the Peloponnesian War is of necessity haunted by Thucydides, although it need not agree with all his judgments.

The focus of this chapter will be the strategy of the combatants in the Peloponnesian War and the course of the conflict. The emphasis will be on naval warfare, although considerable attention will be paid to the war on land as well. Before proceeding to these subjects, a few pages of background are necessary.

ATHENS VS. SPARTA: AN OVERVIEW

The Peloponnesian War of 431–404 is part of the larger history of hegemonic conflict in Greece. The wars between the city-states can be traced back to the late eighth century, and they continued until Philip and Alexander imposed a *pax Macedonica* in the late fourth century. The conflict between Athens and Sparta lasted for a hundred years. It began after these two states had led Greece to victory in the Persian invasion of 480–479. Athens incited Spartan fear and jealousy by its refusal to subordinate its newly won seapower to Sparta's traditional hegemony on land. Athens now stood at the head of a naval confederacy that included nearly all of the Greek city-states of the Aegean islands and coasts (west, north, and east); Sparta was a land power that dominated the Peloponnese and central Greece. The boisterous energy of Athens's increasingly confident democracy also troubled the oligarchy that ruled Sparta.

Cold war broke out into armed conflict in the so-called "First" Peloponnesian War of 460–445. At the high point of this conflict, Athens gained control of the rich city-states of Boeotia to the north and of the strategic city-state of Megara to the west, which controlled the land route to the Peloponnese and protected Athens from Spartan invasion. Athens over-extended itself, however, in a disastrous naval expedition to help Egypt revolt from Persia, and suffered great losses. Megara and Boeotia revolted, a Spartan army invaded Attica, and Athens sued for peace. The resulting Thirty Years' Peace (the Greeks, being realists, put time limits on their treaties), concluded in 445, created a détente between the two power blocs and subjected all future disagreements to arbitration. Neutrals had the right to join either side. Fourteen years later, however, in 431, the peace collapsed.

In 404, Sparta emerged victorious from the long Peloponnesian War. Athens had paid an enormous price in manpower and wealth for its war effort, and ended up losing its fortifications, its allies, indeed its very navy. Yet, nine years after surrendering, Athens emerged at the head of an anti-Spartan coalition, supported by disaffected former allies of Sparta, and fought Sparta to a standstill (in the Corinthian War, 395–386). A quarter-century after surrendering to Sparta, Athens formed a second naval confederacy in 377: never to be as powerful as the first, but still, a significant force. Within a decade, Athens and Sparta had put aside their traditional enmity to face a new threat: Thebes.

Let us turn from this bare-bones account of the long conflict between Athens and Sparta to an analysis of the relative strengths of the two sides on the eve of the Peloponnesian War. By 431, Sparta had been the dominant land power in Greece for about a century. Sparta stood at the head of a loose confederacy of some two dozen states located in the Peloponnese and central Greece, a confederacy known to modern scholars as the Peloponnesian League, and to the ancients as simply "the Lacedaemonians [i.e., Spartans] and their allies." Each of these states had pledged "to have the same friends and enemies and to follow the Lacedaemonians wherever they might lead." In return, the Spartans would protect these states from external threats and from internal revolt. Most of the allies were, like Sparta, oligarchic conservative, generally agrarian regimes. Although a few, particularly Corinth, had navies, the main strength of the Peloponnesian League was in infantry, particularly the redoubtable soldiers of Sparta and Thebes. The structure of the alliance was informal. Assemblies would be called, if needed, to debate important subjects, above all, questions of war. Sparta, the hegemon, collected no tribute, and there was no central assembly.

The Athenian power bloc, by contrast, was newer, more formal, and encompassed a greater number of city-states. In 477, having driven a Persian invasion force from Greece, Athens and some 150 city-states formed an alliance on the Aegean island of Delos. The purpose of the Delian League, as it was called, was (1) to liberate those Greek cities of the coast of Asia Minor that were still under Persian control and (2) to ravage Persian lands beyond the coast for the frank purpose of plunder. The league was meant to last *in perpetuum*—until the iron weights the founding members threw into the sea should rise up again. The league was a free association: Athens, the leading naval power of Greece, was designated hegemon, but in the general assembly of the league on Delos, each city-state had one vote. As hegemon, Athens was to command military operations and to contribute the bulk of the fleet. Most importantly, she was to appoint financial officers and to set the members' contributions. Members could contribute ships, men, or money, but all chose to contribute money, except for the three large and powerful islands of Chios, Lesbos, and Samos. This arrangement naturally increased Athens's military power, but it saved the members a quantity of blood and sweat. The league treasury, located on Delos, amassed a substantial war chest.

By 431, the Delian League had gained a record of success. The membership had more than doubled, comprising over 300 city-states.

Athens had forced the Persians back from the Aegean and extracted at least a *de facto* truce from the Persian king. Yet, at the same time, the league had become more of a coercive, and less of a voluntary association. The league treasury had been moved, with telling symbolism, from Delos to Athens. On several occasions, Athens had put down rebellions, sometimes quite brutally—driving home the point that the allies' promises of perpetual loyalty would be enforced. Athens had encouraged, and sometimes imposed, democratic constitutions on many of the allied states. Some of these states suffered Athenian officials, or garrisons, or colonists, or land speculators—"ugly Athenians," if you will. Pericles proclaimed that Athens was "the school of Hellas." Athenian inscriptions began to refer not to "Athens and its allies" but to "the cities which Athens controls." The Delian League, scholars agree, had become the Athenian Empire.

Analogies to the two leading power blocs of our time, NATO and the Warsaw Pact, come to mind. In both cases, ancient and modern, an oligarchic (if, in the modern case, an ideologically Marxist) bloc, dominant on land, faced a democratic bloc, dominant at sea. In both cases, ancient and modern, the great powers competed for influence among the uncommitted states—of whom the most important in antiquity were, on the eve of the Peloponnesian War, Argos, Corcyra, the Sicilian city-states, and the sleeping giant of Persia. In both cases, the two power blocs endured an uneasy peace.

There are, however, important differences between the two cases. First, in the ancient case, the democratic power bloc was governed by a tyrant: no ally of Athens could leave the Delian League, as France has left NATO's integrated command structure, or Spain and Greece have threatened to. On the other hand, it was possible for oligarchic states to leave the Peloponnesian League, as Corinth, Thebes and other states did for a few years after 421. Indeed, the powerful and wealthy states of Corinth and Thebes had in general an influence over their hegemon, Sparta, unlike that of any member of the Delian League (or of the Warsaw Pact) over its hegemon. Second, in the ancient case, there was no nuclear deterrent: Athens and Sparta did not retreat from war out of fear of mutual destruction. Third, although ideology was present in the ancient case, it was not as profoundly important as it is today.

The fourth, and most important difference, lay in seapower. Whereas today, the Warsaw Pact has, in the Soviet Union, become a formidable naval, as well as a land power, Sparta was almost strictly a land power. True, Corinth, Megara, and other Peloponnesian allies did have fleets, but these were too small and inexperienced to compete with the

Athenian navy. At many points in its history, Sparta had explicitly rejected the opportunity to expand overseas. This rejection was in part the reflex of a land power, in part the product of the fear that if Sparta sent its soldiers too far from home, the huge servile population, the helots, would revolt. Thucydides emphasizes the conservative, hesitating nature of Sparta's landpower, and compares it to the dynamic power of Athens:

> The Spartans proved to be quite the most remarkably helpful enemies that the Athenians could have had. For Athens, particularly as a naval power, was enormously helped by the very great difference in the national characters—her speed as against Spartan slowness, her enterprise as against Spartan lack of initiative.

For Thucydides, seapower coupled with democracy was inherently expansionist. A conservative patriot like Pericles might hold Athens back for a while, but eventually an opportunist like Alcibiades would come forward and lead Athens to expansion. According to Thucydides, Alcibiades said in the Athenian assembly:

> It is not possible for us to calculate, like housekeepers, how much empire we want to have. The fact is that we have reached a stage where we are forced to plan new conquests and forced to hold on to what we have got, because there is a danger that we ourselves may fall under the power of others unless others are in our power.

Hence, the ancient case, at least in 431, presents a more stark contrast between land and seapower than does the current confrontation between the United States and the Soviet Union. Let us look more closely at the nature of Athenian seapower.

THE ATHENIAN NAVY

In 431, Athens had a superb navy. She had at least 300 seaworthy warships, as well as a number of older ships that could, if needed, be repaired and launched. She could call on her allies Chios, Lesbos, and Corcyra to provide more ships, perhaps over 100 in total. Athens had a magnificent harbor in Piraeus and a good one at Phaleron. She had a rich infrastructure of dockyards and ship sheds, and experienced shipwrights and architects in charge of them. She was in control of the sources of raw materials—timber, tar, and pitch—in northern Greece needed to build ships. She had enormous financial resources: an annual income of 1,000 talents of silver and a reserve fund of 6,000 talents, plus uncoined gold and silver worth some five hundred talents.[2]

Equally important, Athens is unusual in naval history in having a citizenry with wide and direct experience of things maritime. A contemporary writer whose name has not survived comments:

> Because the Athenians own property abroad and public duties take them abroad, they and their servants have learnt to row almost without realizing it; for it is inevitable that a man goes on frequent voyages will take an oar, and learn nautical terminology, and the same is true of his servant. Experience of voyages and practice makes them good helmsmen, some learning in smaller boats, others in merchantmen, and others graduating to triremes; the majority are competent rowers as soon as they board their ships because of previous practice throughout their lives.

Even allowing for some exaggeration, this is an impressive statement. It means, first, that the Athenians had a skilled body of rowers and seamen to call on to provide the core of its naval crews. True, the Athenian population was not large enough to fill an entire fleet; consequently, many, if not a majority of the rowers in the Athenian navy, were mercenaries from the allied states. This was not normally problematic, however, since these mercenaries had no other potential employer beside Athens. In the stress of war, though, Athens's dependence upon foreigners could, and did, backfire.

Second, the knowledge of the average Athenian citizen about seafaring gave Athens a rare political advantage in wartime. It meant that the democratic assembly could make unusually informed decisions about naval questions.

Although inferior to the Peloponnesians, the Athenian army was no negligible factor, either in warfare or in domestic politics. Military service was expected of all free men between the ages of 18 and 59. The middle and upper classes served mainly in the army, not the navy: the rowers and most of the other crewmen on a trireme were poor men. The same generals who commanded on land also commanded at sea. As Thucydides, Aristotle, and others write, the Athenians were to a considerable degree a nautical people.

By contrast, the Peloponnesians were deficient in experience of the sea, and in the size and strength of the navy. In 431, the Peloponnesian navy consisted of about 100 ships, most of them Corinthian and only recently built. The general population did not have much knowledge of the sea; the skilled rowers and officers necessary to man ships were in short supply. The likeliest place to find them was in the Aegean area under the control of Athens. With no central treasury, with no individual states to match the wealth of Athens and her maritime allies, the Peloponnesians had no hope of buying these rowers away from the Athenians. On the eve of the Peloponnesian War, Pericles estimated Peloponnesian naval prospects skeptically:

> And as for seamanship, they will find that a difficult lesson to learn. You yourselves have been studying it since the end of the Persian Wars [480–479], and have still not entirely mastered the subject. How, then, can it be supposed that they could ever make much progress? They are farmers, not sailors. . . . Seamanship, just like anything else, is an art. It is not something that can be picked up and studied in one's spare time; indeed, it allows no spare time for anything else.

THE TRIREME

A closer look at the ancient warship underscores the importance of trained, experienced men. The warship of classical Greece was the trireme, an oared warship, light and maneuverable, graceful and deadly, a bronze battering ram at its prow. On the average trireme there were 200 men: 170 rowers, 10 marines, 4 archers, 6–8 petty officers, 2 gangs of 5 seamen each reporting to the helmsman and the bow officer, and the commanding officer—the trierarch. The 170 rowers were arranged in three tiers, one above deck, two below; 64 men in the top pier, 54 in each of the two lower tiers. Thanks to the outrigger that each ship had, the top tier sat farther outboard than the lower two.[3]

Based on the excavated remains of Athenian ship-sheds, we know that the trireme was slightly less than 37 meters long and 6 meters wide. The long and narrow, light-hulled ship was built for maximum speed in battle. Recent estimates of the top darting speed of a trireme under oar range as high as 11.5 knots or even 17 knots (arguing that triremes were light and fast enough to achieve a semi-planing condition). These top speeds could probably be maintained for only 5 or 10 minutes. Based on ancient writings, it seems that a trireme in a hurry could maintain a speed under oar of 8 knots for several days and cover hundreds of sea miles. The normal speed of a trireme was probably less; ships that could afford to take the time would sail instead of row. Still, rowers had to be in top condition, and hence training was essential. Training was also essential, however, because of the coordination and unison among the rowers needed to maneuver the ship: maneuverability and speed were crucial in battle.

As J. S. Morrison has noted, a trireme might employ in battle one or both of two different kinds of tactics. In the first, the "fighting-platform concept," armed men on two ships engaged each other through missiles or hand-to-hand fighting. In the second, the "guided-missile concept," the trireme itself was an offensive weapon, the object being to ram the enemy. Most of the battles of the Peloponnesian

War were fought according to the second tactic, which Athens had perfected; indeed, Thucydides scorns the fighting-platform style as old-fashioned. We shall, therefore, examine the guided-missile concept in greater detail. In a classic naval battle of the Peloponnesian War, as we might imagine it, two trireme fleets would face each other line abreast. This was the usual defensive formation, because it protected the most vulnerable part of the ship, the side. A combatant who could ram the side of the enemy would emerge the victor. The stronger, faster, and more agile fleet would attempt to destroy the enemy's defensive line. He would approach line ahead and then either sail around the enemy to encircle him (the *periplous*) or break through the line head on (the *diekplous*). A second, less-common defensive posture, was to draw the ships into a circle, bow outward, stern inward. This formation not only prevented a faster enemy from outflanking the defender, but it also presented the enemy's side to the defenders' rams, hence allowing a switch over to the offensive. It was, however, a terribly difficult maneuver to execute. Indeed, each of these maneuvers required a disciplined, experienced, and well-conditioned crew as well as intelligent and steady commanders. Small wonder that Pericles, contemplating Athens's fifty-year record of success at sea, had scorn for the Peloponnesians.

LIMITED WAR

Thanks to Thucydides, we think of one Peloponnesian War, 27 years long. In fact, it is necessary to break the war down into four separate periods of conflict. First comes the Archidamian War of 431–421, named for King Archidamus of Sparta. In this period, battle casualties were still relatively limited, although Athens suffered enormous losses in the epidemic of 430–427. Navies played an important role, but the war was decided on land. Next comes a period of uneasy peace, the so-called Peace of Nicias of 421–415. The most important military action of this phase was the infantry battle at Mantinea in the central Peloponnese. In the third period, 415–413, Athens launched the vast armada of its Sicilian expedition, which was defeated both on land and in Syracuse harbor and suffered enormous casualties. The fourth and final phase, the Iono-Decelean War of 413–404, saw important struggles on both land and sea, again with great loss of life, but the war was decided in the Aegean Sea, specifically in the Dardanelles.

Pericles dominates the strategic thinking of the first part of the Archidamian War. Although his plan failed, its boldness and originality are still impressive. For Pericles, Athens not only had to play its strong card, its navy, but to trump the strong card of the Peloponnesians, their army. But how was a state located on the continent, as Athens was, to ignore a continental power? Pericles's answer, by no means flippant, was that the Athenians had to think of themselves as islanders.

The ancient city of Athens, a small place by today's standards, was located in the territory of Attica, about a thousand square miles in size (roughly equivalent in area to Rhode Island). Athens is located inland, about five miles from the sea at Piraeus. Under Pericles' leadership, Athens-Piraeus had been turned into one great fortress, linked by two Long Walls; a third Long Wall went from Athens to the harbor at Phaleron. In the event of war, the city of Athens could be supplied by sea. The majority of the population, however, at least of the citizen population (Athens, a cosmopolitan city, also had many resident aliens and slaves), lived in the countryside, and engaged in farming. These Athenians were vulnerable to a Peloponnesian invasion. Nor could the Athenian army stop the Peloponnesians from attacking. Pericles' novel solution was for the rural population to move inside the Athens-Piraeus fortress during the campaigning season. This would cause considerable distress: the disruption of lives, the cost of moving people and valuables, the need of some to live in squatters' huts and tents, the danger to public health. Above all, there was the physical and psychological cost of watching, from the Athenian acropolis, as the enemy burnt Athenian crops in the field.

Yet, Pericles expected this painful and politically costly strategy to win the war. Athens's control of the sea gave him enormous confidence in the outcome. He considered the possibility of countering the Peloponnesian invasion of Attica with sea-launched Athenian incursions into the Peloponnese, and of countering any Peloponnesian fortification in Attica with an Athenian fortification in the Peloponnese. In truth, however, Pericles expected to win the war psychologically, not by invading the Peloponnese, but by letting the Peloponnesians see how fruitless their invasions of Attica were. As Thucydides writes:

> Pericles . . . said that Athens would be victorious if she remained quiet and took care of her navy, if she avoided trying to add to the empire during the course of the war, and if she did nothing to risk the safety of the city itself.

In short, Pericles planned to wage a defensive war.

In the first year of the war, Pericles led a raid into Megara, Athens's western neighbor and a Peloponnesian ally. He captured a Corinthian stronghold in northwest Greece, and sent a fleet around the

Peloponnese on a raid. This fleet did little damage, but perhaps that was Pericles' plan—not to enrage the enemy, but to give him a graceful out, if not at once, then in a year or two. The Peloponnesian war plan was simpler. Knowing that they could not defeat Athens at sea, they intended to invade Attica, which they expected would bring Athens to its knees, if not at once, then in a year or two. In the event, both plans failed.

In the second year of the war, the Athenians raided the Peloponnese again. They were surprised to discover, however, that far from surrendering, the Spartans launched a sea attack on the island of Zacynthus, an Athenian ally off the western Peloponnese. This attack was unsuccessful, but it marked the beginning of a new Peloponnesian strategy of offensives outside of Attica. Another side of this policy, also a failure, was a Spartan overture to Persia for help against Athens. (Athens captured and executed the Spartan emissaries.) Infinitely more serious, however, was the epidemic that broke out in Athens in the spring of 430. This epidemic (the precise nature of the disease is unknown) would last for several years. Before it ran its course, it would kill between one-fourth and one-third of the population of Athens.

In the summer of 429, the Peloponnesians continued their policy of offensives outside of Attica, this time launching a seaborne attack on Acarnania, an Athenian ally northwest of the Corinthian Gulf. From its base in the Corinthian Gulf, however, the Athenian navy demonstrated its remarkable tactical superiority to the Peloponnesian fleet. The Athenian base was at Naupactus, on the north shore of the Gulf, where Athens had planted a colony of renegade Spartan helots.[4] The Athenian commander was Phormio, later honored for his military achievements with burial in the state cemetery near the grave of Pericles. Phormio had been sent to Naupactus in the winter of 430 to protect the port and to attempt to close off the Corinthian Gulf. His two naval victories in the Gulf in 429 demonstrated that there is no substitute for experience and good leadership. As a consequence, Athens continued to rule the waves.

TIMIDITY AND DARING

Athenian control of the seas was dominant for the rest of the Peloponnesian War. The Peloponnesians were capable of strategic daring, but again and again they were defeated by their own timid tactics. Immediately after their second defeat by Phormio in 429, for example, they organized a naval raid on Piraeus from the port of Megara. At the eleventh hour, however, "frightened by the risk," they set out for the less important target of the island of Salamis—until the first sighting of Athenians, at which point the Peloponnesians fled. Two years later, in 427, they sent out a fleet of 42 triremes under Alcidas in support of the people of Mytilene, in rebellion against Athens. With good leadership, even so small a fleet could have caused serious trouble for Athens, either by helping the Mytilenian rebels or by stirring up a new rebellion on the coast of Asia Minor, which might bring in Persian help. Short of money, Athens faced potential danger. Alcidas landed on the Asia Minor coast. Yet, when the news came that the Athenian fleet was in pursuit, he fled—all the way back to the Peloponnese!

There was still one possibility of action for this fleet. When it returned to the Peloponnese, bolstered by thirteen additional ships and by Brasidas, the Peloponnesian fleet sailed north to Corcyra (modern Corfu), to intervene in a civil war there on the side of the democrats. They easily defeated a force of sixty Corcyrean ships, whose crews were ill-disciplined and even fought among themselves. The presence of twelve Athenian ships, however, as well as Alcidas's timidity, prevented the Peloponnesians from taking advantage of their victory. A day later, when the news came that a relief fleet of sixty Athenian ships was on its way, the Peloponnesians fled.

The Peloponnesian fleet was used only once more during the Archidamian War, this time in response to an Athenian initiative. Beginning in 427, with the emergence of new leaders such as Cleon, Athens adopted a more aggressive strategy. She sent small fleets to the rich agrarian island of Sicily, in the hopes of (a) cutting off grain exports to the Peloponnese and (b) collecting tribute to replenish her depleted treasury. Sparta's friends in Sicily, however, managed to unite and effect a diplomatic rebuff to Athens. A seaborne Athenian attack in 426 on Corinth's allies northwest of the Corinthian Gulf was more successful. Athenian armies denied the Peloponnesians control of a region from which they might have threatened the Athenian fleet's access to Corcyra and Sicily. The most important Athenian initiative, however, and the one that drew a Peloponnesian naval response, was the fortification of Pylos.

In spring of 425, under the command of Demosthenes (not the famous orator of a later century), Athens seized and fortified Pylos, a rocky, uninhabited promontory in the southwestern Peloponnese. Pylos was in Messenia, the Spartan-controlled territory of the helots. Any fort there might be a refuge for runaway helots and was potentially, therefore, a serious threat to Sparta. Pylos was an inexpensive way for Athens to hurt Sparta. It had the additional advantage of being located on the northern edge of the excellent harbor of Navarino Bay.[5]

The Spartans did not wait long to attack the small Athenian force of five ships and several hundred men at Pylos. They gathered sixty ships to use against the expected Athenian reinforcements. Perhaps they considered closing off the two entrances to Navarino Bay, north and south of the island of Sphacteria, which lies just south of Pylos and runs along the western, seaward side of the bay. At any rate, they left a detachment of elite Spartan hoplites on Sphacteria. In the meantime, they attacked the fort at Pylos both with land forces and 43 of their ships. Brasidas purposely ran his ship aground, and encouraged others to do so, in order to make a landing. The Athenians, however, held their ground for two days, until Sparta called off the attack. Thucydides is impressed by the irony of the situation:

> It was indeed a strange alternation in the ordinary run of things for Athenians to be fighting a battle on land—and Spartan land too—against Spartans attacking from the sea, and for Spartans to be trying to make a naval landing on their own shores, now hostile to them, against Athenian opposition. For at this time Sparta chiefly prided herself on being a land power with an unrivalled army and Athens on being a sea power with the greatest navy in existence.

The next day saw the arrival of an Athenian fleet of fifty ships. After a brief withdrawal, in an early demonstration of the power of the offensive at sea, they attacked the Peloponnesian fleet, which occupied a defensive position line abreast in Navarino Bay, and routed it thoroughly. Worse yet for Sparta, 420 hoplites were isolated on Sphacteria. Some of these men belonged to the first families of Sparta, and the government took their plight seriously enough to sue for peace with Athens. In the meantime, a truce handed over to Athens not only all the ships at Pylos, but all the triremes in Spartan territory, a total of sixty.

In the event, the two sides were not able to agree upon peace terms. After a considerable delay, caused in no small part by fear of even a small force of Sparta's formidable soldiers, Athens managed to storm Sphacteria and take 292 alive. This was a tremendous victory. Not only did Athens hold a fort in Spartan territory to which helots could, and did desert, but it held hostages whose safety prevented Sparta from invading Attica again. Furthermore, Athens held the bulk of the Peloponnesian fleet. The Peloponnesians would not be a significant naval power again for the next fourteen years.

Surprisingly, the war did not come to a quick end, nor was Athens able to follow up its famous victory. Athenian attempts in 424 to capture Megara and invade Boeotia both failed, the latter with the loss of 1,000 Athenian hoplites and countless more Athenian lightly armed troops and attendants. The same year, the Spartan general Brasidas led a daring overland expedition over several hundred miles, through hostile territory, towards Thrace, the only part of the Athenian empire accessible to Sparta. Through diplomacy and force, he won over several important Athenian allies in eastern Macedonia. His greatest coup came in December, when he captured the strategic Athenian colony of Amphipolis. This city was important to Athens in many ways, most particularly for its access to a hinterland rich in ship-building timber. Its loss was a major disaster, and it is not surprising that the commander of the region, who failed to bring relief to Amphipolis in time, was cashiered. He was none other than Thucydides, whose twenty-year exile began at that point.

The loss of Amphipolis brought a one-year truce between Athens and Sparta in 423. In 422 the failure of an Athenian expedition to retake the city, as well as the battlefield deaths of the leading war hawks, Brasidas of Sparta and Cleon of Athens, heralded the coming of peace.

PEACE OF NICIAS AND SICILIAN EXPEDITION

The peace negotiated by the weary combatants in 421 was unlikely to satisfy either side. Although it provided for fifty years of peace, the arbitration of differences, and the restoration of prisoners of war and of captured places, neither Athens nor Sparta had accomplished its war aims of 431. Sparta had neither liberated the Athenian empire nor freed the Greeks. Athens had won recognition of its empire from Sparta, but it turned out that the two major Peloponnesian allies, Corinth and Thebes, refused to ratify the treaty. Nor was Athens able to regain Amphipolis, because the residents would not hear of it. In return, Athens refused to give back Pylos, although she did send the Spartan hostages back home. Practically from the start, the peace that Nicias had negotiated for Athens was hanging by a thread.

The next six years were marked by a series of shifting alliances. For a time, it looked as if Athenian diplomacy might break up the Peloponnesian League. Athens won over to its side the neutral Peloponnesian city-state of Argos, which had a good army. A powerful anti-Spartan coalition was formed. Sparta, however, won a smashing victory on land and restored its league at the battle of Mantinea in 418.

Navies played only a small role in these years of neither war nor peace, although it is worth mentioning the Athenian expedition against Melos in 416. A small island, Melos had been neutral until Athens attacked in 426, at which point it joined the Spartans. Now, in 416, its prestige at low ebb after Sparta's victory at Mantinea, Athens sent thirty-eight ships and 3,000 soldiers to finish the job. The occasion leads Thucydides to the famous Melian dialogue, in which Athenians and Melians discuss the brutal reality of power. When the Melians refuse to surrender, Athens besieges their city, and eventually takes it. As punishment, all of the men are killed and all the women and children sold into slavery. War, as Thucydides remarks on another occasion, is a harsh teacher.

A year later, in 415, Athens returned to the idea of gaining control of Sicily. Officially, she was still at peace with Sparta, but a resumption of the conflict seemed likely. At first, Athenian goals in Sicily were limited. The city of Syracuse had considerable military potential. Athens feared that Syracuse might one day intervene in Greece on behalf of its mother city, Corinth. Athenians believed that an aggressive attack force of only sixty ships could thwart this threat by conquering Syracuse neatly.

At first, Athens voted to send such a modest fleet to Sicily. Within a week, however, the assembly reconsidered, and voted nearly to double the size of the expeditionary force—and also, therefore, of the risk.

Athens was now committed to sending at least 100 triremes, some of them troop transports, and to requisitioning other triremes from the allies; a combined Atheno-allied hoplite force of at least 5,000 men, plus light-armed troops, would sail in the armada. According to Thucydides, this huge increase in the size of the venture was the result of a mistake: Nicias, the main opponent of the expedition, hoped to dissuade the Athenians with inflated demands. He was wrong. Led by Alcibiades, a brilliant, dangerous, rogue aristocrat, Athenians began to see Sicily as the royal road to victory. It was wealthy in money and manpower, it controlled grain that the Peloponnesians needed, and was apparently weak and disunited.

As a strategy to win the war, the Sicilian Expedition was risky. If, however, the expedition had been properly led and executed, it had considerable promise of success. Moreover, if Athens had stuck to the original plan of sixty ships, it could have gained access to considerable resources at small risk. The larger fleet offered little military advantage, aroused the fears of the other Sicilians, and increased the risk for Athens. An efficient, small force might have turned the tide in Athens's favor.

The armada set sail from Piraeus in June 415. Thucydides calls this force "by a long way the most costly and the finest-looking force of

Hellenic troops that up to that time had ever come from a single city." No money had been spared, no corners had been cut.

The allied fleet amounted to 134 ships, apparently an overwhelming force. Contrary to expectation, however, Athens did not win a quick victory. The campaign turned into a quagmire and, after two years of fighting, a disaster. The navy played only a limited role. The Athenians engaged in a long, costly, and frustrating siege of the Sicilian port of Syracuse by land and sea.

This is not the place to discuss the campaign in detail. Suffice it to say that by 413, Athens was unable to prevail. Morale had declined considerably, the ships had passed their peak of readiness, and the tide began to turn. Syracuse's army wrested a base in the Great Harbor south of the city, from which they could interfere with the provisioning of the Athenians. Eventually a Corinthian innovation enabled Syracuse to win a major naval victory.

In the continued fighting in the Corinthian Gulf, Corinth had devised a naval defense against the lighter and faster Athenian ships. By reinforcing the bow timbers of their ships, the Corinthians were now able to ram the Athenians head on, and to smash the Athenians' bows and disrupt their oar systems. Corinthian advisers encouraged Syracuse to adopt this new equipment, which turned out to be perfect for the narrow space of the Great Harbor (though not for the open sea, where it would render a ship heavier and less maneuverable). They sank seven Athenian ships and damaged others, and killed or captured many sailors. Syracuse now dominated the Great Harbor.

Athenian reinforcements of seventy-three ships and over 5,000 men now arrived, but were unable to prevail. After a defeat on land, Athens decided to withdraw. In the meantime, however, Syracuse attacked on land and sea. Athenian triremes slightly outnumbered the enemy, eighty-six to seventy-six. Nevertheless, Syracuse broke through the Athenian center, turned on the right wing, and drove the rest of the Athenian fleet ashore in a rout. We may attribute Athens's defeat to moral and material exhaustion on the part of its men, and to Syracuse's heroic exertions. A democracy like Athens, Syracuse gave its all to defend the homeland. In fact, after the victory at sea, Syracuse harried the Athenian army in overland retreat, killing or capturing virtually all of the enemy. Athens, as Thucydides says, was "utterly and entirely defeated."

Athens was defeated only, however, in Syracuse. In spite of its losses, Athens was able to hold out for another nine years, in the last phase of the war, the Iono-Decelean War (413–404). Not only to hold out: Athens won four major naval victories against Sparta, and twice drove

Sparta to sue for peace. It is hard to gainsay Thucydides' judgment that in the end Sparta did not defeat Athens, Athens defeated itself through internal strife—and, it should be noted, through a disastrous loss of discipline in the navy.

If Syracuse had followed up its victory in Sicily with a full-scale attack in the Aegean, then perhaps the Peloponnesians could have brought the war to a rapid conclusion. Syracuse, however, exhausted by its exertions in 415–413, had no taste for such an effort and sent only a small fleet to help. Sparta would have to look elsewhere. Neither the Sicilian disaster nor the revolt of key Athenian allies could win the war for Sparta, because Athens could and did build a new fleet. To win, Sparta would have to destroy that fleet. True, from 413 on, the Peloponnesians had a permanent garrison at Decelea, in the hills above Athens, which did great damage to the countryside. The garrison at Decelea would not win the war, however, because it could not hurt Athens's center of gravity.

CYNOSSEMA AND CYZICUS

Sparta obtained its fleet from a surprising source: Persia. In 411 Sparta surrendered the Greek city-states of the Asia Minor coast to Persian sovereignty, in exchange for a Persian-financed fleet. Previously, fear of Athens had kept Persia neutral. But Athens's current weakness now dictated a policy of building up Sparta as a countervailing force—only, however, to the point of challenging, not defeating, Athens. Persian strategic interests dictated that Greeks be divided and fight each other.

By summer 411, Athenian and Spartan fleets faced each other in the Aegean. Building a fleet had imposed sacrifices on the Athenian treasury. She had lost important allies, and was short of manpower. Nevertheless, recognizing that everything depended on the Aegean, Athens pressed on. The Athenian fleet was based on the island of Samos, while the Spartans were a short distance away in the mainland city of Miletus.

Sparta's strategy was to take control of the Hellespont (i.e., the Dardanelles), probably the weakest link in Athens's vital chain of supply to Ukrainian grain. Athens had established a fort at Sestos, on the central northern shore of the Hellespont. The Peloponnesians had a base opposite Sestos where the straits are about 1 1/2 miles wide. In the summer of 411, Mindarus moved from Miletus to the Hellespont. Together with the Peloponnesian ships from Abydus, Mindarus now had eighty-six ships. An Athenian fleet of seventy-six ships, beached at the mouth of the Hellespont, was ready to engage him. The battle took place in the narrow waters of the western Hellespont, off the Cynossema ("Dog's Tomb") promontory. Despite a promising Spartan initiative, Athens once again demonstrated tactical skill and superb training, which ensured composure in battle.

The two fleets moved towards each other at Cynossema, the Peloponnesians from the northeast, the Athenians from the southwest. They then turned towards each other, line abreast. In the ensuing battle the Peloponnesians were routed. Able to take refuge on the southern shore of the Hellespont, however, the Peloponnesians lost only twenty-one ships, compared to fifteen Athenian losses. Athens not only won a tactical victory, but also a significant moral victory. She came out from under the shadow of the Sicilian disaster and reasserted her naval supremacy.

Athens's second great naval victory over Sparta in the Ionian war took place in 410 at Cyzicus, a Greek city in the sea of Marmara.[6] Having received additional Persian support, the Peloponnesians moved to Cyzicus, which they took by storm. Athenian reinforcements, however, reached their fleet and they meant to take Cyzicus back. The two keys to their plan were surprise and an amphibious landing. The Athenians moved stealthily at night toward Cyzicus.

Upon reaching Cyzicus, they first landed troops to march on the city. Second, they divided the ships into three squadrons. One went ahead, to lure the adversary forces out to battle, while the others waited. When the Peloponnesians approached, the advance squadrons, commanded by Alcibiades, withdrew. Suddenly, at a signal, they turned around to face the Peloponnesians. Meanwhile the rest of the Athenian fleet emerged and cut off the Peloponnesians' retreat to the city. As a result of the battle, which spread from the sea to the land, Cyzicus was taken by the Athenians. The entire Spartan fleet of sixty ships was captured, with the exception of Syracuse's ships, which had been burned. Sparta's utter discomfiture is recorded in a desperate message home intercepted by the Athenians: "The ships are gone, the men are starving. We don't know what to do." Once again, Athenian crewmen had demonstrated their discipline and tactical skill, a skill matched at Cyzicus by their leaders' ingenious and sophisticated strategy. In the aftermath of Cyzicus, Sparta offered to make peace on the basis of the *status quo*. Athens, however, held out to regain full control of its empire.

ARGINUSAE AND AEGOSPOTAMI

The third great Athenian victory took place four years later, in 406, at the Arginusae Islands, off the Asia Minor coast across the strait from the island of Lesbos. Athens did manage to win back some of its rebellious allies. In 407, it sent out a fleet of 100 ships under Alcibiades, who hoped to reconquer the entire empire. The Peloponnesians were still dangerous foes, however, with footholds in the Aegean and Hellespont and with continued Persian support. Athens's position had slipped since Cyzicus. In 407 Sparta built a new fleet and found an able, brilliant, ruthless commander in Lysander. He convinced Persia to raise the pay of a Peloponnesian rower to a level about 25 percent above the Athenian rate. The result was a large-scale desertion of rowers from Athenian ships.

Lysander added a naval victory to this financial one in 407 at Notium, on the coast near Ephesus. Taking a leaf from Athens's book, he lured an Athenian fleet out against a superior Peloponnesian force and sank twenty-two ships. An unexpected benefit was that the Athenian assembly blamed the defeat on Alcibiades, the commander-in-chief, who was absent on another mission. This popular politician and clever general was forced into exile, thereby depriving Athens of a major leader.

In 406, the Athenian fleet, reduced to seventy ships, suffered a further defeat. The Spartan fleet of 140 ships caught the Athenians outside Mytilene harbor, captured 30 ships, and blockaded the rest in the harbor. One bold ship raced its way through the enemy to bring the news to Athens. The assembly reckoned the gravity of the crisis: should Athens lose its navy, it would lose everything. The decision was thus taken to build a new fleet and raise 110 ships within a month. To man these ships it was necessary to enroll not only the upper classes as rowers, but even slaves, who received their freedom in return. The remarkable maritime expertise of the average Athenian saved the day. With the allied ships, the Athenian fleet amounted to more than 150 triremes. The Peloponnesians left 30 ships at Mytilene and moved 120 ships opposite the Athenians at Arginusae.

In the ensuing battle, the Athenians for once had the inferior fleet: slower ships and less-experienced men. They, therefore, were the ones to stand on the defensive. As they saw it, the main Peloponnesian threat was the breakthrough, in which single ships might pierce their lines. To avert it, the Athenians adopted a formation of squadrons in depth. Their center was arranged in a single line, but their wings were in double or perhaps triple file. The Peloponnesians divided their fleet in two and attacked the Athenian wings. After a long fight, in which the Spartan commander (not Lysander but Callicratidas) lost his life, the Athenians prevailed over the Peloponnesian left wing; the right wing broke and fled to the south. The Peloponnesians lost sixty-nine ships, the Athenians only twenty-five. Because of a sudden storm, however, the Athenians were unable to pick up their survivors, so they lost all 5,000 men.

Athens had won a smashing victory, but at a price. An angry assembly blamed the casualties on the generals, not the storm. Five commanders were tried and executed. This did not bode well for the struggle ahead. The Athenians needed to present a united front; instead, they turned on themselves. Five years earlier, in 411, an oligarchy had ousted Athenian democracy for several months. Full-scale civil war was just barely averted, and the divisions smouldered on.

To the careful observer, the strains in Athenian leadership are clear in 405, the year in which Athens lost the war. After Arginusae, as after Cyzicus, Sparta again offered peace terms: the *status quo*, plus the evacuation of Decelea. Again, Athens refused. In late summer 405, Sparta returned to the attack. She had a new fleet of perhaps 175 ships, paid for by Persia and led by Lysander. This force moved on the strategic Hellespont and stormed the city of Lampsacus, located on the Asian side in the northeast. The Athenians hurried after them with 180 ships of their own, hoping to destroy this threat to their vital grain route.

What followed is a classic example of the importance of a united command, of a disciplined crew, and of a firm base of support on the shore. A trireme fleet generally based itself in a city's harbor, where it could find food; it did not carry its own food. In order to pressure the Peloponnesians into fighting, however, the Athenians went past Sestos and landed at a beach opposite Lampsacus near a small village, Aegospotami ("Goat Rivers"). Here, on four mornings in a row, the Athenians crossed the straits and offered battle outside Lampsacus, but Lysander refused. Each afternoon, the Athenian fleet withdrew back to Aegospotami, and the men scavenged for food or napped. The Peloponnesians observed from spy ships.

On the fourth afternoon, the Athenians had an unexpected visitor—Alcibiades—who lived in exile in a nearby fortress. He is said to have urged the Athenians to withdraw to Sestos, where their fleet would not be exposed each afternoon to the enemy. Sound advice, but the Athenians were contemptuous of the Peloponnesians. Worse, after the charges and counter-charges of the Arginusae affair, which general wanted to take responsibility for following the advice of the disgraced Alcibiades? The fleet stayed.

The next day, after the Athenians had returned to Aegospotami in the afternoon, Lysander struck. At the top darting speed of a trireme, he might have been able to cross the straits (about 3 nautical miles wide at Aegospotami) in as little as ten minutes. It is not clear whether, when the Peloponnesians struck, a small contingent of Athenian ships were en route to Sestos, or whether all were on the beach. In either case, the Athenians were shocked. The enemy captured virtually the entire Athenian fleet—apparently, only about a dozen ships escaped—with hardly a battle.

The war was over. It still remained for Lysander to execute those of his prisoners who were Athenians—three to four thousand men—for a Spartan army to lay siege to Athens for several months, and for the Peloponnesian fleet to sail into Piraeus. However dramatic, these events were secondary. The war was decided at Aegospotami.

CONCLUDING NOTE

For the student of maritime strategy, the Peloponnesian War holds several great lessons. First, perhaps most obvious, a war between a land power and a sea power is not easily decided. Each side could do damage to the other, but the Athenian navy could not inflict a decisive defeat on Sparta; nor, owing to strong defenses on land, could the Peloponnesian army crush Athens. To win the war, each side had to confront the enemy in his own element. To do so, given the limited possibilities of economic expansion in antiquity, would require allies.

For Athens, the most promising strategy would perhaps have been to take advantage of the opposition that Sparta's landpower had generated in its neighbors and competitors, and to shape this opposition into an anti-Spartan alliance. Athens began to follow such a policy in the years after the peace of Nicias (421), but only halfheartedly. Instead of sending a large army to support Sparta's enemies at the land battle of Mantinea (418), Athens sent merely 1,000 infantrymen and 300 cavalry, which left the anti-Spartan coalition outnumbered. As a result, Sparta won a great victory.

For Sparta, the most promising strategy was to foment a revolt among Athens's allies, and thereby to create a navy that could challenge the Athenian fleet. The Peloponnesian navy, however, as events proved again and again, was unequal to the task. It lacked ships, money, manpower and above all, experience. Only in the unlikely case of Athens weakening itself could Sparta hope to prevail at sea. This, of course, is precisely what happened. The Sicilian disaster weakened Athens to the point where Persia could intervene on Sparta's side with impunity, and where a Persian-built Peloponnesian fleet could challenge the Athenian navy.

Even then, Athens might have prevailed—so strong was her naval tradition—if not for the cracks in her political and social systems and in the key area of military discipline. The crewmen of the Athenian fleet at Aegospotami were not the superb rowers of, say, Phormio's fleet in 429. Thanks to the epidemic of the 420s and to enormous battle casualties, Athens's military manpower pool had shrunk considerably by the year 405. The best of the mercenary rowers had been lured away after 407 by Persia's high wages. The remainder were put to the test at Aegospotami, and found wanting.

The Peloponnesian War turned out as it did because (a) Athens risked its overwhelming naval superiority unwisely and lost it, which (b) allowed Sparta, a land power, to find backing to build a navy and to keep the pressure up on Athens until she cracked. Although Sparta's army was necessary to close the noose, the noose was tied at sea—of rope of Athens's own making.

NOTES

1. All three-digit dates in this chapter are B.C.

2. Consider (a) that one talent of silver would pay the annual wages of about twenty skilled workmen, or (b) that one talent of silver would pay the wages of the crew of one warship for one month, or (c) that it would take resources of about three-quarters of a talent for an Athenian to be a member of the propertied class. To keep a fleet in service for the full eight-month rowing season of one year would cost 1,600 talents.

3. The Hellenic Navy and the Trireme Trust (Great Britain) are, in a joint effort, reconstructing an ancient trireme. A partial section of a trireme was built and rowed in England in 1985. See John S. Morrison and J. F. Coates, *The Athenian Trireme. The History and Reconstruction of an Ancient Greek Warship* (Cambridge: Cambridge University Press, 1986). A complete trireme was rowed in Greece in the summer of 1987.

4. Students of naval history will note that Naupactus was later renamed Lepanto, and gave its name to the great naval battle of 1571, in which the European powers defeated Turkey.

5. Once again, an ancient site marks the location of a modern sea battle, this time the battle of Navarino Bay of 1827, in which the western powers defeated the Turkish fleet and secured Greek independence.

6. Thucydides died before he could finish his history; his narrative runs out in 411. For Cyzicus and the rest of the naval history of the Peloponnesian War, we must rely on the imperfect, often contradictory accounts of Xenophon and Diodorus of Sicily.

BIBLIOGRAPHICAL NOTE

Modern scholarship on the Peloponnesian War began in the nineteenth century, and the debate continues with vigor today. The student interested in further readings must begin with the ancient sources. Thucydides' *The Peloponnesian War* is indispensable: the longest and most thorough ancient account, and arguably the most brilliant book on war and politics ever written. For a commentary on Thucydides, see the five-volume *A Historical Commentary on Thucydides*. A. W. Gomme, A. Andrewes, and K. J. Dover, eds. (Oxford: Oxford University Press, 1956–81). Thucydides died before he could finish his history, and the narrative is continued from 411 in Xenophon's *Hellenica*—unfortunately, a far less reliable source. The story of the war is also told in the *Universal History* of Diodorus of Sicily, books 12–13. Diodorus lived some 350 years after the war, but he drew his information (sometimes carefully, sometimes not) from the near-contemporary Ephorus, and is therefore a valuable source. Plutarch, also a later scholar but a careful one, provides valuable information in his *Lives* of Pericles, Nicias, Alcibiades, Lysander, and to a lesser extent, Themistocles, Cimon, and Aristides. Aristophanes, the comic playwright, provides biased if vivid pictures of the home front in his comedies *Acharnians* and *Peace*. Aristotle, or at least one of his students, discusses constitutional changes in Athens in his *Constitution of Athens*.

Modern scholarship relies heavily on these literary sources. It also draws much information from epigraphy, the hundreds of contemporary inscriptions, many discovered only in this century, which provide so much useful information about the period. Many of the inscriptions can be found in translation in Charles W. Fornara, ed., *Archaic Times to the End of The Peloponnesian War* (Baltimore: Johns Hopkins University Press, 1977). Archaeology and the study of Greek topography have also made valuable contributions to our knowledge. A good example of this approach may be found in W. Kendrick Pritchett, *Studies in Ancient Greek Topography. Vol. 2: Battlefields* (Berkeley: University of California Press, 1969).

The student interested in additional readings might begin with Thucydides and then turn to Donald Kagan's excellent four-volume series on the history of the Peloponnesian War, *The Outbreak of the Peloponnesian War* (Ithaca: Cornell University Press, 1969), *The Archidamian War* (Ithaca: Cornell University Press, 1974), *The Peace of Nicias and the Sicilian Expedition* (Ithaca: Cornell University Press, 1981), and *The Fall of The Athenian Empire* (Ithaca: Cornell University Press, 1987). The best and most thorough study of the warships of the period is J. S. Morrison and John F. Coates, *The Athenian Trireme: The History and Reconstruction of an Ancient Greek Warship* (Cambridge: Cambridge University Press, 1986). There are many interesting insights, and some controversial theories in Geoffrey E.M. de Ste. Croix, *Origins of the Peloponnesian War* (Ithaca: Cornell University Press, 1969).

Some excellent essays on individual points of strategy and tactics are: Peter Brunt, "Spartan Policy and Strategy in the Archidamian War," *Phoenix* 19 (1965), pp. 255–80; T. Kelly, "Thucydides and Spartan Strategy in the Archidamian War," *American History Review*, 87(1982), pp. 21–42; A. Andrewes, "Notion [Notium] and Kyzikos [Cyzicus]: The Sources Compared," *Journal of Hellenic Studies*, 102 (1982); Josiah Ober, *Fortress Attica* (Leiden: Brill, 1985), chap. 3; Strauss, "Aegospotami Reexamined," *American Journal of Philology* 104 (1983), pp. 24–35; Strauss, "A Note on the Tactics and Topography of Aegospotami," *American Journal of Philology*, 108 (1987), pp. 741–45.

On the social history of the Peloponnesian War, see Strauss, *Athens After The Peloponnesian War: Class, Faction and Policy 403–386 B.C.* (Ithaca: Cornell University Press, 1987), chaps. 2–3. For a general introduction to ancient Greek history, see N. G. L. Hammond, *History of Ancient Greece*, 3rd ed. (Oxford: Oxford University Press, 1986).

5

Maritime Strategy
in the
Punic Wars

BY ALVIN H. BERNSTEIN

HISTORICAL BACKGROUND

"Can anyone be so dull or idle as not to be interested in knowing how and under what form of government the single city of Rome conquered and brought under its dominion almost the whole inhabited world within a period of not quite fifty-three years (219–167 B.C.)?" So wrote Polybius, a Greek, who lived in the second century B.C. He had been held hostage in Rome for sixteen years and his work provides the basis for our knowledge of Rome's wars with Carthage. During his confinement in Italy, Polybius attracted the notice of the famous Roman general-statesman, Scipio Aemilianus, adopted grandson and heir of Scipio Africanus, who finally defeated Hannibal. It was with the younger Scipio's support that Polybius researched and composed his work. While he may have had an axe to grind on behalf of his Roman patron, he must nevertheless have been in a uniquely favorable position to write the history of Rome's Punic Wars. In fact, he bases the part of his work that deals with the so-called First Punic War on two sources—one Roman, Fabius Pictor, and one Greek, Philinus, written from the Carthaginian point of view. Polybius seems to have been sufficiently intelligent, critical, and well informed to have sought verification by balancing the two authors against each other. In this way he created a new and reasonably coherent synthesis.

The epoch-making struggle between the two superpowers of the western Mediterranean, which Polybius records, set the course for the future of Western civilization, for after the defeat of the Carthaginians at the end of the Second Punic War in 201 B.C., no opponent would ever again contest Roman expansion on anything like an equal footing. Moreover, this war gave the West two of its most brilliant military commanders: Hannibal, whose victory at Cannae was the model for Schlieffen's famous plan for Germany's conduct of World War I, and whose campaigns were admired and studied by General George S. Patton; and Scipio, considered superior in generalship even to Napoleon by the famous British strategist, B. H. Liddell-Hart. Rome's use of her navy in this conflict even inspired Mahan's *The Influence of Sea Power upon History*. Certainly, the Punic Wars offer us one of the more interesting anomalies of military history: Rome, known in the ancient tradition as predominantly a military land power, defeated Carthage, one of the greatest naval powers in antiquity, by wresting from her the control of the sea.

ROME BEFORE THE PUNIC WARS

No central power unified Italy in earliest times. Etruscans, Greeks, and various Italic tribes lacked the ability to establish a single, powerful kingdom on the Italian peninsula. In the last quarter of the seventh century B.C. the Etruscans ruled over much of northern and central Italy, including that area called Latium, where the city of Rome was located. When their domination ended, at the end of the sixth century B.C., the Latins of this area feared their return and accordingly sought allies among neighboring tribes. Rome now began a course of expansion and, in a long series of wars, managed to unite and control the Italian Peninsula. During their period of rule the Etruscans left their stamp on the future Roman civilization, while the Greeks, who began migrating to southern Italy and Sicily beginning in the middle of the eighth century, had established about fifty city-states on the southern and western shores of Italy and Sicily. The Romans called the area of southern Italy where they settled *Magna Graeca* ("Great Greece"), and thus gave us the word "Greeks" for the people who called themselves Hellenes. Greek culture from these colonies influenced the Etruscans and, in turn, the Romans. These Greek colonies survived until the third century, when they fell under the hegemony of the Roman Republic just before the outbreak of war with the Phoenicians (hence "Punic") of the western Mediterranean.

In her early history, Rome had followed the traditional Greek pattern of substituting an oligarchy for a patriarchal or hereditary kingship. The centuries before the outbreak of war with Carthage saw a struggle in which a small hereditary upper class, the patricians, battled against the political demands of the much larger class of common people, or plebeians. The Roman tradition records a series of constitutional compromises that led, not to the establishment of many new organs of government, but to admission to the old institutions of wealthy men from the inferior plebeian order. Thus a new patrician-plebeian oligarchy came to govern the Roman Republic. Like the founding fathers of our own country, the prominent plebeian families succeeded in stopping their revolution at the most advantageous point. Not only did the new combined oligarchy of patricians and plebeians retain power but it was able to use the progress of constitutional evolution to hold power more securely.

While the Romans were developing their form of republican government, they were also expanding their holdings on the Italian Peninsula. Except for the Greek city-states in the south and the Etruscan territory in the north, most of the peninsula was occupied by tribes with little organization. The Romans first conquered those in the nearby plain of Latium, then expanded into other territories. The period of conquest was punctuated by one major disaster. In about 390 B.C. a large force of Gauls left their stronghold in the Po valley and captured part of Rome herself. They exacted a ransom as the price of their withdrawal. Rome then renewed her policy of expansion for security's sake, displaying the resilience that made her, in the words of the historian Edward Gibbon, "sometimes vanquished in battle, always victorious in war." Shortly after 300, Rome dominated the Italian Peninsula as far south as the Greek city-states of Magna Graeca.

A series of quarrels led to a war between Rome and these Greek city-states. Thanks to the histories of Polybius, at this point Roman history begins to emerge into clear light—out of the mists of verbal tradition and popular myth—with secure dates and few legendary decorations. The Greek city of Tarentum, founded centuries before by the ancient Spartans, invited Pyrrhus, a prince from the half-Greek region of Epirus (modern Albania), to aid them in their struggle against the advancing Romans. Pyrrhus brought with him a professional Greek army and fought two successful but indecisive battles against the Romans in 280, but at a heavy cost in casualties to his own forces (whence comes the phrase, "a Pyrrhic victory"). When Pyrrhus sent an envoy to demand that the Romans surrender, the aged and blind censor, Appius Claudius, rose in the Senate and declared that he did not understand why Romans were discussing peace terms when an unconquered enemy was still on Roman soil. Pyrrhus might have achieved more than he did if he had pursued his Italian war. Instead he became diverted by military adventures in Sicily, and in 275 B.C. he abandoned Italy, leaving the Romans to their southern conquests. By 265 B.C. Rome had extended its influence to the tip of the peninsula. Only then did she find herself face to face with the Carthaginians, who had recently placed a garrison in the city of Messana, just across the narrow Sicilian straits.

CARTHAGE BEFORE THE PUNIC WARS

Some time during the Dark Ages of Greek history, in the long period between the end of the thirteenth century B.C. and the early Greek colonization of the west that began in the middle of the eighth, bands of Phoenician colonists from the coastal towns of Palestine and Syria began migrating to the western Mediterranean. The expanding populations of the eastern Mediterranean were being harassed by the Philistines and other Sea Peoples (as they are called) and by pressure from the restless inhabitants of the Levantine desert. The Phoenicians colonized in response to these conditions, founding settlements at Utica in North Africa, at Gades on the Atlantic coast of Spain, and later on Spain's Mediterranean coast. Other colonies sprang up along the North African littoral, the most important of which, founded by the inhabitants of the Phoenician city of Tyre in about 814 B.C., was called "New City" or Carthage.

The natives whom the Phoenicians found there when they arrived had formed no extensive political union, although all were of similar racial stock. Predecessors of the modern Berbers, they were racially distinct from the blacks of the sub-Saharan south. In antiquity the Greeks knew these semi-nomadic peoples as Libyans, the Romans, as Numidians. Carthage soon became the dominating power among these peoples, both because of her more advanced civilization and because of her magnificent geographical position. Situated on a peninsula that provided room for expansion and protection from the natives, the city lay sheltered in the heart of the bay. The hinterland was fertile and her prominent position in the mid-Mediterranean allowed her to retain contacts with east and west, as well as to control trans-Mediterranean shipping.

In her early years Carthage maintained a link with her mother city of Tyre but, from the seventh century onwards, Phoenicia lay under the control of a series of eastern empires: Assyria, Babylon, Egypt, and finally, Persia. As a result, the Phoenicians of the west were left to develop independently from their native country. Beginning in the sixth century they came to be united under the hegemony of Carthage. By the time the first war with Rome began in 264 B.C., the Punic empire in the western Mediterranean encompassed an area of about 28,000 square miles and a population estimated at three to four million.

Carthaginian imperial ambitions had extended well beyond the confines of the African continent. During the sixth century Carthage came to the aid of some Phoenician settlers in Sicily, who had been driven to the western tip of the island by advancing waves of competing Greek colonists. In about 480 B.C., the battle of Himera halted Carthaginian counter-advances in Sicily, saving the Greek colonies in the west from being overwhelmed. The struggle between Carthaginians and Greeks in Sicily continued intermittently, however, until the First Punic War, at the end of which Sicily became the first Roman province.

Carthage was also active in Spain, where there was again conflict with rival Greek settlers. Here the Carthaginians were more successful against their competitors. They established settlements not only there but also in Sardinia and Corsica, islands close to the coast of the Italian Peninsula. They destroyed the Greek colonies in Spain and gained in its south an almost inexhaustible source of natural wealth and manpower, as well as control over Atlantic trade. Merchants sailed along the Spanish coasts to explore the tin routes to the north, while others voyaged down the west coast of Africa to bring back gold and ivory. Carthage thus won an impressive overseas commercial empire. In Sardinia and southern Spain some of the natives were reduced to subjection; the rest were forced to contribute mercenary troops.

In Sicily, however, the Carthaginians had to tread more warily. The Greek colony of Syracuse was always a serious competitor for the loyalties of the native population, whom Carthage had to be careful not to alienate and drive into Syracusan hands. Her alliance with some of the Greek and native communities in Sicily therefore consisted in allowing them local autonomy. These allies paid a tribute rather than having to supply troops for Carthage's army and navy.

CARTHAGE AND ROME: EARLY RELATIONS

During this period of external expansion, Carthage first came into contact with Rome. The intermediaries were Rome's Etruscan neighbors to the north, whose ports in Italy had long been open to Phoenician vessels. When the Etruscan dynasty was driven from Rome at the end of the sixth century B.C., Carthage made a treaty with the newly established Roman Republic. The historian Polybius read a copy

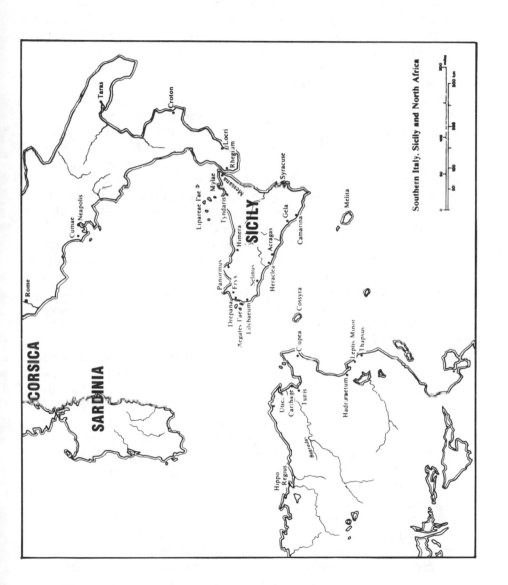

CORSICA

SARDINIA

Rome

Cumae
Neapolis

Taras

Croton

Liparae Iae
Mylae
Tyndaris
Messana
Rhegium
Locri

Panormus
Eryx
Himera
SICILY
Syracuse

Drepana
Lilybaeum
Aegates Iae
Selinus
Heraclea
Acragas
Gela
Camarina

Cossyra

Melita

Utica
Carthage
Tunis
Cupra

Hippo
Regius

Bagradas

Hadrumetum
Leptis Minor
Thapsus

Southern Italy, Sicily and North Africa

0   50   100   150   200   miles

0   100   200   300 km

of this treaty, engraved on bronze, and preserved in the Treasury at Rome. Its terms were obviously dictated by Carthage, since it was wholly in her favor. The Romans agreed to sail neither south nor west of the Gulf of Tunis nor to strike a deal in Libya or Sardinia, except in the presence of a Carthaginian herald. At this early time, the Carthaginians seem to have been attempting to exert control over the region and to exclude any competitive foreign power from offering an alternative to their hegemony. In return, Carthage merely pledged to abstain from injuring certain towns in Latium. When this treaty was renewed in 348 B.C., Rome allowed Carthage to stiffen the conditions considerably. The new agreement excluded Italian traders from Sardinia and Libya and from the western Mediterranean from the Gulf of Tunis to Mastia in Spain. Only Carthaginian Sicily and Carthage herself remained open. Rome was an agrarian society and, for the time being, Roman thoughts turned inward to the affairs of the peninsula, while her future rival gradually transformed the western Mediterranean into something of a Carthaginian lake.

To support her empire, Carthage needed money, men, and ships. Much of the money she derived from customs dues. Her army, originally composed of citizens, was not large enough for her great wars abroad, so that fairly early Carthage began drafting her subjects instead of her citizens: Africans, Sardinians, and Iberians. By the time of the outbreak of the First Punic War, Carthaginian citizens no longer served in the army at all, except as officers or in wars fought in Africa itself. This practice had material advantages for a citizenry that no longer admired the martial virtues, but it had one serious drawback. It created the potential for ambitious generals to use the professional army as a private power base, since the troops owed their allegiance (and sometimes their income) to the commanding officer, not to the state for which they fought. The problem emerged at the end of the First Punic War, when the armies of mercenaries became a permanent feature in Carthaginian politics, and thereafter always presented a potential danger to the security of the state.

As we have seen, the early treaties between Rome and Carthage delineated a Carthaginian sphere of influence and helped to avoid unwanted contacts and conflicts between the two states. Later they may have reached a close political agreement by which the Carthaginians would not interfere in Italian nor the Romans in Sicilian affairs. In 279 B.C. the Romans and Carthaginians reached yet another accord. With Pyrrhus on Italian soil, Carthage and Rome agreed to an emergency measure to keep him in Italy and prevent him from invading Sicily, perhaps in return for Carthaginian naval support. It failed, and Pyrrhus took his army south across the narrow Sicilian straits separating the toe of Italy from the island beyond. When Carthage had to fight Pyrrhus in Sicily, she neither asked for nor received Roman aid, undoubtedly because she did not relish the prospect of bringing yet another competing power onto the island. For similar reasons, the Romans had not asked the Carthaginians to help them against Pyrrhus in southern Italy. Toward the end of the decade, when Pyrrhus left the shores of Sicily on his way back to Greece, having accomplished nothing that lasted, he is reported to have uttered a prescient remark: "What a cockpit we are now leaving for the Carthaginian and the Roman to fight in."

The recent history of the island justified his prophecy. Carthaginian expansion in Sicily had been checked by a strong Syracuse under its king, Agathocles. When he died in 289 B.C., the Carthaginians were again able to advance until driven back by Pyrrhus. After Pyrrhus's departure the Carthaginians defeated the Syracusan fleet, recovered their lost possessions, and reduced the Greek cities of central Sicily. Thus, by 275, Syracuse's influence had shrunk to eastern Sicily and even there she met opposing powers. Some of Agathocles' discharged Italian mercenaries, whom he had hired from the south of Italy to help him fight the Carthaginians, had seized the town of Messana in the northeasternmost tip of Sicily. Styling themselves Mamertines, after the Sabellian god of war Mamers (Latin *Mars*), they settled there and proceeded to plunder the surrounding districts, Carthaginian and Greek alike. In 265, the Syracusans, under a new king, Hiero, conquered the Mamertines and undertook the siege of Messana. At this point the Carthaginians intervened and, with the consent of the Mamertines, put a Punic garrison into the town. Hiero had to return to Syracuse.

The Mamertines, however, had no desire to keep their new garrison and their Carthaginian overlords indefinitely. Some of them advocated reaching an agreement with Carthage by which their autonomy would be respected. Others preferred to seek a different alliance with a people whom they obviously hoped would aid them in removing their Carthaginian liberators. The latter group prevailed, and in 264 B.C. Rome was suddenly faced with a request for an alliance and help against the Carthaginians.

THE APPROACH OF WAR

The historian Polybius explains why the Romans agreed to help the Mamertines now and face war with both Carthage and Syracuse. They feared, he says, the geostrategic advantage that Carthage would gain once it had consolidated its hold on Sicily and taken possession of Messana. With the conquest of Sicily completed, Carthage would control all the islands surrounding the Italian Peninsula, while in Messana she would occupy a position that could serve as a convenient base of operations for her next possible advance—an invasion of Italy itself.

In 264 B.C., an advanced guard of Roman soldiers arrived in Sicily and, with little opposition, forced the commander of the Carthaginian garrison in Messana to evacuate the citadel. The Carthaginians at this stage appeared to have been trying to avoid war with the Romans: they neither contested the Romans' crossing of the straits nor tried to hold Messana against them.

Rome's occupation of Messana provoked a harsh reaction from the government in Carthage, however. They eventually recalled the accommodating Carthaginian commander and crucified him. Neither side had yet declared war, but an unlikely alliance now joined former enemies: the Carthaginians and Hiero, King of Syracuse, made a pact against the Romans, deciding to remove these newly arrived Italian barbarians from Sicily before renewing their own struggle for hegemony of the island. A formidable Punic Army first garrisoned the city of Agrigentum on the southwest coast, then advanced and encamped outside Messana. Hiero also brought an army to Messana from the south, and the new Roman liberators suddenly found themselves besieged, while the Punic fleet anchored to the north to block any further passage of Roman forces across the straits. This was standard operational procedure in antiquity. An army in a city was besieged on land and blockaded by sea until, facing the prospect of starvation, it would emerge and fight its besiegers. In fact, the Romans managed to slip their legions into Sicily at night, and now, with a substantial army of their own at Messana, they sent twin ultimata to the Carthaginians and the Syracusans, ordering both to raise the siege of Messana. These demands having been refused, the Roman consul declared a state of hostilities and the First Punic War began in earnest.

FIRST BATTLES

The Romans divided their forces and attacked the opposing armies simultaneously. Hiero retreated to the safety of Syracuse, while the Carthaginians withdrew their forces to protect their cities in Sicily. In the next campaigning season fresh Roman legions marched towards Syracuse while many of the towns around Aetna submitted to them. Without a formidable naval force to establish control of the sea, however, the Romans would not be able to blockade Syracuse successfully, and there was not much chance that they could take the city by storm. Fortunately for them, Hiero began making friendly overtures, to which they responded. In return for a war indemnity and a promise to help supply the Roman legions, so that Carthage's fleet could not blockade and starve out Roman armies, Hiero won an alliance and control of some 30 miles of territory around Syracuse. The Romans had made him an offer that there was no good reason to refuse.

In the spring of 262 B.C., with the Carthaginians recruiting in Spain, Liguria, and Gaul, the Romans sent both their consular armies to Sicily to attack the Carthaginian base of operations at the Greek city of Agrigentum. After a protracted siege of some seven months—prolonged because supplies filtered through to the Carthaginian army—the Punic commander managed to fight his way out of the city, both sustaining and inflicting heavy casualties. The day after the battle, however, the Romans, as a calculated act of intimidation to any other Sicilian city that might continue to support the Carthaginians, sacked Agrigentum and sold its inhabitants into slavery.

The Romans had won a great victory, but Roman commanders still could not withdraw their legions to Italy confident that the Carthaginians would let Sicily alone. In 261, Rome resolved to drive the Carthaginians from the island altogether. This task would present operational difficulties. At the heart of the problem, as Polybius explains, lay the Carthaginians' undisputed mastery of the sea. Even after Rome's victory at Agrigentum, only the insignificant inland towns would join the Roman side. They feared the powerful and ruthless Roman army on their island, but the larger number of more powerful coastal cities all remained open and loyal to the Carthaginians because they were fortified against land assault and Carthage maintained control of the sea. So long as Carthage had naval access to them, Rome's battlefield victories could not be turned into politically decisive results. The Carthaginians might have been defeated in two land battles but, thanks to their superior naval forces, they could continue to operate in Sicily, return to besiege Messana, and even settle old scores with Syracuse once the Romans withdrew their forces.

Moreover, the Carthaginian fleet now began ravaging the Italian coast, while North Africa remained untouched and untouchable because of Rome's lack of a naval offensive capacity. Increasingly it became clear to the Romans that if they were truly to solve their Sicilian problem they had to choose between two strategic options: (1) They could continue operations on the island in an attempt to drive the Carthaginians permanently from every city that traditionally supported them and force those cities to become, instead, permanent and dependable allies of Rome; (2) they could apply pressure for a lasting cessation of hostilities by raising the stakes and threatening Carthage itself with an assault on Africa. Whichever option they chose they would be obliged to challenge Carthage at sea.

THE ROMAN NAVY

The ancient world did not see Rome as a naval power, but the picture of the Romans as landlubbers was greatly overdrawn. The alliance of which they were the leaders included the seafaring cities of Greater Greece that Rome had just brought under her hegemony— states like Tarentum, Locri, Elea, Naples, and Cumae, with centuries of naval experience and formidable navies of their own. If the Romans, up to this point, had used only land armies for their conquests, that was because their opponents in Italy had all been land powers and they rarely needed to make a naval assault. From her newly acquired Greek allies in the south of the peninsula, Rome now acquired the bulk of her naval forces, though she expanded her own fleet, building an additional 120 galleys. In fact, she was able to accomplish this feat of naval construction without great difficulty, since Rome and the city-states of Latium generally had long seafaring traditions and possessed in abundance the materials needed to step up their shipbuilding. Nevertheless, the bulk of Rome's naval forces and the expertise required for their operation probably came courtesy of her Greek allies in southern Italy.

The galleys of Italy, moreover, now acquired an innovative piece of naval technology—a Syracusan invention perhaps—designed to minimize the greater maneuverability of Carthage's ships. All were fitted with a device called a "raven" or "claw" (Latin *corvus*). This was a movable boarding bridge, about thirteen feet long, which could be rotated about a stump-mast set in the prow of the galley. Beneath its outer end was a sharp spike, which could be raised by means of a rope passing through a pulley set on top of the stump-mast. When an enemy ship came within its reach, it was dropped on her deck, which the spike then penetrated so that it held the enemy ship fast. The Roman soldiers packing the ship's deck could then board and defeat the enemy. The Romans hoped that the raven would provide an answer to one of the favorite tactics of the well-drilled Carthaginian fleet: their better-handled ships would row rapidly through the gaps in their enemy's line—ancient fleets normally advanced towards each other in line abreast—and then, turning quickly, ram their opponents from behind. In a further refinement, the Carthaginians would use the ram as they went past to cripple the oarage on one side of the enemy ship. Whether the Romans' innovative boarding bridge really contributed as much to giving them the upper hand at sea as the ancient accounts maintain is at least questionable. Accounts of the later sea battles do not mention it at all, and the Romans still lost a great sea battle despite it, as we shall see later in this chapter.

In the summer of 256 B.C., a newly organized, newly equipped Roman fleet rounded the east coast of Sicily and encountered the Carthaginian navy just off Cape Ecnomus. The Roman galleys advanced in four separate squadrons on a narrow front, while the Carthaginians formed into one long line abreast, with the intention of outflanking their enemy. The Romans' first wedge-shaped squadron managed to break through the Punic center and thanks, we are told, to the corvus, was soon victorious. Meanwhile, the Carthaginian left wing had forced the Roman second line toward shore, while the Roman third squadron was also faring badly at the hands of the Carthaginian right. The victorious Roman first squadron returned in time to save the third line by driving off the Carthaginian right wing. Then the combined Roman squadrons converged against their enemy's left wing, which was still engaged near the shore. Here they captured fifty galleys, having sunk thirty others, while losing only twenty-four ships themselves. It was a great naval victory with a significant consequence. The Romans now decided to choose the strategic option that would remove the Carthaginian presence from Sicily with a strike at Africa itself.

THE ASSAULT ON AFRICA

The Romans disembarked on the shore of Africa for the first time at Clupea, on the large promontory that juts into the Mediterranean just east of Carthage. When the Carthaginians realized what the Romans intended, they recalled their forces from Sicily and recruited fresh troops, while the Roman commander, Regulus, besieged Adys and, after an initial success against an army sent against him, advanced to Tunis where he encamped for the winter. In the spring of 255 B.C., Regulus's army engaged and was decisively defeated by the Carthaginian force that sallied out against them. The defeat was overwhelming. Only two thousand Romans survived the battle and Regulus along with five hundred others was taken prisoner. A Roman fleet had been prepared to blockade Carthage by sea in coordination with Regulus's army, which was to have besieged the city by land in the traditional manner. This plan fell apart with Regulus's defeat, so that the Roman fleet of about two hundred and fifty vessels sailed to

Africa to face the Punic navy and to rescue the survivors at Clupea. Near the Hermaean Promontory they met and defeated the fleet of perhaps two hundred ships that the Carthaginians intended to employ to keep open their sea lanes of communication against the blockading Romans. Having won yet another naval victory against Carthage, the consuls in command of the fleet rescued the survivors at Clupea and set out to return to Italy. The fruits of victory were short-lived, however. On the way home, off the Sicilian coast, between Camarina and Cape Pachynus, a devastating Mediterranean storm destroyed all but eighty of the Roman vessels. The African campaign had become an extremely costly failure.

LAND AND NAVAL STRATEGIES IN SICILY

That winter (255–254 B.C.), having levied still more taxes to build a new fleet, the Roman Senate reassessed its strategic options. Since they had failed in their attempt to take the war to Africa itself, they decided that they would have to launch a series of campaigns to drive the Carthaginian presence from those Sicilian cities still willing to provide Rome's enemy with a base of operations. In the spring of 254, four Roman legions stormed the Punic base at Panormus (modern Palermo) from both land and sea. The operation succeeded and the thirteen thousand citizens unable to raise the ransom the Romans demanded for their freedom were sold into slavery. Tyndaris and Solus also fell to the Romans. Because the Carthaginians had recalled their forces from Sicily to face Regulus in Africa and because they had been detained there suppressing a Numidian uprising, they could offer their Sicilian clients little help in resisting this latest Roman offensive. The Carthaginians managed one counterattack when they stormed and recaptured Agrigentum. Fearing nevertheless that they would not be strong enough to hold the city, they burned it to the ground. Their reputation among their Sicilian client states was not enhanced either by their weakness or their brutality. At the end of this campaigning season they only held a handful of Sicilian towns.

In 252 the Romans captured Thermae and the Lipari Islands, but they repeatedly failed in their attempts to take Lilybaeum. Meanwhile, another Roman fleet fell victim to a ferocious storm. Because the Carthaginians were too preoccupied with their Numidian problem to take advantage of this Roman setback, they made no serious attempt to regain the ground they had lost, and the next two years (252–250) passed uneventfully. Two years of renewed activity followed this two-year lull. The Romans again sailed against Lilybaeum and tried to blockade it, while an army marched on Panormus. Lilybaeum, however, proved an impossible nut to crack: it was well fortified and its north-facing harbor, though small, was extremely difficult to get at. In 250 the Romans advanced to begin siege and blockade with 120 ships and four legions, but the Carthaginians repeatedly ran the blockade—sometimes with the help of their ally from the Greek island of Rhodes—and succeeded in burning the Roman siege-works, There seemed no easy way for the Romans to dislodge the Carthaginian presence at Lilybaeum.

Realizing the ineffectiveness of this naval blockade, the Romans in 249 decided upon yet another strategy, one Mahan would have applauded. Unable either to take the war to Africa or to drive the Carthaginians from their major Sicilian strongholds, they resolved to advance into Sicilian waters in order to destroy the Punic fleet stationed at Drepana, just 16 miles north of Lilybaeum. The idea was sound, but it was badly executed by the Roman commander and Rome suffered its first major naval defeat of the war. Of the 123 Roman galleys taken to Drepana, 93 were lost. Another storm ravaged almost all that remained of the Roman navy. At year's end only 20 of the 240 galleys with which the Romans started the year had survived. There was no question now of continuing the naval blockade of Lilybaeum. Nevertheless, the Romans sent an army that managed to cut off all the roads that led to Drepana. Although Rome had lost control at sea, the only two towns in Sicily still held by Carthage, Lilybaeum and Drepana, were now isolated from the rest of the island. This tactic at least turned defeat into a stalemate, and although Rome was now too exhausted to build yet another navy, she entertained no thoughts of negotiating a peace settlement. Moreover, Carthage was again too preoccupied with her Numidian problems in the interior of Africa to capitalize on this lull.

New life was infused into what had become a dreary stalemate by the emergence of a new, energetic Carthaginian leader. In 247, Hamilcar Barca took advantage of Rome's naval weakness and raided the coast of southern Italy. By this time Rome had all but abandoned the sea to the Carthaginians. In the next year Hamilcar struck at the rear of the Roman armies besieging Drepana and Lilybaeum by effecting a landing west of Panormus. He fortified a position on the mountain behind the city and anchored his fleet at the foot so that he could collect intelligence against the Romans in Sicily and communicate it easily to the Carthaginian commanders at both besieged ports. This was an important achievement, because from this mountain Hamilcar could direct efforts to thwart Rome's siege tactics. He managed to hold the Romans at bay for three years, harassing their forces and

sending an amphibious assault force to raid the Italian coast as far
as Cumae. In 244 he advanced to Mount Eryx in order to relieve the
pressure of the siege of Drepana. He captured the old town of Eryx
on the northern slopes of the mountain, but the Romans managed
to prevent him from actually breaking their siege. Details of this
struggle, unfortunately, do not survive, but we know that it only ended
with the conclusion of the war itself.

The long years of Hamilcar's campaigns strengthened the conviction within the Roman Senate that the war could be won only at sea.
Since the treasury was exhausted, a collective loan was raised that
would be repayable only in the event of victory. It financed a fleet of
200 warships and many transports, the galleys being of light build
and without *corvi*. In the summer of 242 this new fleet set sail for
Drepana, to attempt once more to engage and destroy the Carthaginian fleet. On arrival it found no Punic navy waiting to face it because
the Carthaginians were using the crews for their wars in Africa. An
attack on Drepana failed but the besieged town was running out of
provisions and it was in danger of falling. By March 241 the Carthaginians, with difficulty, manned a fleet of between 170 and 200 galleys. They intended to land stores in Sicily and then, having embarked Hamilcar and his men in order to compensate for their lack
of marines, to face the foe at sea. Just off the Aegates Islands they
engaged the Roman fleet. Hampered by their makeshift equipment
and heavy freight, they were easily defeated. The Romans sank fifty
ships and captured seventy more. Further resistance was out of the
question. Carthage had shot her bolt; the war was at an end. The
Carthaginian government now gave Hamilcar full powers to negotiate
the peace.

THE SPOILS OF VICTORY, THE COST OF DEFEAT

Rome's victory ought not to be overestimated. Even though, in the
end, Carthage had been defeated on both land and sea, Rome's margin of superiority was never very great. The war had taken twenty-
three years, and only then did Rome's great staying power finally
prevail. Despite the Romans' slight superiority in land warfare, the
Carthaginians had held their own on Sicily until the very end. Neither in Africa nor even in Sicily were the legions able to drive the
Carthaginians completely from their strongholds. The final decision
came at sea, but the decisive factor in the Roman victory was not
military or even naval skill so much as it was simple persistence,
persistence that itself depended on the support and strength of the
Italian confederation the city of Rome had forged. This alliance en-

abled the Romans to launch fleet after fleet to replace those wrecked by storms or defeated by the Carthaginians.

Even in 241 Carthage could probably have continued the struggle, as demonstrated by the sizable war indemnity she subsequently paid to Rome and the Mercenary War she later waged. Continuing to fight was futile, however, for Carthage had no real prospects of victory. At best, she could only have prolonged her resistance and perhaps won another battle. She could not have achieved a decisive political result. Carthage's armies were too weak to wrest the cities and forts of Sicily back from the Romans, while Rome had demonstrated that she could not be brought down simply through defeats at sea. Accordingly the Carthaginians, without being fully defeated, submitted to a peace under relatively mild conditions. To have exacted more would have required that the Romans cross over into Africa—a hopeless undertaking when they could not even drive Hamilcar Barca out of Sicily.

THE INTERWAR YEARS PERIOD: 241 TO 218 B.C.

In 241 Hamilcar Barca and the Roman consul, Gaius Catulus Lutatius, agreed upon conditions for peace. Carthage was to evacuate Sicily, return all Roman prisoners and pay a war indemnity of twenty-two hundred talents in twenty annual installments, a trifling sum for an empire as vast and wealthy as the Carthaginian. Both sides agreed not to attack the allies of the other. Carthage lost and Rome gained the island of Sicily, and the Romans thereby won security for their southern flank, which had been the objective in waging war in the first place. These terms the centuriate assembly in Rome, which had the power of ratifying declarations of war and treaties of peace, later altered. Undoubtedly at the Senate's recommendation, they voted to add another thousand talents to the war indemnity and to cut to ten years the time for repayment. In addition, all the islands between Sicily and Carthage were turned over to Rome, Punic ships were prohibited from sailing in Italian waters, and Carthage could no longer recruit mercenaries in Italy.

The most obvious result of the First Punic War was that Rome gained control of her first territory outside the Italian Peninsula. In Italy, the Roman Confederation had proceeded by requiring subject allies to provide a fixed number of troops for Rome's wars. Instead of applying this system in Sicily, Rome made the Sicilian cities pay an annual tribute. There were good reasons for this decision. Many of the Sicilian natives were politically unsophisticated, and their military qualifications were questionable. Rome probably had no intention of ever calling up their armies. It was simpler to have them pay to Rome the sums they had grown accustomed to paying to Carthage. To collect tribute was the line of least resistance. It might have been chosen without much regard for its long-term consequences—which is not necessarily an argument against it—but in time it revolutionized the whole Roman conception of extended governance. It changed the leader of an Italian confederation into an imperial power, which ultimately used this new principle to facilitate and sustain domination of the Mediterranean world.

Messana and Hiero's kingdom of Syracuse, making up about a quarter of Sicily, fell outside this method of administration. Because of the alliance ties to Rome, the two cities were neither obliged to pay tribute nor even officially to supply troops. Instead, for their exemplary loyalty the two cities were granted a *foedus aequum*, literally an "equal treaty," which in theory acknowledged them as free and equal allies of the Roman People. In practice, however, Rome recognized no equals. The grant was titular only, guaranteeing that these allies would have no formal obligation to fulfill and that Rome would not interfere in their domestic affairs.

THE MERCENARY REVOLT AND THE REBELLION OF SARDINIA, ROME'S SECOND PROVINCE

While the First Punic War had levied a light toll in blood on the citizens of Carthage (since most of the soldiers had been foreign mercenaries), the truceless cold war that followed endangered the city's very existence. Twenty thousand of these mercenaries returned to Africa from Sicily and raised a clamor for their back pay. This motley crew of Libyans, Iberians, Celts, Ligurians, Balearic Islanders, and Greeks found a common bond in their claims on Carthage. They marched on Tunis and fanned the flames of revolt throughout the country. Natives rushed to arms against their overlords, while the Numidians swept over the empire's western frontier. When the North African cities of Utica and Hippo surrendered, the mercenaries moved against Carthage itself from a base of operations they had set up in Tunis. Without command of the sea, however, they had little chance of success.

At the same time, Carthage was further embarrassed by a revolt in Sardinia. In the end, Carthage managed to defeat the mercenaries and drive them out. All African territories were recaptured, but Carthage had paid a heavy price for her victory in terms of her weakness after the war with Rome and the further destruction of her resources, which that weakness now allowed her enemies to exploit. During the years of this struggle Carthage had no trouble with Rome. The rebel-

lion in Sardinia could have been a potential flash point and a vulnerability for the Romans to exploit. The mercenaries there—who had
revolted from Carthage and who had reduced most of the island—
appealed to Rome for help, probably in 239. Then, however, it looked
as though the Carthaginians would be victorious in Africa and would
soon be able to direct all their efforts to regaining control over the
island. Rome rejected their appeal as she did that of Utica, which
also offered to submit to Rome. For the time being, Rome apparently
preferred not to involve herself with the unpredictable bands of mercenaries but to continue to honor the treaty of 241. There were trou-
bles brewing for Rome to the north and the east, and her reading of
the conditions there at this time seems to have kept her from becoming involved in a third, western front.

The skies appear to have cleared in 238, however, and in that year
a second appeal by the mercenaries to the Romans for aid was an-
swered with a Roman declaration of war against Carthage. There was
little likelihood at this time that the battered Carthaginians would
have the heart for yet another conflict, and indeed Carthage suggested that the matter be submitted to arbitration—in vain, however,
as that request was ignored and peace granted only at the price of
yet another twelve hundred talents and the surrender of Sardinia.
Even the very pro-Roman Polybius remarks that Rome's behavior was
"contrary to all justice." In expelling the Carthaginian presence from
Sardinia, the Romans removed another potential base for attack against
the Roman coast.

The pacification of Sardinia was not nearly as easy as the expulsion of the Carthaginians. When Rome set out to take the island, and
Corsica as well, she found that native resistance and the mountain-
ous country made the conquest a slow process. Indeed, Rome began
in 237 and could not gain control of the island until 232, when the
Roman consul in charge gained notoriety by employing man-hunting
dogs against the Corsicans. In that same year Corsica was also paci-
fied, and in 227 the two islands were constituted a Roman province
on the Sicilian model, except that no town had obtained freedom or
immunity.

THE GALLIC INVASION OF ITALY

Throughout the 230s there were rumblings from the north, and
there appear to have been several skirmishes with some Gallic tribes-
men. Toward the end of the decade, Rome had to direct her attentions eastward, but in 226 those attentions were drawn sharply back
to the north. The storm clouds lowered so ominously and quickly

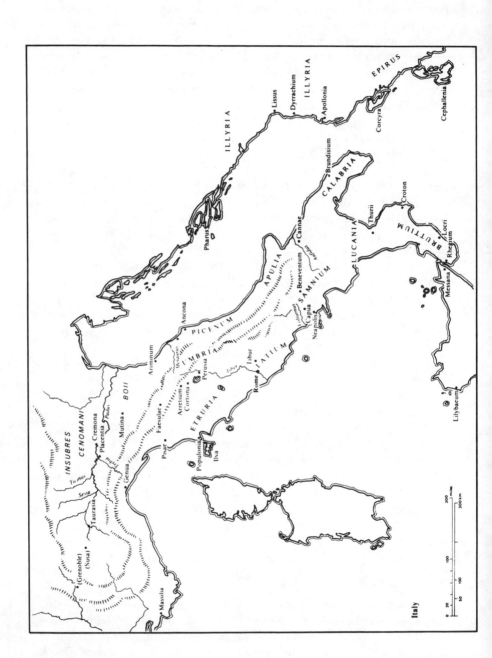

Italy

EPIRUS

ILLYRIA

Cephallenia

Lissus
Dyrrachium
ILLYRIA
Apollonia
Corcyra

Pharus

Brundisium
CALABRIA

Croton
Thurii
LUCANIA
Locri
BRUTTIUM
Rhegum
Messana

Cannae
APULIA
Beneventum
SAMNIUM
Capua
Neapolis

Ancona

PICENTUM

Ariminum

UMBRIA
Arretium
Cortona
Perusa
Faesulae

Tiber
Rome
Tibur
LATIUM

ETRURIA

INSUBRES
CENOMANI
Cremona
Placentia
Mutina
BOII
Genua
Padus

Populonia
Ilva

Trebia

Trebia
Ticinus
Sesia
Taurasia
(Susa)
(Grenoble)

Lilybaeum

Massilia

0 50 100 200 miles
0 100 300 km

there that Rome hastily reached an agreement with Hasdrubal, whose empire-building in Spain was raising visions of new trouble with Carthage. The Gallic clans were gathering; memories and tales of the sack of Rome created panic throughout Italy. A census of all available manpower in the Italian Peninsula revealed almost a million men who might serve under arms.

Rome hastened north to defend Italy. The Gauls advanced over the Apennines and, devastating the country on their march, took the road to Rome, slipping past the two consular legions sent to block their way. These hastened in pursuit, but the Gauls, deciding not to face the consular army in battle, retired with their booty to the Etruscan coast, for the coast offered both further booty and forage for their horses. They proceeded northward followed by a consular army, when they were suddenly surprised to find yet another consular army waiting for them. These were the legions recalled from Sardinia, now marching south to meet the Gauls. A great battle was fought. The Gauls formed two lines back to back to meet the double Roman offensive. Even though one of the Roman consuls was killed, superior Roman discipline and equipment overcame Gallic valor. The Gauls left forty thousand of their fifty thousand soldiers dead on the field, and the other ten thousand were taken prisoner. Only a fraction of the Gallic cavalry managed to break away. Never again did a Gallic army cross the Apennines.

MARITIME STRATEGY IN THE SECOND PUNIC WAR: 218 TO 201

While Rome was thus engaged in Cisalpine Gaul, as well as across the Adriatic in efforts to suppress the fierce Illyrians, Carthage was expanding her holdings in Spain. She undertook operations there in part to offset the loss of Sicily and Sardinia. Her movement through the Iberian Peninsula was swift and deliberate. Hamilcar's successor, Hasdrubal, marched steadily north along the east coast as far as the Ebro river. In 226 Roman ambassadors met him, and a treaty was arranged whereby Hasdrubal promised not to cross the Ebro River in arms and probably received assurances in return that the Romans would not interfere with his conquests south of the Ebro.

In 221 Hasdrubal was assassinated and his place taken by Hamilcar Barca's twenty-five-year-old son, Hannibal, a man soon to enter the lists as Rome's most formidable enemy. Hannibal renewed the expansionist policies of his predecessors, but one of the cities south of the Ebro managed to withstand him: Saguntum. The details have been debated from antiquity to today, but Hannibal's attack on, and siege and plunder of, the city of Saguntum was the proximate cause of the Second Punic War. Even though Saguntum was south of the Ebro River—the demarcation line between the spheres of influence stipulated in the Ebro Treaty—complex relationships and intrigue combined to cause Rome to go to war, paradoxically, over the fall of a city that she failed to defend while it was still resisting. Probably, because as long as Saguntum held out, Rome could feel an ambivalence about its policy there that the fall of Saguntum removed. Now Rome slipped into a war that was to become a struggle for her existence.

THE WAR WITH HANNIBAL

In the settlement following the First Punic War and in her subsequent dealings with Carthage, it became crystal clear that Rome's political strategy was to deprive her traditional enemy of any base of operations against the Italian Peninsula. Not only Sicily but the islands between Sicily and Africa, as well as both Sardinia and Corsica, were now in Roman hands. Since ancient fleets made their way, for the most part, by rowing and sailing close to the coasts, it would be extremely hazardous for the Carthaginians to mount a seaborne attack against Italy without putting its forces at great risk. Rome established sea control by holding the access routes to Italy—the islands between Africa and the peninsula. When war was declared between Rome and Carthage, Rome's superiority at sea and her control of the islands led her to suppose that she alone would decide where the war would be waged. It also meant that the Second Punic War would be a war the Carthaginians would have to wage predominantly on the land.

The Romans decided to confine the war to Spain and Africa. One consul with some twenty-four thousand men and sixty galleys was sent against the Carthaginian armies in Spain. The other was sent with 160 vessels and an army of about twenty-six thousand to Sicily to prepare to journey across the sea to Africa. His strategy would not be to attack the city of Carthage itself: his forces were inadequate for such an undertaking, as the campaigns of the First Punic War had revealed. Instead he was to support and encourage a revolt among the native tribes of the interior.

Rome's naval superiority and her control of seaborne access to the peninsula made it seem likely that Hannibal would try to initiate offensive operations from northern Spain, that he would have to cross the Ebro and advance on Italy slowly, consolidating his communications and keeping a long logistical tail while he marched through Gaul, since he could not count on being supplied by sea. Hannibal,

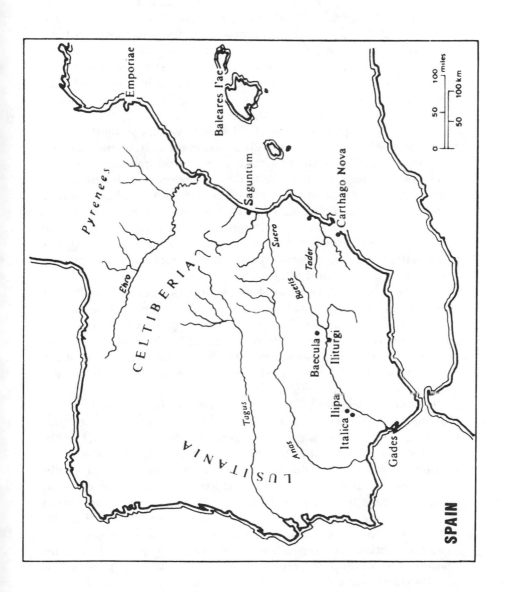

SPAIN

Pyrenees

Emporiae

Baleares I'ae

Saguntum

Carthago Nova

CELTIBERIA

Ebro

Sucro

Tader

Baetis

Baecula

Iliturgi

Ilipa

Italica

Tagus

Anas

LUSITANIA

Gades

0   50   100   miles
100 km
0   50   100 km

however, had no intention of fighting in Spain or Africa. He set out to invade the Italian Peninsula from the north by land, with the intention of destroying the real basis of Rome's naval and military power: the Italian confederacy. He decided to jeopardize his communications, live off the land and swoop quickly down into northern Italy, where he would establish a base of operations rather than rely on maintaining communications with Spain. It was a bold, dangerous plan and in the end it was a very near thing. He left Spain with an army of some forty thousand men. Only twenty-six thousand reached Italy after their trek across the Alps.

At the end of April 218, Hannibal left New Carthage (modern Cartagena) in Spain. He crossed the Ebro river early in June and reached the Rhone in mid-August. A Roman army should have been waiting to contest his passage, but the Boii and Insubres in the neighborhood of the new Latin colonies, Placentia and Cremona, had rebelled, almost certainly at Hannibal's instigation. The legions prepared for Spain had to be diverted to suppress this insurrection. Hannibal marched up the Rhone, but where precisely he crossed the Alps is still a matter of dispute. Most experts think he took the pass between the Little St. Bernard and Mt. Genèvre.

After storming the major settlement of the Taurini (modern Turin), Hannibal was surprised to find that the Roman legions diverted by the local insurrection had managed to catch up with him. A complicated series of maneuvers followed, leading to the battle of Trebia, just south of Placentia, on a bitter December day. Two-thirds of the Roman army that had opposed him was destroyed. Hannibal had won the first real battle of the war.

The Romans decided to abandon the northern plains of Italy, where Hannibal's cavalry and his Gallic allies would prove most useful, and to defend central Italy instead. They could not, however, predict where Hannibal would cross the Apennines. Having advanced to Bononia (modern Bologna), he could have moved either southwest or southeast. Therefore, the Romans split their forces, posting one group to guard Arretium (modern Arezzo), the other to protect Ariminum (modern Rimini). Although the split has often been criticized in retrospect, it is hard to imagine a safer alternative before the event.

In May, when the passes were free from snow, Hannibal abandoned his base camp and crossed the Apennines by the pass of Collina. He deliberately encouraged one of the Roman armies to attack him by exposing his flank as he marched to Cortona and toward Rome. Suddenly he swung off the road to Rome, and headed eastwards toward Perugia along the northern shore of Lake Trasimene.

He marched his forces into a narrow divide between hills that came right down to the lake except where a small plain opened out, more than three miles long. On the hills above this plain Hannibal stationed his troops for an ambush. The Roman legions followed blindly and early on a misty morning they marched in column into the defile. From the hilltops above the mist, Hannibal's troops rushed down simultaneously from all sides. For two hours the battle raged. The Roman commander was killed and only some six thousand of his men managed to cut their way through the enemy, but even they were later rounded up. The disaster was complete; two legions were almost wiped out, although Hannibal granted the surviving Roman allies their freedom. There was no disguising the seriousness of the occasion. In Rome a praetor gravely announced: "We have been beaten in a great battle."

The disaster of Trasimene caused so great a crisis in Rome that the traditional remedy, dormant for thirty years, was revived: a dictator was appointed. The Senate chose Quintus Fabius Maximus, although it gave him a second in command who was out of sympathy with the strategy he had announced: to dog Hannibal's heels and avoid pitched battles at all costs. Unable to bring about a decisive battle, Hannibal moved through Samnium into Campania, one of the most fertile regions of Italy. Fabius followed and looked on while Rome's allies had their lands laid waste. At the end of the campaigning season, Hannibal intended to withdraw to Apulia for the winter, but Fabius held Callicula, the pass by which Hannibal hoped to leave Campania. By a famous ruse, Hannibal by night drove two thousand oxen with burning faggots tied to their horns towards Fabius's camp on the high ground. Roman pickets left their posts in the pass to investigate, and under cover of the resulting surprise and confusion Hannibal slipped through. He marched back to Apulia, crossing the Apennines for the fourth time that year. Although his army was now laden with booty, still none of the towns of Campania had opened their gates to him.

Then news came that Hannibal had captured the Roman depot at Cannae on the right bank of the Aufidus River. The Romans decided to give battle. Four reinforced legions advanced to Cannae. In early August both armies crossed the river and engaged. In a brilliant tactical maneuver, the Carthaginians enveloped the advancing Roman legionaires and cut them to pieces. Twenty-five thousand Romans fell; ten thousand were captured, while perhaps fifteen thousand escaped. So ended the greatest battle the Romans had yet fought. Confidence in Rome's ability to prevail was badly shaken in Italy. Many towns in Samnium and Apulia and nearly all those in Lucania and Bruttium went over to what they took to be the winning side—Hannibal's—and in the autumn Capua, the second most important city in Italy, and some other Campanian towns followed suit. Nevertheless, the whole of Latium, Umbria, and Etruria remained loyal to Rome.

The aftermath of the battle of Cannae vindicated Fabius's strategy of exhaustion. As Rome refused to accept defeat, Hannibal had no choice but to persevere in his attempt to break up the Italian Confederacy. Carthage's lack of control of the sea meant that Hannibal could not be satisfactorily reinforced or resupplied, so he devised a new strategy aimed at embarrassing Rome still further by extending the theaters of operations against the Romans and by raising up a circle of enemies to surround her. In the west the war was to be prosecuted in Spain and a landing took place in Sardinia. In the north the Gauls were still hostile. In the east the Carthaginians sought an alliance with King Philip of Macedon, who would now attempt to expel the Roman forces from Illyria. Even in Sicily the Greek cities were encouraged to revolt to Carthage. Thus, the Carthaginians sought to encircle Rome and to create new theaters of war in Spain, Sardinia, Macedon, and Sicily.

Only part of Spain was involved in the war: the Mediterranean littoral with its hinterland and the rich valley of the Baetis (modern Guadalquivir) in the south where the seat of Carthaginian power lay. A coast road linked these two valleys and the two key towns of Saguntum and New Carthage, the latter serving as the Carthaginians' base of operations for the war. An army invading Spain from the northeast needed three assets: control of the coast road, an adequate base of operations, and command of the sea. Publius Scipio understood the supreme importance of holding the enemy at bay in Spain. He sent his brother Gnaeus there in 218 and joined him the next year. Their task was to prevent supplies and reinforcements reaching Hannibal from Spain, but they did not merely fight a defensive holding action on the line at the Ebro. Instead they launched an offensive designed to break the enemy's power on the Iberian Peninsula.

In his first campaign Publius Scipio not only prevented reinforcements reaching Hannibal, but also won a base of operations and began the conquest of the district north of the Ebro. In 217, Hasdrubal, the Carthaginian field commander, approached the mouth of the Ebro with all his land forces and a fleet. Although his own fleet was quite small, Scipio decided to give battle. He wanted to avoid having his flank turned and understood that he had to have command of the sea to advance any farther south and to prevent Hannibal from receiving support from the sea. Scipio's navy was reinforced by the people of Massilia (modern Marseille), who were well known for their naval prowess and were eager to safeguard their trade with Spain by checking the power of Carthage at sea. Accordingly, the Romans engaged and defeated the enemy's fleet off the mouth of the Ebro. This victory not only allowed them to cross the Ebro in safety but affected the entire course of the war by destroying Hannibal's hopes for success. After a feeble demonstration off Italy this same year, the Carthaginians abandoned any large-scale naval operations, so that Hannibal was left in Italy while Rome continued to control the sea.

In 215 the Carthaginian theater commander, another Hasdrubal, Hannibal's brother, advanced to put everything at risk. He engaged the Roman army on the Ebro. A Roman defeat would wrest back control of Spain for Carthage and allow Hasdrubal to join Hannibal in Italy. Hasdrubal, however, was utterly defeated by the Roman force sent against him. The Scipios had won Rome's first victory of the war in pitched battle: an achievement that would not hurt Rome's image in Italy and would strengthen it in important ways in Spain, where other native tribes now revolted against the Carthaginians. In 212 the Scipios' gradual advance culminated in the taking of Saguntum. From there they planned further offensives to the south and into the hinterland but overextended their forces. In 211 they advanced in two divisions against the enemy. As they penetrated into the south they moved farther from their supply lines and then deeper into territory where the natives had remained loyal to the Carthaginians. In the end, both brothers were defeated and killed in battle, but their accomplishments were substantial. They had prevented reinforcements reaching Hannibal from Spain; they had inflicted two severe defeats on the enemy's forces—by sea off the Ebro, and by land at Ibera; then, taking the offensive, they had captured Saguntum and advanced farther south, wresting from Carthage a considerable part of the Spanish Empire from which Carthage drew so much of her strength.

In Rome during the bitter hours after Cannae, the population did not accept defeat, even though the depletion of Roman manpower had been devastating, Southern Italy had rebelled, and Hannibal was undisputed master in battle. It was now clear that open battle with Hannibal's army must be avoided at all costs: hereafter Fabius's attrition strategy formed the basis of all subsequent Roman operations in Italy. Above all, Rome's naval supremacy had to be maintained. This involved keeping afloat nearly two hundred ships manned by some fifty thousand sailors. Moreover, all the legions abroad had to be maintained there in order to keep the enemy tied up outside of Italy. By 212 the Romans managed to put twenty-five legions in the field (at roughly five thousand men per legion). They allowed even slaves to fight in these dark days after Cannae. Despite Carthage's attempt to encircle Rome with enemies, however, Hannibal had to remain in Italy without outside help and this, in the end, was what guaranteed his failure. The arrival of reinforcements from Spain alone could have changed the course of the war in Italy, and this the Scipios had prevented from happening. So Hannibal, who had vainly tried to take Puteoli and Nola, abandoned his Campanian offensive. He also failed to surprise Heraclea and Tarentum, and the Roman fleet stationed at Brundisium was too quick for him. He could not strike the fatal blow.

In Campania, Capua, and in Sicily, Syracuse had gone over to the Carthaginian side, as had Tarentum in Great Greece, but by 211, the Romans managed to destroy Capua politically and eventually recaptured Syracuse. Meanwhile news of the defeat of the Scipios had come from Spain. Claudius Nero, who had served at Capua, was despatched with reinforcements but took up a purely defensive position to hold the line at the Ebro. Marcellus, the victor at Syracuse, did not try to reduce Tarentum, for the Romans were now war-weary. In 210 twelve of the Latin colonies refused to send their military contingents to help the Romans carry on the war. The next year, though, represented a turning point. While two consular armies held Hannibal at bay, Fabius advanced to Tarentum and, aided by a fleet and by a diversionary attack on Caulonia, moved against Tarentum, which fell by treachery before Hannibal could arrive to help it. The city was sacked. Thus the long war dragged on in Italy, and the Romans' dogged determination had parried Hannibal's offensive thrusts, finally reducing Syracuse, Capua, and Tarentum, and penning up Hannibal in Southern Italy. Meanwhile, news had arrived that the young Scipio had achieved a brilliant success at New Carthage. The whole complexion of the war began to change.

After the loss of the two Scipios, the Romans had forfeited all of Spain south of the Ebro, including perhaps Saguntum. The fall of Syracuse and Capua, however, allowed the Italians to send reinforcements to Spain. Late in 211 an army commanded by Claudius Nero landed there and in the next year tried to secure the land north of the Ebro. Then the son of Publius Scipio, aged twenty-five, was voted an extraordinary command of the forces in Spain. He had fought in Italy but, since he had held only the aedileship (in 213), he was not legally qualified for high command. The details of his election are obscure, but he was enthusiastically nominated to the consular command in Spain. With reinforcements he sailed for Spain where his total force, including the Spanish allies, was just over thirty thousand men. He attacked the Carthaginian base of operations at New Carthage, which contained the bulk of Carthage's money and war materiel as well as the hostages that Carthage held from the whole of Spain. Its harbor was one of the best in the western Mediterranean. Scipio realized that a base of operations that could be resupplied by sea was essential for his success and that his father had failed because Saguntum, his base, had not been far enough south. Thus, one morning in 209, the small garrison of New Carthage awoke to find the town besieged by the Romans by both land and sea. Scipio had marched south with his main army at great speed and arrived simultaneously with his fleet commander and close friend, Gaius Laelius. New Carthage was surrounded by water on three sides. On the next day Scipio vigorously attacked the town from the land while marines from the fleet stormed in with an amphibious assault from the sea. Thereafter, Scipio held the key position in Spain. Besides an immense quantity of booty, money, and munitions, he gained control of the local silver mines and cut deeply into his enemy's revenues. He spent the rest of the year building up a model army, drilling it in new tactical procedures and the use of new weapons.

He now had a base sufficiently far south to justify an assault on Baetica, which he carried out in 208. Although he allowed Hasdrubal's army to escape and cross into Italy, he won a great tactical victory. Early in 206 the Carthaginians decided to stake the fate of Spain on a single pitched battle. Scipio met the combined forces of the Carthaginians near Ilipa (near modern Seville), defeated them, and by a rapid pursuit cut off their retreat. Most of Carthage's Iberian forces were destroyed; the rest surrendered.

The remainder of the year passed in diplomatic arrangements and punitive expeditions. Scipio now prepared for the future by slipping across to Africa to interview Syphax, a Numidian sheikh who had been embarrassing Carthage. A second interview with another Numidian prince, Masinissa, completed Scipio's diplomatic preparations in Africa. The last traces of Carthaginian resistance at Gades collapsed, and the remainder of Carthage's forces sailed off to the Balearic Isles. So fell the Carthaginian Empire in Spain, and Scipio returned to Rome. The collapse of Hannibal's offensive in Italy could not be far off.

Hasdrubal's force, which had earlier escaped Scipio's clutches in Spain, now arrived in Italy and tried to reinforce its commander's brother, Hannibal. It was defeated at the battle of Metaurus and its commander, Hasdrubal, was killed. Victory in Italy was now complete. Rome had won an open battle there for the first time during this long war, and the first serious attempt to reinforce Hannibal had failed. This was a decisive moment. Hastening south, the successful Roman commander, Nero, flung Hasdrubal's head into his brother's camp at Larinum. Thus learning the bitter news, Hannibal withdrew to Bruttium.

Hannibal held on desperately in Bruttium while another Carthaginian army landed at Genoa and tried, unsuccessfully, to reach him. Yet more reinforcements from Carthage intended for Italy in 205 had been driven to Sardinia by a storm and were captured there. All hope of victory in Italy now was gone. In the autumn of 203 Hannibal received orders to return home to defend Carthage. Having kept an undefeated army together in Italy for fifteen years, he at last evacuated the peninsula, and returned to Africa to face Scipio, the most brilliant general that Rome had produced. Hannibal knew well that when they met, both the long war between Rome and Carthage and the future history of the western Mediterranean would be settled.

In 204 a Roman expeditionary force of about thirty thousand men had sailed for Africa. Scipio landed near Utica where he hoped to establish a base and where he was soon joined by Masinissa and his Numidian cavalry. They pressed the siege of Utica by land and sea, but winter arrived and the city still held out. The next spring, Scipio renewed the blockade. When the enemy's suspicions were lulled, he launched a sudden, completely successful attack, and with practically no losses crushed the enemy forces that had been sent against him. There was now considerable alarm in Carthage, for Scipio was not only renewing the siege of Utica but had command of the open country. After yet another battlefield victory, he captured Tunis, from which he commanded Carthage's land communications. The Carthaginians made a desperate attack on his fleet at Utica, but he arrived in time to thwart it.

The situation at Carthage was now critical and Hannibal had been recalled to defend his country, which, while Hannibal was en route, had approached Scipio with peace terms. The Carthaginians offered to evacuate and renounce Italy, Gaul, and Spain, surrender their navy save twenty ships, pay an indemnity of five thousand talents, and recognize the power of Masinissa in the west as well as the autonomy of the native Libyan tribes in the east. Such terms would have made Carthage a purely African power, nominally independent but in practice a client state of Rome. These terms the Romans accepted after some debate, and an armistice was declared. In the winter of

203–202 the Senate officially ratified them. The war seemed at an end.

When Hannibal finally landed, ratification had just taken place, but he renewed hostilities nonetheless. Scipio stormed up the Bagradas valley when he learned of the Punic treachery, cutting Carthage off from her economic base. Thereupon Hannibal advanced to Zama, hoping to cut Scipio's communications and to force him to fight without the Numidian cavalry that was yet to arrive. The sides were evenly matched, each fielding some forty thousand men. When the dust settled after the battle, Hannibal's army had been destroyed and Scipio received a peace deputation at Tunis. He was ready for peace because a siege of Carthage would have involved fresh effort when Italy most needed rest.

A three months' armistice was concluded and Carthage offered to pay reparations for breaking the truce, gave hostages, and supplied grain and pay for the Roman troops during the armistice. According to the terms of the peace, Carthage retained her autonomy and her territory with the "Phoenician Trenches" (roughly modern Tunisia). Thus, Carthage was reduced to the state of a dependent ally of Rome, prohibited from making war outside Africa and able to do so within Africa only with Rome's permission. This brought to an end her existence as a great Mediterranean power and gave her no real guarantee against future aggression. She surrendered her entire navy, returned all prisoners of war to Rome and agreed to pay an indemnity of ten thousand talents in fifty annual installments, which would keep her weak and dependent on Rome for the entire period. In return, the Romans agreed to evacuate Africa within one hundred and fifty days. At last the long war had ended.

SUMMARY OF THE MARITIME STRATEGIES OF THE PUNIC WARS

During the First Punic War, Rome was unable to force a decisive conclusion to her conflict with Carthage until she gained control of the sea. So long as the Carthaginian fleet remained intact, it prevented Rome from delivering a knock-out blow and enabled Carthage to continue military operations in Sicily after her land armies had suffered serious defeats. The Carthaginian navy could even ravage the coasts of Italy itself in response to her Sicilian setbacks. During the course of the war, Rome realized that Carthage would have to be challenged at sea if she were to be defeated decisively. Eventually Rome's maritime strategy gave her a Mahanian, fleet-against-fleet, victory. This final success did not result from Rome's superior seamanship or even from clever technological innovation. It came rather from

Italy's ability to launch fleet after fleet until a conclusive victory was achieved.

In the years between the First and Second Punic Wars Rome pursued a conscious policy of extending her control of the sea by denying the Carthaginians all possible naval bases between Africa and Italy. They thereby forced the strategy of land invasion from the Iberian Peninsula that Hannibal eventually employed. The fact that the Carthaginians had virtually no seaborne access to Italy meant that, throughout the course of the Second Punic War, Hannibal would have difficulty capitalizing on his battlefield victories because he could not be reinforced and resupplied adequately. He might win major battles, but final victory continued to elude him.

Without the naval basing they earlier enjoyed in Sicily, Sardinia, and Corsica, the Carthaginians had only the one remaining avenue for reinforcement and resupply from Spain. The Romans had only to block this avenue and they did so by gaining command of the sea between the Iberian and Italian peninsulas through their victory (helped by the Massilian navy) over the Carthaginian fleet in a battle near the mouth of the Ebro. The army of the Scipios, invading from the northeast, merely needed to control the coast road and establish an adequate base of operations in order to accomplish their crucial task of isolating Hannibal's army in Italy. This they did, and thereafter the Carthaginians abandoned all large-scale naval operations designed to aid Hannibal in Italy. Since only the arrival of reinforcements from Spain could have changed the complexion of the war in Italy, the Scipios' success proved decisive, though it took time. Moreover, Rome's control of the sea between Italy and Spain allowed the Romans to reinforce and resupply their own forces in Spain, so that even after the deaths of the two Scipios in 211, new armies could be sent to attack and take over the Carthaginian base of operations at New Carthage and continue the isolation of the Carthaginian forces in Italy. For all these reasons, Rome's maritime successes were essential elements in her victory over the Carthaginians. Had she not established sea control and sea denial, Rome would almost certainly have lost the Second Punic War.

BIBLIOGRAPHIC NOTE

Any serious study of strategy in the Punic Wars must begin with the two major ancient sources for the wars themselves: the *Histories* of Polybius (Books I–III, VI–XI, XIV–XV) and the *Annals* of Livy (Books XXI–XXX). Accurate translations of both are available in the hardcover editions of the Loeb Classical Library (Harvard University Press) and in paperback translations: *Polybius on*

Roman Imperialism (Regnery/Gateway) and Livy, *The War with Hannibal* (Penguin Books). There is a voluminous modern literature on the period. Among the most useful and readable books for the general student of the Punic Wars are Robert M. Errington, *The Dawn of Empire: Rome's Rise to World Power* (Cornell University Press); William V. Harris, *War and Imperialism in Republican Rome* (Oxford University Press); Brian Caven, *The Punic Wars* (St. Martin's Press); John F. Lazenby, *Hannibal's War: A Military History of the Second Punic War* (Aris and Phillips); T. A. Dorey and R. D. Dudley, *Rome Against Carthage* (Doubleday); Richard M. Haywood, *Studies on Scipio Africanus* (Greenwood Press); Howard H. Scullard, *Scipio Africanus: Soldier and Politician* (Cornell University Press); Basil H. Liddell-Hart, *A Greater than Napoleon: Scipio Africanus* (Blackwood); Johannes H. Thiel, *A History of Roman Sea-power before the Second Punic War* (North-Holland); Brian H. Warmington, *Carthage* (Penguin Books).

ADDITIONAL SOURCES

Adcock, Frank E. "Delenda est Carthage." *Cambridge Historical Journal*, 8 (1946).

Astin, Alan E. "Saguntum and the Origins of the Second Punic War." *Latomus*, 26 (1967).

Caven, Brian. *The Punic Wars*. New York: St. Martin's Press, 1980.

Dorey, T. A. and Dudley, D. R. *Rome Against Carthage*. Garden City, NY: Doubleday, 1971.

Errington, Robert M. *The Dawn of Empire: Rome's Rise to World Power*. Ithaca: Cornell University Press, 1972.

Fritz, Kurt von. *The Theory of the Mixed Constitution in Antiquity*. New York: Arno Press, 1975.

Harris, William V. *War and Imperialism in Republican Rome*. New York: Oxford University Press, 1979.

Haywood, Richard M. *Studies on Scipio Africanus*. Westport, CT: Greenwood Press, 1973 (c. 1933).

Lazenby, John F. *Hannibal's War: A Military History of the Second Punic War*. Warminster, U.K.: Aris and Phillips, 1978.

Liddell-Hart, Basil H. *A Greater than Napoleon: Scipio Africanus*. London: Blackwood, 1930.

Scullard, Howard H. *A History of the Roman World, 753–146 B.C.* 3rd ed. London, 1961.

———. *Scipio Africanus: Soldier and Politician*. Ithaca: Cornell University Press, 1970.

Thiel, Johannes H. *A History of Roman Sea-power before the Second Punic War*. Amsterdam: North-Holland, 1954.

Warmington, Brian H. *Carthage*. New York: Praeger, 1960.

6

England and Spain
1567-1604

BY ALBERTO COLL

The long conflict between England and Spain from 1567 to 1604 was one of the greatest turning points in modern European and world history. Its outcome helped to cement the success of Protestantism in northern Europe, and launched Holland and England on the road to worldwide economic and naval expansion. In the wake of its failed attempt to achieve continental predominance, Spain, defeated psychologically and exhausted financially, began its own long road to decline, reluctantly yielding to France over the next century its cultural and political leadership of Europe. For England, the war was the first of many it would fight over the next four hundred years to maintain a European balance of power favorable to its security. Coalitions of states led by England and backed by English money and seapower were to defeat the aspirations of Louis XIV, Napoleon, Wilhelm I, and Adolf Hitler for mastery over Europe.

While seapower did not provide a decisive resolution to the Anglo-Spanish conflict of 1567–1604, it was perhaps the single most important factor that shaped the war's course and its outcome. Through seapower, England and its Dutch allies frustrated their enemy's efforts to dominate the Netherlands, and resolutely defeated the great Spanish Armada with which Spain intended to conquer England. England also used seapower to put pressure on Spain's weakest point—what Clausewitz would have called its "center of gravity": the far-flung American empire whose gold and silver riches enabled Spain to play the part of a great power far beyond what its own limited economic resources would have permitted it to do. Seapower allowed England to apply this pressure fairly inexpensively, at relatively low cost in English lives or treasure, while forcing Spain to expend in defensive preparations, such as fortifications and naval convoys, resources that it would have preferred to devote to its armies in Europe.

Spain relied upon the defensive use of seapower to keep the English from cutting off its vital lines of commerce and communications with its New World colonies. The English attacks, while costly and inconvenient, did not destroy or even erode the Spanish "center of gravity." Unlike England, however, Spain did not succeed in using seapower offensively to put pressure on its adversary. To some extent, Spain may confirm the dictum of classical seapower theorists such as Mahan concerning the difficulties inherent in the effort to be a great land power and a great naval power simultaneously. Even though between 1583 and 1597 it had a powerful navy with excellent defensive capabilities to protect its home territory and colonies, Spain was never a great naval power in the sense of possessing a successful offensive capacity against the adversary's fleet and its homeland. Having a navy and being a sea power are not the same.

During this period both England and Spain were more successful when they used maritime power defensively than when they used it offensively. Despite the advantages of the offensive, naval power so deployed has the difficulties—by no means insurmountable—of having to operate in a psychologically and geographically hostile environment, often at great distances from land bases of support, against an adversary that enjoys the obverse advantages provided by the defense. In the sixteenth century, offensive maritime strategies faced other problems as well. Ships were at the greater mercy of the weather. They could not be continuously at sea for more than two or three months before their crews began to be decimated by disease brought about by the cramped quarters, inadequate hygiene, and poor food and drink. In the case of England, the Crown did not have enough revenues to support a permanent, fully mobilized fleet even in wartime. The Royal Navy might be fully mobilized to meet the realm's defensive needs; but once the particular emergency receded, the queen, out of financial considerations, had to demobilize the fleet again, leaving only a few warships in full operational readiness. They were not enough, of course, for a sustained maritime offensive. Hence, on the occasions when England undertook naval offensives against Spain, it did so by enlisting the ships and financial support of maritime entrepreneurs and private investors. This was a source of great dynamism to English naval policy, but it also meant that whenever the objectives of personal profit and self-enrichment clashed with those of grand strategy and the national interest, the admirals and captains of the English fleet often chose the former over the latter.

The years between 1567 and 1604 saw the beginnings of a new age of naval warfare. Large sailing vessels capable of circumnavigating the globe, and armed with heavy guns that could sink the enemy's naval forces, made their first appearance and fought their first battles. Seapower could be projected at greater distances than ever before. Despite the limitations of the available technology, the offensive potential of seapower took a giant leap forward. While there was much about the new era of seapower that the brave English and Spanish commanders did not know, and many new strategic and tactical possibilities they failed to exploit, their experience with the new instruments of naval warfare and their tentative wrestlings with the broader strategic implications of these instruments were an essential precondition to the great developments in naval strategy that followed in the seventeenth and eighteenth centuries.

ORIGINS OF THE WAR

Historical mythology to the contrary, the war was not inevitable. Throughout the first half of the sixteenth century, England had viewed Spain as a natural ally against France. In the preceding hundred years, the French gradually had recovered the Channel coast stretching from Normandy to Calais, a territory considered by England to be its first line of defense against France or any other continental power. With the capture of Calais in 1558, France "won control of the entire southern coast of the Channel and removed the land buffer of cross-Channel possessions and satellites that had long cushioned England itself against direct attack."[1]

Queen Elizabeth I (r. 1558–1603), worried that the Low Countries would be the next object of French ambition, as indeed Louis XIV would confirm a century later. As Garrett Mattingly has noted, "in Flanders, Zeeland and Holland were the ports not only through which English goods could most cheaply and safely reach the Continent, but from which an invasion of England could be launched most quickly and easily."[2] To Elizabeth it seemed preferable to have far-away Spain, rather than France, rule the Netherlands. During the reign of Charles I (r. 1517–1556), Spain had exercised its sovereignty rather loosely, benevolently, and with due regard for the religious and cultural differences of the Low Countries. What today is known as Holland and Belgium was then a patchwork-quilt of seventeen different lordships. They were too weak and divided to resist French domination, and from the English viewpoint it was best to have the Spanish bear the burden of protecting them from the French, so long, of course, as Spain did not use the Low Countries as a base for projecting its own military power.

For its part, Spain considered a friendly, or at least neutral, England a valuable counterpoise to French power. Charles I was well aware of the vulnerability of the Low Countries to French expansion. One of his foreign policy maxims was "that at all costs England and the Low Countries should be bound together, so that they can provide each other with mutual aid against their enemies." As he once told his son, the future Philip II (r. 1556–1598), "War with all the world, but peace with England." Charles perceived that a hostile England was easily capable of wreaking havoc with the sea lanes through the English Channel connecting the Iberian Peninsula with the Low Countries. The latter imported annually 60 percent of Spain's total output of raw wool, as well as considerable quantities of produce, cochineal, hides, spices, and sugar from Spain's American colonies.[3] The Netherlands also served as a vital clearinghouse for Spain's importation of cereals and shipbuilding materials from the Baltic, as well as cannon, smaller guns, and other manufactures from elsewhere in Europe.

Relations between the two states began to deteriorate during the early 1560s. The chief catalyst, though by no means the only one, was the revolt in the Netherlands precipitated by Philip II's efforts to impose a greater degree of political control and religious uniformity. It was not in England's interest to allow Spain to tighten its control over the Low Countries. To this key strategic consideration were added ideological ones. The vast number of English traders active in the Netherlands supported the Dutch rebels, partly out of financial motives but also from sympathy with the Protestant cause, much to the irritation of the Spanish authorities. And the growing number of Dutch exiles who fled to London found an equal degree of sympathy for Protestantism mixed with economic and strategic concerns. Meanwhile, many members of England's powerful business establishment were becoming convinced that Spain's rich American empire was vulnerable to English economic penetration, either through peaceful means, which Spain resisted, or by outright plunder and war. They were eager to seize what they perceived as the easy pickings of Philip II's vast colonial realm.

THE COLD WAR (1567–1585)

The turning point came in 1566–67 when Philip II, against the advice of some of his councillors, decided on a policy of total military subjugation to suppress the Dutch revolt, and to that end sent to the Low Countries a large army under the command of the renowned Duke of Alba. As two modern historians have put it:

> England could not stand idly by while a spearhead of Spanish power, hostile to the reformed religion which was identified with English independence, was deployed across the Narrow Seas like a dagger pointed at her heart.[4]

Spain was Europe's greatest military power on land. Alba's 25,000-man army, huge by the standards of mid-sixteenth-century warfare, was composed of some of the finest veterans from Castile, Milan, Switzerland, and Germany. The Spanish Army had a proud tradition of over a century of land warfare, most of it militarily successful, against Moors, Turks, Frenchmen, and Germans. It was a highly professional, seasoned, and disciplined force; its backbone was its brigade-sized formations of heavy infantry (2,500–2,800 strong), the *tercios*, famous for their shock tactics and battle stamina. During the sixteenth century the Spanish Army would count among its ranks such commanders as "El Gran Capitán" Gonzalo de Cordoba, the Duke of Alba, Don Juan de Austria, and Alexander Farnese, Duke of Parma—justly known throughout Europe as among the best soldiers of their respective generations.

England's options were limited. It could neither field an army strong enough to challenge Spain on land, nor count on other states to do so. France was increasingly paralyzed by domestic, civil, and religious strife, and the German states, weak and divided as they were, had their attention centered on the Ottoman threat from the Balkans. The pattern of English foreign policy from 1667 to 1945, in which English financial and maritime assets supported the powerful armies of continental allies against the aspiring hegemonic power, had not coalesced yet. The twin elements of this policy, powerful allied armies on the Continent and an offensive navy, were missing in 1567. English naval capabilities, considerably strong during the reign of Henry VIII (r. 1509–1547), had been allowed to deteriorate during the 1550s. By 1558, Royal Navy tonnage was 35 percent less than a decade earlier, and the number of royal warships had declined from 53 to 26, many of the latter rotten or otherwise in poorly maintained condition.[5] While Elizabeth sponsored a vigorous expansion of naval forces, her efforts took over a decade to bear fruit. As is the case today, a navy cannot be rebuilt overnight; bureaucratic struggles for limited resources, and the long lead time from design to procurement, construction, and final deployment explain some of the difficulties now and then.

Given English weakness on land, and the lack in 1567 of a powerful offensive navy, the queen resorted to a "cold-war" policy of giving financial and political support to the Dutch rebels, while allowing her subjects to harass the Spanish on their trade routes along the Channel between the Low Countries and the Iberian Peninsula. English privateers, operating from the south coast of England and with Huguenot groups from French coastal towns, or acting on their own with letters of marque issued by the rebel Dutch leader William of Orange, wreaked havoc on the Spanish maritime routes. The queen's objective was to pressure Spain into a negotiated political settlement with the Dutch rebels, by which Philip would withdraw his army and restore the "ancient privileges" and political and religious autonomy previously enjoyed by the Low Countries; the rebels, in turn, would lay down their arms and accept formal Spanish sovereignty. At all costs, France was to be kept out.

Even though it was preferable to either inaction or appeasement, the English policy of gradually raising the military and economic costs of Spanish intervention in the Netherlands did not achieve its objectives. Philip responded to the "cold war" by redoubling his military efforts on land and by engaging in various covert activities of his own. Meanwhile, awakened by the cold war on the high seas to Spain's maritime vulnerabilities, he resolved to improve Spanish naval capabilities. Much to Elizabeth's frustration, the years between 1578 and 1585 saw a marked enhancement of Spain's strategic assets, both on land and sea. In 1578, the recently appointed new commander of the Spanish armies in the Low Countries, the brilliant Duke of Parma, began a systematic military and political offensive that slowly brought the southern provinces back into the fold. His forces reached a strength of 75,000 men, and in 1585, after a bloody siege, he captured the important city of Antwerp, dealing a heavy psychological blow to the Dutch rebels and their allies across the Channel.

Meanwhile, following the death of King Sebastian in 1578 without an heir, Philip had become King of Portugal in 1580. He instantly acquired the Portuguese fleet of thirteen heavy galleons capable of long-distance cruising, as well as two key strategic outposts on the North Atlantic: Portugal itself, with its long-established maritime traditions and skills, and the Azores, sitting athwart the sea lanes connecting Spain to its New World colonies. Philip's control of Portugal was important not only for the advantage it gave to Spain, but also for those it denied to its adversaries. A weak, independent Portugal, fearsome of its powerful neighbor to the east, might have tended to ally itself with, or fall under the influence of, the English or the French, allowing them to threaten Spain on its western flank and to cut off its vital trade routes to America.

Thus, as the decade of the '80s opened, Spain's overall strategic position seemed to be improving. One more factor that contributed to this trend was the recrudescence of civil and religious strife in France, which weakened the coherence of that state's foreign policy and invited covert English and Spanish intervention on behalf of opposing factions struggling for control of the monarchy. Elizabeth gave money to the heir-presumptive to the throne, Henry of Navarre, leader of the Huguenots, while Spain aided the Catholic League headed by the Guise brothers. By 1585, the balance of forces within the country seemed to be tilting dangerously towards the Guises. As Spain's military and political presence in Europe grew, the weak French King, Henry III, appeared to have little choice but to gradually surrender power to the Duke of Guise. The shifting international balance of power clearly was having an impact on France's domestic political balance.

Elizabeth responded to this deterioration in England's strategic posture with a sharp escalation of military activities that amounted to open war with Spain. In 1585 she sent 7,000 men to the Netherlands to help the Dutch rebels hold the deep water ports of Flushing and Brill against the relentless onslaught of Parma's *tercios*. Simultaneously, she authorized a naval strike, led by Sir Francis Drake, against Spain's Caribbean territories. Of these two moves, the former, while less spectacular, proved much more significant than the latter. The small English force was decisive in helping the Dutch resist successfully Parma's impressive offensive. Three years later, when the Spanish Armada attempted to escort Parma's army across the Channel to invade England, the lack of a deep-water port under Spanish control spelled failure for the enterprise. Dutch control of these ports was also significant because it enabled the rebels to be supplied by sea regardless of Parma's successes on land. As long as the English fleet was the predominant naval force in the Channel, freighters from England and elsewhere could carry supplies and troops to aid the rebel cause. Elizabeth's moves in 1585–86 rested partly on her knowledge that by now, the slow upgrading of English naval power she had initiated two decades earlier was in place. Never before had England been so strong on the seas, both in absolute terms and in comparison with other powers, including Spain.

ENGLAND'S STRATEGIC WEAKNESSES AND STRENGTHS

In economic resources, population, and capacity to put armies in the field, England was clearly inferior to Spain. Moreover, its geographical position was not free of disadvantages. In 1585 England was not an island state. To the north it had a long border with restive Scotland, which in preceding decades had been an ally of France and hosted a substantial number of Catholic exiles eager to overthrow England's Protestant monarch. Since 1543 French Catholic troops had been successfully conveyed to Scotland six times without English naval interception. To the west were the Irish looking to Catholic Spain for deliverance from English domination. Within England itself there were large numbers of disaffected Catholics, many of them hopeful that Spanish power might be the key instrument that would help them regain political control. Finally, the English monarchy did not have the centralized administrative machinery or vast revenues so helpful in waging war on a grand scale.

There were also, however, significant advantages. The Tudor state, to borrow Bismarck's celebrated description of mid-nineteenth century Prussia, was a "fit frigate" with a prosperous trading and manufacturing economy, an enterprising private sector, and an established naval tradition coupled with a navy second to none in Europe. Its Protestant religion had helped to diffuse throughout all ranks of English society a strong sense of nationalism that was already a dynamic force in the national psyche. The absence of a centralized bureaucracy or of revenues as ample as those of the Spanish monarchy was compensated by a thriving business community eager to finance attacks against Spanish trade and possessions in return for a share of the profits.

One of England's peculiar strengths was the vigorous partnership forged by its merchants, bankers, and investors with the Crown in pursuit of an aggressive maritime strategy against the vulnerable points of the Spanish Empire. The partnership had its informal and formal dimensions. During the 1560s and 1570s the queen, while providing informal encouragement to the predatory activities sponsored and financed by London merchants and investment bankers against Spanish trade, was quick to disassociate herself officially from any responsibility for their actions. To the Spanish ambassador she pleaded powerlessness to control the wayward doings of her unruly subjects. The unspoken assumption was that if Spain would cooperate on the issue of the Netherlands, Elizabeth might find a way to stop her subjects' escapades. The merchants' private war against Spain was an excellent instrument for the queen's cold-war policies. It was efficient enough to complicate and disrupt Spain's commercial and logistical links to the Netherlands and the New World, yet not so outrageous as to provoke Philip into war; after all, it was difficult to prove that Elizabeth was insincere when she claimed she could not control the English "seadogs."

In the late 1570s, several developments converged to strengthen the partnership and turn it into an instrument for the transoceanic projection of English maritime power. First, a leading member of the mercantile establishment, John Hawkins, gained membership in 1577 on the Navy Board, the body charged with overseeing and developing the Royal Navy. He brought a "blue-water" strategic perspective to an entity whose outlook had been primarily one of coastal defense. Hawkins had been a slave trader, and between 1562 and 1568 had made three voyages to the New World, where he had fought the Spanish. He was captivated by the notion that Spain could be crippled if its yearly supply of gold and silver from the colonies was cut off by English seapower. For this, a navy capable of long-range cruising would be necessary, yet many of the existing royal warships were ill-suited for such a task. They had high structures fore and aft and were designed to carry large crews. Such characteristics made them ideal for coastal defensive missions that required boarding enemy vessels and destroying their forces in hand-to-hand combat; but the high structures made them slow and unstable, and the large size of the crew meant they could not be at sea for long periods of time, as rations were consumed quickly and disease spread easily in the vessels' crowded conditions. With the support of Elizabeth's chief minister, Lord Burghley, Hawkins fought inside the Navy Board for lower, narrower, better-sailing ships with smaller crews and heavier guns for the broadsides. Older ships were remodeled and new ones built along these lines, reflecting the shift to an offensive, long-distance maritime strategy. Whereas Henry VIII's ships could stay at sea for only about six weeks, by 1585 Elizabeth's navy was capable of long-range operations against the Iberian Peninsula.

A second important development in the partnership between Crown and merchants was the surge of proposals for transoceanic expeditions that would at once fill the royal treasury and the pockets of investors while weakening Spain's capacity to wage war in Europe. Hawkins's ideas in this respect were not new. In 1558 Henry II of France had given serious consideration to a "western design." Twelve French warships and 1,200 troops would sail to the Caribbean, sack

Santo Domingo and Puerto Rico, and then seize Panama, where the bullion from Peru was regularly stored prior to its shipment to Spain. Although the French king did not carry out this bold operation, modern historians have seen in it "the birth of the 'blue-water strategy,' which was to fascinate seamen and statesmen throughout the sailing-ship era and give to successive European wars between powers having a stake in the overseas world an extra-European dimension within an overall strategic purpose."[6] In 1562, Gaspard de Coligny, admiral of France and a prominent Huguenot, sponsored a project to establish a French colony in Florida that would serve as a base from which to attack the annual fleets carrying silver and gold to Spain as they passed through the narrow Florida Strait. Aware of the dangers posed by such a colony, Philip II ruthlessly destroyed it in 1565.

English merchant-privateers such as John Hawkins and Francis Drake were familiar with these projects, and in the 1570s became leading advocates of joining the resources of the Crown and the business community for sponsoring successful enterprises of this kind. They found support in Sir Francis Walsingham, appointed by the queen as one of her principal secretaries of state in 1572. In his sophisticated, conceptual understanding of the balance of power, his determined anti-Spanish views, and his advocacy of bolder containment policies than the queen was prepared to implement at that time, Walsingham was a sixteenth-century version of the celebrated Sir Eyre Crowe. Eager to exploit Spain's vulnerabilities and to cancel out its predominance on land, Walsingham supported a strong Royal Navy, as well as transoceanic naval enterprises jointly financed by the Crown and the private sector. He was a major investor in, and leading promoter of, Francis Drake's voyage around the world in 1577–80.

The objectives of Drake's famous circumnavigation included probing the east and west coasts of South America for weak points in the Spanish defenses, capturing whatever booty he could find, and searching for new trading opportunities in the Moluccas and China. Drake raided the Peruvian coast and seized a valuable cargo of silver in March of 1579. Upon his return to England in 1580, his financial backers, which included Walsingham and the queen, were delighted with the large returns on their original investment; Elizabeth knighted him, and enthusiasm for future similar ventures mounted. There were also increasingly frequent discussions in court and business circles of establishing colonies or "plantations" on American soil that, among other purposes, would serve as naval bases for attacking Spanish territories and the bullion fleets. The first fruit of such ideas was the establishment in 1585 of a small English colony on Roanoke Island, near the present North Carolina-Virginia border.

Philip's takeover of Portugal in 1580 prompted English schemes for detaching the strategic Azores from his control. In 1581 Walsingham, together with the Earl of Leicester, Hawkins, and Drake, drew plans for naval operations and the landing of forces in the Azorean island of Terceira, which was thought to be loyal to the exiled pretender to the Portuguese throne, Dom Antonio. Terceira would be an excellent naval base for attacks against the Spanish treasure fleets and Portuguese carracks carrying valuable spices and silks from the Orient. Fearing the prospects of open war with Spain as a result of such direct provocation, the queen and Burghley sought an alliance with the French as a precondition for authorizing the project. When negotiations with France failed, the queen ordered the Terceira plan shelved. Dom Antonio, however, acting in his alleged capacity as rightful king of Portugal, issued letters of marque to numerous English sea captains, including several in command of ships owned by the Hawkins family and Sir Francis Drake, authorizing them to plunder Spanish and Portuguese shipping.

By 1585, given Spain's persistent strength on the continent and England's expanding maritime outlook and capabilities, Elizabeth felt both sufficiently pressed and confident enough to authorize, in tandem with the landing of English forces in the Netherlands, Drake's raid against the Spanish Caribbean. While the queen lent some capital and provided several warships, most of the financing came from private investors such as Hawkins, Drake, Walsingham, and other business, naval, and government officials. The bulk of the fleet was composed of privately owned armed merchantmen. En route to the New World, the powerful force of 29 ships and 2,300 men pillaged the Spanish port of Vigo and the port of Santiago in the Portuguese Cape Verde islands. Once it reached the Caribbean, it looted Santo Domingo and the rich city of Cartagena. Drake planned to move on against Panama, where he hoped to find stores of Peruvian bullion worth one million ducats, but the spread of disease among his forces dissuaded him. After contemplating an attack on Havana, he sailed northwards to the Roanoke Island colony, which he hoped to provide with badly needed supplies. On his way he raided San Agustin, the northernmost Spanish settlement in Florida and a threat to the Roanoke plantation. In 1586, Drake returned to England. His Caribbean offensive, intended by Elizabeth as an escalation of her proxy warfare against Philip, cemented yet further the partnership between

Crown and entrepreneurs, between strategy and profit, that was to sustain England in the next long twenty years of open war with Spain.

SPAIN'S STRATEGIC WEAKNESSES AND STRENGTHS

Unquestionably the world's most powerful empire in the sixteenth century, Philip II's Spain also stands in the annals of history as a classic case study of strategic distension. Its sway extended over the proud kingdoms of Castile, Leon, and Aragon, united as recently as 1469; Portugal; the troublesome Low Countries; the Duchy of Luxembourg; Franche Comté, vulnerably wedged between France and the German states; the disparate Italian territories of Lombardy, the Kingdom of Naples, the Kingdom of Sicily, and the Kingdom of Sardinia; several isolated outposts on the North African coast; the Philippines halfway around the world; the Caribbean islands; and the vast, rich colonies of New Spain, New Granada, and Peru, encompassing Mexico, Central America, and much of South America. On its Mediterranean flank, threatening its Italian possessions and Spain itself, the empire faced the Turks, still in a state of dynamic expansion and at war with Spain for most of the sixteenth century. All of Philip's military efforts in the Low Countries and the North Atlantic were complicated by the genuinely defensive needs of what was a perpetual war front in the Mediterranean. Even Spanish successes, such as the great naval victory at Lepanto in 1571, seemed to be only temporary reversals of the persistent Ottoman tide. In retrospect it is amazing that, despite the serious flaws in his statecraft, when Philip died in 1598 only the northern provinces of the Netherlands were missing, by then irretrievably, from the sprawling domains he had inherited from his father forty years earlier.

Inside Spain itself Philip had his share of problems. There were large pockets of anti-Habsburg feeling in Aragon, Castile, and the Basque regions, and substantial minorities of dissatisfied Muslims in Andalucia and Granada. In 1570, a large-scale revolt broke out among the Moriscos of Granada, and civil strife erupted in Aragon in 1591. The Spanish economy was not as vibrant as England's, partly because its manufacturing sector was not as developed, but also because it was overburdened by regulation and taxation.

There may have been much truth to the statement made by the Spanish economist González de Cellorigo in 1600, that his countrymen lived "outside the natural order."[7] In the short period of a few decades, the small backward kingdom of the Iberian Peninsula had been thrust at the head of a sophisticated global empire, not through the organic processes of gradual economic expansion or slow politi-

cal assimilation and consolidation, but as a result of sudden, fortui-
tous events such as the discovery of America and a series of artificial
dynastic unions. The result was serious incongruities and imbalances between the requirements of successful imperial rule and Spain's
economic and technological capacity to meet those requirements.
Thus, for example, in contrast to England, Spain lacked many of the
shipbuilding materials, including vast reserves of timber, necessary to
build a navy for the protection of its trade routes and distant colonies; hence, it had to import such materials from the Baltic. The higher
cost of imports, combined with the higher cost of Spanish labor as a
result of the inflation caused by the excessive flow of gold and silver
bullion from America, meant that it cost three times as much to build
a ship in Spain as in England.[8] Similar inadequacies existed with regard to the design and manufacture of guns. These economic deficiencies were only aggravated by Philip's intolerance toward Jews,
Muslims, and Protestants. Among their ranks were some of his most
enterprising subjects, the nucleus of a thriving business class that
would have served Spain well. Large numbers of them left the Spanish empire during the sixteenth century.

The partly artificial nature of the empire implied endless economic, political, and military exertions to keep it together; yet, the
empire's sheer size and potential power also meant that any such
exertions, if pursued too vigorously, were bound to alarm other states.
This was Philip's dilemma in the Netherlands. The problem was
compounded by Philip's penchant for entangling Spain in too many
conflicts at once, entering new wars before older ones had been won
or settled, and adding new fronts before the previous ones had been
adequately secured.

A strategically distended empire such as Spain, with valuable but
inadequately protected territories strung across the world, needed a
strategy radically different from that followed by Philip. At a minimum, a policy of conserving or reducing enemies, as opposed to
multiplying them, was essential. Weak fronts and vulnerable positions had to be secured prior to further expansion. In practical terms,
this meant that Spain should have consolidated its position in the
Mediterranean and remained on the defensive there. Prior to attempting the invasion of England, it should have secured a victory in
the Netherlands; given the inability of even the Duke of Parma to
accomplish this by 1588, and the fact that Spain already had spent
twenty years and over 100 million florins in the effort, it might have
cut its losses and reached a settlement with the Dutch, acknowledg-
ing the independence of the northern provinces while holding on to

the southern ones that Parma effectively controlled, as indeed Spain was to do twenty years later, in the Spanish-Dutch Truce of 1609.

With the Mediterranean and Dutch fronts quiet, Spain could have reduced its massive budget deficits and growing debts to international bankers that were to drive it eventually into bankruptcy and economic stagnation. It could have poured more resources into strengthening the most valuable part of its empire: the New World, from which it derived the gold and silver that enabled it to be a great power. It is true that Philip spent enough money for a defensive strategy in the New World that kept the English privateers and their fleets from doing any major damage to the imperial territories. The raids by Drake, Hawkins, and others on some of the coastal towns were only pinpricks; moreover, they were one-time events only, as Drake and Hawkins discovered on their 1595 voyage, in which their efforts to repeat their earlier performance were promptly rebuffed by strengthened fortifications and stronger defense forces. Similarly, the Spanish merchant ships occasionally seized by English and French privateers in New World waters stand in remarkable contrast with the failure of the English and French to seize any of the "flotas"—the large convoys that carried to Spain every year the output of the Mexican and Peruvian gold and silver mines.

In 1570 Philip strengthened considerably the convoy system Charles I had instituted in the 1540s. English strategists were correct: the seizure of the flotas one year, or preferably, for two or three consecutive years, would have done Philip incalculable harm. Much of the flotas' cargo was pledged in advance to the Italian and German bankers whose loans paid for Philip's armies in the Netherlands. The loss of the flotas in a given year not only would have hampered Philip's ability to pay the principal and interest due to his creditors that year, but by raising doubts about the future reliability of the bullion shipments, it also would have increased the reluctance among bankers to extend him future loans and, at a minimum, would have raised his borrowing costs. Yet, between 1585 and 1603 more bullion reached Spain than in any preceding or subsequent eighteen-year period, and not a single flota was captured.

Nonetheless, Philip's defensive strategy in the New World, for all its obvious success, still had serious shortcomings. The resources he invested were enough to protect the flotas and coastal towns, but not enough to keep the English out of the area and prevent them from gradually chipping away at Spain's New World monopoly. The Roanoke Island colony in 1585, despite its failure as a result of disease, hunger, and Indian resistance, was a taste of bigger things to come.

An "active" or "forward" defense, something amounting to a sustained offensive maritime strategy, would have been necessary to clear English ships and privateers off American waters and English settlers off American territories. Such a strategy might have used the excellent ports of Havana and Cartagena as naval bases for regular deployments in the Caribbean and the Atlantic waters bordering the eastern shore of North America. England, lacking bases in the New World and preoccupied with the need to maintain the bulk of her fleet close to home waters, would have been unable to respond effectively.

THE ENTERPRISE OF ENGLAND

It is ironic that Spain, weaker than England in naval strength and experience, undertook the boldest maritime offensive move in the entire war. The story deserves to be retold in some detail. With Portugal in his empire after 1580, Philip saw greater possibilities open up to Spain as an Atlantic power. The addition of the Portuguese galleons also encouraged him to build a first-rate Atlantic fleet. In 1581 he ordered nine new warships to be laid down in the Atlantic port of Santander, and in 1582 he gave contracts to private shipbuilders in northern Spain for an additional 15,000 tons of shipping for war service.[9] The idea of using a large armada to invade England was first put to the king by his greatest naval commander, the Marquis of Santa Cruz, in a letter dated August of 1583. Philip was receptive. It was clear to him that English power had provided the Dutch rebels with just the necessary support to avoid defeat at the hands of Parma's army. Elizabeth's decision in 1585 to send English forces to the Netherlands, coupled with Drake's expedition to the Caribbean, strengthened Philip in the belief that Spain had to knock out England first before it could win the Dutch war. Interestingly, Parma, a much better strategist than Philip, saw things differently. In his view, the Dutch could be defeated through a process of slow attrition. The Spanish armies were besieging the major towns methodically, one at a time; through the liberal disbursement of Spanish funds, Parma was bribing enemy leaders into surrender or open treachery; eventually he hoped to have the die-hard pockets of resistance, the provinces of Holland and Zeeland, cornered against the sea, and sooner or later crush them through massive assaults. With the Netherlands secure and its ports in Spanish hands, the invasion of England could then be launched. Nevertheless, the great Parma must be blamed for going along with the king's project for invading England in the near future, and for assuring Philip that his plan, while not free from risks, was quite feasible.

In late 1585 Philip asked Santa Cruz for an estimate of what it would take to carry out a successful invasion. The marquis, who had several decades of experience in naval warfare, was well aware of English capabilities and of the natural advantages the English would enjoy fighting close to their home bases and in defense of their soil. In March of 1586 he submitted his estimate: a minimum of 50 large galleons (warships) and 100 heavily armed merchantmen; 40 heavy transports; 320 smaller auxiliary craft, including numerous shallow-draft vessels for coastal operations; 25,000 sailors; and over 60,000 troops. Although the estimate was realistic and reasonable in view of the armada's difficult mission and the obstacles it was likely to encounter, its price tag was beyond even Spain's resources.

Philip put together what he thought was a more "cost-effective" plan. An armada, much smaller and carrying one-third as many troops, would sail up the English Channel until it reached the waters off the Flemish coast; there, it would meet with a fleet of barges carrying 30–40,000 troops under Parma's command, and escort them to a landing on the Thames estuary. The invasion would be carried out by Parma's forces, reinforced by the 19,000 troops carried aboard the armada. The fleet would stand by to protect the landings, secure Parma's communications with the Low Countries, and repel any interference by English naval forces. While less expensive than the direct invasion of England from Spain proposed by Santa Cruz, the plan had serious flaws. With the armada sailing up the Channel for several days before the landings took place, the element of surprise would be lost. The timing and coordination of the armada's arrival, the departure of Parma's forces, and their rendezvous would have to be perfect, not an easy thing given the slow pace of sixteenth-century communication and logistics. And the English fleet would have plenty of opportunity to interfere with the cumbrous expedition.

By the summer of 1586, Europe was awash with rumors about the armada that was slowly gathering in Lisbon, and many of Elizabeth's advisors thought that England should strike preemptively with a naval offensive of its own. John Hawkins prepared a squadron of eighteen ships with which he hoped to patrol the Spanish coast, blockade it for some time, and then cross the Atlantic for another Drake-style attack on the colonies. He also expected to seize one of the treasure fleets. The queen, however, alarmed by threats of an invasion from France, kept Hawkins in home waters. Nevertheless, the following spring she sent Drake to Spanish waters with a fleet of sixteen warships and seven lighter vessels with the specific objective of disrupting the armada's preparations. Drake swooped down on Cadiz

Bay, where he burned or captured a total of 37 ships; one of these was a magnificent brand-new galleon intended to be the armada's flagship, while most of the others were either loaded with provisions for the armada, or were supposed to join it in Lisbon as auxiliary transports. Drake then seized the strategic Cape St. Vincent on the southwest corner of the Iberian Peninsula, a point by which all Mediterranean traffic bound for Lisbon had to pass. For several weeks his ships prowled the area, capturing a large number of little vessels loaded with nothing more significant than hoops and barrel staves for making casks and water butts. The total cargo of hoops and staves was 1,700 tons, enough for casks that would have carried 25–30,000 tons of food and liquor; Drake had it all burned on the coast at Sagres. As Mattingly observes:

> For the navies of the day casks were a prime necessity, not only for stowing water and wine but for salt meat, salt fish, biscuits and all sorts of provisions. For tight casks, well-seasoned barrel staves of the proper quality were essential. Of this commodity there was never much surplus and the outfitting of the Armada was already creating an extraordinary demand. If, when the Armada finally sailed, its water butts proved to be leaky and foul, if much food spoiled because of green barrel staves and ill-made casks, the smoke which hung over Sagres was to blame. Burning those barrel staves was probably a greater blow to Spain than burning the ships at Cadiz Bay.[10]

By causing Philip to postpone the launching of the armada, Drake's strike seemed to vindicate those among the queen's advisors who were eager to keep up the pressure on Philip by using the navy in offensive missions against Spain's own shores. The tireless John Hawkins proposed a continuous blockade, with squadrons relieving one another every few months. While this idea was truly novel, it was probably beyond Elizabeth's resources and existing naval technology.[11] The queen kept the fleet in home waters.

Meanwhile, determined to launch the armada as soon as possible, Philip kept badgering the Marquis of Santa Cruz throughout January of 1588 to sail forth immediately. The marquis knew better than anyone else Spain's unpreparedness for the great "Enterprise of England," but could not persuade the stubborn king to delay his plans any further. Mattingly has captured well Santa Cruz's growing pessimism:

> The Marquis did not need to be assured that he was fighting in God's cause, but he had seen too many campaigns against the Turks to be overconfident on that score. To be sure of beating the English he had wanted

at least fifty galleons. He had thirteen, and one of those so old and rotten he doubted whether he could get her to sea. He had wanted, besides, another hundred great ships, heavily armed, plus forty hulks for victuals and stores, six galleasses, forty galleys, and some seven- or eight-score small craft. Instead, he had, by the end of January, besides his thirteen galleons, four galleasses and a motley collection of sixty or seventy other ships, hired or commandeered in every sea from the Baltic to the Adriatic, some of them leaky or cranky, many of them slow, clumsy sailors, and the best of them, Oquendo's Guipuzcoans and Recalde's Biscayans, under-manned and absurdly undergunned. Even for such a fleet he had scarcely half the auxiliary small craft he needed.[12]

On February 9th, the old admiral died, and Philip immediately named to his post the Duke of Medina-Sidonia, one of Spain's most distinguished noblemen. The parallels between the duke and the great Nicias, who led ancient Athens's Sicilian Expedition to its defeat, are striking.[13] The duke was a good man of rare honesty and great personal courage, but his heart was not in the "Enterprise," and he tried unsuccessfully to get the king to appoint someone else as commander of the armada; unlike Nicias, the duke had had little military experience, and he complained to the king's secretary that on the few times he had been out to sea, "I am always seasick and always catch cold."[14]

It is unlikely, however, that anyone could have done much better than the upright Medina-Sidonia with the Spanish Armada that sailed out of Lisbon on 28 May 1588. The fleet was impressive enough and had been considerably strengthened in the previous four months. But out of the total of 130 vessels, only 62 were warships, the rest being heavy storeships loaded with troops and provisions, and light frigates useful mostly for scouting rather than battle. There were only thirty-two shallow-draft vessels, scarcely a tenth of the total Santa Cruz had requested in 1586. The English fleet that met the Armada off Plymouth Sound on July 30 had sixty-two warships and forty-three smaller craft; the warships were faster and more leak-proof than their Spanish counterparts, their guns generally better designed and constructed, and they carried more experienced gunners aboard. England had an additional squadron of thirty-five warships hovering around Dover in case the Duke of Parma tried to cross the Channel before the armada reached him. After a week of inconclusive fighting along the Channel, during which the armada lost only two ships (through accidents), it anchored off the neutral port of Calais, near the area where the duke hoped to escort the barges carrying Parma's 40,000 troops to England. This was the critical moment in the entire operation. And it was here that the great Enterprise, so carefully planned, came to grief.

The Duke of Parma was unable to rendezvous with the armada. It was one of history's classic cases of that "fog of war" of which Clausewitz wrote. The Spanish lacked a deep-water port on the Flemish coast. Between the coastal towns they controlled and the Spanish Armada was a wide stretch of shallow water and sand bars, which regular warships could not navigate without grounding. Those waters were effectively patrolled by the rebel Dutch admiral, Justin of Nassau. His heavily armed, shallow-draft flyboats were beyond the reach of the armada's guns, yet were capable of destroying Parma's barges had he dared to sally forth to meet the armada. Parma had recognized this serious problem all along and told the king about it. Philip, impatient to carry out the invasion of England, assumed that Parma somehow could take care of the problem, either by seizing a deep-water port where the armada could meet with Parma's army, or by building a fleet of armed flyboats of his own to face the Dutch. Parma, of course, did not have enough time to do any of these. When the armada anchored off Calais, Parma had no means of reaching it without risking the wholesale slaughter of his army at the hands of Justin's coastal fleet. The armada could have helped, but only if it had had enough of those shallow-draft warships Santa Cruz had initially requested. It did not. At this point, only an extremely bold move by the Spanish, such as the temporary seizure of the deep-water port of Calais from the French, could have remedied the situation.[15] With Calais lightly defended, the armada still in full fighting strength, and Parma's army only 30 miles away in Dunkirk, the Enterprise might have been salvaged.

The English fleet did not give the Duke of Medina-Sidonia and his seasoned squadron commanders the opportunity to ponder any such moves. Now augmented by the thirty-five ships that had been sailing near Dover, the English forces took the offensive on the night of 8 August, sending eight fireships towards the anchored Spanish fleet. It was here that the exceptional English skill for psychological warfare—displayed more recently by Britain during the 1982 Falklands War—paid off handsomely. In the long war of nerves that the English ambassador to Paris had waged with the Spanish ambassador in the previous few years, he had let it be known that England was preparing new, strange fireworks and explosives for use against its enemies. During Antwerp's siege by the Spanish in 1585, the defenders had hired the noted Italian engineer Giambelli, who designed a particularly lethal class of fireships that became known as "the hellburners of Antwerp." Packed with explosives, and with their cannon fully loaded, the sailing ships were set on fire and sent down the current towards a Spanish-held bridge. After hitting the bridge and setting it on fire, the ships began to explode. While the powder packed inside the hulls went off with giant booms, the white-hot cannon fired at random, spreading flaming wreckage for a radius of a mile and killing or wounding many of the enemy. In 1588 the English revealed that Giambelli was in London working for Queen Elizabeth, a fact that did not escape the attention of the armada's crews. As the eight fireships moved towards the Spanish fleet that night, panic spread. Here again were the deadly hellburners of Antwerp, many of the sailors and their officers must have thought. They did not know that these were regular fireships, not very dangerous if one simply moved out of their way and allowed the winds and tides to carry them past one's own ships to shore. Despite the duke's heroic efforts to maintain discipline and his own calm example, many of the captains cut their anchor cables and fled. Great confusion ensued as many of the armada's ships dispersed, some of them colliding with one another. At dawn, while the duke was trying to reorganize his forces, the combined English fleets attacked.

Off the sands of Gravelines they fought all day. It was here that the English advantage in gunnery made a tactical difference that was to have strategic repercussions. As the English closed the range and drew near the Spanish ships, they were able to inflict heavy damage with their guns. When, at the end of the long day of fighting, a violent squall broke up the battle, it was clear that the English had gained the advantage. The Spanish had lost very few ships, but they had taken many casualties and much damage. The duke and his commanders were determined to renew the battle, but the cautious English, running low on ammunition and powder, kept their distance. As the winds changed, both fleets sailed northwards into the North Sea. In Scottish waters the English fleet, short of rations, gave up the chase and turned west to the Firth of Forth on August 12.

The armada's seven-week voyage home around Scotland and Ireland was nightmarish. Due to the defective casks made from unseasoned barrel staves, most of its water and food had already spoiled, and to the privations of dysentery, typhus, scurvy, and influenza were added those of thirst and hunger. Disobeying the duke's command, many ships tried to stop in Irish ports for repairs and provisions. With one exception, they were all shipwrecked, and most of the survivors put to the sword by order of the Lord Deputy who, with his small force of 2,000 English soldiers patrolling all of Ireland, feared that the presence of the Spanish might trigger an Irish revolt. In late September the remnants of the armada began to arrive in Spanish harbors. Of the fleet of 130 vessels that had sailed from Lisbon four months earlier, 44 ships had been lost; from the force of 62 warships, 44 returned. But half of all the ships that made it back were so damaged that they were unfit for further service and had to be broken up. Perhaps more important, given the difficulty of replacing them, was the loss of over half the crews, several thousand excellent infantry carried aboard, and numerous naval and infantry officers that were among Spain's finest. Of the more than 8,000 officers and sailors who manned the armada, very few returned to active service.[16]

In retrospect, Philip's famous naval offensive appears as one of the great acts of military hubris in modern history, alongside Napoleon's and Hitler's invasions of Russia, Wilhelm II's Schlieffen Plan, and Japan's war against the United States. It might have worked, but only if everything had gone right for Spain and wrong for England. The armada was barely equal in numbers to the English fleet, and inferior in the seaworthiness of its vessels and the quality of its guns and gunnery crews. Most Spanish naval officers, including Santa Cruz, knew this; so did Medina-Sidonia who, as late as June of 1588, had begged Philip to call back the fleet and cancel the operation.

From the perspective of grand strategy, Philip's design was also questionable. Even if the armada had been able to escort Parma's forces across the Channel, success would have been far from sure. The English fleet would have done its best to destroy the armada or wear it down through attrition, and prevent it from supplying Parma's forces from the sea. The Tudor state of 1588 was not the England William of Normandy had conquered fairly easily in 1066. Parma would have faced English armies fighting for their own soil and capable of recovering their strength even after suffering tactical defeats. The Dutch provinces that Parma had failed to vanquish in spite of ten years of intense military efforts suggested that much. More appropriate than the frontal assault embodied in the "Enterprise of England" would have been a flanking strategy. The Dutch needed to be subdued in order to secure for Spain the necessary deep-water ports and a long flank along England's eastern shore. Next, an armada similar to that of 1588 could have been launched against Ireland, England's Achilles Heel, where it would have touched off a rebellion that the 2,000 English troops under the Lord Deputy would have been helpless to prevent. Recovering Ireland against a seasoned Spanish army and a Catholic population eager to be free of English rule would have kept England quite busy and might have brought Elizabeth around diplomatically. With its western and eastern flanks covered by the enemy, England would have been in trouble. Indeed, the Spanish eventually attempted an "Irish Enterprise" of sorts when they sent an armada there in 1601. But by then, Spain was exhausted. The naval forces sent were much smaller, hence they had to retreat quickly to avoid the coming English fleet, leaving behind a small army of 4,500 that had landed. English forces then easily defeated the numerically inferior Spaniards.

ENGLAND'S COUNTER-OFFENSIVE OF 1589

In the autumn of 1588 England had an unparalleled opportunity to take the offensive and destroy the Spanish Navy once and for all. The battered ships of the armada that struggled into the Biscay ports of Santander and San Sebastian were all that was left of Spanish naval power; they would lie defenseless in port for a year while they were slowly repaired and refitted. Elizabeth decided to destroy them in the spring of 1589. With Spain's navy so easily and utterly destroyed, England would have been able to keep the Spanish Navy from ever reappearing, the flow of bullion and trade from the New World could have been cut off, and the colonies themselves could have been attacked, isolated, and the weakest ones picked off one by one. It was a historic opportunity much more favorable to England than Philip ever had for his cause.

The great project failed ignominiously.[17] The brilliantly simple strategic goal of destroying the ships at Santander and San Sebastian was joined to the much more ambitious one of invading Portugal through Lisbon. The English maritime community believed their ally, Dom Antonio, pretender to the Portuguese throne, who assured them that the Portuguese people would rise in arms to uphold his cause as soon as he landed with an English army behind him. To Elizabeth's bold courtiers, taking Portugal away from Spain seemed a far more exciting and glamorous enterprise than sinking the crippled warships in the forlorn ports of the Bay of Biscay. Besides, the prospects of booty seemed far greater. Since most of the ships and much of the money for the project came from the private sector, the queen's wishes could not take absolute precedence over those of the maritime entrepreneurs.

Under Drake's command, a powerful armada of eighty-three warships and sixty transports carrying 19,000 troops sailed on April of 1589. Everything went wrong. The armada's large size and the unwieldy nature of many of its cargo ships and troop transports, the westerly winds often prevailing in the Bay of Biscay, and the bay's rough waters persuaded Drake to abandon the objective of attacking Santander and San Sebastian. Alleging the expected arrival of a large Baltic convoy loaded with shipbuilding supplies at the port of La Coruña, Drake struck there instead. He found no convoy, only one large ship and a few insignificant vessels. Then, lured by the hope of booty, he tried to take the town. The siege failed, and many of his sailors and soldiers became sick. After re-embarking, the expedition sailed for Lisbon, which they found alerted and well prepared; thus, they decided to land the troops 45 miles away. Desertions and disease took their toll, and the expected Portuguese uprising did not materialize. Aware of the mounting dangers facing their increasingly demoralized and vulnerable army, the commanders decided to evacuate their forces and bring their ships home. That winter, the silver shipment arrived safely in Spain, and many of the Santander galleons were brought up to service. England's great opportunity had slipped away, and the war with Spain would go on for another fourteen years.

STALEMATE AND EXHAUSTION: 1590–1604

While English advocates of offensive naval power, such as Hawkins, continued to press for a forward maritime strategy of blockade and selective strikes against Spain, the Crown had difficulty channeling resources for such operations in view of the growing requirements of land warfare on the Continent. English money and troops were needed in the Netherlands to hold off Parma's armies. At the end of 1589 France plunged into full civil war, and Spain sent in several armies to support the Catholic League. Between 1590 and 1597 Spanish forces occupied at various times Paris, Rouen, Amiens, Calais, and portions of Brittany and Normandy along the English Channel.[18] England dispatched several armies to France to support the anti-Spanish Huguenots and their leader, Henry of Navarre, and continued to provide heavy subsidies. It was clear to Elizabeth and Burghley, though perhaps not to her naval strategists, that no offensive maritime strategy could be pursued independently of the requirements and priorities of avoiding defeat in the European land theater; in fact, the defeat or neutralization of Spanish power on the continent was the basic cornerstone without which no future offensive maritime strategies could be carried out. Had Spain acquired the Dutch harbors, or had it turned France into a satellite and gained regular access to its Channel ports, the task of defending England by sea would have been complicated immensely.

By 1595, the tide finally began to turn against Spain. Parma had died in 1592, and the Dutch, led by a brilliant military strategist of their own, Maurice of Nassau, swept the Spanish completely out of the northern provinces and increased the pressure on the southern ones. In 1593 Henry of Navarre converted to Catholicism—"Paris is worth a mass," he is reported to have said—and began to rally all Frenchmen to support him as their lawful king and expel the Spanish intruders from their homeland. The Pope's recognition of Henry as Most Christian King of France in 1595 dealt Philip's French policy a devastating blow. England could now spare some resources for a renewed maritime offensive.

Its efforts between 1595 and 1597, however, were frustrated by Spain's resurgent navy and improved fortifications in the New World. A fleet under the joint command of Drake and Hawkins sailed in mid-1595 with the objectives of striking first at Puerto Rico and then Panama. Both attacks, however, failed in the face of stiff Spanish resistance, and the fleet returned home without their illustrious commanders, both of whom died of illness in the Caribbean. In 1596, a powerful Anglo-Dutch armada of over 100 ships (including 47 warships) and 8,000 troops descended, yet again, on Cadiz, Spain's most important port through which passed much of her trade with the New World and the Mediterranean. Led by a brilliant young naval strategist, the Earl of Essex, the expedition destroyed or captured twenty-one major ships, including four large galleons, over twelve million ducats' worth of goods in the harbor, and sacked the city thoroughly. Essex wanted to hold the town and use it as a naval base for further operations; had he done so, he might have captured a large flota that sailed shortly thereafter from the colonies to Spain. Most of his men wanted to go home, however, to enjoy in safety the booty they had seized. Reluctantly, Essex abandoned Cadiz.

Upon his return to England, Essex wrote a paper on naval strategy underlining the importance of securing a base on Spanish soil; only from such a base, he argued, could the fleet carry out the kinds of systematic naval operations required for effective commerce-raiding and blockade.[19] While his broad strategic vision would bear fruit a century later with the English seizure of Gibraltar and the subsequent acquisition by England of a ring of naval bases around the world, it was beyond the capabilities of Elizabethan England. Philip's *tercios* would have quickly swept any English enclaves off the peninsula.

By 1597 a rough stalemate had ensued between the two great antagonists. England had failed to break Spain's empire "to pieces," as Sir Walter Raleigh had wanted. The 1590s were in some respects the golden age of the Spanish Navy. Between 1589 and 1598 the indefatigable Philip built seventy new warships, including a squadron of *galizabras*—fast, light frigates that could elude all English pursuers and were used quite successfully on the trade routes to America.[20] Under the king's direction, the famous Italian engineer Juan Bautista Antonelli drew up in 1587 a comprehensive plan of fortifications for such major colonial ports as Havana, San Juan de Ulua, Puerto Rico, and Portobello, which Philip immediately implemented.[21]

But if England seemed to have reached a dead end in its efforts to bring Spain to its knees, Spain had not done any better. Not one to give up easily, Philip sent two formidable armadas to conquer England in 1596 and 1597. Both were dispersed by storms before they reached the Channel, with much loss of life and ships. In the Netherlands, Spain was barely hanging on to the southern provinces, while the independent Dutch were quickly becoming a major commercial and naval power in their own right. In France, Henry IV and his English allies had gradually defeated the Catholic League and the Spanish forces, and Philip reluctantly acknowledged the inevitable by making peace on May of 1598, yielding the enclaves in French territory still held by his troops. Four months later he died. His son's halfhearted attempt to intervene in Ireland in 1601 failed. When, shortly after Elizabeth's death in 1603, her successor King James I made peace overtures, Spain accepted willingly. Both powers signed a peace accord in 1604. Spain persisted in its ruinous war in the Low Countries until 1609 when, forty years after the Duke of Alba first marched in with his army, it reached a truce with the Dutch. In the 1590s, the wars in France and the Netherlands had consumed 88 million florins from the Spanish treasury. The Castilian national debt, 36 million ducats on Philip's accession to the throne in 1556, was 85 million in 1598.[22] By 1604, both England and Spain were exhausted, the former pausing to climb yet greater heights of power, the latter about to plunge into growing feebleness and decline.

NOTES

1. R. B. Wernham, "Elizabethan War Aims and Strategy," *Elizabethan Government and Society*, S. T. Bindoff, J. Hurstfield, C. H. Williams, eds. (London: Athlone Press, 1961), p. 341.

2. Garrett Mattingly, *The "Invincible" Armada and Elizabethan England* (New York: Cornell University Press, 1963), p. 7.

3. David B. Quinn and A. N. Ryan, *England's Sea Empire: 1550–1642* (London: George Allen and Unwin, 1983), p. 74.

4. *Ibid.*, p. 76.

5. Sterling Hart's, "Armada: The War with Spain 1585–1604," *Strategy and Tactics*, vol. 72 (1979), p. 8, provided this important fact, and was drawn on for further material that appears in the next several pages.

6. Quinn and Ryan, *England's Sea Empire: 1550–1642*, pp. 80–91 and 42–43 underlie my discussion on pp. 140–42.

7. John Lynch, *Spain under the Habsburgs, Vol. I, 1516–1598*, 2d ed. (New York: New York University Press, 1984), p. 366.

8. *Ibid.*, pp. 347–48.

9. Quinn and Ryan, *England's Sea Empire: 1550–1642*, p. 94.

10. Garrett Mattingly, *The Armada* (Boston: Houghton Mifflin, 1959), p. 121.

11. Hart, "Armada: The War with Spain," p. 9.

12. Mattingly, *The Armada*, pp. 203–4.

13. Thucydides, *The Peloponnesian War* (Oxford: Oxford University Press, 1943).

14. Mattingly, *The Armada*, p. 205.

15. Hart, "Armada: The War with Spain," p. 13.

16. Mattingly, *The Armada*, pp. 424–26; Lynch, *Spain Under the Habsburgs*, p. 174.

17. Wernham, "Elizabethan War Aims and Strategy," 362–63; Quinn and Ryan, *England's Sea Empire: 1550–1642*, p. 109–11.

18. Quinn and Ryan, *England's Sea Empire: 1550–1642*, p. 114; Lynch, *Spain Under the Habsburgs*, pp. 350–57.

19. Quinn and Ryan, *England's Sea Empire: 1550–1642*, p. 112–13.

20. *Ibid.*, p. 115.

21. Lynch, *Spain Under the Habsburgs*, pp. 346–47.

22. *Ibid.*, pp. 354–57.

BIBLIOGRAPHIC NOTE

The most thorough and up-to-date treatment of sixteenth-century England's remarkable maritime expansion, and the strategic ideas associated with it is by D. B. Quinn and A. N. Ryan, *England's Sea Empire: 1550–1642* (London: George Allen and Unwin, 1983). The best three works on the Spanish Armada are Garrett Mattingly, *The Armada* (Boston: Houghton Mifflin, 1959), Peter Padfield, *Armada* (Annapolis. Naval Institute Press, 1988), and Colin Martin and Geoffrey Parker, *The Spanish Armada* (London: Hamish Hamilton, 1988). The blend of meticulous scholarship and a lively, engaging style make it difficult for the reader to put these books aside. For a masterful treatment of England's strategic dilemmas throughout the long conflict, see R. B. Wernham, "Elizabethan War Aims and Strategy," *Elizabethan Government and Society*, S. T. Bindoff, J. Hurstfield, C. H. Williams, eds. (London: Athlone Press, 1961), pp. 340–63. John Lynch's *Spain Under the Habsburgs, Vol. I 1516–1598* (New York: New York University Press, 1981) is essential for an understanding of Philip II's foreign policy and strategy, and the difficult problems faced by Spain in keeping its empire together.

ADDITIONAL SOURCES

Bennassar, Bartolome. *The Spanish Character. Attitude and Mentalities from the Sixteenth to the Nineteenth Century.* Berkeley and Los Angeles: University of California Press, 1979.

Elliott, J. H. *Imperial Spain 1469–1716.* London: Penguin Books, 1970.

————. *The Old World and the New, 1492–1650.* Cambridge: Cambridge University Press, 1970.

Guilmartin, John F., Jr. *Gunpowder and Galleys: Changing Technology and Mediterranean Warfare at Sea in the Sixteenth Century.* Cambridge: Cambridge University Press, 1974.

Hart, Sterling. "Armada: The War with Spain 1585–1604," *Strategy and Tactics,* vol. 72 (1979), pp. 4–14.

Kennedy, Paul M. *The Rise and Fall of English Naval Mastery.* London: Allen Lane, 1976.

Mahan, Alfred Thayer. *The Influence of Seapower upon History, 1660–1783.* New York: Hill and Wang, 1957.

Parker, Geoffrey. *The Army of Flanders and the Spanish Road.* 1567–1659. Cambridge: Cambridge University Press, 1972.

————. *The Dutch Revolt.* Ithaca: Cornell University Press, 1977.

————. *Philip II.* Boston: Little, Brown & Co., 1979.

————. *Spain and the Netherlands, 1559–1659.* Short Hills, NJ: Enslow Publications, 1979.

Wernham, R. B. *After the Armada: Elizabethan England and the Struggle for Western Europe 1588–1595.* Oxford: Oxford University Press, 1984.

————. *The Making of Elizabethan Foreign Policy, 1558–1603.* Berkeley and Los Angeles: University of California Press, 1980.

Wilson, Charles. *Queen Elizabeth and the Revolt of the Netherlands.* Berkeley and Los Angeles: University of California Press, 1970.

7

The Anglo-French Wars
1689-1815

BY ROBIN RANGER

Between 1689 and 1815 Great Britain and France fought a protracted conflict, including seven major wars. The conflict was caused by France's bid to become the dominant power in Europe—the hegemon—based on her position as the foremost European land power and as a sea power second only to Britain. As the maritime leader of a series of anti-hegemonic coalitions, Britain opposed France's bid for preponderance. These coalitions enabled the Royal Navy to neutralize French seapower and capture France's overseas empire, while small British expeditionary forces and large British subsidies supported the European land powers opposing French hegemony on the continent.

After one hundred and twenty-six years of conflict Great Britain's grand strategy prevailed. France's last and strongest bid for hegemony, under Emperor Napoleon Bonaparte, was finally defeated on land, at the battle of Waterloo (18 June 1815), nearly ten years after being defeated at sea, at the battle of Trafalgar (21 October 1805).

BRITISH STRATEGY: FOUR THEMES

The following analysis of this protracted Anglo-French conflict uses current geopolitical and strategic concepts to show how Great Britain developed and implemented a strategy, the underlying principles of which can be seen, in the light of this analysis, to be similar to those favored in U.S. grand strategy in the 1980s. Great Britain's strategy in the conflict against France showed, in particular, the importance of four of the central themes of this book. First, sea powers can be defeated at sea by land powers, but they cannot defeat land powers at sea. As a sea power, Britain had to defeat France at sea and help her allies to defeat France on land. But Britain always risked defeat at sea, a defeat that would have permanently crippled the anti-hegemonic coalition.

Second, the offensive is the stronger form of maritime warfare. The Royal Navy's pursuit of the offensive against the French Navy proved much more effective than France's defensive strategy and tactics. By seizing the initiative and increasing its initial advantages, the Royal Navy was usually able to establish effective sea control. When British mistakes, including excessive economies in naval budgets in peacetime, compromised the Royal Navy's supremacy, the French Navy remained psychologically intimidated. The few exceptions when the French took the offensive proved the rule that the offensive is superior at sea.

Third, a major land power with the resources to become a major sea power has the potential to become a successful bidder for hegemony. France's ultimate failure in her bid should not obscure the fact that she came close to succeeding and that a major cause of her failure was her lack of understanding of how to link her seapower and landpower.

Fourth, the balance of advantage swings in favor of a sea power in a protracted conflict for hegemony. The potential hegemon creates increasing opposition in the form of anti-hegemonic coalitions, supported by the sea power's resources. So long as France failed to neutralize Britain, British expeditionary forces and subsidies could support coalition after coalition against France. This happened throughout the protracted conflict as a whole and most notably in its final phase, when Great Britain supported five coalitions against Revolutionary and Napoleonic France.

In addition, Britain demonstrated the importance, for an effective maritime strategy, of striking the right balance between its maritime (including power projection) and continental components. While the maritime component had to be the dominant one, the necessarily limited continental component of Britain's maritime strategy was essential to its ultimate success.

BALANCING THE BRITISH STRATEGY

Great Britain was, in geopolitical terms, an insular maritime power whose security and independence would be threatened if a European land power made a successful bid for hegemony. A hegemonic land power would possess the resources and control the strategically crucial areas of Europe, especially the Low Countries (modern Belgium and Holland), needed to threaten England with defeat by invasion or starvation. So British policymakers in the wars against France had to formulate and implement a strategy that would maximize their contribution to alliances against this European aspirant to hegemony. This strategy also had to recognize the effects of Britain's geopolitical position and the constraints on its resources.

The result was a continuous strategic debate in England between proponents of maritime and continental strategies. As summarized by the distinguished British historian Sir Michael Howard:

> If there was indeed a "British Way in Warfare" it was the outcome of a continuous dialectic between this maritime school and their "Continental" opponents; a dialectic which can indeed be traced back to the Elizabethan Age. . . .Britain's geographical position as an island separated from, yet part of, the European land mass has made this dialectic central . . . to her strategy . . .[1]

The result of this dialectic was a British strategy that was not, because it could not be, a purely blue-water, seapower one. Instead, it was a strategy that recognized that after—but only after—adequate maritime and power-projection forces had been provided, land forces had to be fielded in Europe. This continental commitment was essential if the European allies were to commit their land forces against the potential hegemonic power, keep them in the field, and win the European land wars. Britain's continental commitment had to have a smaller share of her resources because she had to give priority to maritime-force needs, but to be effective this land-force commitment had to be made from the outset. In Michael Howard's words:

> First, a commitment of support to a Continental ally in the nearest available theatre, on the largest scale that contemporary resources could afford, so far from being alien to traditional British strategy, was absolutely central to it. The flexibility provided by seapower certainly made possible other activities as well . . . but these were ancillary to the great decisions by land, and they continued to be so throughout the two world wars. Secondly, when we did have recourse to a purely maritime strategy, it was always as a result, not of free choice . . . but of *force majeure*. It was a strategy of necessity rather than of choice, of survival rather than of victory. It enabled us to escape from the shipwrecks which overtook our less fortunately-placed Continental neighbours; it gave us a breathing space in which to try to attract other allies; it enabled us to run away . . . but it never enabled us to win.[2]

The development of Britain's strategy, balancing the sea and land-force components, can now be traced.

DEVELOPING BRITAIN'S STRATEGY

During the Anglo-French conflict, most of the concepts of British strategy were reformulated and refined. These ideas had been understood, often inchoately, by earlier practitioners of seapower. But it was the British and the French who thought through the implications of these ideas. The French were the better theorists of seapower, but the British were the more effective practitioners.

During this long conflict the British and French navies also made some important technical advances in naval architecture, gunnery, medicine, navigation, and signaling. These enabled them, from the mid-eighteenth century onwards, strategically to wage global war, and tactically to seek and achieve decisive fleet actions—culminating at Trafalgar.

GEOPOLITICAL BUILDING BLOCKS

In geopolitical terms Britain was a natural sea power commanding the major trade routes to and from the northern European sea coasts, with the population and resource bases for a first-class navy. So British policymakers were, by 1689, already thinking of their country as primarily a sea power and only secondarily as a land power. They were also beginning to see the main area of potential economic and territorial gains as lying outside Europe.

In contrast, French policymakers saw France as primarily a European land power and only secondarily a sea power. Yet, while the French Army was the most effective in Europe, its superiority was relative rather than absolute. France was bidding for European hegemony over four other major European powers: the Hapsburg Empire (increasingly based on Austria); Spain (declining but still powerful); Prussia (the rising German power); and Russia (the rising northern European power). Holland was becoming a second-class, but still significant, power, a position she retained until about 1730. Thereafter, Holland became a power of marginal importance except for her small but effective navy as well as her strategic position as a base from which to threaten Great Britain. Outside of Europe, the French Empire had to compete with four other major empires, those of Britain, Holland, Spain, and Portugal. The Portuguese Empire was, however, a spent force by the early seventeenth century because of the Dutch attacks on it in the Indian Ocean.

Although alliances constantly shifted, France was usually allied with Spain (from 1703 to 1808) and always opposed by Britain plus, usually, Austria. Prussia and Russia joined whichever alliance offered them the most gains. So the balance of land forces usually compelled France to concentrate her resources on her army. Only in exceptionally favorable circumstances, which occurred only once—in the War of American Independence (1775–83)—could France free itself from land commitments in Europe.

This combination of circumstances that made France primarily a land power and Britain primarily a sea power gave Britain a significant advantage, because communications were, during their conflict, more effective by sea than by land. So British seapower was relatively more productive of economic and military gains than French landpower.

The French Navy, in second place in the queue for resources, faced three additional handicaps. One was geographic. France had to split her navy between the Atlantic and Mediterranean fleets, based at (mainly) Brest (Atlantic) and Toulon (Mediterranean). After Britain took Gibraltar from Spain (1704), it had a base between the two French fleets and could, weather permitting, concentrate the Royal Navy's main fleet on the Ushant position, dominating the mouth of the English Channel. From this position, the main British fleet could, provided it was superior, carry out its crucial missions: intercept and destroy a French invasion fleet; defend in-bound British convoys and attack in-bound French convoys. Because Brest was located in the west, France did have, unlike Holland, a major naval base with the weather gauge of the British. But this location also facilitated Brest's blockade by the Royal Navy, a blockade that became increasingly effective thanks to technical advances in the eighteenth century. So by late in that century, the Ushant position had become the key to a British system of maritime defense that was so widely understood in the Royal Navy as to offset poor communication. When the strategic situation was particularly uncertain, fleet and ship commanders headed for the mouth of the channel to rendezvous with the western squadron of the Home (Channel) Fleet.

The second handicap was the failure of French strategic theorists and policymakers to fully understand the potential contribution of seapower to France's bid for hegemony. In particular, they consistently failed to understand that if French land and seapower could not combine to neutralize Great Britain at the start of a war, British and allied sea and landpower would eventually block France's expansion. French policymakers thus failed to support their naval and power projection forces, even when these were performing effectively.

The third handicap the French Navy faced was that overall the Royal Navy was usually the superior fighting instrument, collectively and individually. The degree of this supremacy should not be exaggerated: at its peak, in the War of American Independence, the French Navy was nearly the equal of the Royal Navy in combat effectiveness. But even in that war, the Royal Navy proved marginally superior. The reasons for the British naval superiority are complex and are linked to broad geographic, societal, economic, and technical factors. Geography enabled Britain to concentrate her resources on a first-class navy at the expense of her army. British society was also determined to keep the army so small that there could be no repetition of Oliver Cromwell's military dictatorship of the English Civil War. The British economy, based on seaborne trade and individual enterprise, grew rapidly and, by the end of the eighteenth century, was producing new technologies well ahead of France's. Technically, the Royal Navy was an entirely professional service, which rewarded combat effectiveness with prize money from the capture of enemy ships, including merchant ships, and enemy territories.

The effect of these factors was synergistic and cumulative: however large and effective the French Navy was, the Royal Navy was always that bit larger and more effective. Similarly, even when the Royal Navy was suffering from the advance effects of excessive peacetime economies, strategic misdirection, and tactical incompetence, its mistakes would be exceeded by those of the French Navy. It also bears stressing that to field a first-class navy as well as a first-class army would have really strained French resources and taken many years, explaining why this was not often achieved. The result was that French maritime strategic options were usually constrained by their having a less than first-class navy, although this situation also reflected a lack of understanding of their need for one.

The eventual result of the French failure and the British success in understanding maritime strategy was the failure of France's bid for hegemony. It was this sense of the cumulative effect of seapower that Mahan captured in his famous passage. "Those far distant, storm-beaten ships, upon which the Grand Army [of Napoleon] never looked, stood between it and the dominion of the world."[3]

ROUND I: 1689–1697

The War of the League of Augsburg (1689–97) was the first of those in which Britain supported a coalition of continental land powers against French hegemony with major maritime and modest, but significant, land forces.

For France, this war introduced a strategic dilemma that successive governments failed to resolve: should French resources be concentrated on land or sea, to defeat, respectively, her main European land adversaries or her main maritime adversary, Great Britain? As long as French resources were too limited to do both at once, France always had to choose between those two objectives. Yet the French never really recognized that they had to make this choice; they usually tried to achieve both objectives at once, and failed to achieve either.

There was also an ideological element to this war, in the form of religion. Louis XIV was a Catholic who had supported the former British monarch, his fellow Catholic James II. It was fear of Catholicism that led the British aristocracy and army forcibly to replace James II with the Dutch William III, a Protestant, in the Glorious Revolution of 1688. This revolution combined British and Dutch sea, land, and economic power, based on seaborne trade. The Anglo-Dutch union also strengthened the emerging coalition against potential French hegemony, that included Spain, the Hapsburg Empire (including Austria), and some German states.

FRENCH STRATEGY

To eliminate this Anglo-Dutch leader of the anti-hegemonic coalition, Louis XIV and his advisers tried to use a sophisticated combination of maritime, power-projection, and ideological forces. The French Navy, numerically superior to the Anglo-Dutch Navy, would convoy James II and a small French power-projection force (about 7,000 troops) to the largely Catholic Ireland that formed, then—as always, uneasily—part of Great Britain. With the support of the bulk of the Irish population, this French force would tie down or defeat a large part of the Anglo-Dutch land forces. Meanwhile, the French battle fleet would destroy the Anglo-Dutch battle fleet and the French Army would crush the Dutch Army. England could then be invaded. Like successive French strategies for defeating Britain and her allies, that of 1689 was theoretically sound but difficult to execute, given the strength of the relative forces involved, the problems of what would now be called command, control, and communications (C^3), and British plus allied countermeasures.

A French squadron landed the former James II in Ireland in March 1689 and reinforced him. But the French failed to follow up on their initial success with a sound maritime strategy cutting English-Irish sea lines of communication (SLOC). William III then convoyed an army to Ireland in 288 transports with only 6 escorting warships. This Anglo-Dutch army of 35–40,000 troops defeated a Franco-Irish army of 21,000 at the battle of the Boyne (11 July 1690), although it was not until 1691 that the Franco-Irish forces in Ireland finally were defeated. This French use of power-projection forces showed, though, how effective these could be under favorable circumstances.

THE FLEET-IN-BEING

Meanwhile, the English commander-in-chief of the main Anglo-Dutch battle fleet, Admiral Lord Arthur Torrington, devised the concept of the "fleet-in-being" to deter a French invasion. Torrington argued that while he should try to engage the superior French fleet, if he could do so on favorable tactical terms, his overriding objective must be to preserve intact his inferior, but still powerful, fleet. Secure in its defended bases, such a fleet-in-being could deter a French invasion by threatening a sortie in full strength against a French fleet weakened by extensive operations. As Torrington put it on 26 June 1690, the weakness of his fleet meant that:

> . . . if we should fight . . . [we] may not only endanger the losing of the fleet, but . . . the quiet of our country too: for if we are beaten, they being absolute masters of the sea, will be at great liberty of doing many things they dare not attempt while we observe them. [But] . . . whilst we observe the French, they can make no attempt either on sea or shore, but with great disadvantage. . . . I always said, that whilst we had a fleet-in-being, they would dare not make an attempt [at invasion].[4]

The subsequent battle of Beachy Head, on 30 June, and its aftermath, proved the accuracy of Torrington's analysis. He had an Anglo-Dutch fleet of fifty-six to sixty ships against seventy French ships, individually superior, under Admiral Comte de Tourville. Tactical problems caused an English attack to fail and a French counterattack to inflict serious damage on the Anglo-Dutch fleet. Torrington then broke off the action—the strategically correct decision. To continue the action would have been to expose his fleet to defeat and Britain to invasion. By preserving his fleet-in-being he prevented an invasion.

As later used by the French (and other) navies, the fleet-in-being strategy has been misused as an excuse for inactivity. This misuse of what may be an unavoidable strategy under circumstances of temporary inferiority contrasts sharply with Torrington's use of an *active* fleet-in-being strategy. The Anglo-Dutch fleet returned to the offensive as soon as its strength had been built up to the necessary level.

Operationally, this active fleet-in-being strategy was a particularly effective one because fleets were not, then, capable of sustained operations at sea and were regularly laid up in winter.

FROM OFFENSIVE TO DEFENSIVE

In only three years, from 1690 to 1693, French maritime strategy shifted from the offensive to the defensive, a shift that contributed significantly to France's ultimate defeat. French policymakers did not understand how to exploit their temporary maritime superiority. Allied operations against France's land frontiers were not particularly successful, but they absorbed scarce French resources and compelled her to divide her attention between the land and the sea (with an increasing focus upon the former).

Then, in 1692 the French attempted what became their standard plan for invading Britain: a junction between the Brest and Toulon fleets, plus other squadrons from Biscay ports. The French combined fleet would then defeat the Royal Navy, and escort an invasion fleet to the British Isles. Implementing this plan in the days of sail and primitive C^3 would have been difficult even without the Royal Navy's opposition, and it was almost impossible with it.

The French plan of 1692 added a naval attack early in the summer campaigning season, intended to take the Anglo-Dutch fleet by surprise. Admiral Tourville would sortie from Brest with thirty-seven to forty-seven ships, to be joined by thirteen from Toulon. The Toulon squadron failed to join Tourville, and his inflexible orders compelled him to attack with forty-four ships against ninety-nine (sixty-three British and thirty-six Dutch) battleships, odds of more than 2:1 against the French. Despite these odds, the French fleet fought extremely efficiently at the Battles of Barfleur and La Hougue on 29 May and 2 June 1692 and then withdrew, losing only fifteen ships.

A GRAND STRATEGIC DEFEAT

Tactically, France had suffered only a limited defeat, losing fifteen ships but retaining nearly one hundred. These losses could be replaced, as could those of the invasion fleet.

But in terms of grand strategy France suffered a major, almost irreparable, psychological defeat. Louis XIV and his advisers gradually reduced their challenge at sea to the Anglo-Dutch alliance in order to concentrate on the land campaign against Holland. France then made the one-front land campaign a two-front one by attacking another member of the anti-hegemonic alliance, Spain, in 1694.

Once made, the late 1692 decision to accept inferiority at sea took only two years to take effect and lasted for some eighty-six years, until 1778. The decline of the French battle fleet was compounded by a switch from attacks on the Anglo-Dutch battle fleet to attacks on commerce—the *guerre de course.*

GUERRE DE COURSE

After the limited French defeat at Barfleur-La Hougue, the French decided that their naval resources could best be employed for the remainder of the 1692 summer campaign season in attacking Anglo-Dutch commerce. This *guerre de course* was successful and profitable. The temporary French switch to commerce raiding in 1692 became a semi-permanent one in this war and subsequently. The *guerre de course* seemed to offer a chance to attack the seaborne commerce whose profits the British used to fund the coalitions against France, providing instead profits to support France's war efforts, and avoiding the need to fund a large French battle fleet.

The problem with the *guerre de course* strategy was that, in the age of sail, it was a strategy for short-term success and long-term failure. So long as commerce raiders were surface vessels, the dominant British battle fleet could reduce the commerce raiders' attacks to tolerable proportions. The main tactical device for doing so was the convoy, the provision of warships to convoy (escort) groups of merchant ships sailing together. To attack these merchant ships, the French commerce raiders would first have to defeat the British naval escorts and supporting forces, including detached battle squadrons and, ultimately, the main battle fleet. But so long as this British battle fleet was superior to that of the French, their commerce raiding was mainly limited to light forces. These could usually be defended by convoy escorts, although individual merchantmen remained vulnerable. The French could not use larger units, including battle squadrons, for commerce raiding because these would be vulnerable to interception and destruction by the Royal Navy. In addition, Britain could attack such commerce of France and her allies that dared to put to sea.

There was also an ambivalence in French thinking about the *guerre de course* that contributed to their failure to develop a fully effective maritime strategy, complementing their land strategy. The strongest supporters of commerce raiding argued that it should be the preferred French naval strategy and that it could be successful enough to defeat Britain by crippling the seaborne trade on which her economy (and hence her navy) depended. (This view re-emerged in late nineteenth century France as the Jeune École school of thinking on maritime strategy.) More moderate French supporters of commerce raiding argued that it could not be decisive unless supported, ultimately, by a French battle fleet able to defeat the main British battle fleet and so destroy Britain's ability to provide convoy escorts superior to the French raiders. But, the supporters argued, French raiders could do enough damage to British commerce to weaken Britain's will to pursue any particular conflict with France.

Given the naval technology of the Anglo-French conflict, these moderate supporters were correct. Since French commerce raiders had to be surface vessels, the damage they could do to Britain would be limited by the sea control exercised by the superior British battle fleet unless France fielded a fleet able to challenge its command of the sea. But the argument that commerce raiding could be decisive always remained appealing to the French, since it seemed to offer a cheap, simple alternative to fielding a first-class battle fleet. The result was recurrent French attempts to rely on the *guerre de course* and economize on their battle fleet, weakening it and handicapping France's development of an effective maritime strategy and force.

The experience with commerce raiding in the Anglo-French conflict was also important as the basis of two later misunderstandings about such raiding that affected the development of maritime strategy.

TWO MISCONCEPTIONS

Two important strategic misconceptions about commerce raiding are that convoys are defensive and that *guerre de course* cannot be decisive. The first misconception emerged in the Royal Navy after the Anglo-French conflict. This misconception confused the tactical defensive and the strategic offensive. The tactically defensive convoy escorts were, in fact, strategically offensive in a double sense.

The convoys themselves were a form of strategic offense—either projecting British power overseas or supplying the homeland power base. So long as France failed to cut the British SLOC, the British won because Britain was accorded the time, and could accumulate the wealth necessary for the organization and reorganization of the coalition(s) necessary to secure the defeat of the continental powers on land. The convoy *escorts* were also offensive because they forced the commerce raiders to attack the naval escorts, rather than the merchant ships.

The second misconception was that because the French *guerre de course* was not decisive, commerce raiding could never be decisive (a point Admiral Mahan stressed). The French *guerre de course* certainly failed, because the naval technology of the Anglo-French conflict meant that commerce raiding could only be decisive if supported by a French battle fleet large enough to defeat the British battle fleet. But in the twentieth century, new naval technologies made it possible for commerce raiders to operate without challenging the fleets controlling the surface waters and to be potentially decisive at sea.

NET RESULT

The first round of the Anglo-French conflict ended in a draw. The mutual exhaustion of the major European powers led to the 1697 Peace of Ryswick, restoring the prewar status quo. But this apparently inconclusive outcome marked the first of the series of victories for the emerging British maritime strategy, which culminated in that of 1815. France had no territorial gains to show for eight years of war. In contrast, Great Britain made considerable gains. William III's rule over the British Isles, including Ireland, was secured. Britain's seaborne commerce and her North American colonies both increased, and the establishment of the Bank of England in 1694 created a powerful economic weapon.

ROUND II: 1701–13

As its name implies, Britain fought the War of Spanish Succession (1701–13) to prevent a member of the French royal family from succeeding to the throne of Spain, which would give Louis XIV control over a united Franco-Spanish kingdom. In order to prevent this union, Great Britain and Holland allied with the Hapsburg Empire and Prussia against France. Spain was internally divided, but increasingly supported France. As a result, France fought on both its western and eastern land fronts while the allies sought to block French expansion.

At sea, France and Spain tried to protect their overseas empires in North and South America, the West Indies, and the Pacific, to attack Anglo-Dutch seaborne commerce, and to tie down their battle fleets, which were too strong to be challenged—a passive fleet-in-being strategy. The Anglo-Dutch fleets were used to protect and enlarge their overseas empires, attack those of France and Spain, neutralize their battle fleets and support the land war against Louis XIV. An important part of this support was economic. Profits from the seaborne Anglo-Dutch trade and war helped fund further economic growth and subsidize land allies. By the end of this war, Britain was wealthier than when it started while France was bankrupt.

During the war Britain refined its maritime strategy in three ways. First, given the naval weakness of the opposing Franco-Spanish alliance, Britain increased the resources allocated to the continental land-force component of this strategy. Second, it used its naval superiority, including power-projection forces, to acquire geopolitically crucial territories, although Britain also misused its power-projection capabilities to project forces where they were defeated. Third, the Royal Navy confirmed its tactical reliance on the formal line of battle, with important effects.

The continental component of the British strategy had two main characteristics. One was that the resources available for it were still limited by the priority that had to be given to maritime forces, but Britain was able to maintain superiority at sea unusually economically because of her Dutch alliance.

The other feature of this continental component was that, although relatively limited, it was of enormous synergistic value. The forces at the watershed Battle of Blenheim (1704) illustrate this point. British troops comprised between 9,000 and 11,000 (estimates vary), out of the allied army of 52,000 (17–21 percent) versus 56,000 Franco-Bavarians. But without these British forces, plus subsidies, and the Duke of Marlborough's military genius as commander-in-chief, the rest of the Allied Army would not have been there. Nor would they have inflicted the first major defeat French armies had suffered for over forty years. For the next seven years, Marlborough and his colleague Prince Eugene of Savoy were victorious in every battle fought and every siege undertaken. When the new Whig government withdrew British forces and subsidies in 1712, the Grand Alliance collapsed.

GEOPOLITICAL GAINS

Great Britain used its naval superiority to acquire strategic territories, thereby further increasing this superiority. The 1704 seizure of Gibraltar made Britain a major maritime power in the Mediterranean, as well as in the Atlantic and the North Sea. Gibraltar was, as the British Admiral Sir John Fisher later described it, one of the "Five keys that lock up the world: Singapore, the [South African] Cape, Alexandria, Gibraltar, Dover."[5]

The mutually beneficial interaction between the land component of Britain's strategy and this newly acquired strategic base was shown in the allies' 1707 campaign. Prince Eugene led an allied army against France's main Mediterranean naval base, Toulon, while Marlborough and another allied army tied down French forces in the Low Country. The Anglo-Dutch Navy supplied and supported Prince Eugene's army, while blockading the French Navy in Toulon, where the French scuttled fifty fighting ships, a major naval defeat. In North America, British and colonial forces gained control of the Bay of Fundy, increasing Britain's control over the northern coastline of the Atlantic seaboard.

Other significant Anglo-Dutch gains further emphasized how the correct use of maritime forces could strengthen the anti-hegemonic alliance. In 1702 an allied combined operation seized a very valuable Spanish treasure fleet in its Vigo Bay base and destroyed the escort of twenty-four French battleships. This capture also helped Britain to persuade Portugal to join the anti-French alliance (1703), beginning an Anglo-Portuguese alliance that lasted throughout the Anglo-French conflict, and which reflected Portugal's dependence on trade with her overseas empire. Later, in 1708, another combined operation captured Minorca, a Spanish base almost as valuable geopolitically as was Gibraltar.

Britain and her allies did, though, misuse their power-projection capabilities by deploying large land forces to Spain. This secondary theater turned into a Spanish ulcer for the allies and not, as earlier and later, for the French, and the allies were decisively defeated at the battle of Almanza (1707).

TACTICAL CHANGES

Tactically, the battle of Malaga (1704) marked the final replacement of the seventeenth-century melee battle with the formal line-of-battle engagement. The British commander, Admiral Sir George Rooke, defeated the French attempt to relieve Gibraltar through the successful use of the Permanent Fighting Instructions, which he had rewritten, to stress the importance of maintaining the continuity of the line. These instructions thus became the navy's Bible.

Strategically, the line of battle produced a paradoxical result, making it difficult, tactically, for the Royal Navy to achieve decisive results in fleet engagements but making it even more difficult, strategically, for the French to challenge British command of the sea. The French could break off the engagement when they wished, unless the British engaged in a general chase. As a technique for fighting battles without losing them, French tactics were superb; they also made it almost impossible for the French to win battles. Since strategically the French were challenging the British command of the sea, their tactics thus defeated their strategic objective, ensuring that Britannia would continue to rule the most strategically important waves.

NET RESULT

The 1713 Peace of Utrecht formalized a series of significant shifts in the European balance of power. Great Britain emerged as the preeminent maritime power and also as a major European land power. Her North American colonies expanded northwards, into Acadia, threatening the SLOC of the French colonies, which depended on French control of the St. Lawrence River. Britain was confirmed in possession of her new bases at Gibraltar and Minorca. An important economic gain was the Asiento Treaty, giving Britain trade access to the previously closed Spanish Empire.

France's bid for hegemony was contained for over a quarter of a century. No Franco-Spanish union took place, although the two countries remained close allies for most of the next century because of their common interests. France's eastern frontier was not significantly expanded. French armies had been repeatedly defeated, destroying the reputation for invincibility that had underwritten France's politico-military bargaining power. The economic base for France's army and navy was badly damaged, as was the already weak economic basis for Spain's army and navy.

Less obviously, Britain was, by 1713, beginning her successful bid for hegemony at sea via her maritime strategy. This development was underlined in 1718 when Spain tried to challenge the peace settlement by retaking her former possession of Sicily and was defeated at the battle of Cape Passero.

ROUND III: 1740–63

This 25-year war comprised two general European wars fought over a variety of issues, including further French attempts at hegemony, with an armed truce between the two wars, the War of Austrian Succession (1740–48), and the Seven Years War (1756–63).

During the first war, the land component of the British strategy was successful in helping the anti-hegemonic alliance to contain French expansion in Europe. But the maritime and power-projection components were not effectively coordinated, producing an inconclusive outcome. In contrast, in the second war Prime Minister William Pitt—Pitt the Elder—struck exactly the right balance between the sea, power-projection, and land components of his strategy. The land component tied down French forces and resources in Europe, mainly in Germany, while the sea and power-projection components decisively defeated France and gave Britain control over two continents, North America and India. Pitt's strategy also prevented France from making any significant gains in Europe, let alone gains that could offset her losses outside Europe.

GRAND STRATEGY

The twenty-five-year war included two basic conflicts, separate but interrelated. One was between Britain (plus her American colonies) and France (plus Spain) to decide whether Britain or France was to be the dominant imperial power outside Europe. Linked to this conflict was that between Britain and Spain. London was trying to acquire by force the more desirable parts of Spain's massive overseas empire, and began the War of Jenkins's Ear by attacking Spain in 1739.

The other basic conflict was caused by French and Prussian attempts to increase their European territories, France trying to do so on her eastern boundaries, while Prussia sought control of Silesia, which belonged to Hapsburg Austria. It was Prussia's occupation of Silesia in 1740 that triggered the first war, when Frederick the Great of Prussia took advantage of the new, therefore inexperienced, Hapsburg successor, the Empress Maria Theresa.

These conflicts produced a war between a French-led alliance of Spain, Prussia, and most major German states and an Anglo-Austrian alliance. The war was relatively indecisive, but economically exhausting; accordingly, the resulting 1748 Peace of Aix-la-Chappelle largely restored the status quo ante bellum. By retaining Silesia, Prussia alone made a major gain. To recover this territory, Austria reversed her previous opposition to French expansion and allied with France plus the anti-Prussian Russia. Prussia, in turn, reversed her previous alliance with France and switched to one with Britain, still opposing France. Following these diplomatic revolutions, the major powers embarked on the second Seven Years War.

BRITISH STRATEGY

The essence of British strategy and the interdependence of its naval, power-projection, and continental components was captured by the prime minister, the Duke of Newcastle:

> France will outdo us at sea when they have nothing to fear on land. I have always maintained that our marine should protect our alliances on the Continent, and so by diverting the expense of France, enable us to maintain our superiority at sea.[6]

The Seven Years War saw Britain use a fully developed strategy to fight a global conflict with France. William Pitt, prime minister from 1757–62, had a strategic vision:

At last there was a man who could see the war, and the world, as a whole. The vision was so clear it was a wonder no one had seen it before. English trade and money enabled Britain to subsidize allies on the Continent—in this case, Frederick the Great. That kept France busy. France's preoccupation with Germany allowed Britain to rule the seas, and command of the seas enabled her to build up her own empire overseas and destroy the French in the process. The greater the empire, the greater the volume of British trade, and the more money, a self-perpetuating circle that would go on indefinitely and make Britain the chief world power.[7]

The Anglo-French war really began in 1755, with clashes between their forces in North America and at sea, then merged into the general European war begun by Prussia's preemptive attack on Austria in 1756. Strategically, France made a major error by allying with Austria and committing France to a land war against Prussia, as well as to a naval and power-projection war, including amphibious operations, against Great Britain.

The French gamble came close to initial success. A British-Hanoverian army was fielded promptly, but was unable to prevent Austria, France, and Russia from inflicting potentially fatal defeats on Prussia. Prussia was saved by Frederick the Great's victories of Rossbach and Leuthen in 1757. Thereafter, Britain maintained a continental commitment comparable to those of earlier years. Even so, Prussia was on the verge of complete defeat by 1762 and was saved only by a reversal of Russian policy (to supporting Prussia) caused by the death of the Empress Elizabeth of Russia. Yet even if Frederick the Great had been defeated, Britain would still have been unassailable. As an insular sea power, it could thus survive, in the short term, even the complete defeat of its European land allies, provided maritime supremacy was retained. In the longer term, Britain would have been vulnerable to defeat at sea if, as could have happened in 1762, France had been victorious on land, allied to other major European land powers as well as Spanish seapower, and able to concentrate its resources on building a first-class French Navy.

Pitt the Elder's main strategic objective was to use British maritime supremacy to defeat the French empire in North America by a series of combined operations. By 1759 this objective largely had been achieved.

When the war formally started in 1756, the Royal Navy had 130 fighting ships to the French and Spanish navies' 63 and 45, and the British ships individually were superior in combat effectiveness. This superiority rested more on experience and personnel than on naval architecture. The opening naval battle of Minorca was inconclusive, but notable for the subsequent execution of the unfortunate British commander, Admiral John Byng, for failing to do his utmost to engage the enemy, symbolizing the Royal Navy's commitment to the offensive.

Then, in 1759, the year of victories, British maritime and power-projection forces won control of North America and gained complete supremacy at sea. The 1758 recapture of Louisbourg at the entrance to the St. Lawrence River enabled a combined operation to take Quebec City in 1759. This victory gave the British effective control over North America, confirmed by France's 1760 surrender of Montreal.

The British victory at Quebec was the culmination of two years of combined operations aimed at cutting the French SLOC and launching a three-pronged attack on French Canada. Although relatively small by the standards of contemporary European warfare, the forces involved were still large by the previous standards of what was then called colonial (and would now be called Third World) warfare. British maritime command served to provide strategic security for the safe dispatch of 22,000 troops in these operations. In contrast, Montcalm had only 8,000 troops in all of New France. The French Navy was too weak to relieve Louisbourg and lost twelve ships when the fortress fell.

The size of these British forces and their gains is striking when compared to those of the French forces in Europe and their gains. Britain deployed 22,000 troops plus major naval forces to North America and gained control over a continent in a four-year campaign. France deployed armies of 125–150,000 in Germany and gained virtually nothing in a seven-year campaign. The greater leverage from forces correctly employed in power projection was clear.

The interaction between power projection and naval operations was shown by two Royal Navy victories in 1759 that eliminated any French hopes of challenging British command of the sea. In another attempt to unite the French fleet, the Toulon squadron sailed with twelve ships for Brest. They were intercepted by fourteen British ships. Five French ships fled for Cadiz and the remainder were captured or sunk at the Battle of Lagos (18 August 1759). Then, the French Brest squadron tried to sortie, with twenty-one ships, but was intercepted by twenty-nine British ships. In the ensuing Battle of Quiberon Bay (20 November 1759) seven French ships were captured or immobilized, for the loss of but two British combatant ships.

By taking the tactical offensive under appalling weather conditions that represented a real, but calculated, risk, the British Admiral Sir Edward Hawke thus gained a major strategic advantage. Britain proceeded to complete its conquest of North America and of the coastal areas of India where the British and French empires had been competing since 1701. Other effects of the Royal Navy's victories in 1759 were a sharp reduction in the effectiveness of France's *guerre de course*, and the substantial elimination of French seaborne trade.

British maritime and power-projection forces were later, in 1762, transferred to operations against the French sugar-producing West Indies islands (the equivalent, as producers of wealth, of modern oil fields) most of which were taken. Then, in retaliation for Spain's strategically illogical declaration of war in 1761, these British forces attacked the Spanish Empire. Another combined operation, including nineteen ships and 10,000 troops and marines, took Havana, the capital of Spanish Cuba, a major economic and naval blow. This was followed by the loss of Manila, capital of the Spanish Philippines, to another British conjunct expedition. These and other losses combined to compel Spain to join France in suing for peace.

NET RESULT

The 1763 Treaty of Paris represented a major victory for Britain's balanced maritime strategy. France renounced all territories and claims in Canada and the Ohio Valley and all territory east of the Mississippi River, except for New Orleans. In the East, France was reduced to the status of only a minor trading power in India. Spain ceded Florida to Britain, receiving Louisiana in exchange (from France) and the return of Cuba and the Philippines from Britain. Clearly, this was an exchange of geopolitically valuable territories on a grand scale, with the British coming out a long way ahead. Indeed, Britain could have retained even more territories had her new government not been willing to offer France and Spain moderate terms for a general European peace settlement.

In contrast, France gained virtually nothing in return for seven years of war. Spain had incurred serious economic losses in only two years of war. Of the other major powers, only Prussia, allied to British seapower, made any real gains, retaining Silesia.

The success of British strategy in the Seven Years War is remarkable, particularly in the larger perspective of the Anglo-French conflict that had started in 1689. From then until 1763, Britain had led four coalitions against French hegemony in four European wars. In only seventy-four years it had established itself as the dominant imperial power outside Europe, as the dominant maritime power in naval and commercial terms, and as a major European military power. As Mahan was to explain, the triangle of trade, colonies, and navy had been firmly established, and was giving Britain an increasing advantage in the resource base to support sea and land forces.

The role of the continental component of the British strategy was a necessarily limited but crucial one. Britain's land forces and subsidies had indeed been tying down French armies and resources in relatively very unprofitable European campaigns. In the words of Pitt the Elder, "America was conquered in Germany." The key to the successful implementation of the strategy lay in striking the balance between the naval and continental components appropriate to the strategic context of the day.

The only flaw in Pitt's strategy was his diversion of forces to large-scale, ineffective raids against the French coast. These were ineffective because relatively few French forces had to be diverted from the main European campaigns to evict the British from strategically useless territory. Pitt's critics rightly described such raids as the strategic misapplication of resources—breaking glass windows with gold coins.

Ironically, the culminating success of the British maritime strategy in the context of relatively limited warfare was followed by, indeed itself contributed to, Britain's greatest failure in this period: the War of American Independence.

ROUND IV: 1775–83

The War of American Independence demonstrated the potential vulnerability of a dominant maritime power. Such a power could be challenged by a land and sea power with a larger resource base able to concentrate its resources on its navy. The British Admiralty summed up the danger of such a French challenge:

> England till this time was never engaged in a sea war with the House of Bourbon thoroughly united, their naval force unbroken, and having no other war or object to draw off their attention and resources.[8]

The resultant course of the war showed the interdependence of the sea and land components of the British strategy.

There were really two wars being fought; one revolutionary, the other traditional. The revolutionary war was the one for American independence from British rule, an unlimited objective that was achieved. But because this was a revolutionary war, the now established British strategy would not work for two reasons. First, America was not an island or a small overseas territory that could be readily cut off by the Royal Navy. British forces (including the usual mercenaries) could be projected to America but could not win the war except by occupying the whole country—an undertaking beyond Britain's resources. As William Pitt, now Earl of Chatham, said, "You cannot conquer America."

The second reason was that Britain lacked any continental allies to pin down France and Spain in land wars that would absorb their resources, limiting the aid they could send an isolated America.

The traditional war for limited objectives was the one between Britain and France that began three years later. France wanted to reverse her previous defeats, and so aided the American revolutionaries "unofficially" until their 1777 victory at Saratoga made it worth openly allying with the new United States. This 1778 alliance meant that control of the Atlantic SLOC was crucial, particularly for the British. The American commander-in-chief, George Washington, stressed the crucial role of seapower to his French allies:

> In any operation, and under all circumstances, a decisive naval superiority is to be considered as a fundamental principle, and the basis upon which every hope of success must ultimately depend.[9]

But in this round of the Anglo-French conflict, it was the French who were in the stronger overall strategic position. Since France carefully refrained from threatening her neighbors, there was no anti-hegemonic alliance for Britain to organize. Instead, there was Spanish and Dutch resentment both of previous losses to Britain and of the arrogance with which Britain exercised her belligerent's rights at sea, leading these two countries to declare war on Great Britain in 1779.

French resources could thus be concentrated on maritime plus power-projection forces. The rebuilt French Navy's 80 combatant ships were as good as the Royal Navy's 150. The addition of Spain's sixty ships, although of poorer quality, gave the Franco-Spanish-Dutch alliance rough parity at sea. So Britain lost complete control of the sea, although France did not gain it: sea control came to depend on relative local naval strengths. French and British fleets individually convoyed their land forces to fight for control over North America, the West Indies, and India, and fought one another in actions for local sea control.

In home waters, the Royal Navy adopted an active fleet-in-being strategy to deter the combined Franco-Spanish fleet from convoying an invasion force to the British Isles. This strategy was successful, partly because the French were so fixed to a defensive way of thinking that they could not readily switch to an offensive mode. As Rear Admiral Sir Richard Kempenfelt wrote:

'Tis an inferior fleet against a superior fleet. Therefore the greatest skill and address is requisite to counteract the designs of the enemy, to watch and seize the favorable opportunity for action . . . and to oblige them to think of nothing but being on their guard against your attack.[10]

This strategy could not, though, stop Britain's defeat in America by a Franco-U.S. version of the classic British strategy. Their 1781 campaign was a model combined operation, comparable to the British campaign of 1759. General George Washington and the Marquis de Lafayette built up an army of 5,700 Continental Army regulars, 3,000 militia, and 7,000 French regulars (brought by sea). Their forces pinned down General Lord Cornwallis's British army of 8,000 at Yorktown, while Admiral de Grasse's twenty-four French ships blockaded the coast against British endeavors to rescue or assist Cornwallis from the sea.

The British tried to lift the blockade, but with only nineteen ships, under Vice Admiral Thomas Graves. The 5 September 1781 battle of Chesapeake Bay (or Virginia Capes) was a tactical standoff but strategically conclusive. Graves was obliged to break off the action after an unsuccessful attack and withdraw to New York when French reinforcements (eight ships) arrived four days later. As a result, Cornwallis surrendered on 19 October 1781, thereby ending British attempts to control its American colonies.

Elsewhere, the British Mediterranean bases were besieged, with Minorca falling (1782) but Gibraltar holding out and supplied by sea. The West Indies islands were falling to the French until the Royal Navy's victory of the battle of the Saintes (Dominica, 1782). This victory marked the culmination of a campaign in which the Royal Navy initially had been inferior. But it had, by constantly taking the offensive when possible, held off superior French forces until, at the Saintes, the Royal Navy had a superiority of thirty-six to thirty-three ships, each with technical innovations in gunnery that gave them a major advantage. In India, British and French forces were, after French reinforcements, fairly evenly balanced, but Britain gradually gained the upper hand, partly because of her superior integration of sea and land operations.

NET RESULTS

Unable to employ her traditional strategy against America and France, Britain accepted defeat in the form of American independence, but retained Canada. Britain persuaded her European opponents to accept a return to roughly the *status quo ante bellum* as the alternative to the conduct of a prospectively profitless protracted conflict. Their gains and Britain's damage were limited by her stronger strategic, especially maritime, position once Britain's forces were freed from their American commitments.

ROUND V: 1793–1815

This final round in the Anglo-French conflict lasted for twenty-two years, including the brief Peace of Amiens (1802–03). Britain defeated a much more powerful French bid for hegemony, based on revolutionary ideology and mass armies. But Britain had to adapt its strategy to deal with the collapse of its landpower allies in successive coalitions against France.

Essentially, the British adopted a long-haul strategy of refusing to accept French hegemony, waging economic warfare, offering subsidies of unprecedented size to allies, and waiting for France to make major strategic mistakes. To the extent that Britain's continued opposition encouraged France to make these mistakes by overextending itself, British seapower helped to set up the Emperor Napoleon to make them. When he made his first strategic mistake by invading Spain and Portugal in 1808, Britain fielded another continental expeditionary force to support Spanish and Portuguese armies and guerrillas. The Peninsular Army was supplied by the sea and wintered in its impregnable base behind the lines of Torres Vedras. The French Army had to try to neutralize this major base of support for Spanish and Portuguese forces. But the lines were so strong, utilizing the hills of the peninsula between the Tagus estuary and the sea, that they could only be taken, if at all, after a prolonged siege, and the French could not supply a large enough army that far into Portugal. In this strategic extension, British sea lines of communication were superior to French land lines, yet Britain held an asset that the French had to try to retake.

Napoleon's second mistake, his 1812 invasion of Russia, was caused by a complex of reasons. These included Napoleon's inability to tolerate Tsar Alexander I's personal and political position as head of a power as strong as France's and the failure of France's economic warfare against Britain (the Continental System). Tsarist opposition contributed to the failure of the Continental System. British military and economic assistance promptly flowed to Russia. This invasion so weakened Napoleon's Grand Army that Britain was able to form the fifth, and last, coalition against France, hold it together until France was defeated (1813–14) and use it to defeat Napoleon's return from exile (1815).

Britain's wars against Revolutionary France are thus a striking example of the truth of U.S. Admiral Carlisle H. Trost's recent statement that on its own seapower cannot win wars against great continental states, because they can only be won on land.

Because the Revolution destroyed the efficient French Navy of the previous war (1778–83), the sea war was, ultimately, a contest Great Britain was bound to win. The Royal Navy was at the height of its professionalism in the age of fighting sail, a professionalism epitomized by Admiral Lord Horatio Nelson, killed leading his fleet to victory at Trafalgar. Nelson's fleet of twenty-seven fighting ships attacked a Franco-Spanish fleet of thirty-three and destroyed both it and Napoleon's long-term plans to invade the British Isles—the sea campaign of the summer of 1805 already had caused Napoleon to abort his proposed invasion in August.

Establishing this unprecedented degree of maritime supremacy was arduous and resource consuming. But the end result was inevitable, so long as France could not concentrate her resources on her navy for the many years required to rebuild it. British policymakers were, though, always aware of the dangers of France doing so, a danger accurately assessed in the following terms in 1811: if French resources

> . . . which have hitherto been directed . . . to extending her conquests on shore, may hereafter be applied to naval affairs, it seems . . . very doubtful whether we could possibly preserve, for any great number of years, such a preponderance by sea against France . . . there must be . . . in course of time a superiority in number of ships and men on the part of our enemies which . . . no valour nor skill on our part will be able to withstand.[11]

Once established, the British maritime supremacy enabled it to acquire almost all of the overseas empires of France plus her Spanish and Dutch allies. Britain also was able to defeat France's one major power-projection operation, Napoleon's invasion of Egypt. Nelson destroyed the escorting French battle fleet at the Nile (1798), and the French army was contained and defeated by Anglo-Turkish forces, supplied and supported by the Royal Navy.

As in previous wars, the French *guerre de course* was indecisive. Moreover, the maritime supremacy of the Royal Navy enabled it to open up new markets in the Spanish and Portuguese colonies in Latin America when Napoleon's Continental System tried (unsuccessfully) to exclude British goods from Europe.

Yet even this unprecedented supremacy at sea could not directly defeat France on land, although it could guarantee Britain's short-term security against invasion. This security was reflected in Admiral Lord St. Vincent's dismissal of invasion fears, "I do not say that the Frenchman cannot come: I only say that he cannot come by sea."[12]

The balance between the maritime and continental components of British strategy shifted in favor of the naval elements, partly because of domestic political constraints on the size of the British Army and partly because French victories on land deprived Britain of an active fighting front it could join. Thanks to the defensive shield provided by the Royal Navy, Britain was able to avoid fielding much larger traditional or new mass armies. The continental commitment was made in the Low Countries and Germany until Britain's allies there were defeated (by 1797), and then, when Napoleon attacked Spain and Portugal, in the Peninsular War (1808–14). As Sir Michael Howard stressed, ". . . Wellington fought in the Peninsula as the Eighth Army fought in the Western Desert, because it was the only place where he could fight."[13]

The British contribution to the Peninsular War was similar to the earlier contribution to continental campaigns in that it consisted of enough troops and subsidies to ensure her partners' contributions. Great Britain also provided the commander-in-chief of the allied army, the Duke of Wellington. What made this commitment different was that it was so much smaller than those of Britain's European allies, yet was, as the foreign secretary warned, ". . . not merely a considerable part of the dispensable force of this country. It is, in fact the British Army."[14]

The limited Spanish-Portuguese commitment was nonetheless significant in military and political terms. Militarily, it tied down some 200,000 French troops and inflicted an annual attrition of 40,000 upon them—a cumulative total of 280,000. From 1812 onwards, when France invaded Russia, it recreated the French strategic nightmare of a war on two fronts.

The Spanish ulcer did not kill the Napoleonic Empire, but it accelerated its demise. It added to the ultimately fatal attrition inflicted on France's armies and commanders by Austria, Prussia, and Russia in 1809, by Russia in 1812–13, and by all three land powers in 1813–14. In this last campaign, British military assistance expenditures were larger than the total of her expenditure in all four previous coalitions against Napoleon.

Britain's role in the Waterloo campaign symbolized its synergistic value. Britain provided the Allied Army with subsidies, and 30 percent of its troops plus its commander, Wellington, while Prussia provided another army under Field Marshal Prince Blucher. Together, they beat Napoleon's army. Wellington's verdict on his role summarized the rationale for the continental commitment, "I don't think it would have been done unless I [and it] had been there."

NET RESULT

The peace settlement reached at the Congress of Vienna (1814–15) ended France's chances of bidding for European hegemony. Within Europe, territorial adjustments created a barrier against France's expanding into the Low Countries and Germany, backed up by the landpower of Austria, Russia, and much larger Prussia and a much smaller number of more powerful German states. Outside Europe, Britain retained almost all of France's overseas empire. In addition, Britain had established a maritime hegemony that lasted for virtually a century.

Great Britain thus emerged from the Anglo-French conflict not only victorious but more powerful, in terms of its economic and military (mainly naval) resource bases. In contrast, France was permanently weakened by the cumulative costs of her successive bids for hegemony, and never regained her position as the first among the European great powers.

NOTES

1. Michael Howard, "The British Way in Warfare: A Reappraisal," in *The Causes of War and Other Essays* (London: Maurice Temple Smith, 1983), p. 193.

2. *Ibid.*, p. 200, his emphasis.

3. Alfred T. Mahan, *The Influence of Sea Power Upon History, 1660–1805*, Antony Preston, ed. (London: Bison Books, 1980), p. 48.

4. As quoted in Vice-Admiral Philip Colomb, *Naval Warfare* (London: Edward Allen, 1899, 3rd ed.), pp. 115, 122.

5. As quoted in Arthur J. Marder, *The Anatomy of British Sea Power* (New York: Knopf, 1940), p. 473. Fisher added that, "These five keys belong to England . . ." They had done so since the U.K.'s final defeat of France in 1815.

6. As quoted in Admiral Sir Herbert Richmond, *Statesmen and Seapower* (Oxford: Clarendon Press, 1946), p. 117.

7. James L. Stokesbury, *Navy and Empire: A Short History of Four Centuries of British Sea Power* (New York: William Morrow and Co., 1983), p. 149.

8. As quoted in Richmond, p. 151.

9. General George Washington, "Memorandum for concerting a plan of operations with the French army," 15 July 1780, as quoted in Mahan, p. 173.

10. As quoted in Geoffrey Till and others, *Maritime Strategy and the Nuclear Age* (New York: St. Martin's Press, 1982, 1st ed.), p. 114.

11. C. W. Pasley, *Essay on the Military Policy and Institutions of the British Empire* (London, 2nd ed., 1811), pp. 2–3.

12. As quoted in G. J. Marcus, *The Age of Nelson: The Royal Navy, 1793–1815* (New York: Viking Press, 1979), p. 229.

13. Howard, p. 200.

14. Foreign Secretary George Canning's warning was given to Wellington's predecessor, Sir John Moore, killed at Corunna (1808), but it applied equally to Wellington. See Christopher Hibbert, *Corunna* (London: Batsford Books, 1961), p.32.

BIBLIOGRAPHICAL NOTE

The clearest analysis of British maritime strategy as a whole, including its maritime, power-projection, and continental components is James L. Stokesbury, *Navy and Empire* (New York: William Morrow, 1983). He covers the Anglo-French conflict in pp. 80–214 and offers useful "Suggestions for Further Reading," pp. 407–16.

To understand how the Anglo-French conflict looked to the naval commanders and governments fighting it, their own accounts should be sampled and translated into current strategic terms to see how little the principles of maritime strategy change. Two accessible, condensed sources are Geoffrey Till and others, *Maritime Strategy and the Nuclear Age* (New York: St. Martin's Press, 1986, second ed.), Alfred T. Mahan, *The Influence of Sea Power Upon History, 1660–1805* (London: Bison Books, 1980). The broader political-military context is usefully summarized, with excellent maps, in Paul Langford, *Modern British Foreign Policy: The Eighteenth Century 1688–1815* (New York: St. Martin's Press, 1976).

The best account of the Royal Navy at the peak of its power and professionalism in the age of fighting sail, the French Revolutionary and Napoleonic wars, is G. J. Marcus, *The Age of Nelson: The Royal Navy, 1793–1815* (New York: Viking Press, 1979). An additional account, accurate although fictional, was given by the novelist C. S. Forester. He did for Nelson's navy what Tom Clancy has done for the present U.S. Navy in the Horatio Hornblower novels beginning with *Midshipman Hornblower* and ending with *Lord Hornblower*.

ADDITIONAL SOURCES

Barnett, Corelli. *Britain and Her Army, 1509–1970: A Military, Political and Social Survey.* London: Penguin Press, 1970.

Howard, Michael. "The British Way in Warfare: A Reappraisal," in Howard, *The Causes of War.* London: Maurice Temple Smith, 1983.

Hughes, Wayne P., Jr. *Fleet Tactics: Theory and Practice.* Annapolis, MD: Naval Institute Press, 1986.

Kennedy, Paul M. *The Rise and Fall of British Naval Mastery.* London: Allen Lane, 1976.

Mordal, Jacques. *Twenty-five Centuries of Sea Warfare.* English ed. London: Abbey Library, 1973.

Potter, E. B. *Seapower.* Englewood Cliffs: Prentice Hall, 1960.

8

Naval Power in World War I

BY WILLIAMSON MURRAY

For almost one hundred years European society remained largely at peace. From Napoleon's defeat at Waterloo to the outbreak of war in August 1914, few conflicts punctuated the decades of quiet. Only the Crimean War (between Russia on the one hand and Britain and France on the other), the Seven Weeks War (between Prussia and Austria), and the Franco-Prussian War brought major European states into conflict. Even though this was a period of exceptionally rapid technological change, naval activity followed recognizable strategic patterns. The Crimean War and the Seven Weeks War each had some important naval activity. The former demonstrated how seapower might be used to fix enemy ground forces in place, not permitting them to concentrate against friendly forces ashore. It offered examples also of the value of navies in transporting and supporting ground forces over long supply lines, which enabled the French and British to prevail against the Russians in the Baltic and Black seas. The latter conflict demonstrated how a fleet can win a decisive victory at sea and yet fail to affect the war's outcome significantly. The Austrian fleet humiliated the Italian forces at the battle of Lissa, but Austria was unable to prevent Italy from achieving its objectives.

World War I was a massive, protracted conflict between the major nations, and naval power played a crucial role in the evolution of the great land campaigns. By its indirect strategical impact on military operations as well as by its economic implications, naval power contributed critically to the defeat of the Central Powers (Germany and Austria-Hungary) by the Triple Entente (Great Britain, France, and Czarist Russia) and the United States (never directly allied to the coalition but from 1917 to 1918 an associated power in the war).

World War I raised strategic, political, and even technological issues and problems that still confront the use of naval power today. How navies responded to those issues are, thus, of current relevance. The questions that the First World War posed suggest many of the problems that would confront American naval planners and forces in a confrontation with the Soviet Union.

THE BACKGROUND: TECHNOLOGY AND STRATEGY

To understand the difficulties facing the employment of maritime forces in the 1914–1918 war, one must understand two key factors: the impact of technology on naval power, and the adaptation of navies to radical changes in ship and weapons capability. Over the previous decades a technological revolution gathered speed as the navies approached 1914. That revolution radically altered everything from ship design to propulsion and weaponry at an accelerating tempo. With the construction of the *Dreadnought*-type battleship in 1905 by the Royal Navy, the technological race moved even faster than it had at the end of the nineteenth century. The increasing capabilities of ships show most clearly in the range and effectiveness of gunnery. At a range of 6,000-plus yards, U.S. Navy ships in the Spanish-American War had found it difficult to hit their Spanish opponents. At Manila Bay, American ships fired 5,895 shells with only 142 hits; Santiago told much the same story—8,000 shots with only 121 hits. Seven years later at Tsushima Strait, Russian and Japanese ships fought at twice that range. By 1915, the fifteen-inch guns on the British battleship *Queen Elizabeth* could throw a shell 35,000 yards.

Before gunnery ranges began their dramatic upswing, propulsion technology was radically increasing ship speed. By the late 1890s, the introduction of steam turbines enabled destroyers to reach 36-knot speeds, twice what had been possible a decade before. Further complicating technology's impact on the naval scene was the emergence of new weapon systems whose significance was difficult to estimate until tested in combat. The airplane and the lighter-than-air zeppelin made their appearance, while the submarine and torpedo represented significant threats. But what kind of threat and to whom was not entirely clear. Another imponderable further complicated the problem of war at sea. By 1914, radio allowed admiralties on shore and naval commanders at sea to control the movement of ships that were over the horizon. This represented a major break with the past, where naval commanders had to possess discretionary authority because they could not maintain direct contact with command authorities.

The navies of the major powers had to adapt to this revolutionary environment. The dreadnoughts of 1910 bore little resemblance to the ships on which their commanders had begun their naval careers. Moreover, as late as 1911, the British Admiralty possessed no proper staff; as a result, it was incapable in 1911 of articulating an alternative to the wholesale commitment of Britain's land forces onto the continent to defend France. The British Cabinet was so unimpressed with the navy's presentation that it fully endorsed the army strategy and sent Winston Churchill to the Admiralty to create a modern naval staff.

A great naval race between Britain and Imperial Germany marked the immediate period before the First World War. That race was a major determinant in the shape of the coming naval contest as well as in the character and shape of the war itself. At the turn of the century, Britain still enjoyed what her statesmen termed "splendid isolation." But the Boer War, a misdirected and incompetently led conflict to bring all of South Africa under British control, underlined British vulnerabilities. At best, the other European powers regarded the British with suspicion and hostility. The ruthless prosecution of that war further exacerbated Britain's relations with the continental powers. Nevertheless, no matter how sympathetic European powers were to the Afrikaners, without first-class naval power they had no effective means of intervention, and they lacked political leverage.

At this point the Germans launched a great challenge to the Royal Navy's dominance of the world's oceans. Partially as a result of misreading Alfred Thayer Mahan, Germany's leadership embarked on a massive naval program. The key individuals in this program were Emperor Wilhelm II, and Admiral Alfred von Tirpitz. Tirpitz was the architect of the challenge to Britain. Playing on Wilhelm's inclinations and those of others among Germany's political leaders, Tirpitz persuaded the nation that the Reich required a great fleet to ensure herself "a place in the sun." Tirpitz put together a powerful political coalition to support construction of a "High Sea Fleet."

Tirpitz presented his arguments for massive increases in German naval power under the smoke screen of what he termed "the risk theory." Germany aimed to build a large enough fleet that Britain would not dare risk the Royal Navy in war. Even should the British defeat this new fleet, their losses would leave them vulnerable to the French and Russian navies. Therefore, argued Tirpitz, once Germany had such a fleet Britain would never risk war with the Reich, would accept German colonial advances, and might even make an alliance with Germany. Tirpitz's arguments excluded the possibility that the British could join the anti-German coalition of France and Russia; after all, the British had a long tradition of hostility towards those powers.

Tirpitz's real aim most probably was not to build simply a "risk fleet," but rather to build a fleet capable of defeating the Royal Navy in battle. His papers indicate a belief that Germany could outbuild the degenerate British in a sustained armaments race. Moreover, he believed that British commitments in the Far East and in the Mediterranean (against the French and the Russians) would enable the German High Sea Fleet to concentrate superior strength in the North Sea. The Germans could then fight a climactic battle that would destroy British naval power and snatch away the British Empire. Tirpitz's strategic approach rested on a peculiarly German set of assumptions: Britain could not settle her differences with France or Russia; the degenerate British could not match a German naval buildup in either sailors or resources; the continental strategic situation would remain stable and allow Germany to concentrate on a naval buildup with little additional support needed for the army; and the British could never concentrate their naval strength in the North Sea because of worldwide commitments.

Tirpitz's assumptions proved false. The British regarded the naval buildup as a direct challenge. Massive outlays in Germany for battleships met with even greater outlays for the Royal Navy. As Winston Churchill commented on debates in Britain in 1909 about how many battleships were necessary to meet the German naval challenge: "The Admiralty had demanded six ships: The economists offered four: and we finally compromised on eight."[1]

The British did more than accept the naval challenge. With skillful diplomacy, they advanced their naval security in the North Sea and their political connections throughout the world. In 1902, the Anglo-Japanese alliance allowed the return of the Far Eastern squadron to home waters. In 1904, an Anglo-French Entente settled outstanding issues between the two nations. In 1907, an Anglo-Russian agreement did the same for relations with the Czarist Empire. In neither case did Britain make an alliance, but the understandings underlined British strategic support for the Franco-Russian alliance. By 1911, the British had committed their army to fight alongside the French Army.

In 1912, further negotiations with the French culminated in an agreement that allowed the Royal Navy to remove its battleships from the Mediterranean and the French to concentrate their fleet in that sea. The agreement provided that the British would cover the Atlantic Coast of France, while the French looked after British interests in the Mediterranean.

The rising tensions in Europe made clear to European statesmen and generals that war was a real possibility. On the continent, the general staffs did not calculate that naval power would play a significant role in the coming conflict. The French general Ferdinand Foch claimed that the British navy would not be worth "a single bayonet."

Similarly, the German general staff counted the High Sea Fleet as possessing virtually no significance. There was, moreover, no coordination between the German Army and Navy. German operational planning for the outbreak of war (a great invasion of France through Belgium—the infamous Schlieffen Plan) virtually guaranteed that Britain would enter the war at the outset. Despite the fact that as early as 1906 the German general staff calculated that the British would have 100,000 men fighting alongside the French, the army *never* requested that the High Sea Fleet interfere with the transfer of British troops to the Continent. For its part, the navy never asked the army to include in the Schlieffen Plan the capture of the French ports along the English Channel. In August and early September 1914 a few German cavalry divisions could have seized those channel ports all the way to the Somme estuary. When the Germans tried to seize those ports in October, however, they suffered heavy casualties and failed in the attempt.

Germany's naval strategy, like that of the army, rested on rigid assumptions. Tirpitz believed that the Royal Navy would maintain a close blockade of the German coast. After submarines, mines, and torpedoes had inflicted substantial losses on the British, the High Sea Fleet would emerge and in a decisive battle would crush British naval power for all time. As Tirpitz once stated: "In a war at sea, destruction of the enemy rather than territorial gain is the only goal."[2] However, as one historian of the German Imperial Navy notes:

> Seapower, in a word, consists of fleet and position: one is useless without the other. Tirpitz either ignored or never grasped Alfred Thayer Mahan's unwritten presupposition that unfettered access to the world's oceans was the cardinal prerequisite for seapower. Given that Britain was Germany's primary potential opponent, a brief glance at the map will confirm the obvious: the British could bottle up the German fleet . . . in the North Sea if they chose to close the straits of Dover and the waters between

Scotland and Norway. Despite this Tirpitz failed to develop an alternative strategy.[3]

The British came close to playing into Tirpitz's hands. Until 1912, British naval plans involved the immediate imposition of a close blockade on the German coast. Admiral "Jackie" Fisher even suggested landing a portion of the British Army on Germany's Pomeranian coast. Such thoughts were entirely unrealistic. In 1912, however, the Admiralty took the momentous decision to abandon the close blockade. By early 1914, the British had determined that in war their "Grand Fleet" would move to the anchorage of Scapa Flow in the Orkney Islands. A smaller fleet unit would guard the English Channel. Surprisingly, even with this crucial decision, the Admiralty did little to prepare Scapa Flow and anchorages along the Scottish coast. Therefore, few submarine nets and other basic defenses protected the Grand Fleet at Scapa Flow in August 1914. Luckily, the Germans, given their operational concepts, undertook no preparations to attack these crucial bases.

Like the Germans, the Royal Navy expected a great, climactic battle at sea. By imposing a distant blockade in the North Sea (from the Orkneys to Norway) and by closing the Channel, they expected that the High Sea Fleet would come out to break the blockade. The great sea battle would then take place in the middle of the North Sea.

One must have some sympathy with the navies of 1914. None of the senior leadership had been involved in a war involving significant naval forces. The technological revolution had had an enormous impact on fleet capabilities, but prewar exercises and training could give only a dim outline of what admirals could expect in a major battle. If the general staffs were correct, the war would be short and decisive, and naval power would play an unimportant role. If they were wrong, then naval power might play a crucial role in the long-term outcome. But even the admirals had no clear idea of how navies might contribute to victory in a long war.

THE OUTBREAK OF WAR

The assassination of the heir to the Austro-Hungarian throne in June 1914 sent shock waves through Europe. Nevertheless, few in Europe expected that events in the Balkans might spark a great world war. Germany's ambassador in London did make clear to his government that should German armies invade the Low Countries, Britain would enter the war at the side of France and Russia. Coincidental with the growing international crisis, the Royal Navy had scheduled a mobilization of its reserve naval forces. On July 17–18 it held a great review of the fleet at Spithead; thereafter, the reservists were scheduled to demobilize and return home. With Europe tumbling over the brink, Winston Churchill halted the demobilization, and in the early morning hours of the night of July 30 the fleet steamed out to take up its war stations.

In July 1914, the British enjoyed a superiority of twenty to thirteen in modern battleships, and in battle cruisers four to three. In addition, the Royal Navy possessed four battle cruisers on detached duty elsewhere. The British also enjoyed a further advantage in that they had a number of dreadnoughts close to completion (eleven would join the Grand Fleet by the end of the war). Finally, British dockyards recently had completed work on two battleships for the Turks and one for the Chileans. Churchill ordered the navy to seize those ships. That decision was, however, to have important repercussions on events in the Mediterranean and Balkan theaters.

Before turning to the impact of naval power on the war, we might usefully examine the two fleets and their leadership. The Grand Fleet enjoyed a considerable advantage in numbers, one that would grow as the war continued. In terms of materiel, the two fleets were similar. German ships were more heavily armored, but British battleships carried larger guns. While the Germans enjoyed some small advantages in technology such as range-finding devices, these were by no means sufficient to outweigh the Royal Navy's numerical superiority.

The leadership of both navies was also substantially similar. Admiral Lord Jellicoe, commander of the Grand Fleet for the first half of the war, was a highly competent, cautious commander. At Jutland, on the last day of May 1916, he made the crucial decisions that came close to destroying the High Sea Fleet. Nevertheless, he lacked the fire that separates competent officers from truly great commanders. As Churchill noted after the war, "Jellicoe was the only man who could have lost the war in an afternoon"; he did not lose at Jutland, but he failed at that one moment of opportunity to destroy the High Sea Fleet when it was trapped in the North Sea.

Jellicoe was well served by the commander of the battle cruiser scouting force, Admiral David Beatty. Beatty displayed aggressiveness and a willingness to take risks (but never foolish ones). He would lead the Grand Fleet in the last half of the war. Unfortunately, the Royal Navy's staffs and subordinate commanders exhibited a lack of initiative and a tendency to interpret orders with pedantic obtuseness. The weaknesses of the staff work showed glaringly in the failure to incorporate intelligence into operations. At Jutland, even before the sun set on 31 May, the Admiralty possessed intelligence that the German fleet intended to return to port via Horn's Reef. It never passed that information on to the fleet at sea and as a result, the Germans escaped.[4] In addition to the problems in staff work, the decades of peace before 1914 had led the Royal Navy to place an emphasis on obedience to orders above the other characteristics that it sought in its officer corps. The weakness of such an approach in the confusion and complexities of "real" war with its attendant frictions showed most glaringly at Jutland.

The German naval officer corps showed few substantial differences from its British opponents. The Germans had possessed a naval staff for considerably longer than had the Royal Navy, but in Wilhelmian Germany this was not necessarily an advantage. As one historian notes:

> It is symptomatic of the tangled web of German military organization that the navy's highest *administrative* officer, Tirpitz as head of the Navy Office, should have dictated *strategy* to the fleet. It was only the admiral's great influence with the Emperor that permitted this state of affairs to exist. Tirpitz preferred organizational decentralization in order to prevent the emergence of a possible rival. . . . The Admiralty staff, which was charged with developing strategy at sea, was kept powerless by Tirpitz. There were no less than seven different heads of this organization between 1899 and 1915.[5]

As a result, the German naval staff lacked authority, training, and confidence to meet the challenges of war. The failings in German staff work help explain how British cryptographic intelligence was able to break German naval codes for virtually the entire war without the Germans appreciating the fact.

The Royal Navy's decision to maintain a distant blockade undermined the fundamental tenet of Germany's naval strategy. With the British declaration of war on 4 August, the German battleships cleared for action, expecting a sortie into the Heligoland Bight by the Royal Navy. The German emperor, however, refused to allow his admirals to embark on an aggressive strategy in the North Sea for fear that his navy might lose a capital ship. Twice in the first month and a half of war, the British offered battle near Heligoland. On August 28, Beatty with his battle cruisers swept into the waters near Heligoland and sank three light cruisers. Admiral Ingenohl refused to engage, and low tides prevented the High Sea Fleet's dreadnoughts from leaving Wilhelmshaven. Nevertheless, defective Royal Navy staff work and planning resulted in much confusion on the British side and in a lack of coordination—so much so that British light forces operating out of Harwich never knew until action had begun that Beatty's battle cruisers were operating in support.

In the euphoria over the first success, the Royal Navy did not absorb the warning that these considerable defects should have suggested. In fact, with better planning and coordination, the British might have bagged all of the German light cruisers operating near Heligoland. Nevertheless, as Churchill pointed out in his memoirs, the first victory reinforced the Royal Navy's sense of superiority:

> Much more important than these material gains was the effect produced upon the morale of the enemy. The Germans knew nothing of our defective staff work and the risks we had run. All they saw was that the British did not hesitate to hazard their greatest vessels as well as their light craft in the most daring offensive action and had apparently escaped unscathed. . . . The results of this action were far-reaching. Henceforward the weight of the British naval prestige lay heavy across all German sea enterprise.[6]

This start was followed in early September by the picture of the entire Grand Fleet parading off Heligoland at a distance of only twelve miles. German fleet commanders had their hands tied by the kaiser and were obliged to refuse battle.

Inaction in the North Sea masked the fact that throughout the world the British now imposed a general control over the oceans. German and Austrian merchant vessels ran desperately for neutral harbors (over one million tons of the Central Powers' shipping was interned in the United States alone). However, in the Pacific, a German squadron under Admiral Count von Spee caught an inferior British squadron off the coast of Chile at the battle of Coronel. With superior guns, Spee destroyed the British cruisers in short order.

Spee's November victory was short-lived. After being feted by the German colony at Valparaiso in Chile, Spee headed for the South Atlantic. Meanwhile, Admiral Fisher, recently returned as First Sea Lord (commander-in-chief of the Royal Navy), and Churchill acted with dispatch after receiving word of the disaster at Coronel. Despite the narrow balance in the North Sea, Fisher and Churchill ordered out three battle cruisers from the Grand Fleet, one to the Caribbean and two to the South Atlantic. By chance, the latter were coaling at Port Stanley in the Falklands when Spee arrived to shell the port. The two battle cruisers quickly effected the destruction of Spee's squadron. Elsewhere the British hunted down isolated German ships or squadrons. While some German ships, such as the light cruiser *Emden*, enjoyed successful careers as commerce destroyers, the British picked

off *three* times the tonnage sunk by German raiders in the merchantmen they seized in the war's first weeks.

In the Mediterranean, however, the British did not run down the
German ships on station, the battle cruiser *Goeben* and the light cruiser
Breslau. That failure carried weighty consequences.[7] In the confused
days of late July 1914, the Germans neglected to order the *Goeben*
and *Breslau* to leave the Mediterranean until too late. Muddle in London and ineptitude in the Mediterranean allowed the *Goeben* and
Breslau to escape to the Dardanelles. The Turks, angered by the seizure of the two dreadnoughts by the Royal Navy, hesitated for two
days to allow them entrance into the straits, but finally allowed the
Goeben and *Breslau* through the Dardanelles. The Turkish government "purchased" the two ships, but the German crews remained on
board, and to all intents and purposes the Turks had committed
themselves to fight with the Central Powers.

While it is possible that the Turks might have committed to Germany anyway, the *Goeben* and *Breslau* affair forced the Turks to make
a hasty judgment, based largely on prewar prejudices. Pro-German
by inclination, the Turks took their nation into the war. In September
they closed the Dardanelles, and in October the *Goeben* and *Breslau*
attacked Sevastopol, completing Turkey's entrance into the war. The
closing of the Dardanelles cut off Czarist Russia from access to world
markets. She could no longer export her wheat or import the raw
materials and the finished products to make good the weaknesses in
her war economy. The Germans obviously closed the Baltic; Murmansk and the Arctic provided an uncertain route; finally, the Trans-
Siberian railroad, single-track for much of its length, could not carry
the tonnage required to support the weaker areas in the Russian production of munitions. Thus, the failure to catch the *Goeben* and *Breslau* before they reached the Dardanelles had a crucial strategic impact on the war.

The events on land through the late summer and fall underscored
how faulty had been prewar assumptions that a European war would
be of short duration. Nowhere did the great armies achieve a decisive
victory. The German Army won much territory with its execution of
the Schlieffen Plan. Nevertheless, weary German troops had failed on
the Marne and Allied counterattacks battered them back to the Aisne.
Thus, by November a great line of trenches ran from the English
Channel to Switzerland, and the two opposing sides, having done
little to prepare for a prolonged war, now scrambled desperately to
mobilize the manpower and economic resources for a prolonged

struggle. With the Royal Navy's control over the world's oceans, the Allied powers enjoyed the long-term advantage.

GALLIPOLI AND COMBINED OPERATIONS

Turkey's entrance into the war at Germany's side immediately isolated Russia; the Turks also threatened the Suez Canal and the Caucasus. Moreover, by their religion the Turks possessed the means to spread unrest among the Islamic populations of the empires of the Allied powers. As historian Llewellyn Woodward notes:

> For all these reasons the Entente Powers—France and Russia as well as Great Britain—had a direct interest in dealing as rapid and as heavy a blow as possible against Turkey. British seapower offered an opportunity for striking at any one of the vulnerable points of the Turkish Empire without employing a dangerously large number of troops—"dangerously large" in the sense that Great Britain and France could not afford to weaken themselves [on the Western Front].[8]

In December 1914 Churchill focused on the particular impasse to which events on the Western Front had come. Churchill warned the prime minister:

> I think it quite possible that neither side will have the strength to penetrate the others' lines in the Western theater. Belgium particularly, which is vital to Germany . . . , has no doubt been made into a mere succession of fortified lines . . . without attempting to take a final view, my impression is that the position of both armies is not likely to undergo any decisive change—although no doubt several hundred thousand men will be spent to satisfy the military mind on the point . . . on the assumption that these views are correct, the question arises, how ought we to apply our growing military power? Are there not other alternatives than sending our armies to chew barbed wire in Flanders? Further, cannot the power of the Navy be brought more directly to bear upon the enemy?[9]

In early 1915 an advisor to the Cabinet highlighted the Dardanelles as a strategic alternative to the impasse on the Western Front. The Royal Navy, including its commander-in-chief, Fisher, fell into line enthusiastically, but the army proved uncertain and unclear in its support. The head of the War Office, Field Marshal Lord Kitchener, saw some merit in the Dardanelles scheme, but refused to give the full weight of his prestige to the project. The generals on the Western Front adamantly—almost fanatically—argued that nothing could be spared from the fighting in France.

Churchill thought that the navy alone should take the risk of forcing the straits without a supporting ground campaign. Consequently, beginning in February 1915, the British mounted a massive naval assault on the Dardanelles forts. The attacking force was constituted of mostly obsolescent, pre-*Dreadnought* battleships. The assault came close to success, but bad luck combined with a leadership that refused to take risks to defeat the wholly naval enterprise. In Britain the failure furthered a growing rift between Fisher and Churchill, while fueling political dissatisfaction with the conduct of the war at sea.

Once embarked on the venture, however, the British could not easily back away with dignity. Since the naval operation had failed, the government felt obliged to launch an army onto the Gallipoli Peninsula to force the Dardanelles. Kitchener, who reversed his position many times, announced that troops were available: the 29th Regular Division and a corps of Australian and New Zealand troops in Egypt. Unfortunately, Kitchener's reversal had come too late; fully alarmed by the naval bombardment, the Turks, urged on by German advisers, reinforced the defenses on the Gallipoli Peninsula.

Now began the ill-fated campaign on land. Perhaps no campaign of the First World War better illustrates the tactical and operational difficulties of that conflict. A brilliant strategic stroke, that at least held the prospect of breaking the deadlock, failed because of inept tactical and operational leadership and the problems that modern fire power posed to armies mired in nineteenth-century tactical conceptions. In April, two major landings placed large numbers of troops ashore on the tip of the peninsula and up the coast. While these amphibious operations were hardly impressive, they did get the troops, supplies, and equipment onto land. The problem was that tactical leadership on shore was so lacking that victory was thrown away. British and imperial troops failed to capture the heights; the Turks dug in, and the front settled down to trench warfare similar to the Western Front.

Failure at Gallipoli resulted in political crisis in London; the Churchill-Fisher partnership broke down and Fisher's resignation resulted in the replacement of both men. In Fisher's case this was probably not a bad thing; Churchill's removal from the councils of Britain's war leadership was disastrous. Conservative politicians and Western Front generals discredited Churchill and abandoned the assault on the Dardanelles entirely.

The strategic results of failure in the one great joint operation of the war were immediate and direct: Turkey remained unbroken. Her armies posed a direct threat to Britain's vital link, the Suez Canal; and, along with the British need to secure a victory, led the British to mount a far larger expedition into Palestine than Gallipoli had ever been. Material shortages had crippled the initiative in the Dardanelles, yet withdrawal from Gallipoli saved nothing for the Western Front. In the Balkans, moreover, the failure had catastrophic results. Bulgaria, looking at British ineptitude, decided that the Central Powers would win. She joined the Germans, and in the fall of 1915 German, Bulgarian, and Austro-Hungarian armies destroyed Serbia. The results convinced Rumania to remain neutral (for a year, at least). Finally, the lack of an Allied threat in the Balkans allowed the Germans to pound the Russian armies to pieces. Beginning with their Gorlice-Tarnow offensive, the Germans drove the Russians back 300 miles. The defeats inflicted on Czarist armies in 1915 were a major factor in the collapse of that regime in 1917 and the triumph of the Bolsheviks.

In judging Gallipoli, Churchill defended his approach in 1916:

> It is not right to condemn operations of war simply because they involve risk and uncertainty. Some operations can and ought to be made certainties. Others belong to the class where one can only balance the chances, and action must proceed on a preponderance of favorable chances. For instance, the naval attack on the Dardanelles in its final and decisive phase was, of course, a sharp hazard of war. But so were a great many other things done since the outbreak [of war] . . . Withdrawing two battle-cruisers from the Grand Fleet to the Falklands to destroy von Spee was a risk. Every time the Grand Fleet has swept down to the German coast there is a heavy risk. . . . All of these operations, on which the successful prosecution of the naval war has been founded, were pervaded by grave elements of risk in matters of superior importance to the attack on the Dardanelles. Therefore it is idle to condemn operations because they involve hazard and uncertainty. All war is hazard. Victory is only wrested by running risks.[10]

DOGGER BANK AND JUTLAND

The initial contact between the Grand Fleet and the High Sea Fleet had ended very much to the former's advantage. Now at the end of 1914, the complexities of combat intruded themselves on the sensibilities of navies whose preparations remained anchored in the peacetime environment of the prewar period.

The inaction of the High Sea Fleet ended in early November 1914. A raiding force of eight German cruisers crossed the North Sea and attacked Yarmouth. One month later a more ambitious raid hit Scarborough. Ingenohl sent Admiral Franz von Hipper with the German battle cruiser force to execute this mission.

In October 1914 the British had received from the Russians a code book containing the most important operational code of the German

Navy; that same month a British fishing vessel recovered from the North sea's floor another important code, the *Verkehrsbuch* (VB); previously, in early August 1914 the German Admiralty's merchant code had fallen into British hands. For the remainder of the war the Royal Navy deciphered nearly every important signal the German Navy made. Consequently, the British knew about Hipper's raid before he left harbor. What they did not know was that at the last moment Ingenohl decided to take the entire High Sea Fleet out to support his battle cruisers. Thus, for one brief moment, the balance of naval power in the North Sea trembled.

The Admiralty sent Beatty with four battle cruisers and six fast battleships to meet Hipper. The Germans, thus, confronted the tactical situation of their dreams: a detachment of the Grand Fleet was at sea facing the whole High Sea Fleet. The Germans, however, hindered by cautionary orders and the timidity of their commanders, lost the opportunity. When Ingenohl ran into the destroyers screening Beatty's battle cruisers and battleships, he assumed that the entire Grand Fleet was at sea and turned and fled back toward the Heligoland Bight. In effect, he was abandoning Hipper's battle cruisers. Now the British force, between Hipper and Ingenohl, was in a position to destroy the enemy battle cruisers. In the terrible North Sea weather of December, however, Beatty's signals were misread by the light cruisers who had contact with the German raiding force. Turning back on Beatty's forces they lost that contact and the Germans escaped through squalls and heavy showers.

Scarborough, a disappointment to both sides, was soon followed by a major engagement between the battle-cruiser fleets in the North Sea. In mid-January the Germans again raided Britain's east coast. Decrypted signals alerted the British to what was afoot; Beatty with the battle cruisers and Jellicoe with the Grand Fleet up-anchored almost concurrently with the German movement from the Jade in the early evening hours of January 23. In the dawn hours of the next morning the two fleets made contact. Hipper, to his horror, discovered the British reception committee. Moreover, the Germans had taken to sea the *Blücher*, the earliest German battle cruiser, with a top speed much slower than his other ships. Hipper immediately ran for home, but with the *Blücher* holding up the flight he found his ships steadily giving way to Beatty's battle cruisers. The British were soon in range. Despite confusion among Beatty's ships as to which enemy ship was their target, the British gave the Germans a heavy pounding. One of the results of this action was that the Germans changed their procedure for handling ammunition, and emphasized safety in a fashion hitherto not the case. That would prove an important advantage at Jutland.

For the second time in two months the British had been at sea waiting for the High Sea Fleet but had been unable to deliver a decisive blow. That the British had anticipated them should have warned the German naval staff that the security of their signals was in trouble. Nevertheless, as in the Second World War, the Germans explained away their difficulties, not as reflecting of signal compromises but as the result of traitors in the naval staff or of British spies in German ports.

The Battle of the Dogger Bank underlined how difficult it would be for the Germans to achieve a substantial success against the Grand Fleet in the North Sea. The numerical disparity had become great enough so that the Germans now could afford no losses; the British, on the other hand, had such superiority that they could readily accept the hazard of battle—at least on their own terms. The advantages of geography and position allowed them to dominate the High Sea Fleet and effectively shut the Germans off from the world's commerce.

Over the next year the High Sea Fleet remained confined in port as the Germans carried out the first unrestricted submarine offensive. But in spring 1916 with the temporary halt in submarine warfare, and with a new aggressive commander, Admiral Reinhard Scheer, the High Sea Fleet sailed forth again—virtually for the last time in the war. The same factors that had worked against the Germans at the Dogger Bank now worked against them in what was to be known as the Battle of Jutland. For the only time in the war both major fleets were in contact for a substantial period of time, and the Grand Fleet actually maneuvered itself between the High Sea Fleet and its harbors.

Three hours before the Germans were at sea, the Grand Fleet left Scapa Flow. Jellicoe steamed south with twenty-four battleships, three battle cruisers, eight armored cruisers, twelve light cruisers, and fifty-one destroyers. Half an hour later Beatty's force left Rosyth in Scotland with four super battleships (the *Queen Elizabeth* class with the armor of battleships and almost the speed of battle cruisers), six battle cruisers, fourteen light cruisers, and twenty-seven destroyers. The Germans left the Jade several hours later with sixteen battleships, five battle cruisers, eleven light cruisers, and sixty-one destroyers; in addition, Scheer made the mistake of taking along six pre-dreadnought battleships whose speed served only to slow his whole fleet. The nickname of these ships, "five-minute" ships, summed up their crews' expectations as to how long they would last in combat with battleships.

The battle cruisers ran into each other in the early afternoon. Hipper ran south, luring Beatty and his ships towards the High Sea Fleet. In the pursuit south, two of Beatty's battle cruisers blew up, the most probable cause being the inadequacy of safety measures between turrets and magazines. Beatty almost lost his flagship, *Lion*, to the same cause, but a dying turret commander ordered the magazines flooded. At 1633 hours the British spotted the High Sea Fleet behind Hipper. Beatty's force now ran back to the north (not to the northwest and Scotland) with both Hipper and Scheer in pursuit. The only possible explanation for his course lay in a prearranged rendezvous with Jellicoe.

In the early evening hours the two British fleets came in contact with the Germans silhouetted on the horizon. Jellicoe deployed from line to column at exactly the right moment; only a full reversal in course by the German battleships averted a catastrophe for the High Sea Fleet. During a brief engagement the Germans suffered a fearful hammering. The British fleet had now deployed between the Germans and home. Less than an hour later, Scheer tried to force his way through the British line, and this time his "T" was crossed again. The Germans took a terrible battering before they retreated towards the center of the North Sea.

The remainder of Jutland was anticlimactic. The Admiralty failed to provide a clear intelligence picture; Jellicoe persisted in his belief that the Germans would attempt to escape by the Ems route rather than via Horn's Reef; and British subordinate commanders showed a lack of initiative, failing in one case to fire on German ships at almost point-blank range. The material losses for the battle were not all that disparate; in a strategic sense, however, Jutland was a decisive success for the Royal Navy.

> What is crucial about this titanic confrontation involving about 250 ships and 100,000 men, is that it brought the Reich no strategic relief. . . . The Germans had been driven home, and all thoughts about a renewed encounter with the Grand Fleet were equated with a suicide sortie. In fact the High Sea Fleet put out to sea only three times more: in August and October 1916, and in April 1918. And like the French after Trafalgar, the Germans now turned to *guerre de course* in a final attempt to throw off the steel yoke of British naval supremacy.[11]

THE PROTECTION OF COMMERCE

As war extended into 1915, the fundamental assumption with which the powers had begun the conflict had proven wrong; the conflict was going to be anything but short. With unlimited access to world commerce, including the resources of the United States, the Allies could use the world economy to destroy the Central Powers. For the Germans, the defeat of the Schlieffen Plan and stalemate on the Western Front mirrored the bottling up of the High Sea Fleet in the North Sea. The initial blockade aimed at preventing the flow of what international law termed "absolute contraband" onto the Continent—arms, military stores, and so forth. But, the British also attempted to blockade such "conditional contraband" as oil and nitrates. As the conflict lengthened, the British tightened the blockade, so that by early 1915 even foodstuffs fell within what the blockading authorities considered contraband.

As the blockade tightened, the German Navy's helplessness hit home. Tirpitz, who had had such influence on the navy's buildup, now urged that his government use submarines to attack British commerce without warning. On 22 November 1914, the grand admiral gave an interview to an American newspaperman during which, without authorization, he announced a German submarine blockade of Britain. Tirpitz's announcement precipitated a major political argument within his government and eventually a major confrontation with the United States.

The kaiser initially was doubtful about an unrestricted submarine campaign against British commerce. Nevertheless, Tirpitz soon had a host of supporters among the Naval High Command and conservative political leaders. On 1 February 1915 the Germans embarked on unrestricted submarine warfare against the commercial shipping that supported the British Isles. As one historian noted:

> Germany placed its confidence in an incredibly small force. A mere twenty-nine U-boats were available for front line duty early in 1915; . . . German construction [of boats] was slow. Only fifteen boats came to the front in 1915; by May the U-boats had received deck guns. During the course of that year, Germany lost twenty-seven vessels through various causes, and by the end of 1915 a mere fifty-four U-boats were in service. It should be remembered that not even in 1917 did the Reich manage to achieve a ratio of 1:3 in terms of submarine service as opposed to maintenance. The larger submarines were able to stay on station at most twenty days (by the end of the year, thirty-five days) . . . Moreover, torpedo hits amounted to but 40 per cent in 1915 and 50 per cent in 1917.[12]

What is even more astonishing is that the Germans undertook this campaign as if the economic strength and military potential of the United States counted for nothing. In fact, the German Navy discounted not only the merchant vessel strength of the U.S. but the battle strength of the U.S. Navy, which by itself was almost as strong as the High Sea Fleet.

Given available strength, the submarine blockade of the British Isles met with a notable lack of success. In March and April 1915 German submarines sank only 115,839 tons of Allied shipping. This small success, however, nearly brought the United States into the war. After announcing in a front-page advertisement in the *New York Times* that the liner *Lusitania* would be subject to attack due to a blockade, the Germans actually torpedoed and sank her, killing 1,198 passengers (including 100 Americans). Even the left-wing press in Germany celebrated the sinking as a great triumph. By June 1915, however, the possibility that the U.S. might join the war persuaded the Germans to back off from attacking passenger liners; by September the Reich had cancelled unrestricted submarine warfare owing to American pressure. President Woodrow Wilson, however, remained substantially unmoved by an outraged American public opinion, which called for a strong response to German provocations.

If the German Navy had failed in its submarine campaign, nothing in that failure suggested to its proponents that another effort (and the sooner the better) would not win the war or that an American declaration of war might not be disastrous. Throughout 1916, the navy waged an unremitting effort to renew the submarine campaign, using "cooked" figures and estimates to support prospects for an unlimited submarine campaign. Even some German politicians with little military expertise, saw that the navy had left a few things out, including the 1.7 million tons of Austrian-German shipping interned in the United States and the 1 million plus tons yearly capacity of Entente dockyards.

The attractiveness of the navy's arguments to those who ran policy in Germany stemmed from two sources. On the one hand was the desperate strategic situation confronting Germany in the fall of 1916. The battle of Verdun had been a disaster for the German Army—so much so that it would never fully recover for the remainder of the war. In the east, the Russians had achieved a stunning victory against Austria-Hungary; Rumania had joined the Allies; and finally a great British offensive had begun on the Somme. The opening of that attack showed clearly that Britain had harnessed her economic and manpower potential to project a great army onto the Continent. This desperate situation led the German leadership to consider renewing unrestricted submarine warfare. Reinforcing that willingness to take such a risk was the assessment that the U-boats would prevent the U.S. from tipping the scales. The second factor pushing the Germans towards the resumption of unlimited submarine warfare was that the Royal Navy had displayed great difficulty in coming to grips with the limited submarine attacks that the Germans launched in the summer and fall of 1916.

The technology to detect and attack submarines was only being developed at this point. As of fall 1916, no clear means of tracking submarines once they had submerged had been devised. Nevertheless, as long as the Germans did not resort to indiscriminate attacks on merchant vessels, the British and their Allies were able to keep the sinkings at an acceptable level. Surprisingly, given the propaganda campaign waged by the German Navy in public and in the highest levels of the government, submarine construction received low priority in the naval programs of 1915 and 1916. Instead, work continued at full steam on completing a number of capital ships. In 1915 and 1916 the Germans had laid down no fewer than eight new capital ships. In fact, at the same time that the navy was pushing for unrestricted submarine warfare, a number of its senior officers were worrying that a German Navy consisting mostly of submarines would not have positions for admirals.

The navy's campaign for unrestricted submarine warfare reached a peak in the fall of 1916. Even the Reichstag (parliament) declared itself enthusiastically in favor of unrestricted submarine warfare. In December 1916, General Erich Ludendorff (effectively the dictator of Germany from 1916 to 1918) warned the German chancellor: "Our military situation leaves no room for negotiations that would postpone a military measure once it is recognized to be necessary, thereby paralyzing the vigor of our strategy."[13]

On 8 January 1917 the German chancellor, Bethmann Hollweg, found himself summoned for a conference with the kaiser and the high command. There, Ludendorff and Chief of the German General Staff Field Marshal Paul von Hindenburg rejected all counter-arguments about the risks of a submarine campaign. As Ludendorff had remarked to a German industrialist in 1916: "The United States does not bother me . . . in the least; I look upon a declaration of war by the United States with indifference!"[14]

The failure to organize a massive U-boat construction program showed in the fact that Germany possessed barely one hundred submarines in early 1917. When unrestricted submarine warfare began on 1 February 1917, only thirty-six U-boats were available for sea duty. Over the next year German shipyards built eighty-seven U-boats, but the loss of seventy-eight during the same period of time resulted in little increase in the ability to attack Allied commerce. Nevertheless, even with this few submarines the Germans caused a crisis in the movement of commerce across the North Atlantic and from Britain to the support of Allied armies. In February 1917 sinkings soared from 370,000 tons to 540,000 and in March to almost 600,000. In the first half of April the sinkings reached 420,000 tons. Britain and the Allied cause confronted the possibility of defeat at sea. Without a decrease in these merchant vessel losses, the Allies could not sustain the war economically, and the United States, which had finally responded to German submarine attacks with a declaration of war on April 6, could not bring its economic and military weight to bear on the Western Front.

Thus far the Admiralty's approach to the submarine threat had aimed to seek out and destroy the U-boats. Antisubmarine forces discovered that looking for submarines in the wide expanses of the Atlantic was like looking for needles in a haystack; even in areas where submarines had concentrated, hunter-killer groups had a dismal run of success. Meanwhile, Allied and neutral merchantmen sailed independently and suffered excruciating losses.

The Royal Navy's strategy did not represent hidebound conservatism; the introduction of great convoys of sailing merchantmen had finally thwarted the French raiders of the Napoleonic period. Yet in 1917, the Admiralty, under the leadership of Admiral Jellicoe, newly promoted from the Grand Fleet, set itself firmly against any introduction of convoys. It argued that there were too many merchant vessels, that modern merchantmen were too undisciplined to maintain station in convoy, and that the antisubmarine forces could attack U-boats more effectively by seeking them out. Other reasons, such as the requirement for the convoy to proceed only at the speed of its slowest member and of congestion and delays at ports were cited as well.

The Admiralty, however, had overestimated the numbers of sailings of merchant ships from Britain each week; in fact, the number of vessels needing protection was manageable. Merchant vessels in the age of steam found it easier to maintain station than had been the case a hundred years earlier. Finally, to sink any ships German submarines would have to attack convoys; thus, they would have to come to the antisubmarine forces.

The dynamic new Prime Minister, David Lloyd George, stepped in and pressured the navy to try the convoy expedient. As early as February 1917, he urged the Admiralty to experiment with convoys. A number of junior officers within the navy itself were in favor of such an approach. By April, the situation had become so desperate that the Admiralty fell into line. At the end of April, the first convoys sailed from Gibraltar; they arrived in Britain without loss. Not until the end of May did a similar convoy leave Hampton Roads in the United States. All twelve vessels made it without mishap. By early July, four convoys were sailing every eight days from North America.

The use of convoys resulted in an immediate and drastic reduction in merchant shipping losses. In April 1917, U-boats sank 458 ships of 841,118 tons By July the total had fallen to a more manageable 365,000; by September the number of merchant tons sunk had fallen to barely 200,000 tons. In attacks on convoys the Germans had hardly any success at all. In September, 1,306 merchant ships sailed to Britain in 83 different convoys; U-boats sank only ten of that total. In 55 outbound convoys with 789 ships, the British lost only two vessels.

The U.S. Navy played a considerable role in the victory over the U-boats. The German Navy had discounted the role the Americans might be able to play in the conflict. While at first American naval strategy towards Germany was not entirely clear, the U-boat threat concentrated minds upon the essentials. The initial American impulse had been to send the battle fleet to the support of the British; one squadron of America's most modern super-battleships did serve with the Grand Fleet: the *Florida, Wyoming, New York, Texas,* and *Arkansas* under Rear Admiral Hugh Rodman at Scapa Flow.

But the most important American contribution lay in the navy's willingness and adaptability to meet the U-boat threat to the Allied strategic position. Admiral William S. Sims (eventually the commander-in-chief of the American navy in Europe), sent to London in early April 1917 to determine Allied naval needs, immediately recognized how desperate the submarine threat was. He reported back to Washington that what the British needed were not battleships but destroyers and antisubmarine craft. The response was immediate. By the end of April, the United States had dispatched a flotilla of six destroyers to operate on the west coast of Ireland. Within a month, a further twenty-four destroyers had arrived in Europe in support of the British. By July, the American government had decided to stand down battleship construction and launch a massive construction program to build 200 destroyers and numerous other antisubmarine craft.

By the fall of 1917 the British, with significant aid from the United States, had mastered the submarine menace. While losses remained heavy, the U-boats did not sever the sea lines of communications on which Allied security and military power rested. The war in 1918, then, turned on whether the Germans, exhausted by four years of brutal war against the rest of Europe, could gain a victory over the British and French armies before American troops could arrive in substantial numbers. Once the flood of American divisions landed in Europe, the balance of military power would tilt inexorably against Germany. By this point in the war, the Germans were in desperate economic straits. Both the war and the impact of the British blockade had strained the Reich to the breaking point. At home German civilians had suffered through three years of decreasing foodstuffs and other necessities of life. So short of food to feed the population was the German economy that the Germans referred to the winter of 1916/17 as the "turnip winter." The fact that there was a substantial black market and that the upper classes had access to additional rations exacerbated internal discontent.

By 1918 lack of food was having an impact even on the army. The conquest of Rumania and large portions of the Ukraine did not substantially decrease German economic difficulties. It was one thing to conquer territory, but another to force unwilling peasants to part with their produce. Still, there were other areas where the blockade hurt the German military machine just as severely. By 1918, German trucks ran on steel-rimmed tires; no rubber was available. A general shortage of oil could not be alleviated even by the conquest of Rumania. Everything from clothing, to boots, to medicine was desperately short in the German Army. In the face of this grim picture the German High Command, driven by Ludendorff, determined to launch a war-winning offensive in the west before the Americans arrived in very large numbers. They believed that the new tactical doctrine they had developed would allow them to smash the British and French in a few quick and decisive battles.

They came close to achieving their goals. The German offensive began on 21 March 1918 with a massive attack on the British Fifth Army. The Germans did not coordinate that effort with the navy; the High Sea Fleet remained rusting at anchor. Ludendorff's "Michael" offensive achieved a breakthrough and for a time threatened to split the British and French entirely apart. However, Ludendorff could not make up his mind as to the objective and failed to reinforce the major breakthrough. Even more decisive to the failure was that substantial numbers of German troops, on minimal rations for the past two years, stopped to loot British supply dumps. The impact of the blockade had pushed soldiers to the breaking point. In the "Michael" offensive the Germans gained only a huge salient of territory that was harder to defend than the defensive lines they had left on March 21. To achieve these gains the high command had used up precious reserves of their best troops, equipment, and ammunition. The pattern of German attacks in April and May remained the same: major gains in territory, but little of strategic value, a further exhaustion due to heavy casualties, and a dramatic lowering of morale—especially in elite units.

By the late spring of 1918, the American tide was arriving. In March General John Pershing, commander of American forces, had four divisions available. (Each of his divisions was approximately twice the size of a British, French, or German division.) In that month 64,200 American troops crossed the Atlantic; in April the total rose to 93,128; and in May it rose again to 206,287. Thereafter, nearly a quarter of a million American soldiers crossed the Atlantic every month with barely a troop ship damaged—so much for the German Navy's claim that it could prevent the arrival of American troops in Europe. While the chief burden in defeating the German Army rested with the British Army, the American Expeditionary Force played a major role in pushing the Germans back.

By late summer 1918, the German Army in the field faced military defeat. Everywhere on the front Allied attacks battered them back; the German High Command began to unravel. Close to a nervous breakdown, Ludendorff was the first to go. Desperately, a new regime in Berlin sought an armistice to preserve something out of defeat. At this terrible moment, the German Naval High Command, forced to stop unrestricted submarine warfare by the new government, decided to launch the High Sea Fleet on a "death ride" to seek destruction and glory in the North Sea.[15] While the officer corps seems to have reveled in the prospect of a glorious and futile death, the enlisted men had better sense. Revolution broke out in the fleet when the signal came to raise steam. The operation was scrubbed. Revolution then spread from the ships to shore and throughout the land. Germany had been completely broken militarily. For the German Navy, peace brought the final ignominy of internment in Scapa Flow, and then the scuttling of its major units by their crews at that British naval base.

CONCLUDING REMARKS

Seapower alone could not have had a decisive impact on the First World War. However, the exercise of sea control and the economic and strategic implications that accrued to the Allies by that exercise played a crucial role in the defeat of the German Empire and its allies. The initial threat was mastered by isolating the German surface fleet and controlling the entrances and exits to the North Sea. That strategic objective was met in the first days of August 1914. Britain's advantages in geographical position, moreover, forced the Germans either to come out and seek by battle to break the hold of the Royal Navy over the North Sea, or to recognize a *de facto* British control over the oceans of the world. In describing the blockade of Imperial France by the Royal Navy in the first decade of the nineteenth century, Mahan wrote:

> They were dull, weary, eventless months, those months of watching and waiting by ships before the French arsenals. Purposeless they surely seemed to many, but they saved England. The world has never seen a more impressive demonstration of the influence of sea power upon its history. Those far distant, storm beaten ships, upon which the Grand Army never looked, stood between it and the dominion of the world.[16]

His words are as applicable to the First World War as they are to his own time. The grimy, dark line of British battleships blocked the High Sea Fleet and the German nation from access to the oceans of the world. Yet that success represented only a starting point from which the British and their allies could accomplish the defeat of the German Empire.

During the 1930s, a number of British strategists, particularly B. H. Liddell-Hart, argued that in committing a large army to the European Continent Britain had broken with her traditional strategy (termed by Liddell-Hart a strategy of "limited liability") and as a result had suffered needlessly heavy casualties in the terrible fighting in the trenches of the Western Front. In fact, Britain had no other prudent choice. As the historian Michael Howard has noted: "It was . . . precisely the failure of German power to find an outlet and its consequent concentration in Europe, its lack of any significant possessions overseas, that made it so particularly menacing to the sprawling British Empire in the world wars and which make so misleading all arguments about 'traditional' British strategy drawn from earlier conflicts against the Spanish and French Empires . . ."[17] To defeat the German Empire the British had to defeat it on the continent; above all, the nasty business of digging the Germans out of their lairs required the mobilization of national economic and manpower resources to project a great army onto the Continent. It then required the willingness to take the terrible casualties of a great land campaign. On both counts the British proved willing to do what the Athenians refused; the results in both cases speak for themselves.

There was a fleeting opportunity to attack the Germans on the European periphery. The Gallipoli venture represents one of the great strategic might-have-beens of history. The Royal Navy did its part; but the execution of the land portion was so terribly mishandled by the army that the opportunity vanished. All that remained for the British was to see it through on the Western Front.

The Germans, denied access to the world's commerce, did attempt to deny the oceans to the British. Fortunately, in terms of force structure, strategy, and operational concepts, the German Navy functioned with a high level of ineptitude in its submarine campaign. The threat to Allied commerce, though real and life-threatening, was mastered. And the very effort by the German Navy to deny Allied use of the world's great oceanic highways, brought the United States into the war. That fact put the final seal of defeat on the short, catastrophic history of the Bismarckian Reich. Seapower had played a crucial role in the defeat of the Central Powers and the victory of the Allies.

NOTES

1. Winston S. Churchill, *The World Crisis* (Toronto: Macmillan, 1931), p. 28.

2. Quoted by Holger Herwig, "The Dynamics of Necessity: German Military Policy During the Great War," in *Military Effectiveness*, vol. 1, *The First World War* (London: Allen and Unwin, 1988), p. 90.

3. *Ibid.*, p. 90.

4. Arthur J. Marder, *From Dreadnought to Scapa Flow, The Royal Navy in the Fisher Era, 1904–1914*, vol. 3, *Jutland and After* (London: Oxford University Press, 1969), pp. 149–54.

5. Herwig, "The Dynamics of Necessity," p. 119–20.

6. Churchill, *The World Crisis*, p. 353.

7. For an excellent description of the escape of the *Goeben* and *Breslau*, see Barbara Tuchman, *The Guns of August* (New York: Macmillan, 1962), pp. 137–62.

8. Llewellyn Woodward, *Great Britain and the War of 1914–1918* (Boston: Beacon Press, 1970), p. 61.

9. Martin Gilbert, *Winston S. Churchill*, vol. 3, *1914–1916* (London: Heinemann, 1971), p. 226.

10. *Ibid.*, p. 262.

11. Holger Herwig, *Luxury Fleet, The Imperial German Navy, 1888–1918* (London: George Allen and Unwin, 1980), p. 163–64.

12. *Ibid.*

13. Gerhard Ritter, *The Sword and the Scepter*, vol. 3, *The Tragedy of Statesmanship—Bettmann Hollweg as War Chancellor (1914–1917)*, trans. by Heinz Norden (Coral Gables, Fl.: University of Miami Press, 1970), p. 205.

14. Quoted in Holger Herwig, *Politics of Frustration, the United States in German Naval Planning, 1889–1941* (Boston: Little, Brown & Co., 1976), p. 125.

15. After the war the German Navy's leadership was able to sell many gullible historians that the planned October 1918 sortie had a serious military and strategic objective. It is clear in terms of current research that this was definitely not the case. For the best analysis of the thinking that went into the German Navy's last contribution to the defeat of their nation, see Holger Herwig, *The German Naval Officer Corps, 1890–1918, A Social and Political History* (Oxford: Clarendon Press, 1973), pp. 247–79.

16. Captain Alfred Thayer Mahan, *The Influence of Sea Power Upon the French Revolution and Empire, 1773–1812*, vol. 2 (Boston: Little, Brown & Co., 1892), p. 118.

17. Michael Howard, *The Continental Commitment* (London: T. Smith, 1972), p. 32.

BIBLIOGRAPHIC NOTE

By far and away the most important source for the naval conflict in World War I is Arthur Marder's masterful six-volume study *From Dreadnought to Scapa Flow* (London: Oxford University Press, 1969). Paul Kennedy's *The Rise and Fall of British Naval Mastery* (New York: Charles Scribner's Sons, 1976) provides an excellent framework for understanding the overall pattern in which the Royal Navy had developed. For the best one-volume survey of the First World War, Llewellyn Woodward's *Great Britain and the War of 1914–1918* (Boston: Beacon Press, 1970) still provides an excellent description of the war's grand and political strategy from the British perspective. Winston Churchill's *World Crisis* (Toronto: Macmillan, 1931), whether one consults the full six-volume or abridged single-volume version, will still reward the reader with its rich language; there are, of course, some problems with Churchill's defense of his actions, but overall this remains a masterpiece of naval and military history. S. W. Roskill's *Churchill and the Admirals* (London: Collins, 1977), while containing some interesting points, is nevertheless a contentious, one-sided attack on Churchill. For the early portion of the war, James Goldrick's *The King's Ships Were at Sea, The War in the North Sea, August 1914–February 1915* (Annapolis: Naval Institute Press, 1984) is lively and detailed on both sides of the North Sea. For the overall discussion of the Anglo-German rivalry one must consult Paul Kennedy's brilliant *The Rise of the Anglo-German Antagonism, 1860–1914* (London: George Allen & Unwin, 1980). On the contribution that intelligence made to the Royal Navy's victory in World War I, Patrick Beesly's *Room 40, British Naval Intelligence, 1914–1918* (London: Hamish Hamilton, 1982) is outstanding. On the convoy problem in both world wars, J. Winston's *Convoy: The Defense of the Sea Trade, 1890–1990* (London: M. Joseph, 1983) is superior.

On the German side there are a number of important works. Holger Herwig's various works are the best available in English on the "High Sea Fleet" and its troubled history. His *The German Naval Officer Corps: A Social and Political History, 1890–1918* (Oxford: Clarendon Press, 1973) is a first-class examination of the character and flaws within the German naval officer corps. On the German Navy's contribution to bringing the United States into *both* world wars, Herwig has written an excellent study: *Politics of Frustration: The United States in German Naval Planning, 1889–1918* (Boston: Little, Brown & Co., 1976). Herwig has also provided an excellent general history of the "High Sea Fleet," *Luxury Fleet: The German Imperial Navy, 1888–1918* (London: George Allen & Unwin, 1980). For an unveiling of the German Navy's contribution to the revolution in Germany in 1918, Daniel Horn's *The German Naval Mutinies of World War I* (New Brunswick, NJ: Rutgers University Press,

1969) is solid. On the general history of German militarism and the defeat of Germany, Gerhard Ritter's *The Sword and Scepter: The Problem of Militarism in Germany* (four volumes), translated by Heinz Norden (Coral Gables, FL: University of Miami Press, 1969–1973) is worth consulting. Jonathan Steinberg's *Yesterday's Deterrent: Tirpitz and the Birth of the German Battle Fleet* (London: Macdonald, 1965) is also useful. There are a number of important works in German on the role of the "High Sea Fleet" in the history of Bismarck's Reich. The most important is Volker R. Berghahn, *Der Tirpitz-Plan. Genesis und Verfall einer innenpolitischen Krisenstrategie unter Wilhelm II.* (Düsseldorf: Dichte Verlag, 1971).

ADDITIONAL SOURCES

Gemzell, Carl-Axel. *Organization, Conflict, and Innovation: A Study of German Strategic Planning, 1888–1940.* Stockholm: Esselte Studium, 1973.

Hezlet, Vice-Admiral Sir Arthur. *The Aircraft and Seapower.* New York: Stein and Day, 1970.

Marder, Arthur J. *The Anatomy of British Sea Power. A History of British Naval Policy in the Pre-Dreadnought Era, 1880–1905.* New York: A. A. Knopf, 1940.

Pollen, Anthony. *The Great Gunnery Scandal: The Mystery of Jutland.* London: Collins, 1980.

Richmond, Admiral Sir Herbert. *Statesmen and Sea Power.* Oxford: Clarendon Press, 1947.

Roskill, Captain S. W. *Admiral of the Fleet Lord Beatty: The Last Naval Hero.* London: Collins, 1980.

Woodward, Llewellyn. *Great Britain and the German Navy.* London: F. Cass and Co., 1964.

9

World War II: Allied and German Naval Strategies

BY JEFFREY G. BARLOW

PREFATORY REMARKS

In reading this and the following chapter, the reader must remain mindful that in World War II, the Anglo-American allies were waging a global war—one that exacted painful choices from them about how to allocate available military and naval assets in order to defeat enemies operating simultaneously (although not in concert) in multiple regions of the world. The interactive nature of this global conflict meant that events in one theater often influenced, in a positive or negative manner, events occurring in other theaters situated thousands of miles away. One example of this would be a case where a requirement for ships, landing craft, and troops for an operation in the Mediterranean theater might require the postponement or cancellation of an operation in the China-Burma-India theater.

With regard to naval efforts, Britain's Royal Navy, which had faced the German naval menace essentially alone from 1939 to 1941, was forced (with help from its Canadian counterpart) to assume the larger share of the burden in the naval war against Germany and Italy even after the United States entered the war; while, on the other hand, the United States Navy took the dominant role in the war against the Japanese in the Pacific from the beginning of that effort.

A most significant advantage that Britain and the United States possessed in this global war was their status as major maritime powers whose strategic locations and network of bases close to key choke points enabled them to utilize their navies to keep their more geo-strategically restricted enemies from uniting in a coalition war, had they sought to do so. Furthermore, the multi-area flexibility provided by the naval and amphibious forces of Great Britain and the United States allowed them to defend as necessary, to establish local sea control in disputed waters, and to launch assaults on enemy occupied territory at times and places of their own choosing. It was this flexibility provided by maritime ascendancy, for example, that:

- Enabled Britain to withdraw the bulk of its expeditionary force from the beaches of France in the teeth of the German Air Force;
- Allowed the Anglo-American landings in North Africa to take place, even as Montgomery's British Eighth Army was heavily engaged with Rommel's Africa Corps in Egypt; and
- Facilitated the island-hopping campaigns in the Pacific, whereby Japanese island strongholds were bypassed and left to die on the vine as U.S. and allied forces moved ever closer to Japan's final defense perimeter.

In large measure, it was their possession of strong maritime forces that enabled Britain and the United States to rebound so quickly from early defeats at the hands of their Axis enemies and to change over to the offensive.

NAVAL ARMS CONTROL AND GERMAN REARMAMENT IN THE INTERWAR YEARS

In the years between 1919 and 1939 the evolving composition of the fleets of the world's naval powers, and most particularly those of Great Britain and the United States, was affected to a major extent by a series of naval arms limitation treaties. The political leaderships of participating countries had come to terms on these treaties for a mixture of reasons, including support for arms limitation, reduction in national shipbuilding rivalries, and economies in overall defense spending. To the extent that political support for these naval treaties was based upon a belief in the long-term efficacy of arms limitations for reduction of international conflict—and many disarmament advocates saw these treaties as laying the foundation for what was to become a permanent naval limitation regime—it reflected the triumph of hope over reason. Within little more than a decade after the signing of the first naval arms limitation treaty in Washington in 1922, the clouds of crisis that prefigured the onset of the Second World War were already on the horizon.

Britain had emerged from the First World War as she had entered it—the world's supreme naval power. Although more than four years of wartime duties had battered and abraded its forces, the Royal Navy's strength at the time of the Armistice stood at some 1,300 ships, including 42 "dreadnoughts" (post-1906 battleships) and battle cruisers and 109 cruisers. And the British Admiralty was determined to maintain the Royal Navy's superiority over that of other navies.

At war's end, it was the United States, her recent ally, that was Britain's closest competitor in naval strength. Yet it was the United States's potential and not its current strength in capital ships that so concerned the Admiralty. The U.S. 1916 naval shipbuilding program, much of which had been deferred during the war in favor of other naval priorities, was again in force, and it threatened to topple Great Britain from its secure position as the strongest naval power. As the Board of the Admiralty warned the Cabinet in October 1919, if the United States completed its 1916 program and Britain undertook no new naval construction, by 1923 "we shall have passed to the position of being the second naval power."

In July 1921, the United States extended invitations to the eight other countries that had composed the Allied and Associated Powers during the World War to attend a conference on the limitation of armament and on Far Eastern problems. At this conference, which began in November 1921, the five major naval powers—Great Britain, the United States, Japan, France, and Italy—comprised the first committee, dealing with armament limitation questions. The outcome of a month of spirited bargaining, primarily among the delegations of Great Britain, Japan, and the United States, was the drafting of a Five-Power Treaty on naval arms limitation. The Washington Naval Treaty: proclaimed a ten-year capital-ship-building holiday (from November 1921); established a ratio of allowed capital-ship tonnage for the powers of 5:5:3 for Britain, the United States, and Japan, respectively (France and Italy each rated 1.75); set upper limits on the tonnage of individual capital ships (35,000 tons), aircraft carriers (27,000 tons), and cruisers (10,000 tons) permitted during the life of the agreement; fixed the allowable tonnage for aircraft carriers at the same 5:5:3:1.75:1.75 ratio used for capital ships; and limited cruiser armament to guns measuring no more than 8 inches in caliber. The total capital-ship replacement tonnage for the contracting powers was 525,000 tons each for Great Britain and the United States, 315,000 tons for Japan, and 175,000 tons each for France and Italy. The treaty was to remain in force until the end of 1936, provided two years notice of intention to terminate was given.

While the 1922 Washington Naval Treaty curtailed ambitious building programs for capital ships, it had the opposite effect on programs
for smaller ships not limited by the treaty, and because the agreement had established a relatively high individual limit for the tonnage and main armament of cruisers, it provided the signatory powers with a reason to build up to that limit even if their preference (as
with Great Britain) lay more toward building "light" rather than "heavy"
cruisers. It was largely on this second point that the 1927 Geneva
Naval Conference foundered, as the British delegation sought reductions in cruiser size and armament while retaining overall superiority
in cruiser numbers, and the United States fought the size and armament reductions and sought overall parity.

The London Naval Treaty marked a further but only temporary
gain in naval arms limitation upon its signing in April 1930. The five
major naval powers agreed to prolong the capital-ship holiday through
1936 and reached accord on certain restrictions in submarine warfare. Great Britain, the United States, and Japan agreed to scrap by
1933 those capital ships already promised for scrapping by 1936 and
further agreed to limitations in cruisers, destroyers, and submarines,
although Japan was granted parity in submarines and given a 10:10:7
ratio in cruisers and destroyers. However, France and Italy could not
be brought into final agreement on the provisions for destroyers and
submarines.

By the final (Second) London Naval Conference in 1935–1936, the
movement toward naval disarmament had reached its end. The Japanese, who had announced in late 1934 that they would be withdrawing from the Washington Treaty limits when they expired on 31
December 1936, walked out of the London Conference when their
demands for parity were not met. And although Great Britain, the
United States, and France signed the 1936 treaty, it had been drafted
to provide escalator clauses that allowed the signatories to exceed
certain imposed limits if Japan and Italy (as original signatories of
the Washington Treaty) failed to adhere to the treaty's terms by a
fixed date. These escalator clauses subsequently were invoked by the
United States when these countries failed to comply.

By the terms of the Versailles Treaty, which entered into force in
January 1920, the German Navy had been severely restricted. Its fleet
was allowed to consist of only six battleships of an obsolescent type,
six light cruisers, twelve destroyers, and twelve torpedo boats. Warships built to replace these vessels were similarly limited in allowed
tonnage—armored ships could not exceed 10,000 tons in size, light
cruisers, 6,000 tons, etc. And Germany was forbidden to construct or

acquire submarines, even for commercial purposes. The Inter-Allied Control Commission, an official body composed of French, British, Belgian, Japanese, and Italian military officers and men, was detailed to assure compliance with the treaty's terms through on-site inspection. From the first, however, important elements in the German government and the Reichswehr (armed forces) were determined to evade the terms of the hated Versailles Treaty in every way possible.

In the case of the German Navy, a variety of methods was used to evade the treaty's terms without detection. S-boats (motor torpedo boats) first werc built by the Naval Command in the early 1920s under the auspices of the Trayag Yacht Harbor joint stock company. Later, in the early 1930s, the S-boats were tested in a manner designed to camouflage their combat capabilities. As a 1932 memorandum from Admiral Erich Raeder, the chief of Naval Command, to various naval stations noted:

> The torpedo tubes of all S-Boats will be stored in the Naval Arsenal for immediate fitting. During the trial runs the torpedo tubes will be taken on board *one after the other* for a short time to be fitted and for practice shooting *so that only one boat at a time carries torpedo armament.* . . . It should not anchor together with the other, unarmed boats of the Half-Flotilla because of the obvious similarity of type.[1]

Similarly German U-Boat (submarine) construction was initiated through a dummy company set up in Holland. In 1922, a Dutch firm known as *I. von S.* was established at the Hague to act as a German submarine construction office. In the years from 1925 on, I. von S. won contracts to build submarines for Turkey, Spain, and Finland. In all cases, submarine test trials were carried out under the command of former German submarine officers and engineers. The 250-ton Finnish submarines became the prototypes for the first two-dozen German U-boats. The parts for these first twenty-four boats were produced during 1933–1935 and stored unassembled in a specially rented large storage shed in Kiel until early 1935 when the order was given to begin their assembly.

The German Navy had a similar interest in hiding the actual tonnage (hence the amount of armor protection and armament) of its heavy ships. When Germany's first two new battleships *Scharnhorst* and *Gneisenau* were in the planning stage in 1934, Adolf Hitler made it very clear that their tonnages must remain understated. Similar deceptions were provided for other German capital ships.

In the light of this German naval rearmament effort, which by the early 1930s was only semi-covert, it is interesting to note the level of

Great Britain's unconcern. In November 1933, Admiral Raeder had first hinted to the British naval attaché in Berlin that Germany might be interested in a naval treaty with Britain. This conversation was dismissed out of hand by the British Foreign Office. But a year later the idea was more concretely established. Raeder then told the British naval attaché that Germany would welcome direct negotiations with England concerning the strength of Germany's fleet. Events in the preceding months, including the collapse of the Geneva disarmament conference, now made the British more predisposed to listen to such a offer. And when Hitler made it known that Germany should have a fleet only 35 percent the size of the Royal Navy, London began to look on the idea with real interest.

The Admiralty's interest in an Anglo-German agreement centered on the agreement's promises of restraining an otherwise unfettered German shipbuilding effort and offering a more complete transmission of information by the Germans on their current and future building programs. This interest was abetted by some seriously deficient analysis concerning Germany's ultimate intentions for its fleet, which hypothesized that Germany would not only avoid antagonizing Britain with her naval program but that her efforts were directed toward gaining control of the Baltic. It should be noted that from the early 1930s until 1938, the German fleet indeed was being built up to fight the Poles and possibly the French, not the British.

The British government too, despite some objections from the Foreign Office, was interested in seizing the opportunity of obtaining an agreement with Germany that would keep her fleet at the lowest level diplomatically attainable. The ultimate result was the signing of the 1935 Anglo-German Naval Agreement, which provided for a German Navy limited to 35 percent of the British tonnage in each major class of warship (although Germany, under certain circumstances, could go from 45 percent of the British submarine fleet to parity with Britain), with the standard displacement and main-battery caliber of each class of warship conforming to the limits then in force under the Washington and London Naval Treaties. The extent of British naivete concerning German intentions was perhaps best expressed by the words of one British report that stated:

> It is noteworthy that the German representatives have throughout been most insistent on emphasizing the *permanent and definitive character* of the agreement under negotiation. They would scarcely have adopted such a determined attitude on this point throughout the whole of the negotiations had it not been the purpose of the German Government to play fair in this matter and to eliminate all danger of future naval rivalry between the two countries.[2]

Germany was extremely pleased with the terms of the Naval Agreement, and with good reason. It gave quasi-legal sanction to her earlier abrogation of the Versailles Treaty limitations on armament and also provided a diplomatic framework within which Germany could build up its fleet without antagonizing Great Britain. Moreover, as Winston Churchill aptly noted in his memoirs on the Second World War, the agreement allowed Germany a naval building program that would keep her shipbuilding yards working at maximum level for at least ten years. And meanwhile, Germany continued to hide the true extent of her building program from the British.

Until 1938, the actual shipbuilding program remained modest, as each year one or two major units were laid down. But in 1938, the German Navy put forward its first long-term shipbuilding program, which became known as "Plan Z." It was a plan to provide a "balanced fleet"—one equipped with a sufficient number of capital ships to hold its own against a British Home Fleet that was not reinforced by capital ships from the other fleets (which, it was hoped, would be preoccupied with duties elsewhere), and that also contained a large (if not overwhelming) number of U-boats. The period 1943–1944 was expected to be the earliest possible date for the plan's completion.

Nevertheless, during 1938 the "balanced fleet" was only one of two competing conceptions of German naval force structure. The other was predicated upon the need to operate against the enemy's maritime commerce and was centered around large numbers of U-boats, supplemented with pocket battleships—ships like the *Deutschland*, with capital-ship armament (11-inch guns) mounted on hulls only a little larger in tonnage than heavy cruisers—and light forces such as torpedo boats, to act as surface raiders. This latter plan had the support of Karl Doenitz, the flag officer for submarines, and some of the more innovative officers on the Navy Staff, one being Helmuth Heye. As then Vice Admiral Heye explained his thinking on the issue at the end of the war:

> I personally, along with other officers, held the opinion that the composition of a fleet and the types of ship in it must vary according to the geographical position of the country, the possible strength of its fleet, and its dependence on sea routes.
>
> . . . With the standardization of the world's fleets [under the terms of the Washington Navy Treaty], the state which engaged the enemy with the same weapons and the same methods of fighting but with an inferior number of ships was bound to remain inferior. . . . Since the construction of the German fleet was bound to take many years a small fleet consisting solely of types similar to those laid down in [the] Washington [Treaty]

could, in my opinion, scarcely gain successes in defensive engagements. Quite clearly we had to give up the idea of fleet engagements and to operate against the enemy's weak spots. This would have meant for example building first of all a modern U-boat service.[3]

Indeed, in October 1938, Heye had laid out his strategic views regarding a naval war with Great Britain in a paper for Admiral Raeder entitled *Seekriegsführung gegen England*. Its premises were stated plainly: Britain's strengths were her geographical position across Germany's outlets to the open ocean and her strong battle fleet that Germany could not hope to match; Britain's weakness was her dependence on overseas communications. From these premises it followed that the proper form of war at sea for Germany would be a campaign against Britain's economic and military sea communications. Raeder took an academic interest in Heye's thesis but remained committed to Plan Z's balanced fleet effort.

The final decision on which plan to undertake, however, was made by Hitler. He had long favored capital ships and, accordingly, approved Plan Z for implementation. On 27 January 1939, Germany formally notified the British government that she wished to increase her submarine strength to parity with that of the Royal Navy. That same day, the Führer gave Plan Z top priority—new capital ships were added to the program, and the time for completion of the plan was extended to 1949. Three months later (28 April 1939), in a speech to the German government, Hitler announced the cancellation of the Anglo-German Naval Agreement.

Although Raeder and the Naval Staff did not know it, it was, by then, far too late for Plan Z to have any significant effect on the fate of the German Navy. In September, the German armies invaded Poland, and Germany was suddenly at war with Britain and France. That same month, Hitler ordered the original shipbuilding plan modified to the MOB-plan (Mobilization Plan). Priority in the program was switched to U-boat construction, and the plan made no provision for the laying down of new battleships, cruisers, or aircraft carriers. Indeed, only the major ships already nearing completion were to go forward. Thus, it was only in hindsight that Admiral Raeder saw the wrong-headedness of his shipbuilding program. In June 1940 he wrote a letter that touched on this question and had it widely distributed in the fleet. In this letter the commander-in-chief of the German Navy stressed that the naval building program had been directed according to the political demands of the Führer and that the development of events had forced the navy into war while only in the initial stages of its rearmament. Because of this circumstance, however, Raeder noted that those officers who had urged the building up of the U-boat arms appeared to have been right.

WORLD WAR

When Britain and France entered the war as allies of beleaguered Poland on 3 September 1939, it came as a shock to Adolf Hitler, who had convinced himself that the two Western countries would continue their policy of appeasement. Only a few days before, in fact, he had registered an assertion with the leading German military officials at Berchtesgaden to the effect that in the event of a war with Poland, England and France might mobilize their forces and deploy troops against Germany, but this would be merely for show. He had gone on to say that if he thought German actions over Poland would lead to war with the Western countries, he would not undertake them, as "this Polish business is not worth a world war."

The shock was at least as profound for the German Navy and its leader, Admiral Erich Raeder. That very day he wrote a memorandum for the record expressing his feelings on the war. He noted:

> Today the war against France and England broke out, the war which, according to the Führer's previous assertions, we had no need to expect before about 1944. . . .
> As far as the Navy is concerned, obviously it is in no way very adequately equipped for the great struggle with Great Britain by autumn 1939. . . . [T]he submarine arm is still much too weak . . . to have any *decisive* effect on the war. The surface forces, moreover, are so inferior in number and strength to those of the British Fleet that, even at full strength, they can do no more than show that they know how to die gallantly and thus are willing to create the foundations for a later reconstruction.[4]

STRATEGY AND DISPOSITIONS

German naval strategy had developed gradually during the interwar period. It was influenced strongly by studies critical of the overwhelming fixation during the First World War of Germany's High Seas Fleet achieving a "tactical" decision against Britain's Grand Fleet. Postwar thinking, accordingly, moved toward strategies revolving around attack and defense of vital trade routes. One of the pivotal studies of this type was Vice Admiral Wegener's *Seestrategie des Weltkrieges (The Naval Strategy of the World War)*. In this work, Wegener argued that the real purpose of a fleet was to struggle for and eventually assert control of important trade routes and thereby maintain the country's overseas communications. He argued that if during the First World War, Germany had occupied Denmark and then had moved across to take possession of southern Norway, the High Seas Fleet would have been much closer to the British blockading forces and the pivotal Royal Navy base at Scapa Flow—thus, perhaps, in a strategic position to threaten to outflank Britain's blockade of Germany.

Wegener's concern with the struggle for control of trade routes was eventually modified by other naval analysts such as Kurt Assmann (later vice admiral) into a concept of economic or tonnage warfare that sought victory, not through the struggle for trade route control but through the gradual attrition of enemy merchant shipping on all fronts. Ironically, this form of warfare not only avoided contesting enemy naval forces for sea control but failed to envision the attack of enemy shipping at selected key points in its operating chain. During the First World War, such points included the transfer harbors from which the individual ships proceeded to their final destinations once their convoys had disbanded. Indeed, the major German naval critics who gained ascendancy in the navy's leadership failed to grasp the point that had been made by retired Vice Admiral Andreas Michelsen in his 1925 study *Der U-Bootskrieg 1914–1918*, that it had been the administration of the system of convoy (the central direction that coordinated by radio all movements of the convoys, that diverted the convoys from the areas where the U-boats were discovered to be operating, and that provided the personnel in each harbor where shipping was concentrated, in order to organize and instruct the individual convoys) and not the nature of the convoy itself that had posed the greatest difficulty for the German submarines in World War I.

In his study, Michelson had undertaken a comprehensive review of the British antisubmarine organization that had been developed in response to Germany's unrestricted submarine warfare. This review considered not only ship construction and the pace of Allied weapon development but also the extensive apparatus of shipping control devised to maintain the convoy system. None of the influential German naval analysts of the interwar period, however, made a similar effort to analyze the factors that had led to the convoy system's success during the First World War.

In May 1939, Hitler issued directives for economic warfare to the navy and the *Luftwaffe* (German Air Force). In home waters, the German Navy, working closely with the *Luftwaffe*, was to interrupt British blockading efforts through the employment of surprise attacks on inferior naval forces and continuous harassing action. In foreign waters, the navy's task was to attack enemy merchant shipping so as to deprive the Allies of ships and cargoes. Such attacks would dislocate the enemy's trade and serve to dissuade neutral shipping from entering the war zones established around Britain and her Allies.

In the latter part of August 1939, the German Navy prepared for war by sending two of its three pocket battleships—the *Graf Spee* and the *Deutschland*—out into the Atlantic in preparation for cruiser warfare. Similarly, some twenty-one U-boats departed for the Atlantic between 19 and 29 August in order to take up wartime stations before the onset of hostilities. In their initial sorties, both the pocket battleships and the U-boats were able to escape British observation.

At the beginning of the war, the German Navy was a truncated version of its grander hopes. Its forces stood at two battleships (*Scharnhorst* and *Gneisenau*—the British referred to them as battle cruisers because of the state of their armament and armor protection), two old battleships (*Schleswig-Holstein* and *Schlesien*), three pocket battleships (*Deutschland, Admiral Graf Spee,* and *Admiral Scheer*), one heavy cruiser (*Admiral Hipper*), five light cruisers, seventeen destroyers, fifty-six submarines, and assorted torpedo boats, motor torpedo boats, minelayers, minesweepers, and other craft. These forces (aside from those at sea) were deployed at bases at Wilhelmshaven, Brunsbüttel, Kiel, Hamburg, Swinemünde, Stettin, Pilau, and Danzig. In addition to these operational forces, two battleships (*Bismarck* and *Tirpitz*), an aircraft carrier (*Graf Zeppelin*), four heavy cruisers (*Blücher, Prinz Eugen, Seydlitz,* and *Lützow*), and one light cruiser were under construction.

British naval strategy was based on a realistic understanding of the importance of sea communications to the country's economic welfare (indeed, its existence) and on the need to cut German sea communications. As J. R. M. Butler noted:

The Allied staff paper of April 1939 on 'broad strategic policy' had recognized that in the first phase of the war the only offensive weapon which the Allies could use effectively was the economic. . . . Such pressure was envisaged under two forms: the prevention of the supply from without of articles essential to the German war effort, and the destruction of economic life within Germany. The latter task was to be the concern of Bomber Command of the Royal Air Force, but nothing to this end could even be attempted so long as the decision stood to restrict air attack to purely military objectives in the narrowest senses. It was necessary therefore to concentrate on the blockade of Germany.[5]

Imposing a blockade of Germany meant closing the North Sea to all movements of enemy shipping and maintaining contraband control of neutral shipping. The interception of commerce was to be carried out between the Orkney Islands (off the north coast of Scotland) and Iceland and in the Denmark Strait between Iceland and Greenland. A contraband control base was established at Kirkwall in the Orkneys. When war came, this planned British blockade was rapidly established. Within weeks, the overwhelming bulk of Germany's overseas trade had been throttled by the Royal Navy.

In terms of protecting British and Allied shipping, the war plans called for the Royal Navy to be responsible for the Atlantic Ocean and the North Sea, with the French Navy designated to help both on the southerly Atlantic routes and with any efforts at seeking out enemy raiders in the Atlantic. The Mediterranean Sea was to be divided between the two navies, with France securing the western basin and Britain the eastern. Because of uncertainty over the Italians, it was decided to close the Mediterranean to merchant shipping—a decision that would cause merchantmen bound for the Middle East to make the voyage around the Cape of Good Hope. And, this, in turn, established a need for refueling bases and repair facilities on the African coasts.

The Royal Navy's (and the dominions') strength at the outbreak of war was far greater than Germany's, but its capital ships in operation were considerably less modern, in good part because of the effects of the interwar naval treaties. The fleet consisted, in the main, of 12 battleships, most dating from the First World War (although 3 of the *Queen Elizabeth*-class battleships had been extensively modernized by 1940), 3 battle cruisers (including the *Hood*), 6 aircraft carriers (of varying efficiency), 25 heavy cruisers (including 2 Royal Australian Navy ships), 32 light cruisers (including 3 Royal Australian Navy ships), 6 antiaircraft cruisers, 168 destroyers (two-thirds of them relatively modern), 53 escort vessels ("sloops"), and 69 submarines. These were based at a wide variety of ports, with the greatest fleet strengths disposed with the Home Fleet (based at Scapa Flow in the Orkneys), the Channel Force, and the Mediterranean Fleet. In addition to the operational ships (some undergoing refit), there were also five battleships, six aircraft carriers, nine heavy cruisers, and assorted lighter units in various stages of construction.

The French Navy's strength included three newer battleships *(Provence, Bretagne, Lorraine)* and two old ones *(Courbet and Paris)*, two battle cruisers *(Dunkerque and Strasbourg)*, an aircraft carrier *(Bearn)*, ten heavy cruisers and twelve light cruisers. Most of these ships were based in the Mediterranean in September 1939, at ports such as Oran (and Mers-el-Kébir), Algiers, and Toulon. Under construction for the French Navy at this time were the battleships *Richelieu* and *Jean Bart*.

THE NAVAL WAR TO SEPTEMBER 1940: NORWAY AND "SEA LION"

The German invasion of Denmark and Norway in April 1940 ended the period of "Phony War" with a bang. German naval officers (echoing Wegener's *Seestrategie*) had long acknowledged the strategic value of Norway for German naval operations. Admiral Raeder had first broached to Hitler the subject of obtaining Norwegian ports in October 1939. The aim was to see if diplomatic pressure from Germany and the Soviet Union could persuade the Norwegians to offer such facilities.

During the fall of 1939, Germany had been content to let Norway remain "neutral," since it was able to make use of Norwegian territorial waters for its shipping and therefore avoid Royal Navy units and the British-mined international waters. But it was the view of Germany's military leadership that if Britain appeared likely to intervene in Norway, Germany would have to move first. By early 1940, the German Navy was receiving substantial intelligence (of varying quality) that indicated British plans for landings in Norway. This looked extremely serious to the German Naval Staff. As its chief of staff, Admiral Schniewind, later remarked:

> An occupation by the enemy, which by March 1940 was a possibility that had to be taken seriously into account[,] would have been a decisive setback (far more serious than in 1914/18) to Germany's chances of continuing the war at sea. That Norway—and perhaps Sweden too—might enter the war on the side of the enemy, thereby reopening the naval war in the Baltic, did not seem at that time, to be out of the question.[6]

The timing for a German invasion of Norway (and Denmark) was considered critical. In early March 1940, Admiral Raeder stressed that such an operation would be "contrary to all principles in the theory of naval warfare" but urged that it be undertaken anyway. He argued that on many occasions in the history of war such operations had proven successful if carried out by surprise. He noted that the most difficult operation for the German Navy would be its return voyage to German waters, since this would entail breaking through the ring of British naval forces then established. And he stated that all of Germany's modern naval forces would have to combine to achieve this breakthrough. Eventually, the date April 9 was fixed for the operation.

The results of the invasions of Denmark and Norway were very good from the Germans' perspective. Surprise landings along the Norwegian coast from seaborne and airborne forces rapidly achieved their initial objectives. The Royal Navy's intervention against the German naval forces involved was not nearly as damaging as it might have been, in part because the Germans were reading substantial portions of Britain's naval cypher, which provided the dispositions of the Home Fleet's ships. Again and again, German naval forces evaded the waiting British forces. In the end, German naval losses, while serious, were not as heavy as had been anticipated. The Germans lost the new heavy cruiser *Blücher*, two light cruisers, and ten destroyers. In addition, the *Scharnhorst*, *Hipper*, and *Lützow* (the renamed pocket battleship *Deutschland*) were damaged. British losses included the fleet carrier *Glorious* (caught unaware by *Scharnhorst* and *Gneisenau*), two cruisers, and nine destroyers, among others.

Indeed, the Royal Navy was lucky not to have lost considerably more ships to U-boats. Time and again the U-boats lined up on important targets only to have their torpedoes fail. Admiral Doenitz later recounted the submariners' travails: The unexpected high failure rate of German torpedoes allowed British naval units to escape unharmed; this, in turn, caused the U-boat crews to lose confidence in the weapon, and it was necessary for the U-boat commander-in-chief to use his personal influence in order to restore morale.

All in all, the German Navy counted Norway an expensive operation but a necessary one. It had prevented a potential British occupation of Norway, with all its attendant adverse strategic consequences.

Serious German planning for an invasion of Britain (Operation Sea Lion) occurred slightly more than a month after the Norwegian operation concluded. The German Army's unexpectedly rapid progress across France in May-June 1940, and the Royal Navy's highly successful evacuation of the bulk of the British Expeditionary Force (*sans* equipment) from the beaches in the vicinity of Dunkirk, presented Germany with a strategic dilemma—how to compel Britain to sue for peace when the German army could no longer engage British ground forces in battle.

The matter of an invasion of Great Britain was first taken up by Admiral Raeder with Adolf Hitler in late May 1940. Hitler, who expected Britain to seek peace terms when its French ally had gone under and who "fully appreciated the exceptional difficulties" of an invasion of the British Isles, sought to put off further action on the matter. In the following few weeks, as serious service planning for an invasion was undertaken, the Navy War Staff's view of the operation's chances became ever more pessimistic. Unlike the German Army, which saw the operation as not too much more difficult than a river crossing, the navy knew full well the dangers of carrying out an amphibious operation with inadequate resources and across waters guarded by an unbeaten Royal Navy. At a meeting with the Führer on 11 July,

Admiral Raeder informed Hitler that in contrast to the advice that he had given at the time of the Norwegian operation, he could not advocate an invasion of Britain.

Although planning for Sea Lion continued, Raeder acted to dissuade further an already reluctant Hitler from ordering the invasion. He was particularly careful to point out the disparities in planning assumptions held by the army and navy. At a meeting on 31 July he castigated the German Army Staff for continuing to insist on landings on a wide front. He told Hitler that the army had requested that the landing cover a front stretching from the Strait of Dover to Lyme Bay. Such an operation would require moving the troop transports virtually unescorted into the immediate vicinity of main British naval bases. Even weakened British naval forces could wreak havoc with the invasion fleet. In any event, Hitler decided to hold off the invasion until after the *Luftwaffe* had devastated the British Isles. In the end, therefore, it was the evident failure of the German Air Force to break the back of the Royal Air Force's Fighter Command in August and September 1940 that doomed Sea Lion. The decision to launch the operation was pushed back several times and then delayed until spring 1941, when it was finally postponed for good.

The Royal Navy's continuing command of the waters off Britain's south coast had prevented Sea Lion from being anything more than a highly problematical undertaking—as far as the German Navy was concerned. As Admiral Doenitz later recalled: "From the beginning it was clear to the leaders that the invasion could succeed only under certain particular conditions. The navy was certainly not in a position to protect the landing forces against the English Fleet, whose full weight would have to be reckoned with in such an invasion."[7]

In hindsight, it sometimes has been argued that the losses to the German Navy in ships sunk or damaged during the Norwegian campaign (and hence unavailable for operations during the summer of 1940) cost Germany its hopes for a successful invasion of Great Britain later that year. Given this argument, the question arises: Why did Germany squander its naval resources on the Norwegian campaign rather than reserve them for the much more important operations that were to occur during the scheduled German attack in the West?

While interesting as speculation, this argument nevertheless imputes to Hitler and the German High Command a strategic foresight and singleness of purpose that simply was not present in Germany's politico-military leadership. It must be remembered that German military leaders (Hitler excepted) did not expect the invasion of Belgium and France to lead to a swift and decisive victory over the Allies in

France. Moreover, Hitler believed that in the event of a French capit-
ulation, Great Britain almost certainly would be compelled to seek
peace with Germany and thus there would be no need for an invasion of that country. An additional point also should be raised —
even in hindsight, it appears highly unlikely that the German surface
fleet, even had it retained its pre–April 1940 fighting strength, would
have been sufficiently powerful to have supported an invasion of England successfully in the face of an undefeated Royal Navy and a
Royal Air Force that retained local air superiority over Britain's south
and southwest coasts.

Balked in his efforts to settle the matter by main force, Hitler soon
turned his attention eastward toward the Soviet Union. Hitler had
long wanted to settle accounts with the Communist regime there. In
addition, however, if the German *Wehrmacht* could conquer the Soviet Union in a short campaign during 1941, this would eliminate any
chance of Britain obtaining a continental ally with which to continue
its fight against the Axis, since Russia was considered "England's last
resort on the Continent." Hitler may well have felt that such an event
would persuade Great Britain to sue for peace. However, there was
some feeling in the German naval command that even if Britain itself
had been invaded, as long as the Royal Navy remained intact, the
British government under Winston Churchill would continue the war,
operating if need be from Canada and from Britain's possessions in
the Western Hemisphere.

Britain's remaining in the war during the dark days of 1940–1941
was to have a significant influence on the eventual defeat of the Axis
powers. For one thing, it guaranteed that Germany would be faced
with a dreaded two-front war. In addition, Britain's geographical position close offshore continental Europe provided the United States,
once it entered the war, with a secure base from which to mount—
together with its British and Canadian allies—the eventual assault on
German-controlled northwest Europe. The British Empire's geographic, military, naval, and manpower assets elsewhere around the
world also contributed importantly to the successful outcome of the
war.

ANGLO-AMERICAN NAVAL COOPERATION TO DECEMBER 1941

In October 1939, the American Republic approved the Declaration
of Panama, which established a "security zone" around North America (south of Canada) and South America that ranged from 300 to
1,000 miles out to sea (depending upon coastline indentations). The
belligerents were warned to avoid naval activity within this area. The

U.S. Navy was tasked by President Roosevelt with providing the necessary patrol of the security zone.

In the light of the increasingly poor prospects for Britain after April 1940, American strategic planners updated the RAINBOW War Plans, which they had begun drafting the previous year. At the end of May 1940, Plan RAINBOW No. 4 (a hemispheric and Pacific-oriented plan) was submitted to the Joint Army and Navy Board. It visualized two potentially critical dates in the further development of the European war—the date of the destruction or surrender of the British or French fleets and six months after that date, when Germany and Italy could be expected to bring their full seapower to bear in the Western Hemisphere.

In June and July 1940, Winston Churchill requested that the United States furnish Britain with fifty or sixty old destroyers for use against U-boats. This evolved eventually into a destroyers-for-bases deal (signed on 2 September 1940) in which Britain received fifty World War I-vintage, American four-stack destroyers in exchange for giving the United States ninety-nine-year leases to bases in Antigua, Jamaica, St. Lucia, the Bahamas, British Guiana, and Trinidad. The United States was also given rights to use bases in Newfoundland and Bermuda.

In late August 1940, a three-man American military delegation, headed by Rear Admiral Robert Ghormley (who was later designated special naval observer in London), met with the British chiefs of staff in London to discuss mutual concerns. The delegation's first duty was to report back to President Roosevelt on the likelihood of Britain holding out against the Germans. In the course of the talks, the British chiefs presented a very thorough strategic appreciation of the course of the war. The chiefs made it clear to the Americans that the "economic and industrial cooperation of the United States" was fundamental to Britain's whole strategy.

The Americans were told that because of inadequate means, the major British strategy would have to be defensive for some time to come. The foundation of Britain's strategy for the ultimate defeat of Germany was to wear her down by "ever-increasing force of economic pressure" (especially the blockade) and by the pursuit of a continuous and relentless air offensive against Germany and Italy. The British Chiefs summarized the military strategy for the conduct of the war as:

1. To ensure the security of the United Kingdom and our Imperial possessions and interests.
2. To maintain command of sea communications in the oceans, in Home

waters, and the Eastern Mediterranean, and to regain command throughout the Mediterranean.

3. To intensify economic pressure.

4. To intensify our air offensive against both Germany and Italy.

5. To build up our resources to an extent which will enable us to undertake major offensive operations on land as opportunity offers.[8]

During the fall of 1940, the American strategic planners moved ever closer to strategies posited on direct military support of the British Empire. By mid-December, the Joint Board, in its study "National Defense Policy of the United States," set forth the major U.S. national objectives in the immediate future. Among these was the "prevention of the disruption of the British Empire."

From 29 January to 27 March 1941, representatives of the British chiefs of staff met secretly with American military representatives in Washington to discuss the role that each country should play in defeating Germany and her allies in the event the United States entered the war. The report resulting from these staff conversations, known as ABC-1, set forth the basic strategic objectives for the two powers. Among other things, it declared that the Atlantic and European area was the decisive theater of war. It noted also that because of the threat to the sea communications of Britain, the principal task of U.S. naval forces in the Atlantic would be the protection of shipping, particularly in the northwestern approaches to the British Isles, and that American naval efforts in the Mediterranean would initially be considered of secondary importance. The ABC-1 agreements established the essential basis of American war planning for the rest of 1941 and, in broad essence, set forth the fundamental strategy by which the war was eventually fought and won.

In March 1941, Congress passed the Lend-Lease Act, and the U.S. Atlantic Fleet was soon assisting in the convoying of Lend-Lease material within North American waters. In April, the area of U.S. naval patrols was extended farther east to the line Longitude 26 W (which runs through the middle of the Azores). In June 1941 the "Greenland Patrol" was organized, while in July, following the landing of 4,000 Marines in Iceland, U.S. naval patrols and surveillance were extended to Icelandic waters.

In late May 1941, the navy had promulgated Navy Basic War Plan—RAINBOW No. 5, which included as requirements for the navy's General Task: (a) the destruction of Axis sea communications in the Western Atlantic, the Pacific, and the Far East; (b) the protection of Allied sea communications in United States Areas; and (c) support for the defense of sea communications in the United Kingdom and British

Home Waters Area, in the Far East Area, and to the eastward of Australia. Since events necessitated the augmentation of naval forces in the Atlantic, considerable U.S. Fleet forces were detached from the Pacific at about the same time.

The U.S. Atlantic Fleet began wartime convoy duties in mid-September 1941, following the order to execute the current Navy Hemispheric War Plan WPL-51. And a month later, with the activation of Plan WPL-52, the Commander-in-Chief Atlantic Fleet took command of all escort forces in the Western Atlantic Area—both U.S. and Canadian ships. The first task set for the navy by WPL-52 was to protect United States and foreign flag shipping (other than that belonging to Germany and Italy) by escorting, covering, and patrolling and by destroying German and Italian naval, land, and air forces encountered.

Thus, by mid-October 1941, almost two months before the Japanese attack on Pearl Harbor brought the United States officially into the war, the U.S. Atlantic Fleet was fully engaged in combat against Axis forces in the western Atlantic. Yet it was a policy of dire necessity, since the U.S. Navy still lacked the forces to pursue wartime responsibilities in two oceans. As Admiral Ernest King, the Atlantic Fleet's commander, wrote to a friend following the torpedoing of the American destroyer *Kearny* on 17 October:

> I am sure you realize that the KEARNY incident is but the first of many that, in the nature of things, are bound to occur. It is likely that repetition will lead to open assumptions of a war status—and what then? The Navy cannot do much more than is now being done—we are still more than a year away from any marked accession of any ships of the "2-ocean Navy."[9]

THE WAR IN THE MEDITERRANEAN

With Italy's entry into the war on Germany's side in early June 1940, just days before France's surrender, the situation in the Mediterranean changed dramatically for Britain's Mediterranean Fleet. The Germans had been thinking about military cooperation with Italy since the fall of 1939, but by the time of Italy's decision, the German Navy was not favorably disposed to the idea, since with Italy's economic and military weaknesses it was believed that she would soon be needing German help. As far as the German Navy was concerned, however, a neutral Italy would be treated cautiously by the Western powers, and this would force them to hold a certain body of naval forces in reserve in the Mediterranean—forces that would not be otherwise used in the war against Germany.

Italy's naval weaknesses were well known to the Italian Navy general staff and had been brought to Mussolini's attention prior to the decision to go to war. In mid-April 1940, the navy chief of staff, Admiral Cavagnari, had warned Il Duce that it did not seem justified for Italy to enter the war on its own initiative, since there was no possibility of achieving important strategic objectives. He prophesied that Italy would come eventually to the peace negotiations not only without territorial gains but without its fleet and, perhaps, even its air force.

From the first, German strategic thinking concerning the Mediterranean was marked by Hitler's conception of the region as a theater of secondary interest. With Italy committed to using its navy primarily for the defensive purpose of keeping open the shipping routes in the central Mediterranean from Italy to North Africa, prior to mid-1940 neither country seems to have considered using Italy's central geographic position as a base for launching offensive operations against Britain's strategic posture in the Middle East. Indeed, Italy's plan for an advance into Egypt was seen as nothing but a prestige operation by the German military leadership.

The initial plan laid down by the Italian Navy general staff called for the Italian Navy to stay on the defensive in the eastern and western basins of the Mediterranean and on the offensive and counteroffensive in the central Mediterranean. However, the tentativeness with which the Italian Navy fought its ships quickly overcame any advantage in numbers that the Italian Fleet enjoyed over its British counterpart in the central Mediterranean and its eastern basin. Once the British had settled their concerns about possible German use of the interned French Fleet by actions at Oran and Alexandria, Admiral Cunningham was ready to use his Mediterranean Fleet to seize the initiative in those waters. The successful results were so rapidly obtained that the Italian Navy was thereafter entirely reactive in its operations. Indeed, after the British sunk one and heavily damaged two more of Italy's six battleships in a night torpedo and bombing attack on the Italian Fleet at Taranto in November 1940, the head of the German Liaison Staff in Rome was moved to write to Berlin:

> The heavy blow inflicted on the Italian Fleet in harbor, while it was unable to retaliate, must be regarded as the inevitable outcome of the Italian Naval Staff's entirely defensive policy. This policy has assisted the British to build up their strength for offensive operations in the Central Mediterranean. . . . The completely passive attitude of the Italian naval authorities blinds them to a clear realization of the situation and to the logical course of action to be followed. It cripples their ability to make decisions, undermines the morale of the Italian Fleet, and encourages the British to intensify their offensive in Italian waters. . . .[10]

By September 1940, the German Naval Staff had upgraded its view of the strategic importance of Italian operations in the Mediterranean theater and was looking to possible German operations against Gibraltar and the Suez Canal as a way of unhinging Britain's entire strategic position in the area. Hitler and the Supreme Command, however, were too preoccupied with planning for the forthcoming invasion of the Soviet Union to give such thinking any serious attention. Mussolini's disastrous invasion of Greece and the Italian collapse in North Africa were the catalysts that finally brought German military forces into the theater. Ironically, given the German Naval Staff's view of the value of the Mediterranean for Axis strategy, it was disinclined to send German naval units to reinforce the Italians. It wasn't until after mid-September 1941 that German U-boats and light naval forces were sent to support the Italian Navy, and then it was at Hitler's personal urging.

Yet despite its slowness in taking up the challenge, starting in November 1941 Germany sought to win control of the Mediterranean Sea, particularly the vital central Mediterranean, using the Axis naval and air resources available in the region. German U-boats and other Axis forces quickly began taking a toll of British ships. In November 1941, a U-boat sank the aircraft carrier *Ark Royal* of Admiral Somerville's Gibraltar-based Force H, and another sank the battleship *Barham* of Cunningham's Mediterranean Fleet. In mid-December, the British lost the cruiser *Galatea* off Alexandria. Several days later Italian midget submarines successfully penetrated Alexandria harbor and heavily damaged the battleships *Queen Elizabeth* and *Valiant* with delayed-action mines. Cunningham suddenly lacked a battle squadron, and the Admiralty again began seriously to consider withdrawing the Mediterranean Fleet from the eastern basin, holding on only to the Suez Canal and Gibraltar. This was, of course, only days after Japan had attacked British, American, and Dutch possessions in the Pacific, sinking or heavily damaging the American battleships at Pearl Harbor and sinking the British capital ships *Prince of Wales* and *Repulse* off Malaya.

Although control of the Mediterranean remained in dispute for much of 1942, Admiral Cunningham continued to keep the stronger Italian Fleet off balance—the Second Battle of Sirte in March 1942 offering a case in point. Still, it was Britain's continued possession of its facilities on the island of Malta that largely kept Axis plans for the control of the central Mediterranean unfulfilled. Although the Italians and the German Naval Staff understood the strategic importance of Malta to Britain for keeping a secure foothold in the central Mediterranean, Italian military inadequacies, coupled with the German Supreme Command's refusal to commit the necessary air and ground forces to the task of capturing the island while Rommel's requirements in North Africa took precedence, kept the Axis from seizing that vital base.

Similarly, Hitler's unwillingness to coerce Spain's Franco into allowing a German operation against the key strategic target at the western end of the Mediterranean—Gibraltar—meant that throughout the war in that theater, Britain held pivotal bases with which to harry Axis operations in North Africa. With the successful Anglo-American landings in North Africa in November 1942, the handwriting of eventual Axis defeat in the theater was on the wall. Although the addition of German reinforcements to the theater, particularly the *Luftwaffe* units, in the months after October 1941 severely punished British attempts to maintain its Malta outpost (in part due to the inadequate number of British aircraft carriers available to the convoys for contesting local air superiority), Germany was never able to assert control over the central Mediterranean. The combined Anglo-American naval forces available in the theater by 1943 provided the sure underpinning for the landings in Sicily and on the coast of Italy, which ended major Axis naval operations in the Mediterranean. A year later at Normandy, these navies, in landing the armies that were to fight the battles for Northwest Europe, were to help set in motion Germany's final defeat.

FIGHTING IN THE ARCTIC

Germany's invasion of the Soviet Union in June 1941 soon opened up another front to the naval fighting, as Britain and the United States attempted to supply the Russians with essential war material and other goods in order to keep that country in the war. There were only two useful routes by which supplies from Britain could reach the Soviet Union—to Murmansk and the port of Archangel (on the White Sea) in the north, or via the Cape of Good Hope to the Persian Gulf and thence overland for more than 1,000 miles, in the south. The convoying of material to north Russia was seen as an essential means of providing aid at a time when there was little else that Britain and the United States could do to ensure that Russia would stay in the war.

The battle of the Arctic convoys consisted of three phases once the first winter (1941–1942) had passed. During the first phase, lasting from March 1942 to January 1943, German attacks on the British convoys were extremely heavy and included attacks by *Luftwaffe* units,

U-boats, and German surface forces based in Norway. Interesting to note, however, the German surface forces were "handled with marked timidity," in part because of Hitler's strictures on capital-ship employment following the loss of the *Bismarck* in May 1941.

The second phase of this campaign encompassed the years of 1943 and 1944. Because of *Luftwaffe* preoccupation elsewhere, attacks were carried out only by U-boats. The third phase extended from December 1944 to the end of the war. During this period the *Luftwaffe* again was quite active and the U-boats used new and more successful tactics, although the severity of the attacks never attained the levels that had been achieved in 1942. Interestingly, during the entire Arctic campaign, Germany managed to sink only 92 merchantmen (and 18 warships) out of a total of 811 merchant vessels sent to north Russia.

One of the ironic aspects of the convoy operations in the Arctic was the relative passivity of the Soviet Navy in those waters (and indeed elsewhere, except for the Black Sea). The Soviets provided little or no help to the Royal Navy's convoy efforts. This Soviet naval passivity was so marked that Admiral Ernest King remarked in a letter to Admiral Sir Dudley Pound about the incomprehensible Russian attitude, "They will accept no help and yet do little or nothing themselves."

THE BATTLE OF THE ATLANTIC

The "Battle of the Atlantic" was one of the (if not *the*) pivotal naval campaigns of the European war. During several periods of this campaign, German U-boats came close to effectively severing the sea lines of communication to the British Isles.

There were three major phases in U-boat successes during this campaign. The "First Happy Time" (in German submariners' parlance) lasted from June 1940 to May 1941, when the U-boats were fighting in the Western approaches, close to Britain. The "Second Happy Time" occurred from February to October 1942 in American coastal waters, just after the United States had entered the war. And the third phase occurred in the spring of 1943, when the biggest convoy battles of the war were being fought in the middle of the North Atlantic. It is important to note in this connection that throughout the war Doenitz moved his U-boat wolfpacks constantly—keeping them in areas where the targets were plentiful and the enemy defenses weak, but moving them quickly if the pickings became slim or, particularly, if enemy defenses stiffened.

During the first months of the war, German attacks on shipping in the Channel and in the Atlantic had been reduced in effectiveness by two factors: political restraints placed on naval freedom of action by Hitler (who was convinced that events might soon force France and Britain to seek peace), and the very limited number of U-boats available for operations. With regard to the number of operational U-boats, at the outbreak of the war Germany possessed only fifty-six U-boats, and only about a third of this number consisted of submarines (Type VIIC and IXC U-boats) with the range necessary for operations in the Atlantic. Regarding this early period of the war, Admiral Doenitz commented that because of the very small number of U-boats available during this time, it was evident to the U-boat command that they could only inflict "pinpricks" on Britain's trade. In fact, until April 1940 it was the Germans' laying of magnetic mines and not the U-boat that most threatened British shipping.

Despite the changeover to U-boat construction authorized in the Mobilization Plan after early September 1939, the inventory of German boats increased only gradually. Given an expected construction period for U-boats of twenty-one months, it meant that even the U-boats ordered in September 1939 could not be expected to be operational for two years. And although Admiral Raeder urged Hitler's support for an expanded U-boat construction effort throughout the fall of 1939 and winter of 1939–1940, raw-material requirements for the German Army were given first priority. Raeder's feelings on the urgency of this issue were perhaps best demonstrated in a meeting with the Führer on 23 September 1939. At that time he stressed:

> The submarine construction program set up within the framework of the Mobilization Plan, as ordered by the Führer in the conference on 7 September 1939, gives figures which, in the long run, will not keep pace with the anticipated losses. The planned increases are approximately as follows:
>
> 1939—7 submarines
> 1940—46 submarines
> 1941—10 submarines per month
>
> In 1918 the Scheer Program provided for approximately thirty submarines per month. Thus in about two weeks at the latest, when the aforementioned political decision is made, the number of submarines to be constructed must be increased to at least twenty to thirty per month.[11]

German shortages in U-boats did not ease appreciably until early 1941. During the first quarter of that year, the average number of U-boats produced reached ten a month, and by the end of 1941, Doenitz had ninety-eight operational boats available. These numbers continued to improve during the following years. By July 1942 the number of operational U-boats had reached 140 (out of a total of 331) and by July 1943, 208 (out of 415 in inventory).

It is ironic, therefore, that Germany's first major success in the Atlantic battle—the "First Happy Time"—occurred when its U-boat fleet was still very small. In part, this first success (which in terms of tonnage sunk per submarine was never equalled thereafter) was due to factors such as the thorough training and excellent combat skills of the first U-boat captains—men such as Prien, Kretschmer, and Schepke—and the inexperience of the Royal Navy in locating and killing the deadly submarines. During the interwar period for example, Britain had developed a submarine locating device, "Asdic" (later "sonar"), for which it had highly inflated hopes at the start of the war. But clearly, the biggest advantage that the U-boat fleet had, even in those early days, was the German Navy's interception and deciphering of British naval coded traffic relating to convoys. This readily available deciphered information provided the Germans not only with news of convoy routing, but also with warning of enemy reconnaissance, and information on when the enemy became aware of the U-boats and when enemy units were being sent out to oppose them.

This German intelligence success was not unmatched in Britain, where the Government Code and Cypher School (GC and CS) had begun breaking the German naval *Enigma* cipher traffic consistently in April 1941. Through mid-1943, however, Britain faced two difficulties in this communications intelligence contest: first, the Royal Navy remained unaware that Germany was reading its convoy message traffic until December 1942 and thus failed to take the opportunity to increase communications security effectively until late 1942; and second, from early 1942 until December 1942, GC and CS was unable to read U-boat ("Shark") *Enigma* messages. But from May 1943 through the rest of the war, Britain's naval intelligence capabilities raced ahead, while Germany's declined significantly. Britain's ability to read much of the U-boat radio traffic fairly rapidly, when coupled with accurate radio direction finding of the U-boats' transmissions, not only enabled the Admiralty to determine fairly accurately the positions of individual submarines but also to compile information on the U-boats' tactics, their endurance, and their average speed of advance when proceeding to and from patrol.

During the period 1939–1942, the United States played a very important role in the Atlantic war by progressively extending naval patrolling responsibilities to the east. Because Hitler wanted to avoid war with the United States at almost any cost, the imposition of the Pan American security zone and the subsequent U.S. Navy patrolling served to severely hamper U-boat operations in the western Atlantic.

Yet, when Hitler declared war and the United States officially entered the conflict in December 1941, it found itself totally unprepared to protect its own coastal shipping, much less that on the North and Mid-Atlantic Ocean. It was very short of escorts for convoys—the events in the Pacific having necessitated the deployment of many destroyers to that theater, for example—and largely as a result, U.S. coastal and Caribbean shipping largely remained unescorted from January 1942 through May 1942. U-boat sinkings in the Atlantic (the largest proportion during the first seven months from the areas off the east and southeast coasts of the United States), rose from 296,000 tons in January 1942 to a new high of 652,500 tons in June and then slacked off gradually thereafter.

The danger had reached such proportions by mid-1942 that General George Marshall, the army chief of staff, was moved to write Admiral King, now chief of naval operations, that the losses by submarines off the U.S. Atlantic seaboard and in the Caribbean threatened the entire U.S. war effort. He was fearful also that another month or two of these sinkings would so cripple the United States's means of transport that it would be unable to bring "sufficient men and planes to bear against the enemy" in certain vital theaters to "exercise a determining influence on the war."

Measures were slowly being taken in hand on both sides of the Atlantic, however. The Anglo-American military leaders agreed to give escort ships a high priority in construction and to launch heavy bombing attacks against German submarine pens and industry. The Royal Air Force's Coastal Command and U.S. Navy and Army Air Forces bomber units stationed along the North American East Coast, after many months of effort, started obtaining U.S.-built Liberator aircraft equipped with 10-centimeter search radar (which the German U-boats could not detect) in sufficient numbers to close the mid-ocean air gap. With larger numbers of warships available, importantly including the U.S.-designed small escort carriers with their complements of aircraft for antisubmarine operations, convoys now found themselves backstopped by hunter-killer support groups. These were just a few of the more significant measures that eventually furnished success.

In early 1943, despite continued high overall sinking rates of Allied merchantmen, the U-boat fleet found itself taking ever larger losses. Finally, in May 1943, Doenitz decided to pull his boats out of the North Atlantic in a vain attempt to prepare them to reassert German successes there. In late May, Doenitz informed the Führer that he had withdrawn his U-boats from the North Atlantic because of insupportable losses (running at fifteen to seventeen submarines a month), but that he planned to resume operations in that area once the submarines had been equipped with additional weapons that would enable them to hold their own against the deadly Allied aircraft and naval forces.

Nevertheless, not even the addition to the fleet of new submarine improvements over the final two years of the war—including *Schnorkel*-equipped boats capable of running their diesel engines and of receiving fresh air while submerged, boats equipped with heavy anti-aircraft armament for fighting it out on the surface against planes, and new faster methods of underwater propulsion—enabled the U-boat arm to seize the initiative again in the battle over shipping. After many months of fighting, in May 1943 the Allied navies essentially won their hardest campaign.

Indeed, the most severe threat that the U-boat war in the Atlantic posed to Allied strategy after mid-1942 was the threat of sinking enough Allied shipping to delay or curtail projected Allied military operations in the European theaters. Although U-boat sinkings continued at a high level during the rest of 1942 and into the first third of 1943, the shipping losses were insufficient to hamper the buildup of troops and equipment necessary for the Allied landings in North Africa in November 1942 or the invasions of Sicily and Italy in 1943. Interestingly, the plans for the North African operation were so successfully guarded that the German High Command remained unaware of the real purpose of the buildup right up to the start of the landings. For this reason, those Atlantic U-boats that might have been diverted to attack Operation TORCH convoys heading to Gibraltar were left to seek targets among regular merchant shipping convoys in the Atlantic.

And in May 1943, when the U-boats were forced to withdraw from the North Atlantic, Allied antisubmarine activity in the Mediterranean already was beginning to reduce the U-boat menace in that theater to manageable proportions. Thus, the Allied buildups for the invasions of Sicily and Italy were carried out without a significant threat from German U-boats. Similarly, with regard to the Normandy landings in June 1944, the combination of Allied tactical surprise and extensive antisubmarine protection kept the invasion fleet free of attack during its Channel crossing and, furthermore, prevented the Biscay-based U-boats from even penetrating the assault area until nine days after the initial landings had occurred.

CONCLUDING REMARKS

The schizophrenic nature of the German fleet in the first years of the war undoubtedly contributed to the tentative way it was handled during those years. Caught unprepared by a political demarche over Poland gone wrong, the German Navy in September 1939 found itself facing its most dangerous European opponent with a fleet that was but a sad mockery of its dreams. Having chosen the path of a slow-to-build "balanced fleet" rather than a submarine-heavy force better fitted for a strategy of tonnage warfare, Erich Raeder could do little but ask his officers to die gallantly, in service to a reborn navy to come.

The tentativeness with which the German Navy's capital ships were handled throughout the war (leaving aside the fighting for Norway and a few other instances), was indicative of the Führer's and, to a lesser extent, the Naval War Staff's fear of losing them in action. Indeed, it was of a piece with Hitler's tentativeness toward his main enemy during the first year of the war—until much too late in 1940 he retained the hope that Britain would see the futility of the war's prolongation and ask to seek the peace that he was willing to offer. He had not the measure of Mr. Churchill. Thus, early in the war, having sent out his forces to raid Britain's supply lines, he held them back for some days while waiting to see if an early decision in Poland would encourage French and British acquiescence in his conquest. And it was Hitler himself who called for the return of the pocket battleship *Deutschland* to German waters just a month after the war had begun, lest it should be sunk and thereby lower German morale.

Overall, in contrast to Raeder's overly cautious handling of Germany's few capital ships in the first years, Doenitz's handling of the U-boat arm was strong and self-assured. It is important to remark, however, on the lack of a truly strategic perspective shown by Doenitz's economic campaign against the Allies. For example, as late as April 1943, Doenitz was telling the Führer:

> Submarine warfare is difficult. However, it is obvious, that the aim of sinking merchant ships must be to sink more than the enemy can build. If we do not reach this objective, the enemy would continue to suffer severely through loss of his material substance, but we would not be successful in bleeding him to death due to diminution of his tonnage. I therefore fear

that the submarine war will be a failure if we do not sink more ships than the enemy is able to build.[12]

Tonnage warfare is a respecter of neither ship nor cargo; in the slow but steady attrition of the enemy's shipping it matters little in the accumulation of enemy tonnage what targets are attacked. Yet to outlast a country such as the United States in a shipbuilding versus ship-sinking contest, one must possess an almost inexhaustible capacity for replacing submarines and trained crews. Since Germany lacked such capacity, she might better have attempted to determine the weak links of the Allied convoy system and then concentrate her attacks on these. And this she never understood, much less attempted.

It was lucky for Great Britain that the sinking of the passenger liner *Athenia* on the first day of the war forced her to accept convoying at the beginning. And it was fortunate as well that she learned the limitations of Asdic before being forced to confront Karl Doenitz's enlarged U-boat fleet. Fortunately, too, Britain's geographic position astride Germany's routes to the open ocean continued without great change from the first Great War. With the fall of France, Germany indeed gained ports on France's Atlantic (Biscay) coast, but Britain's defenses in the English Channel made transit through the Channel by German surface units moving between Wilhelmshaven, say, and Brest a hazardous experience, and one to which even U-boats were not immune. And even though Germany attempted to break out of the "strategically empty" North Sea by seizing Norway, the U.K. was able to maintain some measure of positional control by moving rapidly into Iceland once Norway had been invaded. Similarly, Britain's retention of Gibraltar gave her close access to ships attempting to enter into or exit from the Mediterranean.

Among the Royal Navy's most serious weaknesses was its antiquated Fleet Air Arm, largely a product of the two decades of neglect represented by its stepchild existence as part of the Royal Air Force. The navy's lack of adequate numbers of aircraft carriers and its woefully obsolescent carrier aircraft until late in the war caused untold grief and many casualties during the naval campaign in the Mediterranean. Interestingly, the German Navy itself sorely felt the lack of an integral air arm, particularly for its long-range reconnaissance requirements. And, too, it saw how quickly its own air priorities could be ignored by the High Command, when, in the midst of its successful attacks against British coastal shipping in 1941, the vast bulk of the *Luftwaffe* units were withdrawn for employment in the Russian campaign.

Given the nature of its entry into the war, the United States Navy found itself balancing its needs in the Atlantic with its more extensive requirements in the Pacific. The overwhelming strengths that the U.S. Navy brought to the European war were its skill in logistics and its superb understanding of amphibious operations. It is interesting to note here, however, that to her German enemies it was America's military-industrial power that held the key to Allied victory. This point was stressed by German Admirals Schniewind and Schuster, who in an intelligence appreciation written shortly after the war, stated:

> The entry of a nation like the USA into the war, as may be concluded in the light of subsequent knowledge, but which was definitely not recognized at the end of 1941, really meant the final overthrow of Germany's prospects of victory. . . . It is the opinion of the authors that in the 1939/45 war as in the war of 1914/18 the entry of America into the war with her enormous arms potential was *the* decisive factor which brought about Germany's defeat.[13]

NOTES

The author would like to thank Bernard Cavalcante, Mike Walker, and Kathy Lloyd of the Naval Historical Center's Operational Archives and the staff of the Navy Department Library for their help in connection with this chapter.

1. (Emphasis in original.) Secret [declassified] NID24/T131/45, "Letter Signed by Raeder on the Disguising of E-Boat Building"; Box T80, German Naval Archives files, Operational Archives, Naval Historical Center, Washington Navy Yard (hereafter NHC).

2. (Emphasis added.) Quoted in N. H. Gibbs, *Grand Strategy, Volume I: Rearmament Policy, History of the Second World War* (London: Her Majesty's Stationery Office, 1976), p. 167.

3. Restricted [declassified], N.I.D. 1/GP/13, 15th October 1945, "Essay by Vice-Admiral Heye on the Naval Aspects of the War," p. 7; German Naval Archives files, Operational Archives, NHC.

4. (Emphasis in original.) "Reflection of the Commander in Chief, Navy on the Outbreak of War, 3 September 1939"; in Confidential [Declassified], *Führer Conferences on Matters Dealing with the German Navy 1939* (Washington, DC: Office of Naval Intelligence, Navy Department, 1947), p. 2.

5. J. R. M. Butler, *Grand Strategy, Volume II: September 1939–June 1941, History of the Second World War* (London: Her Majesty's Stationery Office, 1957), p. 71.

6. Confidential [declassified], N.I.D. 1/G.P/23, 10th November, 1946, "Essay by General Admiral Schniewind and Admiral Schuster on the German Conduct of the War at Sea," p. 17; German Naval Archives files, Operational Archives, NHC.

7. Restricted [declassified], "'The Conduct of the War at Sea, An Essay by

Admiral Karl Dönitz" (Washington, DC: Division of Naval Intelligence, Navy Department, 15 January 1946), p. 8.

8. Quoted in Secret [declassified], Lieutenant Abbot Smith, USNR, "Chapter VI: The Battle of the Atlantic (to April 30, 1943)," *History of the Joint Chiefs of Staff: The War Against Germany and her Satellites.* Unpublished manuscript, Military Reference branch, National Archives, p. 25. This chapter was one of several written for the unfinished JCS history of the war against Germany and thus never received official JCS endorsement.

9. Letter from King to L. F. V. Drake, October 24, 1941; Box 8, Papers of Ernest J. King; Naval Historical Foundation Collection, Manuscript Division, Library of Congress.

10. Restricted [declassified], O.N.I. ref: G.H.S./5, [Vice Admiral Eberhard Weichold] *Axis Naval Policy and Operations in the Mediterranean 1939 to May 1943* (Washington, DC: Office of Naval Intelligence, Navy Department, May 1951), author's collection, p. 18. Weichold was senior liaison officer to the Italian Naval Staff from June 1940 on. From November 1941, he also assumed the command of all German naval forces in the Mediterranean.

11. "Conference between the Chief, Naval Staff and the Führer on 23 September 1939 in Zoppot," *Führer Naval Conferences 1939,* p. 10.

12. "Minutes of the Conference between the Commander in Chief of the Navy and the Führer on 11 April 1943 at the 'Berghof' "; Confidential [declassified] *Führer Conferences on Matters Dealing with the German Navy 1943* (Washington, DC: Office of Naval Intelligence, Navy Department, 1946), p. 20.

13. Schniewind and Schuster, "The German conduct of the War at Sea," p. 30. (Emphasis in original).

BIBLIOGRAPHIC NOTE

Samuel Eliot Morison, whose semiofficial fifteen-volume history of U.S. naval operations in World War II remains a cornerstone of U.S. naval writing, also published a small volume entitled *Strategy And Compromise,* which was based on a series of lectures he gave in the mid-1950s. The portion dealing with "The War In Europe" should be read. Samuel Eliot Morison, *Strategy And Compromise* (Boston: Little, Brown and Co., 1958), pp. 3–60. Herbert Rosinski served until 1936 on the faculty of the German Naval Staff College. Several of his papers were published posthumously by the Naval War College Press. His article "German Theories of Sea Warfare" and its companion "Strategy and Propaganda In German Naval Thought," are both excellent introductions to German naval thinking in the twentieth century. B. Mitchell Simpson III, ed., *The Development of Naval Thought: Essays by Herbert Rosinski* (Newport, RI: Naval War College Press, 1977), pp. 53–101. Captain Stephen Roskill, RN (Ret.) was Britain's Official Naval Historian of World War II. His book *Churchill And The Admirals* provides a fascinating challenge to the traditional view of Winston Churchill's influence on the Royal Navy as first lord and prime minister. His chapter "Return to Power and the Norwegian Campaign 1939–1940" is one of several interesting analyses therein. Stephen Roskill, *Churchill and the Admirals* (New York: William Morrow and Company, Inc., 1978), pp. 93–113. Finally, it is always good to read an article that manages to set conventional thinking on its head. One such article is Alan J. Levine's "Was World War II a Near-run Thing?" *The Journal of Strategic Studies*, vol. 8, no. 1 (March 1985), pp. 38–63.

ADDITIONAL SOURCES

Auphan, Paul and Jacques Mordal. *The French Navy in World War II.* Annapolis, MD: U.S. Naval Institute, 1959.

Beesley, Patrick. *Very Special Intelligence: The Story of the Admiralty's Operational Intelligence Centre 1939–1945.* Garden City, NY: Doubleday & Company, Inc., 1978.

Bragadin, Commander (R) Marc' Antonio, Italian Navy. *The Italian Navy in World War II.* Annapolis, MD: U.S. Naval Institute, 1957.

Clayton, Anthony. *The British Empire As A Superpower 1919–1939.* Athens, GA: The University of Georgia Press, 1986.

Derry, T. K. *United Kingdom Military Series, The Campaign In Norway, The History Of The Second World War.* London: Her Majesty's Stationery Office, 1952.

May, Ernest R., ed. *Knowing One's Enemies: Intelligence Assessment Before The Two World Wars.* Princeton: Princeton University Press, 1984.

Morison, Samuel Eliot. *The Two-Ocean War: A Short History of the United States Navy in the Second World War.* Boston: Little, Brown & Co., 1963.

Padfield, Peter. *Dönitz, The Last Führer: Portrait of a Nazi War Leader.* New York: Harper & Row, Publishers, 1984.

Raeder, Grand Admiral Erich. *My Life.* Annapolis, MD: U.S. Naval Institute, 1960.

Roskill, Captain S. W., RN. *White Ensign: The British Navy At War 1939–1945.* Annapolis, MD: U.S. Naval Institute, 1960.

Ruge, Vice Admiral Friedrich, Navy, Federal Republic of Germany. *Der Seekrieg: The German Navy's Story 1939–1945.* Annapolis, MD: U.S. Naval Institute, 1957.

Wark, Wesley K. *The Ultimate Enemy: British Intelligence and Nazi Germany, 1933–1939.* Ithaca, NY: Cornell University Press, 1985.

10

World War II
U.S. and Japanese
Naval Strategies

BY JEFFREY G. BARLOW

WAR PLAN ORANGE AND THE INTERWAR PERIOD:
U.S. PLANNING

Serious U.S. planning for a war against Japan (ORANGE, in the roster of color-coded war plans) began in 1907, in the midst of a war scare related to strained U.S.-Japanese diplomatic relations. The focus of U.S. concern was the newly acquired Philippine Islands. It was felt that Japanese forces could be assembled to invade the Philippines and defeat the American garrison stationed there. At this time the Philippine Islands were under consideration as a potential location for the United States Navy's major fleet base in the Pacific. However, concerns over the long-term defensibility of sites at Manila Bay and Subig (later Subic) Bay precluded the Philippines being chosen, and early in 1908, Pearl Harbor, on Oahu in the Hawaiian Islands, was selected to be the site of the navy's main base. Nevertheless, the navy had a need for a secondary base in the Western Pacific, and Cavite, on the south shore of Manila Bay, was selected to fulfill this role. The U.S. Army was tasked with the defense of this base, and elected to concentrate its main defenses on islands in and around the bay. The principal strong point was located on Corregidor.

By 1913, scenarios for war with Japan over control of the Philippines had been thoroughly explored and digested. It was not until the conclusion of the First World War, however, that the Joint Army and Navy Board (hereafter, the Joint Board) began refining the elements of War Plan ORANGE in some detail. An ORANGE war was expected to be "[a]n offensive war, primarily naval, directed toward the isolation and harassment of Japan, through control of her vital sea communications and through offensive sea and air operations against her naval forces and economic life." The U.S. Fleet, consisting of a force at least 25 percent superior to the total naval strength of Japan (this figure later was increased to 50 percent), would be concentrated in the Hawaiian Islands and sail rapidly across the Pacific toward Manila Bay. Then, having established itself in Philippine waters, it would relieve the beleaguered defenders, leaving the army reinforcements that had been brought along to recapture seized Philippine territory while it sought out the Japanese fleet and contested it for control of the Western Pacific.

Because the U.S. Fleet was expected to be subjected to a series of attacks by Japanese light forces designed to whittle down its strength during its transit to the Philippines, it would need access to a base in the Western Pacific where it could repair battle damage and refit before engaging the Japanese Navy in a decisive fleet action. The facilities at Manila Bay were the obvious choice, but if these had fallen under Japanese control, another base in the Philippines or elsewhere would have to be used. The army planners in the 1920s were more pessimistic about the likelihood of a Western Pacific base remaining available to the U.S. Fleet than were most of the navy planners. In a 1923 army draft of War Plan ORANGE prepared by Lieutenant Colonel Walter Krueger, the possibility that Japan might seize all U.S. Western Pacific territories in order to forestall early, decisive American action was discussed. The draft noted:

> . . . Japan will probably endeavor, with all the means at her command, to accentuate the naturally great difficulties the United States is bound to encounter in an offensive across the Pacific, that is, that Japan will endeavor to brush aside the precarious foothold of the United States in the Far East in the Philippines, Guam, Wake Island, and Samoa, and will occupy these islands herself, as well as the mandated islands now under her control, thereby making it extremely difficult to penetrate the defensive cordon so formed.[1]

Japan's ability to interdict the U.S. Fleet's movement to the Philippines had been increased in 1919 by the League of Nations' awarding control to Japan of Germany's Pacific possessions in the Marshall and Caroline archipelagoes, in the aftermath of the signing of the Versailles Treaty. Japan's strategic position was further strengthened in 1922 when the Five-Power Naval Treaty was concluded. In this treaty, one of several arising from the Washington Naval Conference of 1921–22, Japan agreed to accept a 5:5:3 (Britain: United States: Japan) ratio in capital ships, in exchange for a promise from the signatory powers that they would maintain the status quo on fortifications in the Pacific region, except for those in the Hawaiian Islands, Australia, New Zealand, the islands comprising Japan proper, and the west coasts of Canada and the United States. This meant that the United States would be unable to fortify further its bases in the Aleutians or in the Philippines, Guam, and other islands to the west of Hawaii. Great Britain was in the same position with regard to its Pacific possessions, except for its base at Singapore, which fell outside the geographic confines of the treaty. Thus, the agreement virtually removed any threat that these Western bases might otherwise have posed to Japan's position in the Western Pacific.

Each year throughout the interwar period, officers attending the senior course at the Naval War College at Newport, Rhode Island, played out a series of war games tied to Plan ORANGE that were designed to test various scenarios as the BLUE (U.S.) Fleet advanced into the Western Pacific to defeat the ORANGE Fleet and recapture the Philippines. By the late 1920s, relatively rapid campaign scenarios involving the ready movement of the fleet to the Philippines had evolved into drawn-out, protracted war scenarios, as the understanding increased that, in any rapid advance the U.S. battle line's initial superiority could be readily drawn down by Japanese attacks launched from occupied islands that flanked the approach routes to the Philippine Islands. By the later 1930s, the war game scenarios were being predicated on conflicts of from three to five years' duration.

There were three basic routes from the Hawaiian Islands to the Philippines—the northern route, the central route, and the southern route. The northern route proceeded from Hawaii to Midway Island and then to Wake Island, and from Wake to Guam in the southern Marianas and finally on to the Philippines. It had the disadvantage of being reverse-flanked throughout by Japanese forces to the south in the Japanese-controlled Marshall and Caroline Island chains and the Palau islands and by the Marianas to the north. The central route, through the Japanese mandated islands themselves and on to the Philippines, would require a frontal attack through Japanese-dominated waters. And the southern route from Hawaii to the south of the "Mandates" and on to the Philippines also was flanked throughout by the Marshalls, Carolines, and Palaus and had the other disadvantage of being bottlenecked against northwest New Guinea.

In 1933, Naval War College student Captain Ernest King (who in less than a decade would be using the strategic insights gained here in his direction of the navy's war), was convinced that a north-central route presented the best approach to the Philippines. In such an approach, a covering force would be sent to the southern Marianas while an occupation force moved to the northwest Marshalls. In phase two, an occupation force would move into Truk in the Central Carolines and establish a base there. These dispositions would allow seizure and occupation, in the third phase of the war, of a triangle based on Guam, Truk, and the Palaus and the eventual safe movement into the Philippines.

Over the course of the twenty-three years from 1919 until the United States entered the Second World War in December 1941, BLUE fleets fought ORANGE fleets in campaign (strategic) war games at Newport 127 times. Yet despite the undoubted repetition of campaign scenarios, the games served to acquaint the participating officers with many of the aspects of moving a fleet across the Pacific, establishing forward bases and maintaining logistics chains (to mention just a few strategic factors) that would be encountered when war came. And as the games themselves were refined, through the incorporation of information based on changing operational realities, they imbued their players with some sense of the prolonged and difficult efforts that would be required to win back captured territories and eventually to defeat the Japanese Empire.

The last version of Joint War Plan ORANGE was approved in February 1938. But by this time, Plan ORANGE was little more than an artifact, because it continued to envision a strategy based on fighting one enemy in one ocean. Alas, the belligerency of German and Italian actions had made the possibility of conflict in Europe all too palpable by the latter half of the 1930s. In November 1938, the Joint Board belatedly directed the Joint Planning Committee to make exploratory studies regarding U.S. courses of action in the event one or more of the Fascist powers violated the Monroe Doctrine and the Japanese simultaneously attempted to assert influence in the Philippines.

The eventual result of these studies was the drafting of the RAINBOW Plans—war plans designed to position American military forces to meet a two-ocean threat, since all the plans were predicated on German, Italian, and Japanese actions in concert against the United States. The first of these plans was drafted during the initial half of 1939 and was approved by President Franklin Roosevelt in October of that year, only weeks after the war's outbreak in Europe. The last of these plans, RAINBOW No. 5, which had superseded the others in mid-1941, was the guiding strategic concept for joint army and navy action at the time the U.S. entered the war. Following the views adopted during the U.S.-British Staff Conversations of March 1941 (ABC-1), RAINBOW No. 5 established the Atlantic and European area as the decisive theater of war. Germany, as the predominant member of the Axis powers, was to be defeated first, and if Japan entered the war, Allied military strategy in the Far East was to be defensive in nature until Germany had been defeated.

JAPANESE PLANNING

After 1907, the Imperial Japanese Navy (IJN) regarded the United States as a country whose interests would likely be in conflict with those of Japan in the Far East. However, this perception of the United States as a significant potential adversary was not shared by the Imperial Japanese Army. The army, consistently focused on events on the mainland of Asia, saw Russia (and later the Soviet Union) as the ultimate potential enemy. Undoubtedly, this disparity of thinking between the two services had much to do with the fact that there was little serious combined (or national-level) war planning for a conflict with the United States during the interwar period. The earliest Japanese Navy plan for a Pacific war was completed in 1909, but the United States was seen as more a "budgetary" enemy than a factual one. And although as early as 1918 Japanese contingency plans included a coordinated army-navy seizure of the Philippines in order to deprive the United States of advanced bases in the Western Pacific, such plans lacked the thoroughness of their American counterparts. In Japanese operational planning after World War I, war against the United States was labelled Operation KO ("A").

Prior to the 1920s, the Imperial Japanese Navy had been fixated on the decisive fleet engagement, as heralded by Mahan and demonstrated by the decisive battle of Tsushima during the Russo-Japanese War, in which Admiral Togo's Japanese fleet devastated the Russian fleet of Admiral Rozhdestvensky, sinking thirty-three of forty-five Russian ships during the two-day fight at a cost of only three Japanese torpedo boats. The great British-German fleet encounter at Jutland during the First World War, although tactically indecisive, further strengthened the IJN's interest in decisive battle. The IJN's basic conception envisioned *strategems* to lure the U.S. Fleet into the Western Pacific. There, having picked the time and place for the battle, the Japanese battle line would annihilate the American battle line in waters off the coast of Japan, using superior maneuverability to overcome the American advantage in firepower.

The signing of the Five-Power Naval Treaty in 1922, however, soon made it necessary for the Japanese Navy to revise its strategic thinking. Under the terms of the treaty, Japan was accorded the right to maintain a fleet of capital ships only 60 percent as large as those of either Britain or the United States. As this significant limitation sunk in, Japanese naval strategists quickly became aware that history showed few, if any, cases in which a navy equipped with a capital ship force representing less than two-thirds of the tonnage of its adversary had emerged victorious in decisive fleet action. Accordingly, a new method of gaining victory was sought. The new concept that emerged was called *yogeki sakusen* (interceptive operations). As refined during 1923–1925 under the direction of Admiral Nobumasa Suetsugu, the head of operational planning on the navy general staff, it involved the adoption of a policy of "offensive defense."

Under this strategy, Japanese heavy units were to remain on the defensive in Japanese home waters. In the meantime, Japanese light forces, including submarines, destroyers, and aircraft, staging out of bases in the Mandates and the Marianas, would attack and harry the U.S. Fleet advancing to rescue the Philippines. The main features of these "diminution" operations would be surprise attacks by submarines, night torpedo attacks by destroyers, and air attacks by land- and carrier-based torpedo- and dive-bombing aircraft. It was expected that such attacks would reduce the U.S. Fleet's offensive strength by some 30 percent by the time it had reached Philippine waters. This attrition of U.S. naval strength would bring the overall ratio of U.S. to Japanese strength close to parity and would enable the waiting Japanese battle line to defeat the Americans decisively.

In addition to annual exercises of the combined fleet, which tested aspects of this "offensive defense" strategy, students at Japan's Naval War College—like their counterparts at Newport—played out numerous war games. Interestingly, however, these games were based on the assumption that an inferior Japanese fleet would clash with a superior American fleet in the decisive fleet engagement. And, too, the greater part of them were tactical rather than campaign games, and the emphasis was put on fleet formations, deployment, and methods of attack rather than on the larger realm of offensive and defensive operations, logistics, and protection of sea lines of communication. In these games it was invariably demonstrated that in engagements between naval forces of similar composition, the side with superior numbers was victorious. This distressing lesson initially caused the Japanese Navy to seek qualitative advantages over the U.S. Navy in things such as firing technique, torpedo attack, and crew training. Eventually, it also led to the search for new and different force compositions. One of the later beneficiaries of this search was Japan's force of aircraft carriers.

During the years from the signing of the Washington Naval Treaty in 1922 until the early 1930s, while the Japanese Navy labored to build its fleet up to the treaty limits in capital ships and aircraft carriers and to expand its cruiser, destroyer, and submarine forces that had not been numerically constrained by the treaty, it was largely unopposed in this building competition by the United States. In part, this Japanese building effort was driven by the government's need to assuage the so-called "fleet faction" that had opposed the 1922 five-power agreement (and which later opposed the agreement reached at the 1930 London Naval Conference).[2] Given this widespread disdain within the IJN for the Washington and London agreements, it is not surprising that in a number of cases Japan evaded the treaty tonnage limits for individual ships under construction. And, while the Japanese Navy expanded in capability, the U.S. Navy lagged behind, hindered by presidents and congresses that believed in the benefits to peace supposedly conferred by naval arms limitation and fleet reductions.

By 1932, U.S. Navy estimates showed that the United States had built to only 50 percent of the tonnage permitted by the 1922 and 1930 treaties, while Japan had 88 percent of permitted tonnage. Japan had invaded Manchuria in 1931, and this and other Japanese actions in the Far East finally aroused Congress to take action to strengthen the navy. In 1934, Congress passed the Vinson-Trammel Act, which authorized the navy, in principle, to build up to treaty levels by 1942. The buildup was gradual, but it increased in intensity toward the close of the decade, as international tensions fueled a Second Vinson Act (1938) and an emergency buildup program (1940). With Europe already at war, it was beginning to look as if the United States soon would be directly involved.

THE WAR AND ITS PROGRESS

Japan's decision to go to war with the United States had been dictated in large part by strategic circumstances. Because of the U.S.-led embargo on the sale of oil and other materials to Japan, the Japanese government looked to the oil-producing and mineral-laden territories in Southeast Asia to make up its losses. Influential Japanese naval leaders believed, however, that a southward thrust could not be taken without eliminating the threat of a flank attack by the U.S. Fleet. Accordingly, it was stressed that Pearl Harbor would have to be attacked and the Allied garrisons in the Philippines and Singapore eliminated as well.

In making the decision to go to war against the United States and Britain, Japan's civilian and military leaders had intentionally avoided one of the most troublesome aspects—how to bring the ensuing war to a successful conclusion. Senior Japanese military officers were very aware of the disparity between Japan's raw-material requirements and industrial capacity and those of the United States. They knew that Japan could not win a war of attrition with the United States. Japanese mobilization plans drawn up in 1940 showed that by the third year of a war Japan would be experiencing extreme shortages of non-ferrous metals and liquid fuel and that shipping losses would curtail coal imports sufficiently to cause a general industrial decline. Similarly, the Japanese Navy estimated that the United States's naval shipbuilding capacity was well over three times that of Japan. Therefore, the IJN was forced to conclude that even under the most optimistic circumstances, Japan's ratio of naval strength would be only 50 percent of the U.S. strength in 1943 and 30 percent or less in 1944. With regard to military aircraft, the situation was expected to be even bleaker, since the United States was estimated to have an aircraft replenishment rate seven to eight times as large as Japan, even after its aircraft commitments to other theaters of war were taken into account.

Admiral Isoroku Yamamoto, commander-in-chief of the Combined Fleet, had told Prime Minister Konoye in September 1940: "If I am told to fight regardless of consequence, I shall run wild considerably for the first six months or a year, but I have utterly no confidence for the second and third years."[3] Yamamoto was not the only senior officer to have deep reservations about the outcome of such a war. More than a year later, in early November 1941, Navy Minister Shimada told assembled Japanese civilian and military leaders at the Liaison Conference between the Japanese Government and Imperial General Headquarters:

> In the event of war, the Naval High Command believes that the Navy stands a very good chance of victory in both the early stage operations and the interception operations against the enemy fleet, with the present power ratio. However, should the war continue into its third year and become a long term war, according to comprehensive research by the various Navy departments, shortages of war materials and the inadequacy of Japan's industrial potential will begin to have their effect on the Navy's strength. Under the latter conditions, it would be difficult for us to have any measure of confidence that we could bring the war to a victorious conclusion.[4]

But the hope at the time the decision in favor of war was made was that somehow Japan's initial victories would lead to such a decline in American (and British) morale that the Western Allies would come to peace terms with the Japanese Empire. Indeed, it was Admiral Yamamoto's secret hope that a decisive attack on the U.S. Pacific Fleet in Pearl Harbor—which was being planned by his staff—might help to serve this function. It was suggested by some officials that Americans, being merchants at heart, would not continue for long with an unprofitable war.

Japan's strategic war aims were equally vague. Stage one of the war called for the elimination of Allied forces in the Western Pacific and in Southeast Asia, enabling access to the region's strategic resources. Stage two contemplated the destruction of the main part of the U.S. Pacific Fleet, thereby strengthening Japan's ability to fight a protracted conflict. It was hoped that when stage two had been reached, the United States would agree to peace terms designed to allow Japan to keep her captured possessions, which would become part of her Greater East Asia Co-Prosperity Sphere.

Specifically the "First Phase" of Japan's offensive operations called for:

- First Period: Invasion of the Philippines, Malaya, Borneo, Celebes, Timor, northern Sumatra and key points in southern Sumatra (Palembang) and the Bismarck Archipelago.
- Second Period: Invasion of Java and occupation, at the opportune time, of airfield in southern Burma.
- Third Period: Pacification of occupied areas and, depending on the situation, completion of operations in Burma.[5]

This was an extremely optimistic military agenda, particularly when coupled with the estimated timetable for accomplishment. Imperial General Headquarters estimated that the bulk of the invasion-related operations in the Philippines could be completed in 50 days, those in Malaya in 100 days, and those in the Netherlands East Indies in 150 days.

Once these initial objectives had been taken, Japan would possess a defense perimeter running from Burma through Sumatra, Java, Timor, Western New Guinea, the Carolines and Marshalls, and Wake Island. The sea areas within this perimeter were thought to be favorable to the establishment of a strong inner defense, except for the line curving north from the Solomons through New Guinea and into the Philippines. The Japanese Navy believed that within this defense zone its fleet, particularly the carrier forces, backed up by land-based air power operating from "unsinkable" island bastions, would be able to operate at great advantage in keeping Allied naval forces from penetrating the perimeter.

Yet, even as Japan was readying itself for the advance to the south, the Imperial Japanese Army, ever wary of the potential threat that the Soviet Union posed to its ambitions in North China, held some 700,000 troops in readiness in Manchuria. There they were to wait throughout most of the war, unavailable for the vital Japanese operations in the South and Southwest Pacific during 1942 and 1943. (When the Soviet Union finally did attack in August 1945, the by-then-depleted Manchurian divisions crumbled under the Soviet onslaught.)

In October 1941, the Konoye government made the decision to go to war with the United States in early December unless last-minute U.S.-Japanese diplomatic negotiations in Washington bore fruit. In early November, imperial sanction was received for the Pearl Harbor attack, the plan for which had been under preparation since early in the year. On 25 November 1941, Admiral Yamamoto issued the order to proceed with the operation, with a provision for calling it off if diplomatic negotiations somehow proved successful. The next day the task force sortied from Hitokappu Bay. The main striking power of the force resided in the six heavy carriers of the First Air Fleet and the twenty-seven submarines of the Advance Force. The bulk of the submarines were to preposition themselves around the island of Oahu to sink U.S. warships attempting to sortie from Pearl Harbor and to intercept shipping arriving from the U.S. West Coast. In the end, however, nothing came from the submarine effort. All the damage done to the U.S. Pacific Fleet in the Pearl Harbor attack was done by Japanese carrier aircraft.

On the morning of 7 December 1941, the naval combatant strengths in the Pacific of the opposing American and Japanese fleets stood as follows: Japan had 10 battleships, 9 aircraft carriers, 18 heavy cruisers, 17 light cruisers, 103 destroyers, and 74 submarines; the United States had 9 battleships, 3 aircraft carriers, 13 heavy cruisers, 11 light cruisers, 67 destroyers, and 53 submarines.[6] A few hours later, following the Japanese surprise attack on Pearl Harbor, the U.S. Fleet based at Pearl found itself with four battleships, a minelayer, and a target ship sunk and another four battleships, three light cruisers, three destroyers, a seaplane tender, and a repair ship damaged. In this single sudden attack the Pacific Fleet had been deprived of its capability to carry out its immediate responsibilities under War Plan RAINBOW-5—responsibilities that included diverting enemy strength by operating against the Marshall Islands, supporting British naval forces in areas south of the equator, and preparing to capture and establish control over the Marshall-Caroline islands area.

The Japanese attack was a tremendous tactical victory for Yamamoto's Combined Fleet force, but it was far less successful in a strategic sense. For one thing, the (unintended) arrival of the attack prior to a formal declaration of war by Japan brought the American people together behind the Roosevelt administration's decision for war as nothing else could have done. And, in a military sense, the attack had not been extensive enough. Though it had destroyed or crippled the American Pacific battle line and had accounted for most of Oahu's military aircraft, it had not touched the navy's oil tank farms or machine shops. If the tank farms had been destroyed, the loss of fuel oil could have prevented the continued use of the Navy Yard as a major naval base over many of the coming months of war. And because the machine shops had not been hit, repair work on the damaged ships could be started immediately. American naval forces had been spared as well. The three U.S. Pacific carriers were not at Pearl Harbor at the time of the attack, and thus were available for defensive and limited offensive defensive operations almost at once. The nine submarines present in the harbor during the attack also were not hit. Both of these forces would find much work to do in the coming months of the war.

There is no denying, however, that the situation in the Pacific was extremely serious for the United States following the Pearl Harbor attack. With its Pacific Fleet virtually immobilized, there was little it could do to stem the rapid Japanese advances to the south. On 30 December 1941, the day he officially took over as commander-in-chief, United States Fleet, Admiral Ernest King sent an important message to Admiral Chester Nimitz, the new commander-in-chief, Pacific Fleet. The message counseled Nimitz that despite other orders he may have received about managing the war in the Pacific, his immediate tasks were reduced to two: first, to hold Hawaii and maintain communications between Hawaii and the West Coast; and second, to keep the Japanese clear of the routes from Hawaii and Samoa, and from there down toward Australia and New Zealand. The purpose of the second task was to maintain contact with Allied forces in the Australian area. As a means of helping to maintain the line of communications to the Southeast Pacific, American Army and Marine reinforcements for U.S. possessions such as Samoa sailed from the West Coast during the first several months of the war.

The Japanese and German navies had been conducting staff talks since early 1941 without producing any significant agreements on common actions. When the Japanese attack on Pearl Harbor occurred, a surprised Hitler was nonetheless ecstatic, since he was convinced that a war with Japan would keep the United States from concentrating all its forces in the Atlantic theater. On December 11th, he declared war on the United States. However, the common military policies that had escaped Germany and Japan before the outbreak of the Pacific War continued to elude them thereafter. Within days, the two countries were at odds over projected spheres of interest and anticipated geographic conquests.

The Japanese "First Phase" operations moved ahead like clockwork. Everywhere—except in the Philippines, where the American and Filipino forces were holding out at great sacrifice on the Bataan Peninsula—the Japanese objectives were attained ahead of or on the projected timetable. From the U.S. Navy's standpoint, actions would have to be taken as soon as possible to stem the Japanese advance. Admiral King was certain that the Japanese would continue to expand their strategic reach until either they had been stopped or they had taken over the entire Southwest Pacific. He expected that the Japanese also had ambitions to take Hawaii, the Aleutians, and even Alaska. One of his first chores was to convince his fellow members of the U.S. Joint Chiefs of Staff (JCS) of the need to beef up the U.S. position in the Pacific. The JCS and the U.S.-British Combined Chiefs of Staff were carrying out the intent of ABC-1/RAINBOW-5 to devote the bulk of their efforts to the defeat of Germany. And General Marshall and General Arnold (in particular), in those first months of the war, were not inclined to put as much military effort into the Pacific war as King thought necessary. Gradually, however, the progress of Japanese advances and Admiral King's arguments won them over to a more active Pacific stance.

On 18 February 1942, King sent a memorandum to General Marshall and Admiral Stark (then chief of naval operations) advocating the occupation of additional islands in the Central and Southwestern Pacific. The memorandum stated:

1. I have come to the conclusion that it will be necessary, as rapidly as possible, for the United States to occupy several additional islands in the central and southwestern Pacific, in order to strengthen the major defensive positions now being garrisoned. The purpose would be to establish a system of groups of islands, whose air contingents will provide mutual support, and which would offer security for the operations of our naval forces and sea communications.

2. The island of greatest immediate importance appears to be Efate in New Hebrides. Of only slightly less importance is Tonga Tabu. . . . It is proposed to employ Army forces as occupational troops, and to station both Army and Navy planes in these islands as soon as these become available.[7]

Admiral King pursued with President Roosevelt the theme of building up a defensive line from which offensive actions could later be launched. On 5 March 1942, only three weeks before he took over from Admiral Stark as chief of naval operations (while keeping his position as commander-in-chief, U.S. Fleet), King wrote Franklin Roosevelt:

1. The delineation of general areas of responsibility for operations in the Pacific is now taking place, in which it appears that we—the U.S.—will take full charge of all operations conducted eastward of the Malay Peninsula and Sumatra.
2. You have expressed the view—concurred in by all of your chief military advisers—that we should determine on a very few lines of military endeavor and concentrate our efforts on these lines. . . .
9. Our primary concern in the Pacific is to hold Hawaii and its approaches (via Midway) from the westward and to maintain its communications with the West Coast. Our next care in the Pacific is to preserve Australasia . . . which requires that its communications be maintained—via eastward of Samoa, Fiji and southward of New Caledonia.
10. We have now—or will soon have—"strong points" at Samoa, Suva (Fiji) and New Caledonia (also a defended fueling base at Bora Bora, Society Islands). A naval operating base is shortly to be set up in Tongatabu (Tonga Islands) to service our naval forces operating in the South Pacific. Efate (New Hebrides) and Funafuti (Ellice Islands) are projected additional "strong points."
11. When the foregoing 6 "strong points" are made reasonably secure, we shall not only be able to cover the line of communications—to Australia (and New Zealand) but—given the naval forces, air units, and amphibious troops—we can drive northwest from the New Hebrides into the Solomons and the Bismarck Archipelago after the same fashion of step-by-step advances that the Japanese used in the South China Sea. Such a line of operations will be offensive rather than passive—and will draw Japanese forces there to oppose it, thus relieving pressure elsewhere, whether in Hawaii, ABDA area, Alaska, or even India.[8]

While the United States was trying to hold the line against expected Japanese attempts to sever the sea line of communications between Hawaii and Australia, Japan's military leaders were discussing new operations. The First Phase operations had proved so unexpectedly successful that the initial war plans were outdated almost from the first few weeks of the war. During late December 1941–early January 1942, medium-term strategic thinking revolved around three competing conceptions. The Japanese Army, which was opposed to any expansion of the Pacific defense perimeter, wanted the navy simply to consolidate in the Pacific while attempting to destroy the British navy in the Indian Ocean. The navy General Staff, which wanted the Combined Fleet's strength preserved for the expected decisive battle with the U.S. Pacific Fleet, favored striking Fiji and Samoa as a means of severing communications between Hawaii and Australia. And the Combined Fleet wanted to pursue the "Eastern Operation"—an invasion of the Hawaiian Islands that was expected to force the U.S. Pacific Fleet into a decisive battle.

By late January 1942, plans were being drafted for a variety of potential operations by the Combined Fleet, including a naval assault on Ceylon, the invasion of Australia, support for the Japanese Army in Burma, and the seizure of Fiji and Samoa. The disparity between army and navy plans was caused by the army's belief that Japan would have to build up an impregnable defense perimeter in order to sustain its position over a prolonged period of war, while the navy (and particularly Yamamoto's Combined Fleet) was seeking the decisive naval battle that would end the war. By early March 1942, an army-navy compromise provided for the IJN's attempting to eliminate British naval forces in the Indian Ocean while avoiding any expansion of the Pacific perimeter in the near future, in exchange for the army's concurring with navy tactical operations beyond the defense perimeter and agreeing to study the feasibility of large-scale invasions of Hawaii, Australia, and Ceylon. This agreement did not keep the Combined Fleet from continuing serious planning for the Eastern Operation, however.

In the last half of March 1942, Japanese forces occupied the Andaman Islands, and a carrier strike force under Admiral Nagumo sortied from the Celebes for the Indian Ocean—specifically, the waters off the coast of Ceylon. There, in operations from April 5–9, Nagumo's force raided the cities of Colombo and Trincomalee, Ceylon, and battered portions of British Admiral James Somerville's Eastern Fleet, sinking the aircraft carrier *Hermes*, two heavy cruisers, and a number of smaller naval vessels. During this same time, surface forces under the control of Admiral Ozawa sortied from Mergui, Burma (in the Andaman Sea across from Ceylon), and attacked merchant shipping in the central Indian Ocean and the Bay of Bengal. Although Nagumo broke off action and retired from the area without having completed the destruction of the British Eastern Fleet, his attacks had been sufficiently serious to induce caution in Admiral Somerville. The British fleet beat a strategic retreat from Ceylon to the port of Mombasa on Africa's east coast, leaving the Indian Ocean to the Japanese, should they choose to follow up their initial sorties.

Japan's victories in the Indian Ocean during April 1942 were of great concern to the British in particular, since they seemed to portend a major Indian Ocean effort by the Japanese. There was a fear that a sustained Japanese assault in the western Indian Ocean could sever Allied lines of communication there and unhinge the Allied position in the Middle East. Such a situation would throw into disarray not only the supply system that sustained British operations in North Africa, but also the Allies' southern supply route to the Soviet Union through Persia (Iran). This also eventually would pose the specter of a German-Japanese linkup in the Indian Ocean area, with even the possibility of a common advance on India itself. It was thus a tremendous relief to the British when Japan failed to follow up on its April successes there.

In early April 1942, the Japanese Navy General Staff drew up the plans for the second phase of the war. It had finally been convinced by the Combined Fleet's logic that the Eastern Operation should proceed. The Indian Ocean and the Southwest Pacific were to be relegated to secondary status. Instead, Central Pacific operations were to have the highest strategic priority. In this phase, Midway Island was to be captured and the U.S. Pacific Fleet destroyed. If this succeeded, in stage three the Japanese planned to occupy Johnson and Palmyra islands, while in stage four the Hawaiian Islands themselves would be assaulted. Concerns about security of the Japanese home islands, following the Doolittle Raid on Tokyo of 18 April 1942, brought army concurrence with this ambitious scheme.

Yet, even as planning for the Midway operation went forward, Japan's luck began to change. American Navy and Army cryptanalysts had begun to decipher portions of messages encoded in the Japanese Navy's fleet operational cipher in January and February 1942. By April, Admiral Nimitz's cryptanalysis staff at Pearl Harbor was reading something less than 20 percent of the intercepted encrypted traffic. It was enough, however, to alert them to the upcoming Japanese plan to capture Port Moresby, New Guinea. In a two-day battle in the Coral Sea (7–8 May), two U.S. single-carrier task forces under the command of Admiral Frank Jack Fletcher fought several Japanese forces, including a two-carrier strike force under Admiral Takaji. The result was a slight tactical advantage for the Japanese forces—they had sunk the carrier *Lexington* and two other ships and damaged the carrier *Yorktown*, while the Americans had sunk the escort carrier *Shoho* and damaged the large carrier *Shokaku*—but it was a strategic victory for the American forces. As a result of the Coral Sea battle, the Japanese *losses at Cord at sea*

called off the Port Moresby operation and never again attempted to capture it by sea. In addition, *Shokaku*'s battle damage and *Zuikaku*'s loss of aircraft and pilots in the operation kept both large carriers out of the Midway operation.

The work of the U.S. Pacific Fleet's code breakers was to prove even more valuable during the battle of Midway, just a month later. On the basis of deciphered message traffic, the cryptanalysts at Pearl Harbor correctly forecast the basic aspects of the Japanese plan for attacking Midway. Thus, when the four large aircraft carriers of the Combined Fleet's *Kido Butai* (striking force) reached their positions 180 miles northwest of Midway, the American carrier forces were waiting only a little more than 200 miles away. Forcefully taking the offensive, and fighting with a good deal of luck in addition to skill, American pilots from the three U.S. carriers *Enterprise*, *Hornet*, and *Yorktown* managed to sink all four carriers in Nagumo's force, with only the loss of the *Yorktown* to mar the surprising victory.

The battle of Midway proved a decisive point in the Pacific war. Japan's Combined Fleet had lost a major portion of its carrier striking forces. The Japanese loss at Midway sounded the death knell for the Eastern Operation—Hawaii was never again seriously threatened. And Admiral Yamamoto, Japan's foremost naval strategist, thereafter became obsessively cautious in his planning and moved toward a strategic defensive posture. (Within a year he would be dead, killed when his aircraft was shot down over Bougainville by U.S. Army Air Forces fighters vectored there through use of deciphered Japanese messages.) On the American side, the victory at Midway signaled the end of the navy's defensive strategy and the beginning of its strategy of the offensive-defensive.

Admiral King began agitating in the joint chiefs of staff for an offensive against the Japanese in the South Pacific area as soon as the favorable results of the Battle of Midway had been received. It was evident that the Japanese were intent on moving down the Solomon Islands chain; they had gone into Tulagi in May 1942, and were beginning to make preparations for an airfield on Guadalcanal. King saw that here was a good chance to push the Japanese off balance and then keep them off balance. He urged that an offensive be undertaken against the Lower Solomons. U.S. forces and supplies available for an offensive operation in the South Pacific were pretty slim in the summer of 1942, and at first the army demurred, arguing that three or four months would be necessary in order to assemble the necessary forces, supplies, and munitions. General Marshall eventually gave in, however. A plan was finally approved for the invasion of

Tulagi and Guadalcanal, with the timing dictated by the need to seize the latter island before its airfield had been completed.

The landings by troops of the U.S. First Marine Division on 7 August 1942 marked the start of a bloody six-month test of wills between the Japanese and the Americans to see who would retain control of Guadalcanal. During these months, the American and Japanese navies fought five major night surface engagements and two carrier duels. Almost to the end, the waters around Guadalcanal remained in dispute. Although the Japanese won a majority of the naval battles, the attrition suffered by ships of the Combined Fleet was high, while on Guadalcanal itself, the piecemeal nature of the Japanese Army's buildup and attacks failed to forestall the gradual Marine encroachment of the island. After November 1942, the Japanese Navy avoided sending combat ships to contest control of the waters off the island; and in early February 1943, it evacuated the remains of the army force left on Guadalcanal. The outcome of the campaign proved to be a demonstration of Japan's tendency, in the months following Midway, to rely on a less than decisive force to achieve decisive outcomes. Having committed its naval forces "too little and too late" at Guadalcanal, the Japanese Navy had been unable to prevail.

"Operation Shoestring," as it had been dubbed by American participants, had succeeded, but it had been a close-run thing for all too much of the time. Yet the fighting for Guadalcanal, as Admiral King had perceived, had already had the strategic effect of throwing off Japan's timetable for further conquests. One immediate result was the cancellation of scheduled Japanese military actions in the Bay of Bengal and further planning for operations against Ceylon and India.

With Guadalcanal secured, Allied preparations were begun for pushing up the Solomons chain. At this time, the Japanese naval and air stronghold of Rabaul, on New Britain, was seen as the logical objective for South and Southwest Pacific Commands' efforts. Seizure or neutralization of Rabaul would be needed before General MacArthur's Southwest Pacific forces could advance farther along the New Guinea coast. On 21 February 1943, U.S. Army and Marine forces occupied the Russell Islands without resistance, in order to secure airfield sites for the next major advance in the Solomons—New Georgia.

By mid-1943, it was evident to senior U.S. naval officers in the Pacific that the Japanese were on the defensive. In early May, Admiral Nimitz wrote to Admiral Bill Halsey, commander South Pacific Area (SoPac): "As I see the general situation the Japs have gone over to the strategic defensive, consolidating their economic and military gains within their present perimeter of control. I expect that they will take vigorous offensive measures to harass us and to prevent us breaking through at any point in the periphery." A week later, Admiral Halsey replied:

> I agree with you that the Japs are definitely on the strategic defensive. I question whether they will take vigorous defensive measures. My opinion is they will wait for us to make the next move. I further believe that when we start up NEW GUINEA and SOLOMONS that they may start a withdrawal action but that they will come down on us with everything they can muster afloat in the usual "save-face" attitude. I am strongly of the opinion that they will do everything they can to maintain their positions, particularly in RABAUL and KAVIENG.[9]

The first U.S. landings in New Georgia took place at the end of June 1943. Casualties in the effort to capture Munda airfield were high, and it was almost the end of August before New Georgia had been secured. The costs incurred in the New Georgia operation led Admiral Halsey's staff to search for ways of bypassing Japanese-held islands and positions not necessary for U.S. offensive operations. This search, in turn, led to the highly successful bypassing of Kolombangara in favor of Vella Lavella. With Japanese positions on Kolombangara and Santa Isabel rendered untenable, the Japanese forces there were hastily withdrawn by sea, suffering severe losses in the process. This bypassing operation was repeated at Empress Augusta Bay on Bougainville in November 1943, and then, most spectacularly, in the case of the major Japanese bases at Rabaul and Kavieng in March 1944.

Initially, General MacArthur and his staff had been adamant about the need to take Rabaul by direct attack. When MacArthur finally was persuaded that Rabaul could be neutralized without its direct seizure, he became insistent that Kavieng would have to be taken by frontal assault. But Halsey managed to convince Admiral King that the seizure of Manus and Emirau would effectively cut off the Japanese forces on both Rabaul and Kavieng from outside support, and when the JCS directive authorizing the substitution of the Emirau operation was received, it was carried out with the predicted results. Interestingly, it had been Halsey who similarly had convinced MacArthur to have his forces make the long jump along the New Guinea coast to Hollandia, thereby bypassing the intermediate Japanese positions along the way.

While these amphibious operations were taking place, U.S. naval forces in the South Pacific were challenging the Japanese Navy up and down the "Slot"—the name given to a body of deep water in the Solomons, of from 12 to 15 miles wide, running between the islands of Choiseul, Santa Isabel, and Malaita to the northeast and the islands of New Georgia, Guadalcanal, and San Cristobal to the southeast. In night battles such as those at Empress Augusta Bay and Cape St. George, well-trained U.S. surface forces demonstrated an ability to defeat Japanese surface forces in night actions that had been largely lacking the previous year off Guadalcanal.

The end of the second phase of the Pacific war for the United States and the beginning of the third phase—the purely offensive phase—was marked by the beginning of CinCPac's drive in the Central Pacific. On 20 November 1943, Marine and Army troops landed on Tarawa and Makin in the Gilbert Islands. Tarawa was secured after three days of bloody fighting. The U.S. Pacific Fleet by this time was dramatically stronger than it had been a year before. It now possessed large numbers of new *Essex*- and *Independence*-class fleet carriers and new battleships, cruisers, destroyers, and submarines. Indeed, the Pacific Fleet was so strong that the Japanese Combined Fleet could no longer chance a direct meeting except in case of the direst necessity. A significant portion of the Pacific Fleet's sustained offensive power, moreover, was due to the development of advanced bases and mobile logistic support forces to maintain the flow of fuel, ammunition, and other war materiel to the forces afloat.

At this point, the drive toward Japan was beginning to proceed along two lines—one under Nimitz, a direct thrust coming across the Central Pacific, and the other under MacArthur, following the perimeter of the land masses to the south. Admiral King was strongly in favor of the Central Pacific offensive because it promised to cut the Japanese sea lines of communication, present the possibility for major combat with the Japanese Fleet, provide air bases from which to bomb the Japanese home islands, and neutralize and occupy Japanese island positions. In practice, this two-pronged strategic offensive served to speed up the rate of the Allied advance, as the Japanese were continually forced to shift the focus of their defensive efforts from one front to the other. This problem was further magnified for the Japanese by their emphasis on over-complex plans, as clearly had been evidenced in mid-1942 by the splitting of the Japanese task forces during the Midway operation.

With the Gilberts under U.S. control, navy attention was turned to the Marshall Islands. In late January 1944, troops were landed at Kwajalein. Eniwetok was taken in the latter part of February, some three months ahead of the previous schedule. By this time the Fast Carrier Task Force was operating as the major offensive power of the U.S. Fifth Fleet.

The Fast Carrier Task Force was perfectly suited for the conditions found in the Central Pacific. With adequate numbers of fleet carriers, the force could neutralize the land-based air power found in the often widely separated Japanese island bastions. As the Naval Analysis Division of the Strategic Bombing Survey (Pacific) explained shortly after the war:

> Here [in the Central Pacific] the immense distances and small and scattered islands with their limited capabilities for defense offered great opportunity for the employment of a mobile force capable of striking at great range, at widely separated points, and with overwhelming power. As the enemy could not be strong everywhere, he was, granting our possession of such a force, strong nowhere. Such a force was provided in our carrier task forces which swiftly beat down enemy air power ahead of our amphibious advance, growing steadily stronger as the war progressed.[10]

With the Marshalls in U.S. hands, the Central Pacific drive moved into the Marianas—the island group Admiral King saw as the key to the Pacific fighting. The major Japanese naval base at Truk had already been deserted by the Japanese fleet. However, U.S. troop landings on Saipan in mid-June 1944 prodded the Japanese Navy into action—the A-GO Operation for a decisive battle with the U.S. fleet was put into effect. It was in the resulting first battle of the Philippine Sea that Admiral Marc Mitscher's carrier aircraft decimated Admiral Ozawa's First Mobile Force. Ozawa lost some 395 carrier aircraft and three aircraft carriers (two to U.S. submarines) at a cost to Mitscher's force of 130 aircraft.

A month later, Guam was assaulted and then Tinian. By the end of July 1944, the Marianas were firmly in U.S. hands and preparations were being made for building the airfields from which Army Air Forces B-29s could be launched to bomb the Japanese home islands. Then, in preparation for supporting MacArthur's Southwest Pacific drive into the Philippines, the Central Pacific offensive was directed into the Western Carolines. In mid-September 1944, Peleliu was attacked, at the cost of sizable U.S. casualties, and then Anguar. Ulithi was simply occupied.

In mid-October 1944, General MacArthur's forces, bypassing the Philippine Island of Mindanao, landed on Leyte. This set into motion the Japanese Sho Operation No. 1 for defense of the Philippines. The IJN's operational plan was very complex, involving five groups of ships arriving from several different directions and operating together to catch the American invasion force in a pincer movement. Its complexity magnified the plan's other deficiencies, and in a series of separate engagements, the Japanese task forces were soundly defeated—

although not before Admiral Kurita's strong surface force had given a decided scare to the inadequately protected U.S. escort carriers operating in Leyte Gulf in support of the American landings.

This last-ditch attempt to prevent the penetration of its inner defense zone rendered a failure, the Japanese Navy pulled back to await the inevitable. Other U.S. landings in the Philippines took place at Ormoc, Mindoro, and Lingayen, and the consolidation of the U.S. position in the Philippines soon followed.

Meanwhile, Nimitz's Central Pacific forces invaded Iwo Jima in February 1945, taking a large number of casualties from heavily dug in Japanese forces despite extensive naval gunfire support. And in April, the Central Pacific drive ended with the assault on Okinawa. It was during the eighty-two-day struggle for Okinawa that the U.S. Pacific Fleet suffered significant damage from Japanese kamikaze (suicide) aircraft and boats, and from other desperation weapons. In all, 36 U.S. ships were sunk and 368 damaged during the operation.

In the last several months of the war, U.S. fast carriers and surface action groups ranged off Japan's coasts almost at will, softening up the home islands prior to the scheduled invasion. Japan's merchant shipping had long since been decimated by the deadly U.S. submarine fleet and, late in the war, by air-delivered mines dropped in Japan's Inland Sea primarily by Army Air Forces B-29s. Although the two atomic bombs dropped on Hiroshima and Nagasaki provided the final impetus for the Japanese government's decision to surrender, the Japanese military situation in the Pacific area had been rendered untenable months before.

FORCES, TACTICS AND TECHNIQUES: SURFACE FORCES

The Japanese Navy had trained and equipped a superb surface fleet during the interwar period. Given its emphasis on the importance of light forces in the "diminution operation," the navy had provided extensive training for its cruisers and destroyers in night attacks. Indeed, Japanese battle training was marked overall by its rigorousness and realism—taking place in remote locations and often under harsh weather conditions.

By way of contrast, the U.S. Navy during this period normally had carried out its peacetime exercises in southern waters or in other areas where good weather prevailed. It had not regularly practiced night operations. Indeed, special care had been taken in such exercises to avoid personnel casualties that could generate adverse publicity for the U.S. armed forces.

Much of the equipment furnished to the Japanese surface ships was superb. Especially worthy of note were the Japanese Type 93 Long-Lance 24-inch torpedo, which had a top speed of 49 knots and a range at that speed of 24,000 yards (almost four times the range of the U.S. 21-inch torpedo at top speed), and Japanese optical sighting equipment.

The principal technical advantage enjoyed by U.S. surface forces during the war was radar, although its use was not properly understood by most commanders until early in 1943. Later in the war, when coupled with shipboard combat information centers (CICs), radar provided invaluable service not only for aimed gunfire but also for a variety of important anti-air warfare tasks.

The Japanese night surface action victories in the waters off Guadalcanal in the fall of 1942 were due to a combination of superb training, good equipment, and sound tactics. This was the opposite of the case with American surface units during that period. One reason for the repeated U.S. defeats at this time was the decision of American commanders to keep their destroyers close in to the main bodies of heavier ships, rather than freeing them to launch independent torpedo attacks prior to opening fire with the main batteries of their cruisers. An equally significant factor, and one produced by the overall shortage of destroyers in the Pacific Fleet in that first year of the war, was the inability to keep together and train destroyer divisions and squadrons as units. Because destroyers from different destroyer divisions regularly were cobbled together to form task units for upcoming actions, they did not share the same standard operating procedures and consequently were unable to operate together with a requisite amount of teamwork. This problem was understood by Admiral Halsey, who took over SoPAC in mid-October 1942. As he wrote to Admiral Nimitz in January 1943:

> I am quite in accord with your ideas about the offensive potentialities of our destroyers in battle. As a destroyer sailor of long service it has broken my heart to see the way these ships were of necessity abused materially and in the way of personnel.
>
> In accomplishing this abuse, all squadron and division organization has been terrifically disjointed. This was enough to prevent them giving their best in battle. With our new organization, which I shall use my utmost endeavor to keep going, this handicap should be overcome. In other words, I believe at long last we are in sight of a position where we can use destroyers as they should be used.[11]

With the advent of increased quantities of new destroyers and cruisers in the theater in 1943 and the arrival of consummate surface warfare tacticians such as Arleigh Burke, the situation started to turn around, and the Japanese Navy began to suffer increasing numbers of surface action defeats.

AMPHIBIOUS FORCES

The amphibious forces utilized by the United States in the Pacific during World War II were so superior in organization, training, and equipment to those of the Japanese Navy and Army that direct comparison is of little value. The largest share of the credit for the success of the wartime U.S. amphibious operations would have to go to the U.S. Fleet Marine Force. Starting in 1920, the Marine Corps had built its officer education program around the objective of developing experienced amphibious commanders and staff officers in all ranks. Marine Corps field units were devoted to the development of new and improved amphibious doctrines and techniques. This was fully in accordance with its belief that in a future war the Fleet Marine Force would have to be responsible for seizing and holding the numerous island bases that would be needed to sustain a U.S. Navy advance into the Western Pacific.

When the war came, it was necessary to perfect amphibious warfare in the Pacific under combat conditions—a task that took some two years. At the war's end, CinCPac's Public Information Office used a theatrical analogy to describe the perfecting process that had taken place from one operation to the next. It equated the Guadalcanal landing to a first reading and a walking through the lines of a new play (on an all but bare stage); the Gilberts-Marshalls assaults were likened to a dress rehearsal of the play in which some cues were missed; and the Marianas operation was compared to the finished performance. But if the U.S. Navy's amphibious forces had much still to learn early in the war, they were head and shoulders above the similar forces of the enemy.

CARRIER FORCES

The carrier forces of both countries were well trained at the time of the Pearl Harbor attack. During the first year of the war, however, Japan's Zero fighter outclassed all of the U.S. Navy's fighters. The introduction of F6F Hellcats in mid-1943, when coupled with the ready availability of F4U Corsairs by that time, ensured that by the end of the Pacific war's second year the Zero no longer possessed superiority.

The carrier battles in the first months of the Pacific war were learning experiences for both sides. At Coral Sea, Midway, and Santa

Cruz islands, the U.S. and Japanese navies were taught painful lessons about such things as the control of multi-carrier task forces, the nature of adequate antiaircraft defenses, and the importance of ship damage control. These lessons proved invaluable to the U.S. Navy in 1944 and 1945 when the U.S. Fast Carrier Task Force was operating in areas close to major concentrations of Japanese air. Just how much had been learned about operating the carriers in maximum combat conditions was demonstrated by the fact that during the fleet's hammering by Japanese kamikazes off Okinawa not a single aircraft carrier was sunk—despite the large number of hits sustained by the carriers.

The decimation of Japan's first-line pilots in the battles at Coral Sea and Midway quickly reduced the overall level of professionalism in the Japanese Naval Air Arm. Unable from this point on to provide a level of training during wartime commensurate with that provided by its adversary, Japan found itself slipping further and further behind the United States in the combat capability provided by its carrier aviation. Similarly, Japan could not hope to match the carrier building rate reached by the United States. During the Second World War the U.S. operated 110 carriers of all types. Of these, 33 were fleet carriers designed for offensive combat operations.

This decline in Japanese aviation capability was reflected in the changes made in its offensive air tactics during the course of the war. From December 1941 to the beginning of 1943, the Japanese primarily relied upon daylight dive-bombing and torpedo attacks by carrier groups. Because of high aircraft attrition rates and the loss of most of its first-line carriers, however, and with the approach of U.S. naval forces within range of Japanese shore-based aircraft, in January 1943, Japan shifted to relying upon night attacks by land-based medium bombers and available carrier aircraft.

In February 1944 this tactic, which had achieved only limited success, was replaced in turn. Japan reverted to daylight attacks—but in the form of sneak hit-and-run attacks by fighter bombers and carrier-type aircraft on enemy naval forces that were now operating even closer to the Japanese inner defense zone. Japan reached the nadir of its offensive air capability with its disastrous losses in the Battle of the Philippine Sea in June 1944. In October 1944, in desperation, she began relying upon suicide attacks, using relatively inexperienced pilots in obsolescent aircraft to crash into the enemy's warships, in a last, hopeless attempt to turn aside the increasing weight of Allied maritime power that was already positioning itself for the final thrusts at Japan's home islands.

SUBMARINE FORCES

At the beginning of the Pacific War, Japan possessed about twice as many submarines as the U.S. had in the Pacific. Interestingly, the Japanese Navy lacked a central operational command for its submarine force. And from the first, the employment of this large submarine force was hampered by the Japanese Navy's narrow strategic conception for its use. The submarine arm was viewed largely as an adjunct to the Japanese surface fleet. Accordingly, the Japanese subs were used extensively for scouting and reconnaissance in advance of the surface units. Offensively, the submarines were to be deployed in lines across an enemy fleet's track to attack its major surface combatants. However, little attention was paid by the IJN to the submarine's role as a means of attacking the enemy's sea lines of communication. The result of these factors, from almost the first days of the war, was a dissipation of the Japanese submarine effort on a variety of piecemeal, tactical responsibilities. Accordingly, by the middle of 1942, the submarines could no longer be considered an effective offensive branch of the Imperial Japanese Navy.

In contrast, the fifty-one U.S. submarines in the Pacific in December 1941 were controlled by commanders who understood the nature of commerce warfare. Within six hours of the start of the Pearl Harbor attack, the chief of naval operations had issued dispatch orders authorizing unrestricted air and submarine warfare. During the first months of the war, if Japanese merchant shipping losses mounted only gradually, it was largely due to flaws in the submarines' Mark XIV Mod 1 torpedoes. The torpedo's depth-setting equipment and magnetic exploders were malfunctioning. Nevertheless, these problems had been corrected by mid-1943 (and others plaguing new U.S. torpedoes were overcome later), with the result that, by war's end, American submarines had accounted for 1,113 Japanese merchant vessels sunk (47.4 percent of the total destroyed from all causes). Indeed, the U.S. submarines of the Pacific and Southwest Pacific Commands contributed substantially to the progressive strangulation of the Japanese home islands' economy, months before long-range air power was positioned to begin the systematic destruction of Japan's urban-industrial centers.

CONCLUDING REMARKS

Japan had entered the Second World War with a powerful navy but without carefully thought-out strategic goals and, more importantly, without any realistic idea for bringing the war to a successful conclusion. Overwhelmed by the success of its "First Phase" operations and seized by a "victory disease," Japan continued to expand the defensive perimeter it had established in the heady first weeks of the war until checked at Coral Sea and Midway.

The United States, having entered the war with its Pacific battle line in tatters, remained on the defensive only as long as the Japanese Fleet was advancing. With its strategic concepts soundly forged by years of carefully played ORANGE war games, the U.S. Pacific Fleet took advantage of Japanese hesitation in the weeks after Midway to stage an earlier-than-expected counteroffensive at Guadalcanal. And once sufficient Allied forces had been built up to sustain a two-pronged offensive, Japan never again had a chance to regain the initiative.

To its dismay, the Japanese Navy discovered that the island bastions composing its defensive perimeter could be neutralized by fast-moving, mobile carrier air power of a strength sufficient to overwhelm locally deployed, land-based air forces. Under such circumstances, its "unsinkable carriers" became strategic liabilities, capable of consuming more military resources than they were worth.

In the end, for all its tactical skill in surface engagements, the Japanese Navy found itself being whittled away by carrier air power of a quality to which it could no longer aspire and a submarine offensive the nature of which it had never fully grasped.

NOTES

The author would like to thank Bernard Cavalcante and Mike Walker of the Naval Historical Center's Operational Archives and the staff of the Navy Department Library for their help in connection with this chapter.

1. Secret [declassified], Joint Army and Navy Basic War Plan Orange—2d draft W. P. Orange prepared by Krueger, 7 Nov. 1923, p. 2; War Department Operations Division files, Box 182, R.G. 165, Military Reference Branch, National Archives.

2. With regard to the 1930 London Naval Treaty, two of the countries that had signed the 1922 Washington Naval Treaty—France and Italy—could not be brought into final agreement. However, the "big three"—Britain, the United States, and Japan—did agree to its provisions. In the 1930 treaty, all classes of combat vessels were brought under "limitation" for the first time. The ban on capital-ship construction was extended to the end of 1936. Additionally, the three powers' battleship strengths were to be reduced at once from a ratio of 20:20:10 to 15:15:9. In cruisers and destroyers, a tonnage ratio was set at 10:10:7, with each country to be allowed more of the cruiser type (8-inch "heavy" or 6-inch "light") it preferred. And in submarine tonnage, Japan was allowed parity with Britain and the U.S.—each was authorized 52,700 tons of these vessels. In general terms, the 1930 agreement was notable for two things. First, Britain gave formal acquiescence to full U.S. parity in all classes of ships. Second, the tonnage ratios that it set provided a distinct advantage to Japan over what had been provided in the 1922 Washington Treaty.

3. Quoted in Samuel Eliot Morison, *The Rising Sun in the Pacific 1930–April 1942*, vol. 3 of *History Of United States Naval Operations In World War II* (Boston: Little, Brown & Co., 1948), p. 46. Morison is here citing extracts from an early postwar Japanese printing of the Memoirs of Prince Konoye. However, this is a widely used comment from Admiral Yamamoto and can be found in sources, with many substantial variations in the exact wording.

4. *Quoted in Political Strategy Prior to Outbreak of War, Part V*, Japanese Monograph No. 152 (Tokyo: Military History Section, Headquarters, [U.S.] Army Forces Far East—Distributed by Office of the Chief of Military History, Department of the Army, 1953), p. 1; reprinted in *War In Asia And The Pacific, Volume 2: Political Background Of The War* (New York: Garland Publishing, Inc., 1980).

5. *Nampogun Sakusen Kiroku* (Southern Army Operations Record), 1st Demobilization Bureaux, July 1946; cited in *Reports of General MacArthur, Volume II—Part I: Japanese Operations In The Southwest Pacific Area* (compiled from Japanese Demobilization Bureaux Records) (Washington, D.C.: Department of the Army, 1966), p. 60.

6. Allied naval strength in the Pacific increased U.S. battleship strength by four, carrier strength by one, heavy cruiser strength by four, light cruiser strength by twenty, destroyer strength by twenty-one, and submarine strength by about fifteen. Confidential [declassified], "Naval Combatant Strength, *Pacific Ocean,* as of December 7, 1941," part of Exhibit No. 86; U.S. Congress, Joint Committee on the Investigation of the Pearl Harbor Attack, *Pearl Harbor Attack: Hearings*, Part 15, 79th Cong., 1st sess., U.S.G.P.O., 1946; p. 1906.

7. Secret [declassified], FF1/A16–3/F-1, Serial 00105, February 18, 1942, from Commander in Chief, U.S. Fleet to the Chief of Naval Operations and Chief of Staff, U.S. Army, Subject: "Establishment of a United States Garrison in Efate, New Hebrides Island"; Box 35, Papers of Ernest J. King, Naval Historical Foundation collection, Manuscript Division, Library of Congress.

8. Secret [declassified], "Memorandum for the President," March 5, 1942; Ibid. Admiral King's draft of this memorandum is in Box 14.

9. Secret [declassified] & Personal, letter from Nimitz to Halsey, May 7, 1943, and Secret [declassified] and Personal, letter from Halsey to Nimitz, 14 May 1943; both Box 15, Papers of William F. Halsey, Naval Historical Foundation collection, Manuscript Division, Library of Congress.

10. "Naval Analysis Division Final Report Tentative Brief, Draft—25 November 1945," p. 3; Box 2, Papers of Ralph A. Ofstie, Operational Archives, Naval Historical Center, Washington Navy Yard.

11. Secret [declassified] & Personal, Letter from Halsey to Nimitz, 11 January 1943; Box 15, Halsey Papers, Manuscript Division, Library of Congress.

BIBLIOGRAPHIC NOTE

Michael Vlahos has written extensively about the U.S. Naval War College during the interwar period. A recent article of his has some interesting things to say about the evolution of ORANGE-related wargaming at the War College. Michael Vlahos, "Wargaming, an Enforcer of Strategic Realism: 1919–1942," *Naval War College Review*, vol. 39, no. 2 (March-April 1986), pp. 7–22.

Herbert Rosinski's insightful writing about naval strategy included not only his several interesting essays on German naval thinking but one on Japanese strategy written for *Brassey's Naval Annual* in 1946. Herbert Rosinski, "The Strategy Of Japan," in B. Mitchell Simpson III, ed., *The Development of Naval Thought: Essays by Herbert Rosinski* (Newport, RI: Naval War College Press, 1977), pp. 102–20.

Samuel Eliot Morison's contribution was based upon a lecture (one of two) given at Oxford University in May 1957. In this lecture, expanded upon for publication, Morison attempted to encapsulate views on the Pacific war gained during the writing of his fifteen-volume history of World War II U.S. naval operations. Samuel Eliot Morison, *Strategy and Compromise* (Boston: Little, Brown & Co., 1958), pp. 61–120.

ADDITIONAL SOURCES

Buell, Thomas B. *Master of Seapower: A Biography of Fleet Admiral Ernest J. King.* Boston: Little, Brown & Co., 1980.

———, *The Quiet Warrior: A Biography of Admiral Raymond A. Spruance.* Boston: Little, Brown & Co., 1974.

Costello, John. *The Pacific War.* New York: Rawson, Wade Publishers, Inc., 1981.

Dull, Paul S. *A Battle History of The Imperial Japanese Navy (1941–1945).* Annapolis, MD: Naval Institute Press, 1978.

Evans, David C., ed. *The Japanese Navy In World War II.* 2nd ed. Annapolis, MD: Naval Institute Press, 1986.

Hayes, Grace Person. *The History of the Joint Chiefs of Staff in World War II: The War Against Japan.* Annapolis, MD: Naval Institute Press, 1982.

Hiroyuki, Agawa. *The Reluctant Admiral: Yamamoto and the Imperial Navy.* Tokyo: Kodansha International, 1979.

Layton, Edwin T., with Roger Pineau and John Costello. *"And I Was There": Pearl Harbor and Midway—Breaking the Secrets.* New York: William Morrow and Co., Inc., 1985.

Lewin, Ronald. *The American Magic: Codes, Ciphers and the Defeat of Japan.* New York: Farrar Straus Giroux, 1982.

Morton, Louis. *Strategy and Command: The First Two Years. United States Army in World War II: The War in the Pacific.* Washington, DC: Office of the Chief of Military History, Department of the Army, 1962.

Morison, Samuel Eliot. *The Two-Ocean War: A Short History of the United States Navy in the Second World War.* Boston: Little, Brown & Co., 1963.

Pelz, Stephen. *Race to Pearl Harbor: The Failure of the Second London Naval Conference and the Onset of World War II.* Cambridge, MA: Harvard University Press, 1974.

Potter, E. B. *Nimitz.* Annapolis, MD: Naval Institute Press, 1976.

Prange, Gordon W., with Donald M. Goldstein and Katherine V. Dillon. *At Dawn We Slept.* New York: McGraw-Hill Inc., 1981.

Spector, Ronald H. *Eagle Against the Sun: The American War with Japan.* New York: The Free Press, 1985.

Stephen, John J. *Hawaii Under the Rising Sun: Japan's Plans for Conquest after Pearl Harbor.* Honolulu: University Of Hawaii Press, 1984.

III

CONTEMPORARY MARITIME STRATEGY

11

Seapower
and
Western Defense

BY COLIN S. GRAY

AMERICAN INSULARITY AND THE MARITIME ALLIANCE

To understand the security problems and opportunities of the United States, one has to begin with geography—political, physical, economic, cultural. In the most direct terms, the United States is an insular superstate and the principal organizer and only possible leader of, and by far the largest security provider for, a truly global maritime alliance. The United States occupies a central geographical position *vis à vis* regions of great security interest, and the oceanic trade (and power-projection) routes of the world form the internal lines of communication of the U.S.-led maritime alliance.

Although the United States occupies a central position with respect to lines of communication to Eurasia, it is no less true that the Soviet Union—occupying the Eurasian Heartland—holds a central position and has advantageously interior land lines of communication *vis à vis* much of the periphery of Eurasia. The concepts of interior lines of communication and depth of territory (or extent of sea) for defense do not lend themselves to easy translation into military advantage. Japan discovered that distance, or strategic depth, can mean weakness if reliance is placed upon far-flung and static garrisons insufficiently supported by powerful mobile strike forces. In the absence of fleet superiority, the Japanese concept of a far-distant defensive barrier was a prescription for military disaster.

The Heartland position of the Soviet state looks very menacing on a map, *vis à vis* the Eurasian Rimland arc of U.S. security clients ranging from Norway around to South Korea. But, the depth of geography that renders power projection for conquest into the Soviet Heartland so impractical also renders multiple-frontier defense very difficult for Moscow. In the Crimean War of 1854–1856, for example, maritime power projection by Great Britain and France was logistically far superior to landpower projection by Imperial Russia. In 1904–1905, Imperial Russia was neither able nor willing to wage more than a distinctly limited war in Manchuria and Korea against Japan. Furthermore, notwithstanding the advances registered since 1904–1905 in transportation technology, in the Soviet/Russian industrial base, and in relative Soviet/Russian military power compared with her potential enemies, it is clear that the U.S.-led maritime alliance could project military power more economically to and across the frontier of the Soviet Far East than could the Soviet Union itself. An important reason why the Soviet Union maintains such large forces in her Far Eastern territories is because in time of war that very large area could be isolated from reinforcement and resupply from European Russia.

Location of national territory obviously is important, but so is distance. In terms of defense logistics in Eurasia, the Russo-Japanese War has much to say for today. However, the strategic meaning of geography has to be specific to political context. Soviet ability to project power from, or defend, its borders in northern Europe, southwest Asia, and northeast Asia, is not just an elementary matter for logistic calculation. What is the political-military context? If the Soviet Union is fighting, or anticipating having to fight, in central, southern, and northern Europe, her ability to do more than hold her own—and probably not even that—in northeast Asia, *inter alia*, must be in doubt.

There are basic, enduring attributes of the United States that flow from geography. Strategic geography typically is Janus-like in its implications, as some of the points discussed below illustrate.

First, the United States is strategically insular. The military weakness of Canada and Mexico, effectively—though to a diminishing degree, given the disorder in Central America—renders the United States an island nation.

Second, for reasons of geography the United States has to be a maritime power if it is to be a military power capable of influencing security conditions in Eurasia. Today, as in World War I and World War II, if the United States and her allies do not enjoy a "working" quality of sea control, then U.S. overseas garrisons cannot be supplied and relieved, expeditionary forces cannot move or be supplied and reinforced—and, if need be, rescued so that they might fight again. Changes in transportation technology in the twentieth century have not altered the validity of the proposition that freedom in U.S. use of the world's ocean highways is the *sine qua non* for any of the strategy designs of the leading contending schools of thought on U.S. defense policy.

Third, because of the continental extent of its territory, the immigrant character of virtually all of its people, a liberal-idealist tradition, and the blessings of geographical distance, the United States is not reconciled either to maintaining its current "guardian" role with respect to Eurasia for as long as objective conditions require, or to the proper use of all of the instruments of statecraft necessary for effective guardianship. American insularity has bred powerful variants of isolationism and unilateralism on both the political left and right.

Fourth, the specific course of American history necessarily has been influenced powerfully by geographical factors. American physical geography enabled political separation from the British Empire. U.S. geographical location allowed the Royal Navy to sit astride the choke points through which the naval power of any European state had to transit—and thereby protect the coasts of the United States as effectively as it did the coasts of Britain. Geography has provided the economic sinews of American power; influenced greatly the outlook, attitudes, and expectations of the American people; and in large measure prompted the selection of foreign allies and foes.

Fifth, the insular U.S. strategic condition is either a strength or a weakness, depending upon U.S. maritime power. The paradox is a familiar one. As was stated in chapter 1, the U.S. Navy could not defeat the Soviet Union strictly through action at sea, any more than the Royal Navy could defeat *directly* the landpower of continental Imperial, and later Nazi, Germany. But, the U.S. Navy would need to win at sea—which, at minimum, would mean securing a working measure of sea control when and where the Western Alliance would require it—if the war in general were not to be lost. Should Soviet maritime power succeed in its denial strategy on key sea lines of communication, then the West must either lose or seek conflict resolution through desperately dangerous, vertical (nuclear) escalation.

Sixth, geostrategically the U.S. security community is both blessed and cursed by distance. The notion that strength erodes proportionally as distance increases requires careful application to particular cases, but it remains a general truth about transportation and logistics. The oceanic distances from North America to other continents that are a hindrance to attack plans of overseas enemies, particularly when confronted with superior U.S. naval power, also restrain the projection of American power. Even with considerable host-nation support, U.S. forces in Europe must function and, if need be, fight as expeditionary forces. The need for airlift and sealift can be minimized, however, the more one is able to secure forward garrison locations for people and equipment. Forward garrisons, however, tend for political reasons to become fixed in location and in size. Their subsequent impact on policy and military posture, because of this inflexibility, might be very costly.

On the one hand, valid geopolitical generalities may be offered about the comparative U.S. advantage in maritime power over the Soviet Union—ease of access to the open ocean, absence of land-frontier military distractions, and so forth—as may plausible lectures on the central geostrategic location of U.S. seapower *vis à vis* Rimland Eurasia. On the other hand, those valid generalities and plausible lectures have to be considered in the context both of the fact that the maritime alliance of the West faces an awesome landpower threat on one geographical axis of potential advance in particular, and of the proposition that that threat must be countered *directly* at very heavy costs. Specifically, it is fairly orthodox to maintain that peninsular NATO-Europe is the proximate (not ultimate, for Americans) prize in the Soviet-American struggle, that it faces a landpower threat of daunting proportions, and that there could be no imaginable compensation available elsewhere to the United States, for political loss of Western Europe to Soviet territorial control or political domination.

GEOPOLITICS, FREEDOM OF ACTION, AND ALLIANCE

It is partially correct to consider the maritime power of the United States as the functional successor to the maritime power that Great Britain exercised, to the benefit of international order from the very late seventeenth century until the middle of the twentieth century. British maritime power, a concept and a force traditionally held to be synonymous with British national power, was directed consistently in an anti-hegemonic role. In the multipolar world of post-Westphalian (1648) Europe, an anti-hegemonic policy generally meant an anti-French policy, given that France after 1689 was the country most threatening to the continental balance of power. The First (1905) and Second (1911) Morocco Crises registered publicly, and underlined, the extent to which British threat identification had switched from the traditional to a new enemy: Germany.

From the sixteenth century, when she was only a fairly minor power, to the mid-twentieth, when she was advanced in her *relative* economic decline, Great Britain sought to deny success to territorial or hegemonic imperialism on the part of any continental country or coalition—a policy, or really precept of statecraft, that could require considerable diplomatic agility. The same rationale that for four hundred years moved British statesmen to join or organize coalitions to deny continental hegemony has been the geopolitical motive for American international security policy since the time (1917) when a continental superstate might be able, if unopposed on land, to translate superior landpower into superior seapower. This was why Britain fought in the First World War, and why successive British governments refused to accede to a historic bargain with Nazi Germany that allowed her a free hand in Europe. As a consequence of victory on land, Germany would then have been at liberty to generate the material basis for victory at sea.

In geopolitical perspective, the Soviet challenge to American security is the same as was the German. Notwithstanding the more obvious differences between the Third Reich and the USSR, both have sought—and, in the case of the latter, is still seeking—political preponderance in Eurasia for a truly secure continental base. The structural rigidities in the international system did not permit Britain to play the role of the agile power balancer in twentieth century European diplomacy. In a similarly structured situation, the United States is required to oppose, indeed to organize and lead opposition to, the Soviet drive for hegemony if that drive is to be contained or reversed.

At this juncture it is important to recognize the somewhat changing geopolitical significance of nuclear weapons for American security over the past forty years and, by logical extension, to the end of the century.

From the end of World War II until the mid-1960s, nuclear weapons served persuasively—both in contemporary analysis and in retrospect—as an effective equalizer for the maritime alliance of the West in its endeavor to organize and hold a forward, on-shore containing line in Eurasia protecting the Rimland. It should be recalled that in the late 1940s and through much of the 1950s, both the material and political basis for a balance of power in Eurasia was critically dependent upon American forward commitments and the "extended deterrent" of strategic nuclear forces that underwrote those commitments. The U.S. nuclear arsenal was *the* security guarantor for Rimland-Eurasia against Soviet continental conquest or domination. British, and later American, seapower historically had been effective in laying siege to continental landpower, but that seapower required allies on the continent to provide distraction for the landpower enemy. The Anglo-

American air and maritime threats to Hitler's European fortress, for instance, proved decisive when much of Germany's military strength was detained elsewhere.

The Western problem after World War II, once the U.S. expeditionary forces had been demobilized, was that there was no adequate Eurasian distractor of Soviet military effort available, or even prospective. Atomic weapons provided the United States and its economically exhausted European clients with what appeared to be a relatively inexpensive and very credible means of containing further realization of Soviet hegemonic ambitions in Europe. In effect, nuclear weapons assumed much of the role formerly filled by militarily strong continental allies. The strategic rationale for "The Great (Nuclear) Deterrent" functioning as an "Extended Deterrent" was eminently reasonable, while the United States enjoyed what is termed strategic superiority. In the jargon of modern strategic theory, the United States could extend nuclear deterrence to cover the territories of distant allies because it had, or was believed to have, "escalation dominance."

In Soviet geostrategic perspective, from the late 1940s until the early-to-mid 1960s a NATO-Europe vulnerable to invasion was hostage to moderation in U.S. strategic nuclear behavior. Until the Soviet Union acquired a secure second-strike capability against the United States in the mid-1960s, U.S. freedom of direct military action against the Soviet homeland was offset by the damage that Soviet armies could do to vital U.S. interests in peninsular Europe. In American perspective, unmatched U.S. strategic nuclear prowess offset the continental imbalance in conventional capabilities. U.S. strategic nuclear superiority, translating into anticipation in the East and the West that the United States could exercise escalation dominance in any trial by combat, meant that U.S. risks and U.S. interests were tolerably evenly in balance with respect to the security implications of alliance ties.

The rout of American isolationism by Franklin Roosevelt, critically assisted by the abysmal statecraft of Japan and Germany, was confirmed by the Truman Doctrine of 1947, reconfirmed by the outcome of the great debate over the NATO Treaty in the spring of 1949, and then was set in concrete with the activation of SHAPE in 1951 in the immediate aftermath of the invasion of South Korea by North Korea. "Atlanticism" in the 1950s and through much of the 1960s could claim, with justification, that the denial of Soviet hegemony over Western Europe was a vital interest of the United States—that is to say it was an interest well worth fighting to protect (after all, the United States already had fought two wars within living memory for the geopolitical purpose of thwarting hegemonism in Europe). It would be in the self-interest of the United States to wage as much war as might prove necessary in order to protect that interest. Escalation dominance refers to the ability deliberately to prosecute a war at higher and higher levels of violence in reasonable expectation of securing thereby an improved political outcome. U.S. strategic superiority, although more and more dependent upon securing a favorable operational context (i.e., who launched first), meant that the United States was not risking literally the survival of American society with the strategic-nuclear threat it posed to the USSR in support of NATO in Europe.

Since the late 1950s, the value of the United States's geographically forward-located security clients in Europe and Asia has greatly increased on most figures of relative merit. Whereas the *glaçis* of the Soviet homeland in Europe comprises unwilling (i.e., unreliable) and relatively poor satellite states, the United States has a group of security clients who are willing and generally very economically successful allies. However, Soviet achievements in competitive armament of all kinds since the early 1960s have wrought an unacknowledged revolution in the relationship between risk and interest in the formal security connection of the United States with Western Europe.

What has altered since 1949, and even more dramatically since the mid 1960s, is the quality of risk for the United States that is attached to the NATO commitment—at least for as long as the structure of NATO's military strategy remains unaltered in its essentials. Over the course of the past twenty years the Soviet Union has constructed a comprehensive, multi-level nuclear counterdeterrent that threatens to negate the effectiveness of the architecture of NATO strategy. Flexible response is good enough while Soviet leaders lack a truly powerful political incentive to consider very seriously a military solution to a close-to-intolerable political problem. In political and military logic, NATO's flexible response strategy should no longer "work," owing to the existence of a powerful Soviet intercontinental nuclear arsenal. Nevertheless, the risk remains for the Soviet Union that NATO countries, and particularly the United States, might offer military resistance of a kind and quantity that would be contrary to logic.

In American perspective, denial of Soviet hegemony over Western Europe is an interest worth fighting for, but it is not an interest measured in terms of direct and immediate *survival* value for American society. Given that proportionality is an important principle for the guidance of statecraft, the quantity of sacrifice the United States should be prepared to make in defense of an interest ought to be roughly proportional to the "worth" of that interest. The Soviet military buildup and modernization program has raised the *possible* price of alliance to an intolerable level for the United States. This is the core of the strategic logic of neo-isolationism, whose banner carriers for "America First" in the 1980s include commentators and theorists of both liberal and conservative political persuasions.

Until the advent of intercontinental air power and missile power in the 1950s, insular strategic geography permitted a voluntarism for the United States, a freedom for unilateral decision, that geographical contiguity of threat has not allowed to Eurasian continental states. Even in the missile age, it can be argued that nuclear weapons function, or should function, quite strictly as *counterdeterrents*, thereby failing to effect a revolution in the likely time scale (and geographical scope) of war. Just as British "blue water" theorists and practitioners for four hundred years forged a unilateralist tradition in the selection of its strategy—although definitely not an isolationist tradition in the practice of its foreign policy—exploiting the inherent flexibility and superior mobility of seapower over landpower, so there is an analogous American school of thought today.

The United States has a geostrategic "long-suit" of central maritime position between Asia and Europe-Africa and global security concerns. Since the Soviet defense perimeter is so extensive (and so substantially flanked by a major, if second-class, enemy in China) that it invites threats on multiple axes, the United States cannot help but be interested in avoiding so heavy a specific forward defense commitment that many of her geostrategic advantages effectively would be foresworn. The dilemma is a familiar one.

In World War I, Britain had to make an enormous continental landpower commitment to the defense of France, because defeat on the Western front could have meant general defeat in the war. But, the scale of the British commitment to France was so great that potentially important efforts on the flanks of the Central Powers—the amphibious expedition to Gallipoli in 1915 standing as the most obvious example—were virtually condemned to be conducted too late with too little. The United States today has to decide where to strike the balance between allocating scarce resources to the defense of the vital NATO center and allocating assets for flexible exploitation of its comparative (maritime) geostrategic advantages.

THE SUPERPOWER CONFLICT

By far the most important fact about the structure of the U.S. security condition for the next several decades pertains to the basic character of the Soviet-American antagonism. One cannot frame geostrategic propositions soundly in the absence of a clear understanding of the foundations of that antagonism. Such understanding has to provide the framework within which scenarios are generated and in the light of which advice on strategic policy must be assessed.

For reasons both Soviet and Russian, the Soviet Union's quarrel with the United States is that the U.S. exists as the only country currently capable of organizing and executing effective resistance to the expansion of the Soviet empire. The Soviet Union may or may not be an historically familiar, typical great power; it really does not matter. The great powers in the European balance-of-power system were restrained in the scope of their ambition by the countervailing endeavors of the other great powers. The basis for U.S. hostility to the Soviet Union lies both in the nature of the Soviet system as an actor in world politics—with the motives for outward pressure endemic in the domestic stability requirements of that system—and in the bipolar structure of the contemporary international security system. The Soviet Union is the enemy of the United States because of capabilities of all kinds, actual and potential. Soviet-American antagonism superficially will be to a degree specific to time and place, but the superpower quarrel is not "about" Berlin, relative influence in Beijing, or any other geostrategic particular. Soviet power is self-justifying and has no formal geostrategic bounds to its ambition short of achievement of global imperium. There is much to recommend the following argument advanced by Robert V. Daniels:

> Americans must face a basic fact: Russia is a mammoth power that will not disappear or cease to challenge the United States, regardless of the colorations of its government. The contest for world influence between the United States and Russia is grounded in history—indeed it was foreseen by writers in Europe and America more than a century ago. Russia will continue to be guided by the pride, ambitions, and interests that have carried over from pre-revolutionary times—and no mere alteration in regime or ideology will quickly eliminate them.[1]

Recognition of the systemic character of bipolar superpower conflict does not carry necessary, specific implications for U.S. military strategy and force structure. However, decisions on strategy and posture are unlikely to be correct if the character of the conflict is not assessed accurately. It would be difficult to improve upon Clausewitz's statement that:

> The first, the supreme, the most far-reaching act of judgment that the statesman and commander have to make is to establish . . . the kind of

war on which they are embarking; neither mistaking it for, nor trying to turn it into, something that is alien to its nature.[2]

The United States could have chosen to wage only a limited war of strategic position against Japan in 1942. For very understandable reasons, the United States elected to wage total war; it was Japanese statesmen who misunderstood the nature of the war that they had unleashed. The war in peace that is Soviet-American security relations fits by analogy neither U.S. nor Japanese intentions in 1941–42. Soviet intentions, unlike those of the Japanese at that time, are not geographically bounded, and the military expression of those intentions does not lend itself to definitive overthrow in decisive battle.

The United States is at considerable liberty to decide where, how, and with what it will oppose Soviet hegemonism, but it is not at liberty to withdraw from a condition of opposition. The central fallacy of neo-isolationism is that the United States can enhance its security by withdrawing from those foreign security commitments that, purportedly, give offense in Soviet eyes. The fallacy lies in the belief that it is the geostrategic detail of the U.S. guardianship role that is provocative in Moscow. Soviet hostility towards the United States, however, will continue at least until the structure of the world balance of power is altered radically.

A Soviet Union essentially left in charge of security in Eurasia would not have attained thereby any facsimile of a natural security perimeter. U.S. statesmen, thinking that they should not risk American survival in defense of interests of less than immediate survival quality, would find that they would have shifted the geographical terms of superpower competition, inevitably, towards contention over assets closer to survival quality than had been judged to be the case with respect to Rimland Eurasia.

Today one may be sure that the Soviet Union regards her friends and allies-of-convenience in the Caribbean and Central America as a useful and highly expendable diversion for limited U.S. policy energy. However, in the event of a comprehensive U.S. security withdrawal from Eurasia, Soviet statecraft should be expected to begin in earnest to lay siege to the American homeland. Theorists of international relations differ over the probability of major shifts in the balance of power promoting yet greater shifts in the same direction, as "fence-sitting" states elect to join the bandwagon in fear that, if they do not, the bandwagon may roll over them. A no less popular view holds that an imbalance in power tends to be self-correcting, as successful aggrandizement triggers the very opposition that must arrest its progress. In an extreme form, this latter argument holds that should the United States decide no longer to lead an intercontinental western Alliance, but rather to laager its wagons, or carrier task forces perhaps, around the Western Hemisphere, Soviet efforts to exploit this historical development inexorably would cause such security alarms in Western Europe, China, and Japan, that that which had been politically impossible while the United States played alliance leader, would then be clearly necessary. In this hopeful view, a European Defense Community would be forged in tacit coalition with a Sino-Japanese alliance or, at the least, *entente très cordiale.*

As a Panglossian vision, this happy prospect has everything to recommend it. Unfortunately, responsible U.S. planners can have no confidence that the United States in fact would be able to pass the security organizer's baton to the leaders of new architectures for collective defense in Europe and Asia. There can be little doubt that the continuation of a U.S. definition of its security perimeter as lying onshore in Rimland Eurasia from Kirkenes to Seoul, does serve effectively to discourage local defense initiatives. But, it is a great leap of political faith to proceed from recognition of major incentives for Eurasian-Rimland countries to take charge of their own regional security interests, to belief that the necessary creativity and determination would occur in a timely fashion.

It is probable that the United States cannot remove itself from the status of Soviet "public enemy number one" simply by redrawing the geographical perimeter of U.S. vital interests. In Soviet calculation, actual and potential U.S. capabilities define the U.S. role as the principal threat. For ideological and for *realpolitik* motives, the Soviet Union will never voluntarily permit the United States a quiet retirement from the perils of nuclear-age power politics, wherein "life, liberty and the pursuit of happiness" can be pursued by a country determinedly inoffensive to Soviet interests in world affairs.

STRATEGIC GEOGRAPHY

There is something to recommend a geopolitical perspective upon the superpower antagonism that argues that, in Soviet eyes, the proximate American offense is its preservation of a large, prosperous, and well-armed bridgehead in NATO-Europe. Security and stability in Soviet political (and strategic) culture flows from Soviet preponderance. Pluralism in security frameworks is as alien to Soviet state wishes, as would be genuine pluralism in the domestic political system of the Soviet imperium. However, the geopolitical referents of Soviet-American competition are not confined as by some law of geopolitics to

U.S. security bridgeheads in Europe and Asia. After the tide of battle turned definitively in World War II with the failure of the last great German offensive in the east (Kursk) in July 1943, the Soviet Union has secured the Eurasian Heartland, has moved from the status of a regional great power to being *the* regional great power, to being *the* second-class superpower, to being a global superpower. But, to be a global superpower of first-class rank, the Soviet Union must transcend its landlocked condition and break convincingly out of the Heartland.

Although the United States has enormous positional and logistical advantages over the Soviet Union *vis à vis* potential conflict in the Western Hemisphere and its maritime approaches, it is well to remember that the strategic meaning and value of geography can alter dramatically with political, as well as technological, circumstances. The disadvantages under which the U.S. Navy would labor in seeking to exercise sea control, or to project power, in waters very close to the Soviet homeland are obvious. However, critics of extant U.S. foreign security entanglements tend to forget, or at least to neglect, the no-less-obvious contemporary advantages enjoyed by the U.S. Navy. Those advantages include choke-point control denying Soviet forces access to the open ocean that is scarcely less impressive than that exercised by the Royal Navy in its heyday. The surface navy of Imperial Germany could not sortie onto the sea lines of communication of the Western allies, except through the unacceptable tactic of offering itself up to a very strong probability of total destruction in a decisive battle in the North Sea. Without denying the survival risk to the United States that is inherent in opposing Soviet hegemonic policies in Eurasia, the fact remains that the forward-located allies and friends of the United States are denying Moscow access to geography critical for global power projection. The allies provide large naval, land, and airpower barriers to Soviet access to the oceanic approaches to the Americas. On the positive side, the Eurasian allies of the United States provide a forward geostrategic basis for U.S. access to the Soviet imperium.

Neo-isolationists, and even unilateralists who tend to disparage the security value to the United States of the NATO alliance, need to recognize some geopolitical considerations of enduring relevance for the very structure of American security. First, the beginning of wisdom is recognition of the validity of Nicholas Spykman's 1944 dictum that the United States's

> . . . main political objective, both in peace and in war, must therefore be
> to prevent the unification of the Old World centers of power in a coalition
> hostile to her own interests.[3]

Spykman is simply repeating for the United States what had been the overriding operating principle for British statecraft since the time of Henry VIII.

Second, the greatest twentieth-century geopolitical theorist, Sir Halford Mackinder, recognized as early as 1943 that this time, predicting Soviet power in the future, the wolf truly would be at the Western door.

> All things considered, the conclusion is unavoidable that if the Soviet Union emerges from this war as conqueror of Germany, she must rank as the greatest land power on the globe. Moreover, she will be the power in the strategically strongest defensive position. The Heartland is the greatest natural fortress on earth. For the first time in history, it is manned by a garrison sufficient both in number and quality.[4]

Mackinder did not know about the Manhattan Project and—one should note—his conception of a Heartland to the "World Island" (the dual continent of Europe-Asia, plus Africa) originally was presented in 1904, before the maturing of heavier-than-air flight. Nonetheless, this brief passage of 1943 vintage points directly to the third enduring truth of geopolitics relevant to U.S. security. Preponderant landpower, if substantially uncontested and distracted by continental adversaries, may be the basis from which superior seapower is developed and exercised. (See the extensive discussion of this point in chapter 1.)

If the United States were expelled, or chose to withdraw, from European and Asian security entanglements, there would be a severe danger that the Rimlands not only would no longer serve to support purposes congruent with U.S. interests, but also might be enlisted for active participation in support of a new phase of Soviet *Weltpolitik*. Nuclear-armed, the United States should be secure against invasion. If the Soviet Union were conceded preponderance in Eurasia, however, it would have the geostrategic position, it might achieve the economic strength, and it certainly should have the military basis for initiating a serious challenge to the United States in the Americas. Soviet maritime and mercantile assets no longer "locked up" or blockaded, in the Arctic, the Baltic, the Black Sea, the Sea of Japan, and the Sea of Okhotsk would no longer be hostages upon the high seas in time of crisis; nor would they be compelled to behave as fugitives in time of war if they sailed outside the Soviet Union's coastal sea bastions.

Overall, it cannot be doubted that the European and Asian allies of the United States, to greater and lesser degree, expend proportionately fewer national resources upon a supposedly common security enterprise than does the United States. Furthermore, these Rimland allies constitute a geographically fractured chain of relatively exposed outposts (or U.S. bridgeheads in the Soviet view). Commitment to the forward defense of those allies reduces greatly the flexibility with which American policymakers might otherwise choose to direct the application of military power.

NATO's Central Front, covering assets absolutely essential to the viability of the Alliance, simply has to be defended with the utmost determination. Soviet strategic planners, while hoping—though probably not expecting with total confidence—to achieve a *Blitzkrieg* victory on the Central Front, might suspect that in the event of failure to secure a rapid and fatal rupture of NATO's linear, hard-crust defense, they could impose a theater-wide "Verdun" (a grinding battle of attrition) upon their enemies. In other words, Soviet planners probably expect that NATO would expend all available effort to attempt to hold as far forward as possible on the Central Front: this would not be a battle, or campaign, that NATO could afford to concede in order to fight again another day on more advantageous ground.

The Soviet military experience against Germany in World War II was of a broad-front attritional struggle against a materially inferior enemy massively distracted by the need to garrison virtually the whole of southern, western, and northern Europe, eventually to defend Italy and France against invasion, and to employ more than 65 percent of its air force in homeland defense. Soviet political and military leaders, prudently recognizing that war is an uncertain business, have to be aware of the possibility that a short-war *Blitzkrieg* could fail. In that event, they would be confronted with the dilemma of choosing among initiating nuclear escalation in an effort to snatch victory out of stalemate, accepting a protracted ground war of attrition in Europe with an enemy with a truly global reach, or seeking prompt war termination by negotiation. In the course of a protracted war of attrition, the enemy economies that would be conducting crash-scale military mobilizations would not resemble the Axis powers of 1941–45, but instead would be the world's economic leaders. Soviet strategic culture may have some difficulty believing that the Soviet Union could lose a prolonged conventional war, but the dominant Soviet military experience was of a one-front war against an underequipped, undermanned, and poorly commanded Germany. The differences with a putative World War III should be awesome and profoundly deterring in Soviet perspective. Nevertheless, whether or not the maritime alliance of the West will act to provide itself with the strategy, the ready military means, and the defense-economic mobilization plans and preparations that would make a reality of the possible Soviet anxieties sketched here, remains a matter for conjecture at the present time.

U.S. military commitments to an on-shore perimeter that runs essentially from the North Cape of Norway to eastern Turkey, risk the U.S. ability to "roll with the punch" and recover, because too great a percentage of U.S. deployed and readily mobilizable military power might be lost in the first battles. Given the advantages of the initiative for Soviet arms, in the context both of very considerable initial numerical ground-force superiority and in ease of rapid reinforcement, it is obvious why the forward defense commitment to NATO-Europe could place the U.S. homeland at survival risk after the passage of only a few days of theater combat.

Nevertheless, Americans critical of NATO-European efforts for the common defense, and understandably worried lest there is today a foolish asymmetry between the quality of U.S. risks and the quality of U.S. interests in Europe, should remember that the allies of the United States are contributing their national territories as potential battlefields for the forward defense of the Americas. Furthermore, it should be understood that a redefinition of the U.S. defense perimeter would simply alter the geographical locale for agonizing decisions. It would not permit the United States to evade indefinitely the harder problems associated with maintaining its security in the shadow of nuclear threats. So great would be the perils of a drastic scale of withdrawal of U.S. security guarantees—from a known containing line to what?—and so much is it to the U.S. advantage to keep the Soviet Union essentially landlocked, that there is everything to be said in favor of exploring rigorously how national U.S. and allied military strategy can be improved in order better to balance ends and means. There is no compelling case for the United States to begin the unraveling of the geopolitical architecture of the maritime alliance of the West. Readers should ask themselves: if the United States flinches from the prospect of nuclear escalation in defense of Norway, West Germany, or Turkey, what risks would be run for Spain, Portugal, the Azores, Venezuela, or Panama?

ON STRATEGY

Common sense as well as contemporary defense reformers remind us that strategy is an exercise in the making of choices. In practice, many important choices are, and should be recognized as, foreordained by geopolitics. Moreover, U.S. freedom of action in choice of strategic objectives is constrained by the fact that the overall strategic posture, and certainly the political purpose of the Western Alliance, is defensive in character. To the substantial degree to which the U.S./ NATO choice of strategic objectives must flow from the scale, kind, locations, and assessed intentions of a Soviet attack, Western strategy generically is reactive in nature. The flexibility with which superior naval power can be applied is important in principle, as the United States and NATO seek to shape an overall strategy that leans on relative Western strengths and exploits relative Soviet weaknesses. But, the strategic value of superior naval power is *to a degree* offset both by the substantial inaccessibility of the core areas of power in the Soviet Union to the *direct* application of pressure from the sea, and the geostrategic vulnerability of peninsular Europe to the long-suit of Soviet power: mechanized ground forces.

The principal restriction upon choice of strategy for NATO and for the United States is geopolitical in nature. Whatever the U.S./NATO choice among military instruments and the operational methods chosen for their employment, the primary immediate objective of the alliance has to be to defeat a Soviet invasion of West Germany. Insofar as NATO is concerned, Western Europe from the Baltic to the Adriatic prospectively comprises the main theater of operations. Arguments over the implications of this inalienable fact are at the heart of the debate over U.S. national military strategy. Much of this debate— between continentalists/coalitionists and maritime advocates—has reflected considerable mutual misunderstanding, the attacking of imaginary debating positions, and an absence of history-based prudence. A maritime-oriented analysis of the geostrategic situation of the West yields a number of important propositions.

First, allied maritime advantage is critically important—not just desirable, but literally essential—for the deterrence of war. The credible promise of the U.S. exercise of sea control is a necessary precondition for the conduct of protracted armed conflict in and about Eurasia-Africa. Needless to add, perhaps, Western ability to enforce a long war on the Soviet Union could be defeated if U.S. strategic nuclear forces were insufficient to impose escalation discipline, or if the United States were denied working control of the key sea lines of communication.

Second, if NATO's ground and tactical air forces go down in defeat in a matter of days, U.S. and allied naval forces cannot provide strategic compensation through the achievement of success of comparable strategic value elsewhere. Furthermore, there is no way in which NATO's maritime assets could be employed in the course of a European campaign of, say, two-weeks' duration, such as to have a truly major impact on the battle of the Central Front. There is nothing very surprising about this: British naval power could not intervene directly to thwart the execution of the Schlieffen Plan in August-September 1914, the Ludendorff Offensive of March 1918, or the unfolding of the Manstein Plan in May 1940.

Third, if NATO's ground and tactical air forces can remain "in the field" somewhere in Western Europe, U.S. and allied naval power would play an essential role in NATO's military recovery. This would take place by securing working control of the SLOCs and, increasingly, through flexibility in sea-based power projection against a Soviet imperium vulnerable to attack on many geographical axes. Some proponents and critics of recent trends in the strategic thinking of the U.S. Navy have tended to conduct debate with insufficient reference to its appropriate operational context. U.S. and allied naval power is not going to save NATO-Europe in the event of a May 1940–style catastrophe on the Central Front. But, sensible proponents of the case for the importance of Western maritime preponderance do not claim otherwise.

Fourth, U.S. working control of the relevant lines of maritime communication will be essential whether or not a Soviet ground-forces' offensive can be held in Central Europe. In U.S. perspective, war in Europe might be only a campaign, it need not comprise *the war*— and it is very important for deterrence that Soviet leaders understand this point. Always assuming the functioning of strategic nuclear counterdeterrence, in the event of U.S. military expulsion from continental Europe the U.S. Navy again would assume its historic role of being the first line of the nation's defense.

Fifth, contemporary U.S. debate over maritime strategy allegedly "versus" continental strategy, misses the point that the debate should not be over the relative merits of landpower or seapower in U.S. national military strategy. The United States cannot be a land power beyond North America unless she is a sea power, and seapower has strategic meaning only insofar as it has influence on events on land.

Altogether, there is today in the United States an obsession with one, admittedly exceedingly important, problem—the difficulty of holding and repelling a Soviet ground assault in Central Europe. Of course one must recognize the strategic importance to the United States of keeping the Soviet Union essentially landlocked, and healthily distracted by continental security problems (NATO in the West, China in the East, unstable clients in Eastern Europe, and fanatical Moslems to the South) from the full-fledged exercise of *Weltpolitik*. However, that recognition, and acknowledgment that the cutting edge of Soviet military power lies in its ground forces, should not translate into an argument for a stronger U.S. Army and tactical air force at the expense of the U.S. Navy.

These points bear repetition:

- The prospect of protracted armed conflict should prove particularly deterring to the Soviet Union. The entry price the United States must pay in order to threaten plausibly to impose such a conflict, comprises a very convincing strategic nuclear counterdeterrent and preponderance at sea.

- It would be vastly preferable for the United States were the Soviet Union to confront the prospect of a protracted conflict with a U.S. bridgehead intact in continental NATO-Europe. But, the case for a U.S. Navy able to ensure U.S. use of maritime communications for transportation and for power projection is equally strong, whether or not the protracted conflict includes an active continental NATO-European dimension. There is a wide world beyond Europe.

- The argument that the U.S. Navy could sink a substantial proportion of the Soviet Navy and yet still contribute not at all to the defense of NATO's Central Front, is a popular trivialization of strategy discussion. The same point can be made, for example, with reference to the Royal Navy's Grand Fleet of 1914–1918, with equal lack of cogency. Lest the point is still obscure: only ready, deployed, and rapidly transportable ground and tactical air forces can preclude a Soviet *Blitzkrieg* victory in a one-to-two-week war in Central-Western Europe. U.S. and allied maritime power is only marginally relevant to that mission. The case for very strong U.S. naval forces is: (a) to ensure that U.S. reinforcements arrive rapidly in order to avoid a short-war defeat for NATO; (b) to keep NATO "in the field" in a war that lasts more than a few weeks; (c) to exploit Soviet weaknesses on its flanks (in Europe and Asia) in a protracted war; (d) to apply pressure on the Soviet Union for war termination through the sinking of more and more of its SSBN force; (e) if needs be to enable the United States to wage a protracted war in Asia and Africa should Europe fall; and (f) truly in *extremis*, to contest a siege of the Americas if the Soviet Union should achieve hegemony over Eurasia and set about the translation of her superior continental landpower into a challenge for maritime command.

As happens frequently in defense debates, orientation towards disagreements over naval force posture, operational deployment, and missions (e.g., over large carriers versus small carriers, power projection versus sea control) has had the effect of putting the debate over national military strategy out of focus. From the public literature of the 1980s, one could derive the impression that the case for and against a 600-ship U.S. Navy with fifteen carrier battle groups hangs critically upon the answers to such questions as these: Should the navy promptly assault the home bastions of Soviet naval power in the event of war? And, could success on "the flanks" contribute vitally to the defense of NATO's Central Front in a short war? This is a classic example of the wrong questions generating irrelevant answers.

NATO and the United States cannot, or cannot sensibly, choose between strength at sea and strength for the holding of Western Europe on land. Why? Because NATO cannot hold on land for very long if it cannot control its transatlantic SLOC. Moreover, the severity of Soviet security problems in East Asia easily could be exacerbated by the ability of the U.S. Navy to use the transpacific SLOC. Soviet problems in East Asia would bear noticeably upon Soviet freedom of action in Central Europe. A very strong maritime dimension to its strategy is mandated for the United States by reason of the geography of its competition with the Soviet Union. Some critics of U.S. naval augmentation and modernization are committing the error of reducing hypothetical future war almost strictly to a brief campaign for an initial (and possibly definitive) decision in Central Europe, neglecting to consider what might happen next.

Given the plausibility of the propositions that the ability to sustain a protracted global conflict may be critically important for the deterrence of war, and that nuclear counterdeterrence renders protracted U.S.-Soviet armed conflict probable—*whether or not NATO holds in Western Europe*—several caveats must be noted concerning the development and operational uses of naval power.

First, the Western Alliance as a whole obviously should not construct a reply that is overbalanced in the maritime region to what is, in the first instance, essentially a landpower threat. However, it does not follow from this elementary point that the United States should not have a maritime-heavy orientation in *its* general-purpose forces.

Second, U.S. and NATO maritime power should not be used in such a way as to enhance the prospect of a precipitate rate of vertical escalation. For the enhancement of prewar deterrence it is important that Soviet leaders should anticipate their Western foes being willing to adopt any and all means necessary to defeat Soviet strategy. Those means include endeavors to exploit differences of interest and commitment within the Soviet empire, denial of absolute sanctuary status to Soviet home territory, and willingness to use nuclear weapons. In operational practice, however, the United States and Great Britain may choose to accord Soviet territory sanctuary status in order to minimize the risks to American and British territory.

Lest there be any misunderstanding, the second caveat reflects no more than a concern for due consideration in planning and force execution. Certainly it does not assume that assaults against the Soviet coasts must be unwise under all circumstances, that freedom of choice necessarily will rest with the United States, and certainly it does not assume that the U.S. Navy is committed to an immediate offensive against the coastal bastions of Soviet seapower, regardless of strategic conditions or tactical circumstances.

CONCLUSIONS

Even if the essence of strategy, or perhaps of the quality required of a strategist, is the moral courage to make difficult choices, the real scope for strategic choice in U.S. national military strategy is rather less than is frequently asserted to be the case. If the United States continues down the path of global containment of Soviet power, employing a mix of multilateral and bilateral alliance ties as the political framework, and notwithstanding some historical ebb and flow in U.S. domestic enthusiasm for forward military commitments outside the NATO area, geostrategic and political considerations serve vastly to narrow the scope for U.S. innovation in strategy. As the center of gravity of a global coalition of states knit together by sea lines of communication, the United States is obliged to have what amounts to a maritime emphasis in its national military strategy. However, endorsement of such an emphasis, with its proper expression in force structure, does not mean that one: is blind to the essentially land-power character of the Soviet threat to the territorial integrity of NATO-Europe and of China; fails to recognize the relative inaccessibility of much of the Soviet imperium to pressure directly from the sea; or, least of all, that one is determined to hazard U.S. carrier task forces in prospectively very severely contested areas on the Soviet maritime frontier at the very outset of a war. The case for a maritime emphasis in U.S. national military strategy rests upon the following considerations:

- Recognition that it is politically essential and militarily efficient for regional allies in Europe and Asia to provide the overwhelming majority of the ready and rapidly mobilizable ground forces for local defense.
- Recognition that working control of key SLOCs would be absolutely essential if NATO were to be able to sustain a conflict in Europe, and/or if the United States were to prosecute a more pro-

tracted war—regardless of how the campaign in Europe had developed.

- Recognition of the likely global character, or certain global *potential,* of a protracted conflict, and of the importance of providing such strategically useful distraction on the very far-flung flanks of Soviet power as could be achieved at tolerable cost. If NATO can hold in the center, it will begin to be very important indeed that Soviet leaders should feel pressed in the Far North, in southern Europe, and—above all—feel generally overextended in the European theater of operations as a consequence both of U.S. operations in the northeast Pacific and of the Chinese threat that flanks their entire position in the east.
- Appreciation of the fact that although the benchmark for adequacy in military preparation would be provided by the test of battle in the event of a Soviet invasion of Europe, the United States and her allies are operating day by day in a condition of war in peace. There are few security problems in peacetime to which U.S. naval power is not relevant.

NOTES

1. Robert V. Daniels, *Russia: The Roots of Confrontation* (Cambridge, MA: Harvard University Press, 1985), p. 358.

2. Karl von Clausewitz, *On War,* Michael Howard and Peter Paret, eds. (Princeton, NJ: Princeton University Press, 1976), p. 88.

3. Nicholas John Spykman, *The Geography of the Peace* (New York: Harcourt, Brace, 1944), p. 45.

4. Halford J. Mackinder, *Democratic Ideals and Reality* (New York: W. W. Norton and Company, 1962; first pub. 1942), p. 33.

BIBLIOGRAPHIC NOTE

The proper roles for, and relative importance of, seapower in Western defense, is a topic that has attracted a great deal of attention in recent years. Distinctive views are presented in Robert Komer, *Maritime Strategy or Coalition Defense?* (Cambridge, MA: Abt Books, 1986); Jeffrey Record, *Revising U.S. Military Strategy: Tailoring Means to Ends* (Washington, DC: Pergamon-Brassey's, 1984); Zbigniew Brzezinski, *Game Plan: A Geostrategic Framework for the Conduct of the U.S.-Soviet Contest* (Boston: Atlantic Monthly Press, 1986); and Colin S. Gray, *The Geopolitics of Super Power* (Lexington, KY: University Press of Kentucky, 1988).

ADDITIONAL SOURCES

Atkeson, Thomas B. "Hemispheric Denial: Geopolitical Imperatives and Soviet Strategy." *Strategic Review,* vol. 4, no. 2 (Spring 1976), pp. 26–36.
Claude, Inis L., Jr. "The Common Defense and Great-Power Responsibilities." *Political Science Quarterly,* vol. 101, no. 5 (1986), pp. 719–32.

Gray, Colin S. *The Geopolitics of the Nuclear Era: Heartland, Rimlands, and the Technological Revolution.* New York: Crane, Russak (for the National Strategy Information Center), 1977.

Kennedy, Paul. *The Rise and Fall of British Naval Mastery.* New York: Charles Scribner's Sons, 1976.

Krauss, Melvyn. *How NATO Weakens the West.* New York: Simon and Schuster, 1986.

Parker, Geoffrey. *Western Geopolitical Thought in the Twentieth Century.* New York: St. Martin's Press, 1985.

Parker, W. H. *Mackinder: Geography as an Aid to Statecraft.* Oxford: Clarendon Press, 1982.

Spykman, Nicholas John. *America's Strategy in World Politics: The United States and the Balance of Power.* Hamden, CT: Archon Books, 1970; first pub. 1942.

Trofimenko, Genrikh. *The U.S. Military Doctrine.* Moscow: Progress Publishers, 1986, pp. 29–67.

Vlahos, Michael. "Maritime Strategy Versus Continental Strategy?" *Orbis*, vol. 26, no. 3 (Fall 1982), pp. 583–89.

Zoppo, Ciro E., and Charles Zorgbibe, eds. *On Geopolitics: Classical and Nuclear.* NATO ASI Series. Boston: Martinus Nijhoff Publishers, 1985.

12

Soviet Maritime Strategy

BY ROGER W. BARNETT

Chto nuzhno, chtoby stat' velikoy morskoy derzhavoy? ("What is needed in order to become a great sea power?") The Soviet Union maintains today in numbers of ships the world's largest navy. It also counts in its inventory over 2,500 merchant ships of 1,000 gross tons and larger, which is 10 percent of the world's total and second only in ranking to the 3,500 ships of the same description registered in Panama.[1] In fishing, the Soviet annual catch is exceeded only by Japan, and it is more than twice as large as that of the United States. The Soviet oceanographic research fleet exceeds in size the total of the rest of the world combined. Yet, the Soviet Union is not ordinarily thought of as a great sea power. "What," admirals of the Soviet Navy must be asking, "does it take?"

Since the time of Peter the Great (1689–1725), the leaders of the Russian and then Soviet state have often either maintained or sought to acquire a large fleet of combatant ships.[2] The rise and fall of the fortunes of the Russian Navy, great both in amplitude and in frequency during the first two and a half centuries of its existence, have begun to stabilize in the last several decades. Of late the Soviet Navy has prospered, thanks in large measure to the late Admiral of the Fleet of the Soviet Union Sergei G. Gorshkov. Admiral Gorshkov led the Soviet Navy from 1956 to 1985, a period marked by significant overall economic growth. A foundation has thus been laid to sustain a large, capable navy into the indefinite future.

The Soviet Union commands its own chapter in this book for two reasons: first, because the Soviet Union, as the major military competitor to the United States in the world today, maintains the world's only other first-class navy. At present, all navies other than those two must be judged distinctly second-rate or less by comparison. The Soviet Navy is of high interest in the second place because the competition between the Soviet Union and the democratic West must be considered both structural and enduring. Although the Soviet leadership has from the time of Lenin claimed that it follows a policy of "peaceful coexistence," and although it has rationalized its actions on the world scene in such terms, to Western observers the Soviet approach might not appear so benign.[3] The competition between the two superpowers, moreover, is *classical* in the sense that it centers on the relative competitive positions of two superstates—much like the competitive tensions that have existed between major powers through the ages, many of which have been addressed in earlier chapters.

THE SOVIET APPROACH TO STRATEGY

Soviet strategists take a very different approach to their subject than do their Western counterparts. They emphasize conceptual rigor and careful, consistent employment of terminology. Soviet strategists would never mistake *tactics* for *strategy*, or either of them for *doctrine*. Western strategists, as a group, are often insensitive to those differences, or to why they matter. Precise definitions are not central to this discussion, however. The point is that the Soviet approach to strategy seeks and purports to be *scientific*. Military science in the Soviet Union takes as one of its major purposes the identification of laws of war and principles of armed conflict. The Soviet overall approach to conflict seeks to describe objectively the relative capabilities of adversaries, and to assess them by means of scientific and historical analysis based on principles of Marxism-Leninism. Military science in the Soviet Union endeavors to ensure that lessons hammered out painfully in combat will be neither forgotten nor ignored. The briefest sampling of Soviet military writings will serve to illustrate the point.

It should be understood, therefore, that a Soviet military man will be conditioned by the need to commit fully to the objectives that have been established for him by the political leadership. He might be tempted, but his training will not countenance his being diverted by matters not central to his purpose. Ever mindful of his mission priorities, he should be expected to seek ways to draw on his training—peppered heavily with historical anecdote—rather than to innovate.

Soviet seapower cannot be analyzed adequately without an understanding of the features that have tended over time to shape the direction and content of Soviet naval policy. First and foremost has been the long-standing debate on the question of the value of the navy. No one disputes the fact that the development of the Soviet Union into the largest organized state in the history of the world took place with minimal participation by Russian maritime forces. Russia amassed no far-flung colonial empire, no mercantile network linked together by the sea lanes, and no great merchant fleet had a place in its heritage. Consolidation of the largest empire the world has ever known took place on the land; it was accomplished by the army and through coercive diplomacy. The navy's part in expanding the borders of the Russian state was virtually non-existent, and the Soviet Union today does not maintain an overseas empire. Likewise, that the Soviet state is and has always been essentially autarkic underscores the fact that it has had neither large external commercial dealings that require ships to service, nor the need to import raw materials. The closest it has come over time to a position of import dependency has been its rather recent requirement to import grain, owing to chronic agricultural problems.

It would be both fair and accurate to characterize the Soviet Union as an exemplary great land power. Acquiring and consolidating, and then organizing, controlling, defending, and administering the 8,600,000 square miles that today constitute the Soviet polity consumed much of the available energy of the Russian leadership for century upon century. Interests abroad were generally minimal, and as a consequence the need for large inventories of ships for any purpose was not viewed as great. Conquest took place and threats originated primarily on the land. Enemies such as Sweden in the eighteenth century or Turkey in the eighteenth and nineteenth centuries occasionally mounted military efforts against Russia from seaward axes, yet no threat had ever emanated from across wide oceanic expanses. Accordingly, a continuing debate raged within government councils concerning the value and importance of a navy for other than coastal defense.

The value and importance of *access to the sea* was not at issue. Russian history is peppered with examples of recurring efforts to secure reliable, long-term access to the sea, and thus to the benefits that might be garnered by maritime intercourse. Each of the important maritime areas of today's Soviet Union was at one time the site of a struggle for access to the sea. While the historical evidence is scanty (even though the folklore is very rich) that the Russians have persistently sought a "warm-water" port, just the opposite is true with regard to access to the sea. Whether in the White Sea, Baltic, Black, or Pacific regions, Russia has always coveted outlets on bodies of water adjacent to land areas over which it maintained political control.

Typically, and understandably, the czars and the Politburo alike have consistently accorded the navy a lesser status than that of the ground forces. Today, to underscore the point, the navy stands last in relative priority among the five Soviet armed services. Most experts agree that the relative standing starts with the Soviet strategic rocket forces and then, in order, the army, air defense forces, air force, and navy. For the most part, the navy was considered a supporting arm of the army, and it remained under the firm command of the army. Stalin referred directly to the Red Navy as the "great and faithful helper of the Red Army," and to this day naval spokesmen give substantial weight to the task of the navy that calls for it to support the army from seaward axes.

The widely distributed series of writings of Admiral Gorshkov over the past decade and a half have sought to demonstrate the value of seapower in general, and the navy in particular, to the Soviet Union. Doubtless, however, more than a few non-believers still occupy the upper echelons of the Soviet military hierarchy. It is not difficult to speculate that geography, politics, and tradition will help ensure that priorities currently existing among the Soviet armed forces will not change appreciably in the future. Thus, one can suggest with confidence that the overall control of the Soviet armed forces will remain with those who are basically oriented landward, not seaward.

Why, then, should the Soviet Union desire to maintain a large, very capable navy? In *Seapower of the State*, Admiral Gorshkov sets forth a series of reasons. First and foremost, of course, is the contribution the navy makes to the defense of the Motherland against attacks from the sea. Second is the ability to mount attacks against adversaries from the sea. These will be considered in detail later in the chapter. Admiral Gorshkov, however, sought to inform his readers of the potential of maritime forces in other areas, and thus to recruit some additional supporters, when he claimed:

> For the Soviet Union, the main goal of whose policy is the building of communism and a steady rise in the welfare of its builders, seapower emerges as one of the important factors for strengthening its economy, accelerating scientific and technical development and consolidating the

economic, political, cultural and scientific links of the Soviet people with the peoples and countries friendly to it.[4]

Admiral Gorshkov appeared on the scene at a very propitious time for the Soviet Navy. His timing was somewhat analogous to that of Alfred Thayer Mahan's for the U.S. Navy. He was in the right place at the right time. He succeeded, in the almost thirty years of his tenure, in leading the Soviet Navy to a position as one of only two first-rate navies in the world. This is a noteworthy, and, considering the checkered histories of the Russian and Soviet navies, a truly amazing accomplishment.

THE TRADITIONALIST-MODERNIST DEBATE

Throughout its history the value of a navy to Russia has been the subject of recurring debate, with the composition of maritime forces prominent as the central issue. That is, the major question generally has concerned the type of units that should constitute the navy. The value of the navy was argued in terms of what proponents and opponents believed the navy's force structure should be, which stemmed from their respective views about what the navy might be tasked to accomplish in time of war. The debate polarized along lines that recur frequently in the history of maritime force structuring in many countries: the "traditionalists," or Old School, versus the "modernists," or Young School.

Traditionalists in the Soviet Union argued for high-quality seapower characterized by a fleet capable of operating on all the oceans of the world, not just a fleet for use on lakes and territorially adjacent seas. They maintained that the navy should have a greater share of military funding and decision-making authority, that a future war would have an important maritime component, and that excessive attention to the land battle would result in incomplete strategies for waging war. In their view, important strategic factors—such as the geography and strategy of potential enemies—should be taken more fully into account. Nevertheless, they generally agreed that building a large, capable fleet depended greatly on overall economic well-being, and that it should be accomplished gradually, not all at once. That the navy should be able to conduct operations independent of other armed forces, and that the Communist Party should be a secondary force in the command system for military matters, also stood high on the traditionalist agenda.

In sharp contrast, *modernists* contended that land battles historically had been, and would continue in the future to be, decisive for victory. In their view, maritime forces could play no central role in the course or outcome of war. They rejected doctrines that called for command of the sea; championed a highly mobile fleet of light, inexpensive surface ships, mines, submarines, and aircraft to defend the coastline; argued vigorously against offensive capability for the navy; based much of their argumentation in Marxist economic terms; and believed strongly that the navy should remain subordinate to the army. Modernists took the position that Communist doctrine should guide, and the Communist Party should play an important role in, maritime affairs.

The modernists generally were successful in the debates that transpired early in the life of the Soviet state. They were also alert to take advantage of the appointments of M. V. Frunze—a modernist who succeeded Leon Trotsky as head of the Soviet armed forces in 1924— and of R. A. Muklevich, an outspoken modernist as people's commissar for the navy in 1926, to influence the naval construction program of the first Soviet Five Year Plan. For the next twenty interwar years the pendulum oscillated between the two schools. First the modernists, then the traditionalists were more influential and effective.

Overlaid upon, but in some ways separate from the modernist/ traditionalist debate in shaping the course of the navy, was the impact of direct political interference. Stalin's purges of the navy in the 1930s and Nikita Khrushchev's interest in submarines—inasmuch as Khrushchev was a thoroughgoing modernist—spring immediately to mind in this regard. Since the time of Khrushchev, however, there has not been a Soviet head of state who was either clearly enamored of or obviously hostile to the idea of broad-gauged Soviet seapower. Recall, on the other hand, that it was Khrushchev who promoted Gorshkov to lead the Soviet Navy, a position he retained for almost thirty years.

Finally, after World War II—the "Great Patriotic War" in Soviet parlance—a compromise was effected between the two schools. This new understanding called for constructing a fleet balanced between large and small surface ships and submarines. Detail on what a balanced fleet was supposed to accomplish, however, had to await the writings of Admiral Gorshkov. The consensus on a balanced fleet appears to be holding today, at least as nearly as one can tell by observing Soviet shipbuilding programs and reading the open Soviet literature.

THE PERVASIVE IMPORTANCE OF GEOGRAPHY

While the modernist-traditionalist debate in the Soviet Union seems at least for the present to be resolved in favor of the latter persuasion, there is a more enduring feature that shapes Soviet maritime policy and strategy: geography. Geography imposes a triple burden on Soviet maritime affairs owing to the wide separation of the four fleet areas, the effects of climate on the various fleets, and the fact that each of them is isolated from the open oceans by geographic choke points.

The four Soviet fleets and one flotilla—as the Soviets call them, the Red Banner Northern Fleet, the Twice-Honored Red Banner Baltic Fleet, the Red Banner Black Sea Fleet, the Red Banner Pacific Fleet, and the Red Banner Caspian Sea Flotilla—are so widely dispersed that any possibility of mutual reinforcement in time of war must be considered to be low at best. The advice Mahan offered to the U.S. Navy not to divide its fleet simply cannot be followed by the Soviets, who have no such option. The two largest and most capable of the four fleets are the Northern and the Pacific, by reason of the fact that they have the easiest access to the sea.

Severe climate takes its toll on navies by not permitting them to maintain their ships as well as they might, by damaging them in high winds and seas, and by reducing the opportunity for at-sea training. Of course, it would be foolhardy to train to fight only in fair weather. On the other hand, much training is compatible with either good or bad weather, and it is far easier to accomplish when the seas are flat and the winds are calm. None of the Soviet fleets is located in a temperate climate; all have winter problems with storms. Some, in fact, are icebound in port for months at a time, completely unable even to move.

Geography also takes a toll by providing a gamut for each of the Soviet fleets to run in order to reach the open sea. In the Pacific, the main naval base is at Vladivostok. Ships located there must transit straits controlled on at least one side by an ally of the United States. On the north, the La Pérouse or Soya Strait is an international strait. The strategic sensitivity of this area is punctuated by the fact that the Soviet Union and Japan have not to this day concluded a peace agreement ending the Second World War, owing to a territorial dispute over islands located at the northern tip of the Japanese island of Hokkaido. Several of these islands have been stoutly fortified by the Soviets. Tsugaru Strait, between the Japanese home islands of Honshu and Hokkaido, permits passage of Soviet ships in peacetime, but its availability to the Soviets in time of war would be problematical at best. Of all the Pacific straits, or choke points, it would be the easiest to interdict.

The Korea Strait, or Straits of Tsushima, lies between U.S. allies, Korea and Japan. Altogether the widest—120 miles at its maximum width—the Korea Strait offers the shortest route from Vladivostok southward. Soviet peacetime traffic patterns show use, over a period of time, in the ratio of 6:3:1 for the Soya, Korea, and Tsugaru passages, respectively. It should be clear that these choke points hemming in Vladivostok in time of war would be key to the war effort of both sides.

Petropavlovsk, the other major Soviet Pacific Ocean port, is home port for submarines and small surface ships. It suffers from nasty weather much of the year, the requirement for icebreakers to keep access to the sea open in the winter, and the fact that it is completely isolated by land. There are no good roads and no railways that serve Petropavlovsk. All materials must come either by air or sea; and, as is characteristic of intercontinental commerce the world over, the bulk of the cargo for Petropavlovsk is transported in ships.

The Black Sea Fleet is bottled up by the Turkish Straits. Even when ships negotiate those narrow waters, they find themselves in another enclosed sea, the Mediterranean. Moreover, movement through the Turkish Straits is controlled in peacetime by the Montreux Convention of 1936, which regulates the number, size, and type of ships that may pass. As a consequence of all these hindrances, the Soviet Navy does not assign the most capable of its fleet units to the Black Sea Fleet. For example, although they were built there, no *Kiev*-class aircraft carriers sail as part of the Black Sea Fleet, there are no *Kirov*-class cruisers or other nuclear-powered ships home-ported there, and strategic ballistic missile submarines do not operate there. In fact, a provision of the Montreux Convention prevents the Soviets from using Black Sea Fleet submarines with their operational Mediterranean unit, the Fifth Eskadra. Consequently, Soviet submarines deployed to the Mediterranean must be provided from elsewhere.

The Baltic Fleet sits at the eastern end of that body of water. Its access to the North Sea is blocked by the Danish Straits, flanked by neutral Sweden and NATO allies Denmark and Norway. Of course, access to the North Sea does not guarantee access to the Atlantic, as the Royal Navy demonstrated to the German Navy through two world wars. Consequently, the Baltic Fleet, like the Black Sea Fleet, does not number the newest and most capable Soviet ships in its inventory.

Finally, in the north, those Northern Fleet units based at Murmansk enjoy ice-free access to the southwestern Barents Sea and then into the Norwegian Sea. Ice closes the White Sea for five to six months a year, but Murmansk, a vital port of debarkation in both world wars for resupply to the Soviet Union, remains open year-round. Access to the Barents and Norwegian seas, however, is also not access to the broad Atlantic. Ships of the Northern Fleet must first traverse the so-called Greenland-Iceland-United Kingdom (G-I-UK) (sometimes referred to as the Greenland-Iceland-Norway or G-I-N) Gap. While not as narrow as the other Soviet accesses to the sea, the G-I-UK passage commands great attention for its strategic value, since it marks the gateway to the transatlantic sea lanes. Like the Pacific, Black Sea, and Baltic, it, too, is flanked by U.S. allies. The only other outlet from the Northern Fleet area, traversing from west to east along the top of the Eurasian continent, known as the "Northern Sea Route," is unattractive. This passage is open only about two months a year and is nearly 7,000 miles in length.

The strategic importance of choke points is accentuated by the presence or absence of out-of-area naval bases and long-range logistic forces. To illustrate the point, take the case of the submarine. If the Soviet submarine is to be employed to interdict the oceanic sea lanes, it must in every case (except the base at Petropavlovsk in the Pacific) pass through a geographic choke point en route to its objective area. As it passes in wartime it would be subject to attrition by adversary forces stationed to guard the passage. The need for the submarine to return to its home base will be governed by logistics: fuel, repairs—requiring equipment and/or expertise—food, expendable weapons, and the ability to replenish these somewhere other than home base. Sooner or later, even a nuclear-powered submarine will need logistic support. Either a tender in a secure location or a base an out-of-area submarine might use would be a valuable operational asset, so that it did not have to transit the choke point twice more—risking attrition each time—to return to station and conduct another mission. The historical record indicates that the country or coalition obliged to protect the sea lanes, however, has expended great energy to ensure that there are few sources of repair or resupply in waters remote from the adversary's homeland, thus forcing enemy ships periodically to return to base. Geography renders this a particularly thorny problem for the Soviet Navy.

Sensitivity to the strictures of geography has long influenced Russian thinking on the deployment of their navy. During the U.S. Civil War, for example, which coincided with an uprising in Poland in 1863, the Russians perceived a danger of war against Great Britain and France. As a consequence,

> Five new steam-driven ships of the Baltic fleet were sent over to New York and five other steamships from the Pacific squadron were sailed to San Francisco. This was not so much a demonstration of Russian favor for the Union in the American Civil War as many Americans thought, but an at-

tempt to have the ships best suited for raiding operations in friendly ports outside the British blocking line.[5]

Thus, sensitivity to choke points, and the Russian interest in obtaining the capability to service and resupply ships that might be deployed out-of-area, have long histories.

DEMANDS FOR LARGE MARITIME FORCES

Accordingly, the evolution of Soviet naval doctrine, rationalizing the acquisition and prospective use of maritime forces, took place against a backdrop of political and geographic handicaps. Clearly, a navy is useful for defense of the homeland from attack by seagoing enemies. Building a great navy, however, historically has required additional stimulus—from the need to amass and protect an empire, from the concern about the security of a network of commercial shipping, or from a requirement to support allies in a balance-of-power system across the highways of the sea. None of these are adequate to explain the Russian interest in a large navy.

The czars and the commissars pursued their own agendas. At the end of the Second World War, however, for the first time in its history Russia's main adversary was oceans away from the continental land mass, in a position the Soviet Union could not reach without great difficulty. Small wonder that the Soviet Union was the first to put cruise missiles in submarines, the first to put ballistic missiles in submarines, and the first to develop intercontinental missile and space technology. The Soviet leaders were seeking a way to reach their new adversary. Small wonder, also, that the Soviets were alert to U.S. forward deployments of ships and aircraft that could strike the Soviet homeland. The need to establish a credible, effective counter to U.S. long-range striking power, of course, places Khrushchev's attempt to place missiles in Cuba in proper strategic perspective.

The Soviet military rationalizes its need for large and strong military forces by claiming that they are necessary as long as imperialism—the final and most dangerous stage of capitalism—exists, and as long as its aggressive nature remains unchanged. In addition, Admiral Gorshkov has written: "The seapower of our country is directed at ensuring favorable conditions for building communism, the intensive expansion of the economic power of the country, and the steady consolidation of its defense capability."[6] As one who must rationalize Soviet naval programs, he goes beyond the questions of direct protection of the homeland and projecting Soviet power across the distance that divides the superpowers. He recalls the classic reasons states have listed for requiring use of the seas—to support friendly, "progressive" forces abroad, mercantilism, and "defense of state interests in peacetime."

HOW MARITIME FORCES MIGHT BE USED

At this point it seems appropriate to ask: How did the Russian and Soviet navies go about preparing themselves for the tasks they foresaw? Here one is obliged to assess not just declaratory policy—what they say they are planning to do with their navy—but also the wherewithal. If the instruments of warfare do not correspond to the rhetoric, then actual policy and action can be no more than problematical. Still, this also is a dynamic as well as a static area for analysis, and a time dimension must be taken into account. In many instances Soviet spokesmen claimed a certain capability or intention for which they did not then have corresponding capability, but over time the capability appeared. One should not conclude that the appearance of new capability that supports earlier expressions of interest or intent to be the result of sheer coincidence.

According to Soviet theoreticians, matters of strategy for the use of maritime forces were not formalized until the revolution. It is not to be doubted that some of the new rulers of Russia were keen to develop a new, scientific, uniquely Marxist approach for the use of Soviet armed forces. It is also well known that there were those who argued the contrary; that is, others maintained that there was no such thing as a military doctrine that was unique to political ideologies. In any event, it should come as no surprise that, like Soviet overblown or false claims in other areas, they could give no credit to their predecessors or non-Marxists who, by definition, were not invested with the "truth." In the words of Admiral Stalbo, a leading naval writer,

> The role of the old Russian Navy's theoretical heritage was limited to operational and tactical bounds. Naval thought assumed more natural outlines corresponding to a new type of Armed Forces as Soviet military doctrine formed and as new systems of arms were developed and its own experience expanded.[7]

Admiral Stalbo is telling his readers that the Russian Navy had no *strategic* outlook, its intellectual frontiers were confined to *local* and *theater* considerations. His interest, in part, is to ensure that his readers recognize not only that there was a sharp break between the naval policy and actions of the czars, but also that the old Russian approach had been a very narrow one.

THE EARLY SOVIET NAVY AND LEGACIES
FROM THE CZARIST FORCE

The post-revolution legacy to the Soviet leadership from the czar's Imperial Navy was over two hundred ships, a tally that included six battleships, five cruisers, fifty-four destroyers, and twelve submarines. This, by the way, from an armed force that had suffered one of the most devastating defeats in the history of maritime warfare only twelve years earlier at the Battle of Tsushima. Admiral Stalbo might be correct in his assertion that Russian military thinkers neglected strategy in favor of tactics and operational art, but there can be no gainsaying that an abiding interest in naval warfare extended through a chain of activities right back to Peter the Great. Table 1 offers a select list.

While the number of ships passed down to the Bolsheviks by their czarist predecessors was large, they were substantially undermanned, untrained, and in a poor state of material upkeep. Until the post–World War II time frame, these qualities typified the Russian Navy. Large in numbers, it was consistently deficient in operational capability.

The wartime performance of the Russian Navy in World War I had been, in a word, undistinguished. Reflecting the great concern of the Russian leadership about attack from the sea in the Baltic area, the czar subordinated the entire navy to the land forces, placed the Baltic Fleet under the army commander responsible for the defense of St. Petersburg, and issued orders that capital ships in the Baltic could not be moved except by direction from army headquarters. Thus, minefields were laid in echelon at the entrance to the Gulf of Finland in the shadow of the guns of the coastal batteries. What sparse naval operations the czar's fleet performed in the war invariably were related to mine warfare—either defensively to protect the ports and approaches to Russian territory, or offensively to hamper German use of the sea lanes in the Baltic for movement of troops and war material. Overall, however, considering what the Baltic Fleet commander had to work with, and considering that the navy was undermined after 1917 by mutiny and revolutionary activism, it is unlikely that Russian forces there could have accomplished substantially more.

In the post-revolutionary Soviet state, desperate economic conditions alone would have militated against devoting large amounts of funds to building a navy. Consequently, a weakened navy was obliged to adopt the so-called "fortress-fleet" concept. The fortress fleet was one that remained in port, protected by coastal fortifications under the umbrella of shore batteries. It was not long, however, before mod-

TABLE 1.
EARLY SEAMARKS OF THE RUSSIAN NAVY

- 1703: Russian forces take Swedish fortress on the Baltic, rename it St. Petersburg, and thus gain access to the Baltic. Peter built an 800-ship fleet, fought Swedes and Turks.

- 1720: Peter I printed the first official document in the history of the Russian Regular Navy, which generalized the experience of its combat actions and was a documented expression of naval thought.

- 1769: Catherine the Great established a permanent Russian fleet presence in the Black Sea. Ordered Count Orlov to take the Baltic fleet into the Med to bring pressure on the Turks from their rear. This was the first Russian Navy operation outside contiguous waters, and a classic use of seapower to affect the struggle on land.

- 1802: Establishment of the Ministry of Naval Forces.

- 1803–1806 Two ships complete first circumnavigation.

- 1827: Establishment of the Naval Academy.

- 1827: Establishment of the Naval Scientific Committee.

- 1848: Appearance of *Morskoi Sbornik (Naval Digest)*.

- 1853: Battle of Sinope against the Turkish Navy. Last major Russian or Soviet fleet victory.

- 1863: Baltic Fleet ships sail to New York and San Francisco.

- 1898: Port Arthur occupied.

- 1905: Destruction of the Russian Fleet at Tsushima.

- 1909: New naval building program begun. Included mainly defensive vessels such as submarines and minelayers.

- 1912: Fleet bill called for construction by 1930 of eight battleships, four battle cruisers, four light cruisers, thirty-six destroyers, and twelve submarines. All to be based in the Baltic. Only one ship was complete when World War I erupted.

ernists set forth a doctrine of "active defense," one in which the navy would function defensively to protect the revolutionary gains that had been secured, and, in keeping with the Party line and the fervor of the times, might be called upon to support revolutionary uprisings in other countries. To accomplish the first part, the plan was to use submarines to weaken an enemy in advance of his approach to Soviet territory, to constrain his movements with minefields, and then to deliver strikes against him using surface ships, torpedo boats, coastal artillery, and aviation. One suspects that not even the most activist Communist Party ideologue had the slightest notion of how the Soviet Navy would go about effecting its second task, that of aiding revolutionary activity abroad.

The initial Soviet shipbuilding program, laid out in 1926 was, as noted earlier, a victory for the modernists and their doctrine of active defense. It contained provisions for construction only of patrol and torpedo boats and submarines, all of which were optimized for coastal use. The cruisers and battleships (the ships around which the fortress fleet was organized and for which there were no evident roles in the "active defense") were accorded funding in the plan for modernization and upkeep, but there were no intentions to build more of them. Even the modest goals of the first five-year shipbuilding plan went unrealized.

The second five-year shipbuilding plan was, in essence, a repeat of the first one, except that while the emphasis remained on small ships and submarines, their numbers were to be substantially increased. This plan was approved in 1933. Remarkably, it set as its goal the completion of over 350 submarines by the end of 1937. However unrealistic, the submarine building program did proceed apace in the early 1930s, and the inventory of submarines rocketed during the period of the second plan from about twenty to nearly one hundred and fifty—well short of the goal, but the largest submarine fleet in the world at the time by a significant margin.

INTERWAR CONSOLIDATION, GROWTH, AND CONTINENTAL DEBATE

The 1930s were a time of great activity for the Soviet Navy. Two new fleets were added to the organizational structure: the Northern and the Pacific. The former was formally designated a fleet in 1937; the latter, leading from the assembly of ships at Vladivostok in 1932, had become the Pacific Fleet in 1935. (The Black Sea Fleet, which had been decimated during the civil war, had been reestablished in 1930.) Then, in 1938, following Stalin's purge of the remaining czarist naval officers, the navy was granted its organizational independence. It was no longer to be completely subservient to the army. Of interest, however, is the fact that the attainment of organizational independence by the navy equated to an increase in party control over the navy. According to one expert, "Before 1938 the party did not have a great deal of formal control over the navy, since there was a system of separate political administrations for each fleet, which were only indirectly connected to the naval command structure."[8] This establishment of an independent naval commissariat also marked another swing in the pendulum, the ascendancy of the traditionalists. As a consequence, the Third Five-Year shipbuilding plan would emphasize large ships formed into fleets to sail the open seas.

In 1938, the new commander-in-chief of the Soviet Navy, Admiral P. A. Smirnov, issued the following declaration:

To ensure the impregnability of the sea approaches to our sacred land, to guard the motherland from attempts of attack from the sea by the fascist plunderers, to guarantee the normal travel of trading vessels under the red flag in any part of the world. This is the sacred responsibility of our Navy.[9]

This interest in protecting commercial shipping at great distances from Soviet shores rubricated the ascendancy of the traditionalist school, reflected in the Third Five-Year shipbuilding plan, which in 1937 had called for new construction by the beginning of 1943 of 16 battleships, 13 cruisers, over 100 destroyers, 120 submarines, and over 400 smaller ships of various classes. This famous plan, one of the most ambitious naval building plans ever adopted by any country, even included the intention to begin construction of aircraft carriers in 1942. By the end of the Third Five-Year Plan, the number of new submarines in the fleet would have been nearly 350.

Because of this shift to the traditionalist agenda, on the eve of the Nazi attack on the Soviet Union in June 1941 the Soviet fleet tally stood at 3 battleships, 7 cruisers, nearly 60 destroyers, over 200 submarines, and in excess of 2,500 aircraft. The assault by the *Wehrmacht* caught the Soviet armed forces basically in disarray, and the Soviet Navy large, but, as usual, untrained and untested. Stalin had earlier demonstrated his core thinking about the war clouds on the horizon and his vision for the Soviet Navy when in the fall of 1940 he curtailed all construction on large surface ships and accelerated efforts on submarines and small combatants.

WORLD WAR II

During the war, ships of the navy were not employed outside of their respective immediate fleet areas. The preponderance of naval activity took place on the rivers and other internal waters of the Russian interior and in protecting the immediate coastline. Although for the three European fleets the war lasted four years (rather than the one week for the Pacific Fleet), and although 400,000 navy men were pressed into augmenting army units, the Soviet Navy as a force accomplished remarkably little. In fact, Western historians and strategic analysts are in broad agreement that the Soviet Navy could have made a significantly greater impact than it did in the Black Sea, the Baltic, and in the Northern Fleet approaches to the very important cargo-receiving port of Murmansk.

Throughout the Second World War only a few independent, modest offensive operations were undertaken by the Soviet Navy. Most of these involved amphibious operations in the Black Sea. In fact, Stalin himself, echoing the czar's World War I decree, issued an order in 1943 that forbade the use of surface ships larger than destroyers. This virtually took the surface navy out of the war. Submarine operations—even in the absence of Stalin's intervention, the only way the Soviet Navy might mount an offensive with an impact on the war—were sporadic and in the main unsuccessful. No major Axis warship was sunk by Soviet naval action, yet the Soviets lost 104 submarines over the course of the war. As one analyst has written:

> The Soviet war records show that it protected an impressive total of 1,600 convoys involving 4,400 ships, yet there never seemed to be many Russian warships or aircraft around in 1942 when Allied convoys—including some Soviet merchant ships—were running the German blockade to bring supplies to Murmansk and Arkhangelsk.[10]

Surface-ship operations ranged from poorly executed to non-existent. The rapidly moving German armies bypassed the Black Sea Fleet and outflanked the Baltic. For the most part the *Luftwaffe* ruled the skies over the Baltic and Black seas. In addition, the Germans succeeded in evacuating over 100,000 troops from Sevastopol in 1944, and over two million soldiers and civilians from various parts of the Baltic during the last half year of the war, virtually without opposition.

That the Soviet Navy was kept in fetters throughout the war either by political control or by its enemies is not surprising. Yet, even with thirty-five years of hindsight, we find Soviet writers making claims such as this:

> The Soviet Navy made a worthy contribution to the victory over Nazi Germany and Imperialist Japan. It inflicted heavy losses on the German Navy in the Barents, Baltic, and Black seas and covered the strategic maritime flanks of Soviet land forces.[11]

One need not make claims unsubstantiated by history to recognize that the Soviet Navy, configured and situated as it was on the eve of war, alone could neither have won nor lost the conflict with Germany. As the Soviets put it, the navy could not have had an important effect on either the course or the outcome of the war. As it developed, the war demanded that the bulk of the navy be used to assist directly in the land battle—as land forces. The only remaining criticism, then, centers on the unaggressive, unimaginative, unsuccessful employment of those naval units that were operational during the war. Even Admiral Gorshkov has levied criticism in that regard.

POSTWAR ACTIVITY: A SERIES OF TRANSITIONS

Recovery from the devastation of war in the Soviet Union did not include a high priority for the immediate rebuilding of its navy. Nevertheless, Soviet state interests were becoming more outward-looking. Elimination of the German threat and the partition of Germany; expansion of the Soviet zone of security by the addition of buffer states; incorporation of weapons, technologies, and trained personnel of former enemies; precipitate, deep disarmament of the Western Allies; and significant domestic economic improvement—all contributed to expanding the vistas of the Soviet leadership.

Stalin eventually opted for a compromise position between the traditionalist and modernist school, prompted by an assessed inability to follow a more aggressive approach to fleet building. Initially, giving scant recognition to the lessons of seapower illuminated by the war, Soviet military leaders envisioned nothing other than "more of the same" for the Red Navy. That is, the navy was to be the handmaiden of the army, with no independent tasks to perform in conducting the defense of the Motherland. By 1950, however, no doubt stimulated by the Truman Doctrine, the Atlantic Alliance, the routine deployments of the U.S. Sixth Fleet in the Mediterranean, the emplacement of U.S. naval presence in the Persian Gulf, and the growth of the U.S. Seventh Fleet in the Pacific, Stalin reestablished an independent naval ministry and approved a major ten-year naval construction plan that included four aircraft carriers. In addition, the balanced fleet plan called for significant numbers of large and small cruisers and destroyers, plus over thirty medium-range submarines *per year*.

U.S. carrier air power became the focus of Soviet attention starting in the 1950s, and Soviet ship, land-based naval aviation, and weapon programs reflected this emphasis. The U.S. Navy undertook tasks that required strategic weapons late in the 1940s by deploying P2V Neptune aircraft on some of its aircraft carriers. The P2V, a patrol aircraft, was used because it was the only navy aircraft that could deliver an atomic bomb. Introduction of the first carrier-based attack aircraft with atomic weapon capability occurred in 1950 with the appearance of the AJ-1 Savage. Antiship cruise missiles were developed, and the capability to carry and launch them from air, surface, and subsurface platforms appeared concurrently. The first Soviet antiship missiles appeared in the late 1950s. The air-to-surface beam-rider AS-1 Kipper, carried by the Badger aircraft, was first observed in 1958. Submarine-launched cruise missiles made their debut on Whiskey-class submarine conversions about the same time, while surface ships also were outfitted with antiship missiles.

Broadly described by Western observers, the Soviet Navy's central efforts were directed toward *sea denial*. It seemed evident that the Soviet leadership had not factored into its thinking prospects for controlling sea areas distant from Soviet shores, or for protecting Soviet sea lanes in open ocean areas. Soviet objectives, in the near term at least according to this mind set, could be secured if the Soviet Navy could be used selectively to deny the use of the seas by Soviet adversaries. Thus, *sea control* would be unnecessary; *sea denial* would suffice.

Yet, the seeds of change for the navy had already been sown. Because land-based missiles of intercontinental range were expected to take a long time to develop, in the interim it would be necessary to take weapon-carriers to the vicinity of their targets. Thus, long-range bombers and ballistic missile-launching submarines became the instruments of Soviet strategic reach. However small, for the first time the Soviet Navy could participate in defense of the *Rodina* (Motherland) in a truly *strategic* way by deploying ballistic missile submarines in missile range of targets in the United States.

The lack of a solid navy constituency within the Soviet government, and the basic antipathy of the marshals returned to the forefront of policy significance immediately on the death of Stalin. The independent ministry once again was dissolved, the navy was subordinated to the army, and Stalin's ambitious building plan was discarded. Even though little specific information is available about an intra-governmental struggle, if in fact there was one of any importance, by the time of Party General Secretary Khrushchev's visit to the United States in 1959 it was apparent that the pendulum had swung again toward the modernists. From what is known, it seems as if the decision to abolish the naval force structure Stalin had sought was taken for reasons that had little to do with maritime interests. Beset with economic difficulties, Khrushchev desired to leapfrog into the missile generation, marrying the nuclear warhead to the long-range weapon in what Soviet military writers termed the "Revolution in Military Affairs."

Combining the striking power of a nuclear warhead and the speed of a ballistic missile, it looked to Khrushchev and his military advisers, notably Marshal Zhukov, that perhaps the modernist school approach had appeared about thirty years before its time. Khrushchev saw this as an opportunity to break with the policies of Stalin and to economize by not investing in expensive naval forces, while at the same time taking advantage of the march of technology. The maritime forces selected to support a strategy that emphasized nuclear strike weapons would be submarines and land-based aircraft. To cement the divorce, in 1956 Khrushchev replaced the head of the Soviet Navy, Admiral Kuznetsov, a favorite of Stalin, with Admiral Sergei Gorshkov, Commander of the Red Banner Black Sea Fleet.

There followed a period of adjustment. As the postwar recovery of the Soviet economy was building momentum, the Soviet Armed Forces underwent several across-the-board reductions in personnel strength, and the new navy leadership consolidated its power. There were lessons a-plenty owing to the Cuban missile crisis of 1962, not only at the strategic level, but also for the employment of maritime forces.

At about this time appeared the first comprehensive publication in the open literature on the subject of Soviet strategy, Marshal Sokolovskiy's *Military Strategy*.[12] This was a watershed publication in many ways, but, of course, it had been written before the Cuban Missile Crisis. For the navy, it went further than previous open publications in admitting to roles for the navy that exceeded coastal defense and support of the ground forces from seaward. To be sure, navy tasks would include those central ones, but now they would also allow for some independent maritime actions to combat the enemy fleet—especially aircraft carriers and missile-carrying submarines—to disrupt sea lanes, and to strike adversary homelands. Evidence was mounting that the Soviet leadership was coming to grips with the question of what it would take to confront, and to fight if necessary, an enemy not located on the Eurasian continent. Long-range, nuclear-tipped rockets would be required, of course, but it would be important also to be able to deal with opposing navies and the plan of the United States to resupply allies across wide ocean expanses. With the addition in the 1970s of a task of defending ballistic-missile submarines, these have continued to be the Soviet Navy's primary missions.

Just about the time (1962) that the United States redefined its strategic targeting to downgrade the carriers in the strategic integrated operation plan (SIOP) in favor of ballistic missiles, the Soviets shifted emphasis to defense against missile-launching submarines. The first evidence of this shift appeared in 1963–1964. As many observers of the changes in Soviet doctrine noted, Soviet shipbuilding, missile, and aircraft programs were altered to support the redirected emphasis.

Recognizing the advantage that might be gained by prompt offensive action and the savings that were apparent in naval acquisition costs to obtain such capability, Soviet planners emphasized that they must win the "battle for the first salvo." Accordingly, whether their primary focus while concentrating on defending the homeland was on the adversary aircraft carrier or on missile-firing submarines, the approach was similar. Operational patterns that centered on sea denial and early assumption of the offensive, weapons with powerful striking capability, and naval forces with minimal defensive capability and logistic sustainability were characteristic of the Soviet Navy for about twenty-five years after the Second World War. Soviet naval strategy mirrored these patterns and capabilities.

DEFENDING SUBMARINES: A NEW STRATEGIC TWIST

The task of defending ballistic missile submarines was one that, while it might make sense to a Soviet planner, was for a long time completely unrecognized by U.S. experts. The mirror image was strongly enough polarized to prevent U.S. appreciation of this Soviet innovation. While innovative, the plan was adopted out of weakness: the Soviet Union appreciated that it had a large investment—both monetarily and strategically—in strategic missiles placed in submarines, but that those submarines were not as invulnerable to attack as they might have hoped. The advent of multiple independently targeted reentry vehicles (MIRV) for U.S. ballistic missiles made Soviet insecurity about their *land*-based missile force more acute, and U.S. advances in antisubmarine warfare aggravated their concern about their sea-based forces.

The development of a long-range missile for the strategic submarine force (the SS-N-8, first deployed in 1973) offered the Soviets the opportunity to operate strategic submarines close to their own coastline. Thus, they decided to do something quite radical from a U.S. point of view: to defend ballistic-missile submarines in three dimensions. Such a scheme was attractive from several points of view. First, submarine missiles could reach their targets when fired virtually from home waters, and the ships would not have to take up stations close to adversary territory. This alone—because no transits would be required through geographic choke points and because the opposition would have to come to them rather than vice-versa—would be beneficial and attractive.

Second, the forces to defend them would not have far to go. Whereas submarines on-station in the Atlantic and Pacific oceans far from Soviet territory could not be protected adequately from enemy attack, if ballistic-missile submarine deployment areas were nearby, land-based air from fields in the Soviet Union could provide the requisite air umbrella. Soviet surface ships, notoriously deficient in their ability to operate at distances far from the homeland because of short logistic legs, could be concentrated and easily supported in friendly waters.

And the entire inventory of submarines, including short-range diesel-powered ones, might be brought to bear.

Third, if the strategic submarines were close to Soviet territory, communication with them would be simplified. The major weakness of a submerged, nuclear, ballistic-missile launcher is that communications with it are tenuous at best. But if the submarine were not far away, the forces that deployed to protect it also could be used to communicate with it. Even in the age of communications satellites, moreover, the reliability of communications is related to the distance from the transmitter to the receiver measured on the globe. To the Soviet military, the option of placing strategic submarines close to the Motherland rather than deploying them at great distances must have been very attractive.

Finally, if the strategic ballistic-missile submarine force constitutes part of the Soviet *strategic reserve*, then it must be protected at all costs. A short digression on the question of strategic reserves is necessary at this point, because it is important to the analysis.

Soviet strategists by the 1970s had opened a lead on their Western counterparts in their ability to think their way through the difficult questions of nuclear warfighting. There were several reasons for this, foremost of which was the adoption by the United States of a strategic policy of mutual assured destruction. This ill-starred policy tended to choke off both interest and debate in nuclear warfighting. It contended, in short, that so long as both sides maintained a secure second-strike capability, deterrence was stable, and no one needed to think further about strategic nuclear war. That is, to the question: What if deterrence fails? the answer would be given: It cannot fail so long as an assured destruction capability is maintained by both sides. All other thought and analysis was thus shunted to ground.

The Soviets were not a victim of this mindless paralysis. They said, in effect, if a nuclear war were to be fought, just as in land warfare with which we are so familiar and expert, the advantage will go to the side with the secure strategic reserve force. Strategic reserves must be *secure* so that they can be used to influence war outcomes. (Westerners never asked about war outcomes because they could not admit that wars could begin in the first place—war would be *deterred*.) Accordingly, if one side has a secure strategic reserve force of adequate size and capability, it can force war termination by suggesting to its adversary that its strategic reserve can be brought to bear in an effort to win the *last* battle. Thought of in this way, there are only two conditions under which a strategic reserve force can be committed: to avoid defeat in the last instance, or to secure victory with a high probability of success. Submarines are attractive as a secure strategic reserve because they are relatively less vulnerable than land-based missiles. Whatever vulnerability they have can be offset by protecting them. In essence, this is what expert opinion today believes is the Soviet interest in protecting their strategic submarines, although Soviet spokesmen have never been so candid.

Western observers were slow to understand this approach because, as was noted, they wore mutual assured destruction blinders. In addition, the U.S. has always considered its own ballistic-missile submarine force to be independently secure. That is, the vulnerability of U.S. submarines has been assessed as low enough that additional protection for them has not been provided. Indeed, the Soviets fielded an echeloned three-dimensional defense for their sea-based missile force, yet little evidence exists to suggest that the U.S. has seriously even examined the question.

While much of Soviet naval thought about protection of ballistic-missile submarines *as a strategic reserve force* must be inferred from Soviet open-source publications and from the observation of operational patterns, since the early 1970s a great deal of other material has appeared in the Soviet literature. In particular, the major 1972–1973 series of articles in the main Soviet naval professional magazine, *Morskoi Sbornik (Naval Digest)*, by Admiral Gorshkov, and his subsequent book *Morskaya Moshch' Gosudarstva (The Seapower of the State)*, the first edition of which appeared in 1976, offered the first comprehensive revelations about Soviet thinking about the use of their navy in war and peace.

FLEET AGAINST THE FLEET AND FLEET AGAINST THE SHORE

Admiral Gorshkov's analyses of how a navy might be strategically employed remain essentially unchallenged as the manner in which the tasks of the Soviet Navy are defined and prioritized. A straightforward dichotomy was devised by Admiral Gorshkov to describe and explain the navy's tasks. He called them "fleet against the fleet" and "fleet against shore." Introducing his analytical categories, he wrote:

> The main tasks of land forces, as is known, has always been the destruction of the opposing foe in order to take over his territories and possessions. . . . This is not so in the sphere of the navy. As well as the tasks of fighting an enemy fleet, it is also faced with tasks associated with the operations against territories and groupings of troops therein.[13]

Lest there be any misunderstanding, moreover, the relative importance between them was expressed unequivocally:

. . . the operations of a fleet against the shore have assumed paramount importance in armed conflict at sea, governing the technical policy of building a fleet and the development of naval art.[14]

The difference between "fleet against the shore" and "fleet against the fleet," however, is not entirely intuitive. For example, offensive operations by strategic submarines obviously fall into the former category. By a short stretch of argument, moreover, protecting strategic submarines—what Admiral Gorshkov describes as providing them "combat stability"—can also be included as "fleet against the shore." On the other hand, it is more difficult to understand instinctively that operations against the strategic submarines of the other side fall into the "fleet against the shore" rather than the "fleet against the fleet" task.

Soviet naval strategy for war can be compressed into a succinct list. In descending priority order, Soviet forces must:

1. Defend Soviet territory from seaborne attacks, by air, surface, or subsurface forces. This would include attacking enemy missile-launching submarines;
2. Deliver offensive missile strikes against enemy territory from submarines, if called upon to do so;
3. Protect strategic missile submarines from attack by hostile forces;
4. Provide support from seaward to Soviet ground forces, which is obviously the primary mission for the essentially land-locked Baltic and Black Sea fleets, including amphibious operations on the flanks of the Red Army and to secure various theater objectives;
5. Attack enemy sea communications; and
6. Protect Soviet sea lanes.

This hierarchy reflects the Soviet belief that a war between opposing coalitions would probably break out after a period of tension, be short in duration if nuclear but perhaps prolonged if conventional, and global in its geographic dimension. There is a conviction that permeates the literature, moreover, that such a war would be fought to a conclusion, and it would be decisive for the victor. While Soviet naval leaders make much ado about conducting combined operations with other Soviet military forces, the list above does not appear to offer much opportunity for joint efforts.

Thus, unlike the pre–World War II Soviet Navy, or the czar's navy before it, the Soviet Navy today enjoys truly *strategic* missions—ones that can have an important effect on both the course and the outcome of war. Unlike earlier force structures, moreover, the fleet today is said to be *balanced*. According to Admiral Gorshkov, it has been possible ". . . to establish a balanced navy consisting of nuclear submarines, surface vessels, missile-carrying and ASW naval aviation, naval infantry and coastal missile-artillery troops."[15]

Finally, in peacetime the Soviet Navy has assumed an important function as an active instrument of state policy. This is a relatively new role. For example, Soviet Navy full-time presence in the Mediterranean began afresh with the positioning of eight Whiskey-class attack submarines in Albania in 1958. When Albania broke away from the Soviet orbit in 1961, both the deployment opportunity and the submarines were lost, and continuous presence in the Mediterranean was not reestablished until 1964. The first Soviet Navy routine operations to the Indian Ocean began in 1968 (the U.S. Navy has maintained continuous presence there since 1948), and the first of what have become nearly annual visits to the Caribbean area began only in 1969.

Overarching the wartime and peacetime employment of naval forces stands, in Admiral Gorshkov's view, the central importance of the historical meaning of seapower to the general well-being of a country that features itself to be prominent on the world scene. He argues, therefore, not just for naval military power, but also for all the other diversified modalities that comprise seapower: merchant ships, fishing fleets, marine industries, oceanographic research and exploration, and shipbuilding.

Only twenty years ago Admiral Arleigh Burke, retired chief of naval operations and American naval hero, penned these words in the foreword to the seminal book in the English language on Soviet naval strategy:

> The Soviets will . . . have to decide what they think they can do to prevent our Polaris submarines from destroying a large part of the Soviet Union immediately following the initial Soviet attack. Without carriers and a very much larger ASW force (and more protection for it than they now have) they cannot prevent the Polaris submarines from launching. . . .
> Then why have the Soviets developed a navy at all? To defend the waters contiguous to her shore line. To support her ground forces. To conduct short-haul amphibious operations close to territory she holds. To destroy Free World merchantmen and naval ships in the event of a "conventional war." To dominate the waters of her adjacent nation neighbors, and, thus, to intimidate them.[16]

Well, evidently the Soviets have made the decision to adopt as a mission to seek out and destroy U.S. ballistic missile submarines, and to place in the field a large fleet of strategic submarines of their own.

Four small aircraft carriers are currently in their inventory, and two large aircraft carriers are under construction. The Red ASW Fleet is large, capable, and growing. But Admiral Gorshkov's vision about his navy stands as a striking example of a much larger vista than the one employed by Admiral Burke: the relationship of seapower to national greatness and destiny. According to Admiral Gorshkov:

> The strength of the fleets was one of the factors helping states to move into the category of great powers. Moreover, history shows that states not possessing naval forces were unable for a long time to occupy the position of a great power.[17]

Unwittingly, Admiral Gorshkov has suggested another central theme for this book. Yet, his successor, Admiral Chernavin, commands a navy that has no tradition of victory at sea under the czars, and under the hammer and sickle has not fired a shot in anger in over 40 years. The haunting question thus returns: *Chto nuzhno, chtoby stat' velikoy morskoy derzhavoy?*

NOTES

1. In terms of total deadweight tonnage, the Soviet Union's merchant fleet accounts for only 3.6 percent of the world's total, ranking behind Liberia, Panama, Greece, Japan, and Norway, reflecting the small average size of the Soviet ships.

2. Throughout this chapter the convention has been adopted that when it is important to distinguish between them, especially between the Imperial or Russian Navy and the Soviet Navy, care has been taken to use the correct terms. Where it has not been important, the terms "Russian" and "Soviet" are used interchangeably.

3. This contemporary quotation from a well-known book is typical: "Our progressive Marxist-Leninist military theory provides a scientifically based nature for Soviet military doctrine which derives from the peace-loving policy of the CPSU and the Soviet government. The adherence to the cause of peace and peaceful collaboration with other countries is determined by the essence and nature of the socialist society. In our nation there are no and cannot be any persons interested in an aggressive policy and war. The defensive focus of Soviet military doctrine stems invariably from this. . . .

"Over all its history the USSR has never threatened anyone with a war and has attacked no one and this in actuality shows the focus and nature of Soviet military doctrine." Colonel General Makhmut A. Gareyev, *M. V. Frunze—Military Theorist* (Moscow: Voyenizdat, 1984), p. 342.

4. Admiral of the Fleet of the Soviet Union S. G. Gorshkov, *The Seapower of the State*, 1st. ed. (Oxford: Pergamon Press, 1979), p. 1–2.

5. Jürgen Rohwer, "Admiral Gorshkov and the Influence of History Upon Sea Power," United States Naval Institute Proceedings (May 1981), p. 155.

6. Gorshkov, *Seapower of the State*, p. 284.

7. Stalbo, Vice Admiral K., "From the History of the Development of Russian Naval Thought," *Morskoi Sbornik*, no. 8 1985, pp. 31–32.

8. G. Hudson, "Soviet Naval Policies Under Lenin and Stalin," *Soviet Studies*, vol. 28, no. 1, January 1976, pp. 57–58.

9. *Ibid.*, p. 57.

10. David Fairhall, *Russian Sea Power* (Boston: Gambit Inc., 1971), p. 181.

11. Captain 1st Rank G. A. Ammon, Rear Admiral Y. A. Grechko, Captain 1st Rank (Ret.) M. I. Grigoriev, Colonel (Ret.) N. G. Tsyrulnikov, *The Soviet Navy in War and Peace*. Translated from the Russian by Joseph Shapiro. (Moscow: Progress Publishers, 1980), p. 82.

12. Translated and published in the West as V. D. Sokolovskiy, *Soviet Military Strategy*, 3d. ed., edited, with analysis and commentary by Harriet Fast Scott. (New York: Crane Russak & Co., c. 1968.)

13. Gorshkov, *Seapower of the State*, p. 213.

14. *Ibid.*, p. 221.

15. Admiral of the Fleet of the Soviet Union Sergei G. Gorshkov, "The Experience of the Great Patriotic War and the Present Stage in the Development of Naval Art," *Morskoi Sbornik*, no. 4, 1985, p. 19.

16. Robert Waring Herrick, *Soviet Naval Strategy: Fifty Years of Theory and Practice* (Annapolis, MD: U.S. Naval Institute, 1968), p. ix.

17. Gorshkov, *Seapower of the State*, p. 59.

BIBLIOGRAPHIC NOTE

In English, the primary work on Soviet Maritime Strategy is the now-dated *Soviet Naval Strategy: Fifty Years of Theory and Practice*, by Robert Waring Herrick (Annapolis, MD: U.S. Naval Institute, 1968). More recently have appeared: Bryan Ranft and Geoffrey Till, *The Sea in Soviet Strategy* (Annapolis, MD: Naval Institute Press, 1983), and James L. George, ed., *The Soviet and Other Communist Navies: The View from the Mid-1980s* (Annapolis, MD: Naval Institute Press, 1986), the latter of which devotes but a quarter of its length solely to discussion of Soviet doctrine and strategy, and the rest to hardware, theaters of operations, and navies of other Communist countries. For an analysis of Soviet operations in the Second World War, Friedrich Ruge, *The Soviets as Naval Opponents 1941–1945* (Cambridge: Patrick Stephens, 1979) is excellent, but for an unparalleled overview of both history and strategy, Donald W. Mitchell's *A History of Russian and Soviet Seapower* (New York: Macmillan, 1974) remains the classic work. The official U.S. government view is presented, quite expertly and with many illustrations, pictures, and other valuable information, in *Understanding Soviet Naval Developments*, now in its fifth edition, April 1985. It is published by the Office of the Chief of Naval Operations under document number NAVSO P-3560, and is for sale by the Superintendent of Documents, U.S. Government Printing Office, Washington, D.C.

For the Soviet view, Admiral of the Fleet of the Soviet Union S. G. Gorshkov's, *The Seapower of the State*, 1st. ed. (Oxford: Pergamon Press, 1979) (in English) remains the most important single book published on the subject. The insights provided into Soviet naval art cannot be duplicated elsewhere, but the historical parts should not be read uncritically, for they are Soviet interpretations of history, which do not always correspond to agreed Western interpretations. Historical works, not as rich in discussion of matters of strategy, include Captain 1st Rank G. A. Ammon, Rear Admiral Y. A. Grechko, Captain 1st Rank (retired) M. I. Grigoriev, Colonel (retired) N. G. Tsyrulnikov, *The Soviet Navy in War and Peace*. Translated from the Russian by Joseph Shapiro (Moscow: Progress Publishers, 1980), and V. I. Achkasov and N. B. Pavlovich, *Soviet Naval Operations in the Great Patriotic War 1941–1945*. Translated from the Russian by the U.S. Naval Intelligence Command. (Annapolis, MD: Naval Institute Press, c. 1981.) In addition to the occasional book, articles about maritime strategy appear frequently in the Soviet Navy's journal, *Morskoi Sbornik*.

ADDITIONAL SOURCES

Bathurst, Robert B. *Understanding the Soviet Navy*. Newport, RI: Naval War College Press, 1978.

Dismukes, Bradford and James M. McConnell, eds. *Soviet Naval Diplomacy*. New York: Pergamon Press, 1979.

Kime, Steve F. *A Soviet Navy for the Nuclear Age*. National Security Affairs Issue Paper 80–1. Washington, DC: National Defense University, April 1980.

MccGwire, Michael, Ken Booth, and John McDonnell, eds. *Soviet Naval Policy: Objectives and Constraints*. New York: Praeger Publishers, 1975.

McGruther, Kenneth R. *The Evolving Soviet Navy*. Newport, RI: Naval War College Press, 1978.

Murphy, Paul J., ed. *Naval Power in Soviet Policy*. Studies in Communist Affairs, vol. 2. Washington, DC: U.S. Government Printing Office, 1978.

Polmar, Norman, *Guide to the Soviet Navy*, 3d ed. Annapolis, MD: Naval Institute Press, 1983.

United States, Department of Defense. *Soviet Military Power*. Washington: U.S. Government Printing Office, annual.

Watson, Bruce W., and Susan M. Watson, eds. *The Soviet Navy: Strengths and Liabilities*. Boulder, CO: Westview Press, 1986.

13

The Maritime Strategy of the U.S. Navy Reading Excerpts

BY ROGER W. BARNETT AND JEFFREY G. BARLOW

SOME INTRODUCTORY COMMENTS

During the first two years following the end of the Second World War in September 1945, the U.S. Army and Navy suffered precipitous declines in combat capability as they responded to national demands for rapid demobilization. The navy, whose manpower strength at the end of the war had stood at almost 3,900,000 plummeted to a strength of some 478,000 by mid-1947. In mid-1945, the U.S. Fleet had comprised more than 8,000 vessels—some 1,200 of them principal combat vessels, including some 26 fleet aircraft carriers, 23 battleships, 66 cruisers of all types and 754 destroyers and destroyer escorts. By August 1947, however, the navy was estimating that in the event of a war in the European theater, it could muster within the first 60 days a striking force of only 11 fleet carriers, 4 battleships, 16 cruisers, and 82 destroyers and destroyer escorts—even counting the reinforcements available from the Pacific Fleet.

This overall weakness in operational forces (for all three services), when compared with U.S. foreign policy and occupation commitments in the early postwar period, remained a fact of life until the U.S. combat involvement in the Korean War pushed national defense spending to higher and more realistic levels in the months after June 1950. In this period, the navy was also faced with a challenge to its traditional role as the country's first line of defense by the emergent

U.S. Air Force, which was arguing that the atomic bomb had invalidated conventional military force and that only an atomic weapon-armed strategic striking force could preserve the peace.

By the early 1950s, however, increased defense-spending levels and renewed shipbuilding and procurement programs had reinvigorated the navy. Under the Eisenhower administration's "New Look" policy, while the army found its ground forces being cut back alarmingly, the navy's nuclear-armed carrier task forces found a secure place as part of the country's arsenal for deterring general war. And yet, by the middle of the decade the navy was beginning to argue that it needed a fleet with increased capabilities to handle lower-intensity wars and contingencies in the Third World that would not be expected to escalate to general war.

READING EXCERPTS

In June 1945, the army and navy were busily occupied with attempts to flesh out the first Joint Basic Outline War Plan, code-named PINCHER. Given the large disparity between Soviet ground forces in Europe and U.S. and British occupation forces there, PINCHER envisioned an extended period during which Soviet forces would be in control of most of Western Europe, and the U.S. and allied forces would remain on the defensive. In a conference with Vice Admiral Forrest Sherman, the deputy chief of naval operations (Operations), the navy's director of strategic plans (OP-30) discussed the situation, and this discussion demonstrated clearly the strong imprint the course of the Second World War had had on navy strategic thought. As seen in paragraph 2:

> (b) How do we get to the situation where we can take up the offensive leading to the ultimate defeat of the enemy?
>
> (d) We must consider what we actually have in the way of disposable forces at all times, remembering that many ships are now practically demobilized due to lack of personnel, training, etc.
>
> (e) What do we do in case hostilities break out over Trieste, for instance? Same for other trouble spots, such as Turkey, Middle East, Balkans, Korea, etc.
>
> (f) We should have plans for withdrawal of occupation forces from Europe and Korea and disposal of forces in North China.
>
> (g) The British will probably have primary responsibility in case it is necessary to withdraw occupation forces through the channel ports.
>
> (h) Work out problem of sending task force to the Mediterranean. COMNAVMED [Commander Naval Forces Mediterranean] will probably be the light force commander for inshore, with carrier strikes to back him up.
>
> (i) All available CVE's [escort carriers] except those especially equipped

for ASW [antisubmarine warfare], will probably be required to transport Army aircraft.

(j) In the Pacific, hold Aleutians, Japan, Ryukyus, Philippines line. Withdraw from Korea. The last place to get out of is the Shantung Peninsula (Tsingtao). The Carrier Task Force in the Western Pacific should be able to wipe up the Russian Fleet Bases. We will probably redeploy the Eastern Pacific carriers to the Atlantic, leaving one CTF [carrier task force] in the Western Pacific.

(n) We will have to force the Portuguese situation. If necessary we will take the Azores, Cape Verdes, and Iceland. In any event we must reinforce Iceland and Azores.

(o) We must hold the British Isles, the Mediterranean, and Spain. We can then set up air bases for long-range air bombardment.

(p) The Russians can probably take the Dardanelles. Turkey should be kept in the war if possible.[1]

Included within this framework are the sinews of the maritime strategy the United States has pursued for the past four decades.

In January 1947, Admiral Sherman briefed President Truman on the probable character of a major war in the next few years and on navy tasks in such a war. He stated:

In the event of war with Russia, the naval tasks we currently consider most essential are:

(a) To protect the United States;

(b) To control essential sea and air communications;

(c) To evacuate our occupation forces from Europe;

(d) To assist in protecting the United Kingdom;

(e) To assist in holding Japan and in providing for the safety of our forces in China and in Korea;

(f) To assist in retarding Soviet advances into Norway, Spain, Italy, Greece and Turkey, and toward Suez;

(g) To prevent Soviet use of sea communications; and

(h) To seize and defend positions from which subsequent offensives may be launched.

We envisage that from the naval point of view such a war would have four distinct phases.

The *first phase* would be one of initial operations by our existing forces, of stabilization of the Soviet offensive, and of mobilization and preparation of additional forces, and of expansion of production of war material. The nation would be on the strategic defensive but our naval and air forces should assume the offensive immediately in order to secure our own sea communications, support our forces overseas, disrupt enemy operations, and force dissipation of enemy strength. In this phase the navy would have a tremendous initial responsibility. Early offensive blows would be of extreme importance in shortening the war.

During this phase the Reserve Fleets would be activated as expeditiously as possible in order to provide our minimum requirements. For the Atlantic these include a carrier task force of 16 carriers with suitable support ships, and for the Pacific approximately half that number. Strong submarine forces would be required for such tasks as destruction of enemy controlled shipping, reconnaissance, and inshore work, sea-air rescue, patrol of advanced areas and bottling up the Russian Navy. Our active amphibious forces and Fleet Marine Force should be ready with naval-air and gunfire support to move promptly to occupy advance bases. Anti-submarine operations would commence immediately. . . .

Specific targets for early carrier attacks might include objectives in Manchuria, North Korea and Siberia to cover withdrawal of our forces from Korea and North China; and objectives in northwest Germany and in northern Italy to cover the retirement of our occupation forces.

Our submarines would be deployed promptly to bottle up the Russian forces in the Far East, the White Sea, the Baltic and the Black Sea and to patrol the approaches to Alaska and the Aleutians. Anti-submarine measures would be instituted promptly along the routes over which our troops and vital shipping must pass.

The *second phase* would be one of progressive reduction of Soviet war potential and build-up of our own. Operations would be characterized first by increased offensive action by naval and air forces and by joint forces, and subsequently by general advancement of our base areas as our military power permits. During this phase, large elements of all services would be moved overseas; advanced bases would be established and stocked; and requirements for shipping of all sorts and for naval escorts would increase rapidly.

The *third phase* would involve continued and sustained bombing offensive. The Dardanelles would be opened and limited positions seized in Europe and in the Middle East as desired. Naval activity would consist of maintaining our overseas lines of communications, protection of troop movements, gunfire support for amphibious landings, carrier action against appropriate objectives, and submarine operations to prevent enemy use of coastal waters.

The *final phase* would comprise the systematic destruction of Soviet industry, internal transportation systems, and general war potential. As naval targets disappeared, our naval operations would become more thoroughly integrated with ground and air operations, the need for maintenance of heavy carrier striking forces would decrease; while the need for ships for transporting forces and supplies, and for close-in escort and support would remain high.[2]

In 1948 the navy's General Board issued an important study on "National Security and Navy Contributions Thereto," which had been conducted under the leadership of then Captain Arleigh Burke. It discussed a wide variety of political, economic and military factors. With regard to carrier task forces, the study noted in paragraph 4:

(a) Within the foreseeable future it will be necessary for the United States to control the high seas if we are to project our offensive to the enemy in sufficient strength to be decisive. Sea or air raids will not likely bring about the defeat of a strong enemy. Sustained heavy attacks will be necessary which will require shipping to support. The Soviet Union can presently and within ten years challenge our control of the seas only by submarines and by air.

(b) Carrier task forces will be required to assist in destruction of enemy submarine bases if submarines are a threat to our freedom of the seas, as it now appears they will be. Destruction or blockading of submarine bases can be accomplished by atomic bomb or radiological attacks or by mining.

And in discussing antisubmarine warfare, it stressed:

1. General.

The next war will likely demand much increased emphasis on antisubmarine warfare. We cannot win a war by only defeating the enemy's submarines, but we assuredly will lose a war if we cannot defeat them. . . .

2. Russian Submarine Capabilities

(c)(6) In any case, it is most important that Russian submarines not be permitted to take the high seas. These dangerous weapons are much more easily destroyed in their bases than when they are in the operating areas.[3]

The navy discussed its thinking with regard to naval air power in a future war before the Eberstadt Committee in October 1948. It stressed:

IV. *Navy Analysis of Character of Future War*

B. Our thinking about the organization and employment of our air power must start with a survey of the basic geographical, economic and political facts which enter into the development of our strategy.

Geographically we are an island outpost lying offshore of the Eurasian land mass. Our island position has in the past dictated that our strategy be that of a maritime power. Technical advances in aviation have modified the demands of geography but have not surmounted them. Naval air power is blended with seapower in a way that makes geography work for us— not against us . . .

The extent to which we have control of the sea determines how soon and in what degree our land and air forces can be used. Defensively, if we control the sea and the advance bases from which an attack may come, we need only minor land forces and an air force for fighter defense. Offensively, we must have ready land forces to capture and consolidate advance air bases and an air force for use against strategic targets. . . .

I. *The Nature of a Future War*

2. In any war in which the U.S. (or any other democracy) may become engaged, the phases encountered will be as follows:

(a) Phase I—Defensive withdrawal.

(b) Phase II—Consolidation and establishment of advanced bases.

(c) Phase III—Counterattack.[4]

Not quite a year later, the chief of naval operations was forced to reiterate the vital importance of the navy to U.S. strategy in a memorandum to the secretary of defense that protested proposed cuts in the Navy Fiscal Year 1951 budget. Admiral Louis Denfeld told the Secretary:

Command of the Sea

4. The major task of the navy in any war is not merely the protection of certain sea lines of communications, a defensive task. Instead, it is the broader task of gaining and maintaining control of the sea; i.e., the ability to use the sea for whatever purposes are necessary to us and the ability to deny its use to the enemy. That control is attained by a combination of various operations and under various degrees and conditions of enemy opposition. Anti-submarine warfare limited to the defensive aspects is the most costly means of combatting the submarine threat. In certain sea-areas, control may be attained and exercised with minimum combatant effort. In other areas, such as the Northeastern Atlantic and the Northwestern Pacific, enemy surface and air opposition may be expected; in the Mediterranean, control would probably be vigorously disputed by intensive air effort not only on the part of the Soviet naval air arm but also by the Soviet army air. We cannot cut our naval cloth to the pattern of only one type of enemy opposition.

5. Elimination of offensive naval forces from the NME [National Military Establishment] would permit us only a limited use of the seas at the cost of continued, unremitting, *defensive* efforts; and it would completely destroy the capability—which we now possess of using the seas for offensive operations and as an area under our control from which to project and establish elements of the army and air force on the Eurasian continent. The elimination of offensive naval power throws away at one stroke a major component of our greatest strategic asset, which is our capability of exploiting the elements of mobility, concentration, surprise, and economy of force.

6. For our offensive-defensive tasks in Western Eurasia in the early days of a war, an offensive naval force is equal in importance to the atomic bomber force.[5]

The need for command of the sea was also emphasized to the public at large. In April 1950, the vice chief of naval operations told a Naval Civilian Orientation Conference:

I do not consider that there is need to more than mention to this audience what an implacable, and potentially strong, enemy we have in this world. Nor, what disaster he can quickly bring to us unless our forces and our attitude make him doubt his success.

The fact that he is situated on an island called Eurasia and we on an island called North America makes command of the sea, and thus the navy, vital to us and our allies. . . .

Though not a maritime power, historically, our potential enemy is strong enough to challenge seriously our use of the sea, particularly in the terminal areas where our ships and other forces must go. Enemy submarines, aircraft, and mines can cause in many respects a greater threat than a strong surface navy. . . .

Exercising control of *all* the seas, as we must, is going to be a mammoth task. Note that I say *exercise* control. To do this we must *have* the control from the beginning, not fight for it for four long years as we did in the Pacific in World War II. . . .

The usual peacetime task of the navy is to train diligently for war. This we are doing. But there has always been, and now exists in important degree, a peacetime task which only the navy can perform, namely, that which is broadly termed "showing the flag." A naval force is the only one which can move at will throughout the world without violating the neutrality or sovereignty of another nation. The navy is thus an important tool of diplomacy.[6]

In October 1951, the new Commander in Chief of the Atlantic and the Atlantic Fleet talked about his fleet's wartime responsibilities with the students of the U.S. Naval War College. He said:

I think it is interesting to note that the broad wartime task of the overall Naval Commander in the Western Atlantic has been essentially the same since the battle of Santiago in 1898. It is largely one of supporting active and wide-spread combat on the other side of the Atlantic, with enemy submarines as the chief combatant threat on our side of the ocean. . . .

Task Number III [Augmentation and support of forces in Europe and Africa]. . . .

Within the confines of this task, the Atlantic Command exhibits its definite offensive potentiality. By this arrow, we indicate our readiness to deploy striking forces to the forward area. They would most probably be fast carrier task forces aimed at operations along the Western European coast or against some of the northern islands such as Spitzbergen. . . .

Likewise, amphibious attack forces might well be built up here for direct transit to the objective area. . . .

As you all know . . . the United States has maintained a naval force in the Mediterranean since the end of the last war. We call it the Sixth Fleet, and it necessarily looms large in our European strategy.

This force, in conjunction with those of our allies, by maintaining control of the Mediterranean, would furnish security to General Eisenhower's right flank, now under Admiral Carney as Commander-in-Chief Southern Europe. In addition, it would probably have an important role in the Eastern Mediterranean.[7]

The navy's director of strategic plans set forth the navy's wartime tasks in general war in a 1954 memorandum to the director, General Planning Group. He stressed:

In the event of general war, the navy must be prepared to perform three broad tasks:

First, the navy must dominate the seas to maintain the flow of men and materials to theaters of war, and the return flow of our supply of strategic raw materials. It must be prepared to counter the probable capabilities of the enemy to challenge our control of the seas and especially the sea areas near foreign ports used by our shipping. We must deny our most probable enemy the effective use of his submarines, and his growing fleet of surface ships, and must counter his mining effort and his air threat to shipping and naval forces.

Second, the navy must land combat forces where and when they are required, assist in providing for their security and assist in providing combat support to U.S. and Allied land forces, including air and gunfire support, as the situation may require. Protection of the sea flanks of our overseas forces against enemy forces which attempt to interfere with naval operations, shipping or naval support of our ground forces, is an important navy responsibility.

Third, the navy must, by offensive operations, control the sea areas, that the enemy wishes to use, denying him the use of these seas and permitting their use by our own naval forces, as avenues into enemy territory.[8]

A year and a half later, the deputy chief of naval operations (Fleet Operations and Readiness) sent a memorandum to the chief of naval operations highlighting the need for increased amphibious warfare capability. He noted:

5. For the past several years we have been conditioning our armed forces to handle nothing but an all-out war accompanied by a liberal sprinkling of atomic and thermonuclear weapons by both sides. All our thoughts have been channeled toward how best we can project our atoms against the enemy while at the same time preventing him from projecting his atoms against us . . . We have been so engrossed in this fascinating subject that we have all but lost sight of the fact that we are also faced with other problems which may in the end prove more important. In the ten years since World War II our principal problem has not been all out atomic war. On the contrary, what we have been faced with daily is the peripheral type war, the limited war, the brush fire wherein atomic weapons

have not been used and probably could not be used without risking expansion into an all out atomic war. And this may be the type of war with which we will be faced for many years to come. In fact there is growing doubt in the minds of many officers that we will ever become involved in an atomic exchange unless we allow ourselves to get in a position where we are not equipped to fight any other kind of war. And that is the trend at the moment. For, except for the limited capability of the army's airborne divisions[,] about the only means we have for handling peripheral wars is with our Fleet Marine Forces, transported, landed and supported by our Amphibious Task Forces. And the ability of the navy to provide the necessary combat support for such operations is rapidly dwindling.[9]

In 1961, Admiral Arleigh Burke, the chief of naval operations, spoke about the strategic mobility offered by the navy. He commented in these terms:

The geographical position of the United States, between two oceans, is one of our country's greatest assets. . . . These great oceans offer us military freedom of movement—a strategic seagoing mobility—to use as needed to insure the security of the United States and the Free World. . . . But in time of war, a nation can use the seas only so long as that nation has the *naval* power to do so. And no matter what kind of military power we project overseas—naval, ground, or air—we are going to have to use the seas to sustain that power.

And that means we must be able to control the seas, that we must be able to keep them free for *our* use and to deny that use to any enemy. Control of the seas is the Navy's primary mission. . . .

All of our naval forces have the tremendous advantage of mobility. Moving at sea our ships have no fixed address. They cannot be targeted in advance, for attack by long-range ballistic missiles. And our submarine retaliatory forces at sea have another, most significant advantage. They can be concealed, submerged in the depths of the seas—silent, ready, and invulnerable. . . .

But POLARIS is not our only seagoing asset for nuclear war. In addition, our powerful, versatile attack carriers contribute to our country's retaliatory capability. These carriers and their aircraft form the backbone of our naval striking power: power that can be projected overseas, power that can carry the fight to the enemy, power that can be used in wars of every kind. . . .

But aggressors are apt to strike in areas where we are not so well covered, in areas far away from concentration of land-based American fighting power. And that is why our *mobile* naval forces are so very important. Our Navy/Marine Corps amphibious capability, one unique to the United States, can supply armed strength from the sea ready to fight. . . .

Naval forces are essentially self-contained offensively, defensively, and logistically. This staying power is an important feature of our modern navy, which insures that United States strength and influence can always be exerted where and when needed.[10]

The need for an offensive naval strategy was at the focal point of an article written by the vice chief of naval operations in 1963. He pointed out:

> The primary role of seapower in our national military strategy is to contribute to our national readiness to project U.S. power overseas. Sea areas lie between us and any prospective allies. Extensive use of the seas is necessary for support of our allies and for the support of our own military forces on their soil. . . .
>
> These factors dictate an offensive naval strategy. Our Navy must be designed to carry the war to the enemy, both at sea and on land.
>
> In our early history the navy was frequently forced into a coastal defense strategy.
>
> It was only after we shook off the shackles of these defensive concepts that we were able to exploit our full potential and perform our primary mission—control of vital sea areas.
>
> In World War II, the greatest of all naval wars, this offensive philosophy paid great dividends. . . .
>
> Technological advances since have reinforced the validity of this offensive strategical concept. No weapon is foreseen that will change that philosophy in the future. . . .
>
> This offensive naval philosophy is not restricted to wartime operations, but extends into the area of peacetime tensions short of a shooting war. We have found it extremely beneficial and helpful to American and Free World policy to keep naval forces capable of conducting offensive operations deployed thousands of miles from our shores in the Far Western Pacific and in the Mediterranean. . . .
>
> When force is needed, prompt action is most important, because timely action by comparatively small forces usually precludes the need for larger forces later. By exploiting the quick reaction capability of naval forces, we can either prevent hostilities or contribute greatly to keeping them confined.[11]

Relatively speaking, however, the decade of the 1960s represented the high-water mark for the postwar U.S. Navy. The legacy of maritime forces from World War II had been spent, and the navy found itself embroiled in a war in Southeast Asia for much of which it was ill-prepared. By the end of the decade the focus was on the obsolescence of a U.S. fleet that, while still very large—almost 900 ships— was also old. Almost two-thirds of the ships were approaching the twentieth anniversary of their commissioning. The downward trend in numbers of battle force ships was to continue for the decade of the seventies as well. Figure 13-1 portrays the decline graphically.

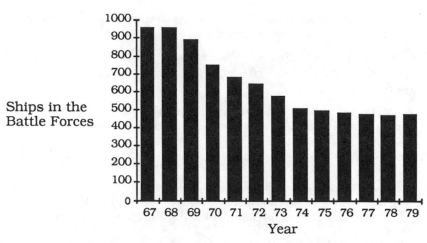

Ships in the Battle Forces

Year

Figure 13-1. U.S. Navy Battle Forces, 1967–1979.[12]

During the decade of the 1960s the entire force of forty-one fleet ballistic-missile submarines became operational, relieving the aircraft carrier of its primary nuclear attack mission. This was the time, in 1962, of the navy's participation in the successful quarantine of Cuba in order to require the Soviet Union to remove the offensive weapons they had emplaced there, and which were en route by sea. This was also the time of the sea-based NATO Multi-Lateral Force (MLF), which found tangible expression in a U.S. guided-missile destroyer with a multi-national crew for the period of one year, 1964–1965. The central idea of the MLF, establishing a multi-national sea-based nuclear-deterrent force for the NATO alliance based in surface ships at sea, however, was never implemented—largely owing to French hostility to the idea—and the experiment foundered.

Although the U.S. blue-water fleet was obsolescent, it was capable and proficient enough to support the land war in Vietnam. Strategy for use of the seas was nonexistent in this war because, even though an attack at sea (the Tonkin Gulf incident of August 1964) triggered greatly increased U.S. involvement in the war, there was virtually no opposition at sea.

The 1960s also witnessed a new emphasis on rationalizing and analyzing defense programs rather than on formulating and articulating the strategic use of military forces. "In my mind, I equate plan-

ning and budgeting and consider the terms almost synonymous,"
secretary of defense McNamara testified before the Congress in 1961.
Consumed by a war that struck hard both at morale and at force
structure, and forced to meet analysts of the office of the secretary of
defense in pitched battle on the budgetary front, maritime strategists
in the United States retreated into almost total silence for better than
a decade.

Admiral Elmo R. Zumwalt, Jr., became the youngest chief of naval
operations in the summer of 1970, and as one of his first acts he
commissioned a comprehensive plan for his four years as CNO, to be
accomplished within two months of the time he was sworn into office. "Project 60," as it became known, set forth four explicit missions
for the navy:

- Strategic Deterrence,
- Sea Control,
- Projection of Power, and
- Naval Presence.

These were set forth as new definitions—clearly in reaction to the
OSD systems analysis approach—and they were defended by members of Zumwalt's staff:

> To those accustomed to phrases such as "seapower," "command of the
> seas," "commerce warfare" and "amphibious warfare," the new terms may
> seem to be just a new jargon. Not so . . . there has been a redefinition of
> traditional roles and missions. The primary purpose is to force the Navy
> to think in terms of output rather than input . . . Why must we measure
> output? . . . so skeptical taxpayers can measure the output in terms of
> national objectives . . . and rationally decide what resources should be
> allocated to the Navy. . . .
>
> Focusing on missions helps the tactical commander keep objectives in
> mind, establishes priorities for allocating resources at macro- and micro-
> levels, assists in selecting the best among competing systems. . . .

It was intended that there be a clear distinction between:

> Sea Control which is concerned with what happens on, under, and over
> the ocean surface, and Projection of Power which is concerned with the
> impact of naval focus on land forces and is divided into three categories;
> amphibious assault, naval bombardment, and tactical air.

There was no question where the emphasis should be placed,
moreover. Zumwalt was unequivocal:

> I feel that the sea control mission has now become paramount more
> than the projection mission of the carrier, because the power of the Soviet
> Navy has grown so dramatically . . . They have a very believable prospect

of severing our sea lines of communication. Therefore, the first mission and role of the carrier must be to try to keep open the sea lanes to the United States and to our allies.[13]

Power projection was rarely discussed as pertaining to conflict with the Soviet Union. It was to be used in other areas of the world in support of the Nixon Doctrine.

Meanwhile, the central fact for the navy was the decline in fleet size, especially in light of concurrent increases in Soviet battle forces. In an extraordinary memorandum, Admiral Zumwalt wrote to Secretary of Defense Laird in 1971, with respect to the Fiscal Year 1973 budget then in preparation:

> I have informed you repeatedly of my concern for the continuing degradation of naval capabilities. In my judgment, the end-FY '70 forces gave us a 55 percent probability of success if we became involved in a conflict at sea with the Soviet Union. Since that time, naval forces have been reduced for fiscal reasons by 111 ships including four carriers; the FY '73 Base Case [the Five-Year Plan] requires a reduction of twenty-eight ships and the decrement [the billion-dollar cut] a cut of thirty-six to seventy-three ships including four to five carriers. While I judge our naval forces today have only a 35 percent chance in an engagement with the Soviet Union, that level of confidence is reduced to 20 percent based on the potential consequences of the Tentative Fiscal Guidance. It is perfectly clear that we are unable to support the fighting of a war overseas by the U.S. or allied forces should the Soviet Union challenge the U.S. for control of the seas . . . The decremented forces would, for all practical purposes, constitute a one-ocean navy.[14]

A January 1977 classified study undertaken by the National Security Council staff as the Ford administration was drawing to a close served to highlight many of the issues about the navy's roles and missions, and the comptroller general's report and commentary to the Congress on the study underscored the fundamental differences in the way contributions of the navy to national security were perceived. The study, much of which was declassified in the comptroller general's report, framed the questions thus:

> The navy is the principal force used to achieve and maintain maritime superiority on which the nation relies. Its mission is to be prepared to conduct prompt and sustained combat operations at sea and defeat any force that curtails free use of the seas. . . .
>
> The navy performs four functions to achieve its mission. Two of these—sea control and power projection—are wartime functions.
>
> Sea control is the fundamental function of the navy; it connotes control of designated air, surface, and subsurface areas. It does not require simultaneous control over all waters but is exercised where and when needed.

Sea control is achieved by engaging and destroying hostile aircraft, ships, and submarines at sea or by deterring hostile actions by the threat of destruction.

Power projection operations primarily use tactical air and naval gunfire in direct support of land operations and/or amphibious forces used in land assault operations. Power projection and sea control are interrelated because sea control is necessary in areas where power is to be projected, and, conversely, power projection may be needed to assist efforts to control the sea.

The second two functions—presence and crisis management—are peacetime functions. Presence is the non-hostile use of naval forces to support U.S. foreign policy. Crisis management is the use of naval forces to stabilize critical situations to avoid escalation into war.

Navy Roles

In the functional exercise of its mission, the navy is responsible for:

—Providing a strategic nuclear deterrence.

—Providing naval components of U.S. overseas deployed forces to support allies and protect U.S. interests.

—Assuring the security of the sea lines of communication (SLOC).

The NSC study concluded that low fleet force levels of 1976

. . . provide a slim margin of superiority over the Soviets and that without a program to increase force levels, this superiority will be lost in about 5 to 10 years.

The NSC study, which forms the basis for the navy's 1978 fiscal year 5–Year Shipbuilding Program provides for a force level of about 600 ships by 1990. This force level is not unlike today's force structure in that it is centered around 12 carrier task groups.

In its commentary, GAO

. . . found that the study left unresolved the following important issues:

—Should the navy continue to rely on the carrier for offensive capability? The navy may be structuring a carrier-oriented force that would be best suited for power-projection and for peacetime and minor conflicts instead of a force built for its major role—protecting the sea lines of communication.

—Could and should forward deployment of high-value forces be accomplished with less valuable assets? Forward deployment could expose high-value forces to high-intensity cruise missile and aircraft attacks.

—Why does the study assign a large number of ships to protect naval shipping? There is reason to believe that sea-line interdiction is not a primary Soviet intention and will not be attempted until U.S. carrier and strategic submarine forces are neutralized. . . .

GAO concluded:

. . . Without procuring any additional carriers, the navy could continue to have more than 10 aircraft carriers operational through the 1990s. The study considers this level adequate for basic sea control in a North Atlantic Treaty Organization War.

The appropriate congressional committees should hold extensive exploratory hearings to examine the impact of these issues on the future naval force size and composition. . . .[15]

Admiral James Holloway succeeded Admiral Zumwalt as chief of naval operations and set about to redefine questions about the navy's missions, functions, and tasks. In 1978 Holloway signed NWP-1 (Rev. A), *Strategic Concepts of the U.S. Navy,* in which the relationship of the navy's mission to national military strategy was detailed, and the navy's "functions" were clearly spelled out. They contrast sharply with the discussion immediately above. Here is an excerpt:

3.1 U.S. NAVY FUNCTIONS

In order to achieve the basic military objectives of the United States, the respective Services are tasked with specific primary and collateral functions by Department of Defense Directive 5100.1. The Department of the Navy is tasked:

To organize, train, and equip navy . . . forces for the conduct of prompt and sustained combat operations at sea, including operations of sea-based aircraft and land-based naval air components—specifically, forces to seek out and destroy enemy forces, and to suppress enemy sea commerce, to gain and maintain general naval supremacy, to control vital sea areas and to protect vital sea lines of communication, to establish and maintain local superiority (including air) in an area of naval operations, to seize and defend naval bases, and to conduct such land and air operations as may be essential to the prosecution of a naval campaign.

Briefly, the navy's two basic functions are sea control and power projection. The ability to perform these functions is a requirement if the U.S. is to utilize the seas to support its national policies and to defeat the forces of any state that would deny such use. The functions of sea control and power projection are closely interrelated. Some degree of a sea control is necessary in the sea area from which the power is to be projected, depending on the type of force to be employed. Conversely, the capability to project naval power was developed in naval forces largely as one means of achieving or supporting sea control. . . .

3.2.1 Sea Control. Sea control is the fundamental function of the U.S. Navy and connotes control of designated air areas and the associated air space and underwater volume. It does not imply simultaneous control of all the earth's ocean area, but is a selective function exercised only when and where needed. Sea control is achieved by the engagement and destruction of hostile aircraft, ships, and submarines at sea, or by the deterrence of hostile action through the threat of destruction. Sea control is a requirement for most naval operations. It is required so that the U.S. Navy may have operating areas that are secure for the projection of power, such as carrier strike or amphibious assault, and sea lines of communication that assure buildup and resupply of allied forces in the theater of operations, and free flow of strategic resources. Effective sea control also enhances security for the nation's sea-based strategic deterrent.

3.2.1.1 Prerequisite. Sea control is a prerequisite to the conduct of sustained overseas operations by U.S. Army and U.S. Air Force general-purpose forces. Modern land warfare generates logistic requirements of such proportions that the overwhelming amount of material needed must be supplied by sea.

3.2.1.2 Implementation. Sea control is achieved by the destruction or neutralization of hostile aircraft, surface ships and submarines which, by their presence, threaten U.S. or friendly forces operating in those maritime areas which the United States must use. Sea control can also be effected by deterring the intrusion of hostile forces into those areas. However, deterrence is less effective than destruction in that it permits the enemy to retain a threatening force in being.

3.2.1.3 Application. For analytical purposes sea control may be categorized as area or local. Area sea control includes extended operations to engage and destroy hostile forces, such as seizure or neutralization of enemy bases or denial to the enemy of access routes to the sea. Local sea control includes close defense of U.S. and allied naval and merchant units and of friendly forces engaged in other operations, such as amphibious assault and mine warfare. Sea control can be achieved or supported in several ways:

1. Sea control is primarily effected by operations designed to locate and destroy hostile naval combat units on the high seas.
2. Barrier operations are designed to deny enemy naval forces access to open oceans or specific areas, taking advantage, where possible, of geographic choke points.
3. Sea control is also accomplished through the use of moving screens to clear the sea area surrounding ships in transit such as military or commercial convoys and amphibious or support forces.
4. The utilization of mines in such areas as harbor entrances and choke points is an important means of sea control.

3.2.1.4 Power Projection as a Part of Sea Control. The use of carrier and marine amphibious forces in the projection of military power can be an absolute necessity to ensure control and continued safe use of the high seas and contiguous land areas essential to control of the seas. This entails destruction of enemy naval forces at their home bases or enroute to those ocean areas which the United States desires to protect, destroying their logistic support, or preventing the approach of enemy forces within range from which their weapons can be employed against U.S. forces.

3.2.2 Power Projection. As an independent function, power projection is a means of supporting land or air campaigns utilizing capabilities designed for naval tasks. Power projection covers a broad spectrum of offensive naval operations including strategic nuclear response by fleet ballistic missile forces, employment of carrier-based aircraft, amphibious assault forces and naval bombardment with guns and missiles of enemy targets ashore in support of air or land campaigns.

3.2.2.1 Sea Control as a Prerequisite for Power Projection. An essential element of power projection is the navy amphibious ship with marines embarked, the nation's only means of inserting U.S. ground forces into the hostile environment of an opposed landing operation. Carrier aircraft, in the power projection function, are able to strike land targets with a variety of weapons, conventional or nuclear. The ultimate means of power projection is the Fleet Ballistic Missile (FBM) submarine force, one element of the U.S. strategic offensive force mix. Each element of power projection requires a measure of sea control for its effective execution, and that function can be exercised simultaneously with the projection function, if necessary. . . .

3.3 U.S. NAVY ROLES IN THE NATIONAL MILITARY STRATEGY

In the functional exercise of its mission responsibilities within the national military strategy, the U.S. Navy has three main roles: strategic nuclear deterrence, to provide overseas-deployed forces, and security of the sea lines of communication (SLOCs).

3.3.1 Strategic Nuclear Deterrence. The effectiveness of the submarine launched ballistic missile combined with the virtual invulnerability of the SSBN provides the strongest deterrent in our strategic nuclear forces, and thus a stabilizing factor in the strategic nuclear balance.

3.3.2 Overseas Deployed Forces. The navy provides operationally ready naval components of overseas deployed U.S. forces to support allies and protect U.S. interests. These fleet elements are deployed to locations where they can engage hostile forces at the outbreak of hostilities and rapidly support forward-positioned U.S. ground and air forces, as well as U.S. allies.

3.3.3 Security of the Sea Lines of Communication (SLOCs). The success of a forward military strategy depends upon the navy's ability to maintain the integrity of the sea lines of communication between the United States and its forward deployed forces, its allies, and those areas of the world essential for the supply of imports. The most vulnerable segments of these SLOCs are the overseas portions lying closest to potential hostile bases and farthest from friendly territory where land-based air and control combatant craft can assist in the protection of shipping. The protection of these most vulnerable sea areas requires that U.S. Navy forces be present in sufficient strength to defeat hostile air, surface, and submarine threats. . . .

In the interest of forging a coherent navy position for use in strategy and budgetary battles with the Carter administration, a broad-gauged study entitled SEA PLAN 2000 was undertaken by the navy. Although the study remains classified, an unclassified executive summary was produced and disseminated. SEA PLAN 2000 suggested three national security objectives, against which were arrayed seven missions for the navy:

OBJECTIVES AND MISSIONS

Security Objective	Naval Mission
—Maintenance of Stability	—Forward deployments
—Containment of Crises	—Calibrated use of force against the shore
	—Superiority at sea in a crisis setting
—Deterrence of a Global War	—SLOC defense
	—Reinforcement of allies
	—Pressure upon the Soviets
	—Hedge against uncertainties of the distant future

No priority among the missions was advocated. The maintenance of stability, the containment of crises and the deterrence of global war were as tightly interwoven as are the international politics and economics of today's world.

SEA PLAN 2000 then presented three options based upon budgetary growth rates of 1 percent, 3 percent, and 4 percent greater than the rate of inflation. The options were said to be balanced so that no mission would be neglected; they differed in degrees of risk and versatility as well as cost. The options are of interest in the light of force goals subsequently adopted by the navy.

- OPTION 1 (1 percent real growth) called for 11 large aircraft carriers and a total active force level of 474 ships. It was "judged to be a high-risk option with a low degree of flexibility, with minimal capability across the range of naval tasks."
- OPTION 2 (3 percent real growth) listed 13 large aircraft carriers and 579 ships in the inventory. It "hovers at the threshold of naval capability across the spectrum of possible uses, given the risks associated with technical and tactical uncertainties."
- OPTION 3 (4 percent real growth) showed 15 large aircraft carriers, 631 total ships (585 active), and was said to provide "a high degree of versatility in the form of a wider range of military and political actions at a moderate increase over Option 2."

The next chief of naval operations, Admiral Thomas B. Hayward, began his term in early 1979 with optimism about the state of the navy and for the near future, and in his posture statement for Fiscal Year 1980 set forth his "Fundamental Principles of Naval Strategy":

> I am pleased to report that there is agreement within the U.S. government today on the proposition that maritime superiority must be the foundation of our national naval policy. This proposition recognizes the strategic realities of our geographic position as an island nation, connected to overseas allies by two oceans, and confronting a great land power which has chosen—for reasons of its own—to challenge our traditional supremacy on the seas.
>
> Maritime superiority means the capability to use the world's oceans, for military or economic purposes, whenever and wherever our national interests require, against whatever opposition may be brought to bear. It does not mean that we must control all the vast ocean expanses simultaneously. It does mean that we must have the ability to control those sea areas which are important to the United States and its allies, whenever it is necessary to do so . . . In this task we look to our allies and sister services for important support. But in the final analysis, the United States must have the clear ability to prevail over any maritime adversary in order to protect its vital interests worldwide, and to deter actions which could lead to a major war. I believe the explicit recognition of the requirement for maritime superiority is a major milestone in the evolution of our national strategic thinking. . . .
>
> The statutory mission of the U.S. Navy is to be prepared to conduct prompt and sustained combat operations at sea in support of U.S. national interests and the national military strategy. In the discharge of this mission, a number of principles, discussed below, guide planning for the employment of Navy forces. . . .
>
> To achieve maritime superiority, the United States must maintain naval forces, as well as other forces with maritime application, sufficient to defeat Soviet or other hostile maritime forces which threaten our ability to use the major ocean areas for a variety of offensive, defensive, and economic support tasks. In conjunction with allied maritime forces and facilities, our capabilities must be sufficient to put at risk the survivability of Soviet maritime forces even in their coastal waters and bases. . . .
>
> A basic premise of U.S. Naval Strategy is that a conflict between NATO and the Warsaw Pact, in all probability, will be worldwide in scope. This proposition is consistent with Soviet doctrine, which contemplates preemptive attacks against U.S. and allied forces wherever they may be located around the periphery of Eurasia at the outset of a war . . . from a broad strategic viewpoint, there is clear advantage in maintaining a worldwide U.S. naval strike capability which threatens potential enemies from a number of widely dispersed directions. . . .
>
> Fundamental to current naval strategy is the principle that U.S. Navy forces must be offensively capable. The geographic range of the Navy's responsibilities is too broad, and its forces too small, to adopt a defensive,

reactive posture in a worldwide conflict with the Soviet Union. We must fight on the terms which are most advantageous to us. This would require taking the war to the enemy's naval forces with the objective of achieving the earliest possible destruction of his capability to interfere with our use of the sea areas essential for support of our overseas forces and allies. In this sense, sea control is an offensive rather than a defensive function. The prompt destruction of opposing naval forces is the most economical and effective means to assure control of those sea areas required for successful prosecution of the war and support of the U.S. and allied war economies. . . .

Related to the preceding principles is the fact that the U.S. Navy is outnumbered and is likely to remain so for the foreseeable future. . . .

We must exploit Soviet disadvantages and should continue to deploy naval forces in locales which provide us strategic advantage. It is important that we make the Soviets understand that in war there will be no sanctuaries for their forces. We cannot allow them to exploit asymmetries in force structures by, for example, attacking our carriers with land-based air in the expectation that we will not respond with strikes against the aircrafts' bases. Keeping the Soviets preoccupied with defensive concerns locks up Soviet naval forces in areas close to the USSR, limiting their availability for campaigns against the SLOCs, or for operations in support of offensive thrusts on the flanks of NATO, or elsewhere such as in the Middle East or in Asia. . . .

Our plans must take into account that we have no substantial reserve of U.S. forces to draw upon at the outset of war. We will fight with essentially what we have . . . Given the long lead time for production of today's complex ships and aircraft, neither side will have a substantial opportunity to reconstitute major naval units, even if the war is relatively protracted in duration. Every major naval engagement must, therefore, be regarded as potentially decisive in terms of its impact on the naval balance, and every U.S. naval unit must have the maximum offensive capability we can build into it consistent with its mission. . . .

Given the nature of the U.S./Soviet naval balance and our essential inability to reconstitute battle losses, U.S. tactical commanders must be governed by the principle of calculated risk. That is, they must select engagement opportunities which promise attrition ratios clearly favorable to the U.S. side. This principle—which Nimitz enjoined Spruance to follow at the Battle of Midway—is classic guidance for a force which does not enjoy a broad margin of superiority over an enemy. . . .

The inherent mobility of naval forces, and their relative lack of need for land bases, would make them particularly useful in a post-conflict environment. Assuring that the U.S. emerges from the conflict with an adequate residual naval force is, therefore, an important planning consideration. . . .

Flexibility in concepts for force employment must be a central principle of navy planning and for force structure development. . . .

The role of naval forces becomes increasingly important as the conflict progresses and seaborne reinforcement/re-supply of ground theaters becomes more critical. Employment of naval forces in the early stages of conflict must be predicated, in part, on long-term objectives, including residual naval force requirements, early sealift for high-demand cargoes at the start of the war, and growing sealift requirements as the war continues. . . .[16]

Finally, in an unprecedented article published in 1986, Chief of Naval Operations Admiral James D. Watkins provided "the most definitive and authoritative statements of the Maritime Strategy that are available in unclassified form." His article, accompanied by companion pieces authored by Secretary of the Navy John F. Lehman, Jr., and Commandant of the Marine Corps General P. X. Kelley with Major Hugh K. O'Donnell, Jr., merits extended quotation here. It is striking not for its unique approach but for its broad, long-term continuity with navy thinking illustrated throughout this chapter.

By its peacetime presence throughout the world, the navy enhances deterrence daily. Our forward deployments maintain U.S. access on fair and reasonable terms to oil, other necessary resources, and markets, and deter and defend against attempts at physical denial of sea and air lines of communications critical to maintenance of the U.S. and allied economies. They provide a clear sign of U.S. interest in a given nation or region, and of U.S. commitment to protect its interests and its citizens.

One key goal in our peacetime strategy is to further international stability through support of regional balances of power. The more stable the international environment, the lower the probability that the Soviets will risk war with the West. Thus our peacetime strategy must support U.S. alliances and friendships. We accomplish this through a variety of peacetime operations including naval ship visits to foreign ports and training and exercises with foreign naval forces. . . .

The heart of our evolving Maritime Strategy is crisis response. If war with the Soviets ever comes, it will probably result from a crisis that escalates out of control. Our ability to contain and control crises is an important factor in our ability to prevent global conflict. . . .

- Forward-deployed posture and rapid mobility make naval forces readily available at crisis locations world wide, providing significant deterrent value and reducing the likelihood of ambiguous or short warning.
- Naval forces maintain consistently high states of readiness because of forward deployments, ensuring operational expertise and day-to-day preparedness.
- Naval forces increasingly operate with friendly and allied armed forces and sister services.
- Naval forces can be sustained indefinitely at distant locations, with logistics support relatively independent of foreign basing or overflight rights.

- Naval forces bring the range of capabilities required for credible deterrence. Capabilities demonstrated in actual crises include maintaining presence, conducting surveillance, threatening use of force, conducting naval gunfire or air strikes, landing Marines, evacuating civilians, establishing a blockade or quarantine, and preventing intervention by Soviet or other forces.
- Perhaps most importantly, naval forces have unique escalation control characteristics that contribute to effective crisis control. Naval forces can be intrusive or out of sight, threatening or non-threatening, and easily dispatched but just as easily withdrawn. The flexibility and the precision available in employing naval forces provide escalation control in any crisis, but have particular significance in those crises which might involve the Soviet Union. . . .

If our peacetime presence and crisis response tasks are done well, deterrence is far less likely to fail. Deterrence *can* fail, however, and we must consider how the navy would be used in a global war against the Soviets. . . .

Should war come, the Soviets would prefer to use their massive ground force advantage against Europe without having to concern themselves with a global conflict or with actions on their flanks. It is this preferred Soviet strategy that the United States must counter. The key to doing so is to ensure that they will have to face the prospect of prolonged global conflict. Maritime forces have a major role to play in this regard. The strategy setting forth their contribution consists of three phases: deterrence or the transition to war; seizing the initiative; and carrying the fight to the enemy. There are no fixed time frames associated with these phases; they provide a broad outline of what we want to accomplish, not an attempt to predict an inherently unpredictable future.

Phase I: Deterrence or the Transition to War: The initial phase of the Maritime Strategy would be triggered by recognition that a specific international situation has the potential to grow to a global superpower confrontation. Such a confrontation may come because an extra-European crisis escalated or because of problems in Europe. In either event, this phase of the Maritime Strategy deals with a superpower confrontation analogous to the Cuban Missile Crisis of 1962, where war with the Soviets is a real possibility.

The goal of this phase is deterrence. Through early, worldwide, decisive use of seapower we—along with sister services and allies as appropriate—would seek to win the crisis, to control escalation, and, by the global nature of our operations, to make clear our intention to cede no area to the Soviets and to deny them the option to engage in hostilities on their terms. While seeking to enhance deterrence at the brink of war, we must also consider that deterrence may fail. Thus preparing for the transition to war, specifically to global war, is an integral aspect of this phase.

Keys to the success of both the initial phase and the strategy as a whole are speed and decisiveness in national decision making. The United States must be in a position to deter the Soviets' "battle of the first salvo" or deal with that if it comes. Even though a substantial fraction of the fleet is forward deployed in peacetime, prompt decisions are needed to permit rapid forward deployment of additional forces in crisis.

The need for forward movement is obvious. This is where the Soviet fleet will be, and this is where we must be prepared to fight. Aggressive forward movement of anti-submarine warfare forces, both submarines and maritime patrol aircraft, will force Soviet submarines to retreat into defensive bastions to protect their ballistic missile submarines. This both denies the Soviets the option of a massive, early attempt to interdict our sea lines of communication and counters such operations against them that the Soviets take.

Early embarkation of Marine amphibious forces takes advantage of their flexibility and would be matched with forward movement of maritime prepositioning ship squadrons toward most likely areas of employment. . . .

Forward deployment must be global as well as early. Deployments to the Western Pacific directly enhance deterrence, including deterrence of an attack in Europe, by providing a clear indication that, should war come, the Soviets will not be able to ignore any region of the globe. . . .

Phase II: Seizing the Initiative: We cannot predict where the first shot will be fired should deterrence fail, but almost certainly the conflict will involve Europe. If war comes, we will move into the second phase of the strategy in which the navy will seize the initiative as far forward as possible. Naval forces will destroy Soviet forces in the Mediterranean, Indian Ocean, and other forward areas, neutralize Soviet clients if required, and fight our way toward Soviet home waters. . . .

The Soviets will probably focus their offensive on Central Europe, while attempting to maintain a defensive posture elsewhere. Instead, we must dilute their effort, divert their attention, and force them to divide their forces. We must control the type and tempo of conflict, making sure the Soviets understand that they can take no area for granted. . . .

Phase III: Carrying the Fight to the Enemy: The tasks in this phase are similar to those of earlier phases, but must be more aggressively applied as we seek war termination on terms favorable to the United States and its allies. Our goal would be to complete the destruction of all the Soviet fleets which was begun in Phase II. This destruction allows us to threaten the bases and support structure of the Soviet Navy in all theaters, with both air and amphibious power. Such threats are quite credible to the Soviets. At the same time, antisubmarine warfare forces would continue to destroy Soviet submarines, including ballistic missile submarines, thus reducing the attractiveness of nuclear escalation by changing the nuclear balance in our favor.

During this final phase the United States and its allies would press home the initiative worldwide, while continuing to support air and land campaigns, maintaining sealift, and keeping sea lines of communication open. . . .

The goal of the overall Maritime Strategy, particularly of Phase III, is to use maritime power, in combination with the efforts of our sister services and forces of our allies, to bring about war termination on favorable terms. In a global war, our objectives are to:

- Deny the Soviets their kind of war by exerting global pressure, indicating that the conflict will be neither short nor localized.
- Destroy the Soviet Navy: both important in itself and a necessary step for us to realize our objectives.
- Influence the land battle by limiting redeployment of forces, by ensuring reinforcement and re-supply, and by direct application of carrier air and amphibious power.
- Terminate the war on terms acceptable to us and to our allies through measures such as threatening direct attack against the homeland or changing the nuclear correlation of forces.[17]

Thus, from this series of excerpts it seems clear that the preferred strategy for the U.S. Navy since the time of the Second World War has been one that emphasizes deterrence, and if deterrence should fail, fighting far forward with the assistance of allies. Sea control has always been a central function, and during those periods of time when the navy was clearly preponderant or on the upswing it has emphasized both forward offensive operations to secure control of the seas and power-projection operations against enemy forces or territory. At times when the international and budgetary climates were not favorable for seapower, the navy leadership has retrenched. Then, it appears that the navy has either been forced to adopt a less aggressive strategy, or the leadership decided that the best it would be able to do, in view of the forces available and the prevailing threat, would be to forgo—or at least to de-emphasize—forward offensive operations. What is most striking, in the final analysis, is the similarity between the strategic vision of Admiral Watkins and Admiral Sherman—not the differences.

NOTES

1. Top Secret [declassified], Memorandum by Colin Campbell Op-30B, "Conference with Op-03 on War Planning," 7 June 1946; A16–3(5) folder, 1945–1946 Strategic Plans Division Subject and Serial Files, Operational Archives, Naval Historical Center, Washington Navy Yard (hereafter NHC).

2. Top Secret [declassified], "Presentation To The President 14 January 1947, Vice Admiral Forrest Sherman, U.S. Navy, Deputy Chief Of Naval Operations (Operations);" CNO Chronological File, Post 1 Jan. 46 Command File, Operational Archives, NHC.

3. Confidential [declassified], "Working Papers of CAPT A. A. BURKE on General Board, serial 315, 'Study of the National Security of the UNITED STATES within the next ten years and the Navy's most effective contributions to National Security.' " Papers of Arleigh A. Burke, Operational Archives, NHC. *Note:*

The quoted material is from a draft of Serial 315. In the final version of paragraph 4.b. above, conventional bombing was added as a means of attacking Soviet submarine bases.

4. Secret [declassified], Op-56, (SC)A21–1, "Presentation before the Eberstadt Committee on 18 October 1948 Justifying the Navy's Position Regarding Air Power and the Organization of the Air Forces," 4 Oct 1948; A18, A21 Legislation, Conferences, Aviation 1948–1949 folder, Box 3, John L. Sullivan Papers, RG428, Military Reference Branch, National Archives. This document was the compiled outline material for the navy's presentation.

5. Top Secret [declassified], Limited Distribution, Op-03, (SC)A16-3, Serial: 0097P03, Memorandum For the Secretary of Defense: "Naval Forces for Fiscal Year 1951 Program," 27 July 1949; Box 19, Papers of Arthur W. Radford, Operational Archives, NHC.

6. "Address by Vice Admiral L. D. McCormick, USN, Vice Chief of Naval Operations at the 13th Naval Civilian Orientation Conference at Headquarters, Fifth Naval District, U.S. Naval Base, Norfolk, Virginia, on Friday, 28 April 1950 at 7:30 p.m. (EST)"; speeches folder, Box 3, papers of Lynde D. McCormick, Manuscript Division, Library of Congress.

7. Confidential [declassified], *The Atlantic Commands* Delivered at U. S. Naval War College By Admiral L. D. McCormick, U.S. Navy, 4 October 1951"; Speeches folder, Box 3, Papers of Lynde D. McCormick.

8. Enclosure to Top Secret [declassified], OP-301C1, Ser: 00051P30, "Status of U.S. Programs for National Security as of 31 December 1953," 21 Jan 1954; "1954 Top Secret Spindles 0001 to 000300" folder, 1955 Strategic Plans Division Subject and Serial Files, Operational Archives, NHC.

9. Secret [declassified], OP-343, Ser 00368P34, "New Concept of Amphibious Warfare; requirements for support of," 21 Sep 1955; A3 folder, 1955 Strategic Plans Division Subject and Serial Files, Operational Archives, NHC.

10. "Address By Admiral Arleigh Burke, USN, Chief of Naval Operations, Armed Forces Day—Salt Lake City, Utah—17 May 1961"; "SPEE-8" file, Papers of Admiral Arleigh A. Burke, Operational Archives, NHC.

11. Claude Ricketts, Admiral, U. S. Navy, "Naval Power—Present and Future," U.S. Naval Institute *Proceedings*, vol. 89, no. 1 (January 1963), p. 37.

12. Desmond P. Wilson, *Naval Budget and Cost Constraints: Effect on Ship Force Levels* (Alexandria, VA: Center for Naval Analyses, 1982), p. 23.

13. U.S. Congress, House, *Hearings*, Committee on Armed Services, 92nd Cong., 2d sess, 1972, p. 11415.

14. Elmo R. Zumwalt, Jr., *On Watch: A Memoir* (New York: Quadrangle, The New York Times Book Co., 1976), pp. 337–38.

15. Report to the Congress by the Comptroller General of the United States, *Implications of the National Security Council Study "U.S. Maritime Strategy and Naval Force Requirements" On the Future Naval Ship Force* PSAD 78–6A (Washington, U.S. General Accounting Office, March 7, 1978) *passim*.

16. A report by Chief of Naval Operations Admiral Thomas B. Hayward, U.S. Navy, on *The Fiscal Year 1980 Military Posture and Fiscal Year 1980 Budget of the United States Navy* (Washington, DC: Navy Internal Relations Activity, 1979).

17. *The Maritime Strategy*, Special Supplement to the U.S. Naval Institute *Proceedings*, January, 1986.

BIBLIOGRAPHIC NOTE

In the same special issue of the U. S. Naval Institute *Proceedings* in which Admiral Watkins's article appeared, there was a bibliographical compilation of contemporary U.S. Naval Strategy by Captain Peter M. Swartz. Subsequent to the appearance of that annotated listing, the Naval Institute has published a comprehensive addendum to the bibliography. (At this writing, the U.S. Naval Postgraduate School at Monterey, CA, has undertaken to keep the Swartz bibliography current.) The addendum is broken into twelve areas, including army and air force published views on the strategy, contributions, and views of the allies, Soviet strategy and views, war gaming, antecedents (many of which appear as references in this book), etc. This compilation of materials must be assessed as invaluable to all students of the theory and practice of strategy by maritime forces.

14

Maritime and Continental Strategies: An Important Question of Emphasis

BY ROGER BARNETT

In today's world, how should national leaders go about providing for the security of their state? The question is not merely a variant of "How Much Is Enough," but more fundamentally one of "What should be done and why?" In the past, democracies in particular have found this a vexing question. Striking the balance between satisfying domestic needs and rising expectations on the one hand, and the demands for security from external threats on the other, stands high on the governmental agenda—and probably always will.

Is it guns or is it butter? Can security and welfare be more optimally matched by entering into bilateral international security arrangements, by a network of multilateral alliances, or by avoiding such entanglements altogether? Once national objectives have been agreed upon, should a strategy that relies first and foremost on highly capable maritime forces to secure those objectives be adopted; or, alternatively, should land-based army and air forces receive the major emphasis? Offensive or defensive, counterforce or countervalue, nuclear or conventional, maneuver or attrition—which approach holds the least risk and maximizes the probability of prolonging the peace at the lowest cost? The simple-minded seek to understand complex relationships by narrowing their essence down to binary choices. Those who have responsibility for the process, and who feel the weight of the issues, on the other hand, are more frequently impressed with their richness and durability.

For totalitarian countries the struggle to answer such questions is not nearly so difficult. While democracies take as their goal maximizing the well-being of their citizens, nondemocratic states attempt to maximize governmental power and control over their domestic populations, and also over other sovereign states. The issues appear from time to time, but the totalitarian (or authoritarian) approach to answering them is vastly different from that of free, democratic states.

THE IMPORTANCE OF GEOSTRATEGIC SETTING

In the West, difficult decisions must be faced on a frequently recurring basis, both by individual states and by alliances as a whole. Geostrategic considerations strongly influence choices about national defense. History, geography, economics, and politics, together with a wide menu of other factors, define the range of those strategic decisions. Context is all-important, for without a contextual setting actions can become incomprehensible. Thus, where in the world one lives and the nature of one's government must be considered crucial.

Historically, enemies have tended to be neighbors. This was because the application of force across short distances was considerably less difficult than across long distances. States nearby were familiar, their capabilities could be more easily assessed, access to them was much less complex, and opportunity to take action against them often became irresistible. Until this century, instances of combat at long range against opponents not territorially adjacent were extraordinary. Almost without exception, such conflict took place on the sea or with significant support from seaward. *Seapower permitted geographically widely separated states to reach one another,* some times with commerce, other times with military power. Today air and missile power—accompanied by their individual advantages and shortcomings—offer alternative methods of reach.

While enemies customarily live next door, allies frequently do not. States seek allies to offset or divert the strength of hostile or potentially threatening neighbors. States that have common borders with a third state tend to be natural allies. Moreover, offshore sea powers seek land-power allies against antagonistic land powers, and continental states often ally with sea powers to oppose other sea powers.

Since the time of the Roman Empire no single state has enjoyed preeminence both on land and on the sea. Preeminence in one or the other environments evokes feelings of anxiety or envy on the part of competing powers, and offers the stimulus for counter-coalition. Every superstate that appeared to be first class both on land and sea in reality has been either a sea power with a large and competent army, or a land power with a large and competent navy. It is truly rare, moreover, to find a country that has been in any serious doubt about whether its more pressing dangers—its more dangerous enemies—were on the sea or land. The location and capability of the prime adversary has not always been the strongest determinant of how a country provides for its national security, however. History offers many instances of states fully aware of dire threats to their existence that nevertheless failed to make adequate provision for their own defenses.

Constellations of important considerations about security align themselves not in accordance with some scientific law, but in accordance with national self-interest. Where a state is located in the world influences greatly who its enemies and friends are and will be.

THE IMPORTANCE OF SYSTEMS OF GOVERNMENT

Systems of government also play an important part in influencing a state's security policy. Democracies—driven by pursuit of equality, justice, individual freedom, and liberty—tote extra baggage in international affairs, because they lean toward the end of the spectrum that is more satisfied with the status quo than their nondemocratic counterparts. In the absence of an unequivocal threat, democratic governments find it difficult to give high priority to military requirements in the competition for budgetary resources. Many have noted these characteristics and tendencies. None have put them so eloquently or forcefully as Alfred Thayer Mahan. He wrote, in this regard:

> Whether a democratic government will have the foresight, the keen sensitiveness to national position and credit, the willingness to insure its prosperity by adequate outpouring of money in times of peace, all of which are necessary for military preparation is yet an open question.[1]

The question remains open today.

THE EXAMPLE OF GREAT BRITAIN

> We should be mad to
> entangle ourselves in a
> continental strife on
> land. Our medium is
> the ocean way.
>
> LORD ESHER[2]

For nearly its entire history, the United States has been graced with secure borders and the absence of a threat on land. To invade the continental United States would require an expeditionary force brought across the oceans in ships, for airlift would be insufficient for such a task. Foreseeably, therefore, a direct assault on the territory of the United States with occupation as its objective must come from seaward. In its national security complexion, and in its reliance on offshore sources of raw materials and on commercial relations of global scale, the United States exhibits genuinely insular characteristics. The United States is, in most important ways, an island nation. Throughout its history it has sought to take advantage of its geostrategic insulation against direct aggression. Of late, however, the security problems and stresses of the United States have mirrored those that faced decision makers in another island nation—Great Britain— for centuries: how best to balance the requirements for forward continental defense on the one hand, and for "blue-water" maritime defense on the other. The British example is instructive, and will be examined in some detail.

The dilemma for Great Britain pivoted on the question of how militarily involved it should be in affairs on the European continent, while still paying adequate attention to the direct defense of its home islands. Tending to the demands of maintaining a global empire also complicated the question significantly for policy makers in London. British statesmen had recognized for centuries that hegemonic power on the continent would be life-threatening for British sovereignty. The long-standing British policy of balancing landpower in Europe by means of variable alliance systems, while maintaining superior forces at sea, demonstrated British sensitivity to events on the continental land mass. The most serious debates and internal struggles have arisen for the British when they have been forced to deal with the issue of how to afford an army (an air force, or a strategic missile force, for that matter) with sufficient capability to count as a meaningful weight in the continental balance or to keep wavering allies in the field, while at the same time exercising preeminence at sea.

Some well-intentioned British citizens argued that no occurrences elsewhere in Europe could genuinely endanger British security. Similar voices, and transoceanic echoes of them, can be heard today. Asserting that Britain could not be defeated in Flanders Fields (let alone in faraway places in central Europe with strange-sounding names), they argued that, therefore, land presence on the continent should not be purchased at the expense either of the well-being of the British populace or of other military capability. Some who favored strong emphasis on seapower were explicit in making clear their preference for seapower as an alternative, not as a supplement, to a balance of power policy.

The terrible experience of the First World War resurrected long-standing British prejudices against continental commitments. In this view, the United Kingdom would maintain its independence behind the shield of a Royal Navy that would stave off enemy invasion. Thus, there would be no need to maintain a large army for home defense.

In 1919, in fact, the British War Cabinet decided explicitly *not* to maintain ground forces earmarked for a continental commitment. Mr. Duff Cooper, financial secretary to the War Office, observed in 1933: "The British Army is not designed for Continental wars. The purpose of the British Army is to maintain order in the British Empire only. . . . The Army is not likely to be used for a big war in Europe for many years to come."[3] This decision was not altered until the winter of 1938/39 after Munich, when it was much too late to have either a deterrent effect on Hitler's aggressive designs, or to make much of a difference in the defense of France against the *Blitzkrieg*. Deployment of the British Expeditionary Force to France began in September 1939. By the time of the German attack in May 1940, ten ill-equipped, under-trained British divisions were in place, only to have to be evacuated from channel ports by June 4. British policy, having deliberately opted against a strong continental commitment, had failed.

Subsequent to the war, under the terms of the Brussels treaty of 1948, Britain agreed to provide three divisions and a tactical air force in West Germany, thereby for the first time undertaking a treaty commitment to station troops for forward defense on the continent. As a direct consequence, the British Army on the Rhine currently numbers 55,000—a total that stands unchanged since the commitment was assumed, when British armed forces were significantly larger. This commitment has contributed to the telescoping of the Royal Navy both in size and in capability, to the point where it now has but sixty major surface ships, and fewer than thirty submarines, manned by 70,000 sailors. Prospects for near-term rejuvenation of the Royal Navy are not promising, for it has become amply clear that such a large presence on the continent has been maintained deliberately in order not to provide an example that might prompt the reduction of *U.S.* forces there, and some of the bill has been paid at the expense of the navy. Today a superior Royal Navy sailing in all the world's oceans and the glories of empire are both only fading memories.

After the turn of the century, Britain continued to be whipsawed between the need to provide for the Royal Navy, to secure the empire, and to defend the home islands. It was able to perform each only marginally. The Royal Navy, in retrospect, peaked as a fighting instrument at Trafalgar, and has been in decline ever since. The empire is no more, but the continental commitment and, more recently, an independent nuclear capability have received the lion's share of the United Kingdom's expenditures for national security. All things considered, there was never enough money allocated to the British armed forces to accomplish everything that appeared to be necessary, and Britain made her choices.

APPLICATION TO THE UNITED STATES

The security environment of the United States exhibits many features in common with the British situation and experience. An off-shore sea power, it faces a powerful continental Eurasian hegemonic empire. The United States therefore requires, as Britain did in so many instances before it,

- *Continental allies and military presence on the continent* to offer a purchase with which to grapple Soviet landpower; and
- Sufficient *seapower* to enable it to conduct mutually beneficial commerce with its overseas allies in peacetime, facilitate their support and reinforcement in time of war, and project military power inland from seaward axes.

This sets up a dialectic similar to the one that caused British governments great anguish for centuries. It has become an issue in the United States only over the past four decades—since the formation of the North Atlantic Treaty Organization (NATO).

The debate hinges on the budgetary emphasis that should be given to one or the other side of the discussion. At its roots this is an economic argument: for what purpose scarce resources are to be spent. The lines of the current debate are fairly easily drawn, and comprehended. They polarize around, and are summarized below as "schools" of thought without attribution, for they are not the views of any single person, but of a mind-set.

THE CONTINENTAL SCHOOL

The so-called "continental school" argues that control over land area is the organizing principle of nation-states and politics. Man lives on the land, not in the sea, and control of the land far supersedes in importance control over maritime areas or lines of communication. In historical perspective, conflict has taken place almost exclusively with control over territory as the stake in the contest.

The situation on the Eurasian landmass today is one in which the Soviet Union enjoys control of Mackinder's geopolitical heartland, fields massive conventional and nuclear-armed military forces, and maintains a political system and philosophy that is hostile to Western political structures and values. To resist the powerful flux fields of Soviet power, and to prevent the Soviet leadership either from engaging in military adventures or from attempting to intimidate its adversaries requires strength on land, at every possible point of attack. Obvious weakness in ground forces and supporting air forces in the center of Europe risks sending to the Soviet Union and its allies the unintended and inappropriate message that NATO will not stoutly resist aggression.

Land strength, manifested by armies and air forces, sufficient to provide the counterweight to Soviet might cannot be provided by any Western country acting alone; coalition is required. The alliance must be bound firmly together, offering the appearance of unshakeable indivisibility. As Article 5 of the North Atlantic Treaty demands, NATO must be seen as "all for one and one for all."[4]

The military balance on the land is unfavorable to NATO, and has been so throughout its history. The ratio of fully reinforced ground forces in the NATO/Warsaw Treaty Organization (WTO) area favors the East by 1.3 to 1. In tanks, the cutting edge of landpower and the basic instrument of rapid exploitation of surprise attack, the advantage is more than 2:1 in favor of the WTO and growing. On almost every static index—artillery, surface-to-surface missiles, anti-tank weapons, armed helicopters, surface-to-air missile launchers, and tactical aircraft, to name the most important—the WTO is preponderant. Of course, such indicators do not provide a reliable measure of fighting strength, which is a product of material and less tangible but very important factors such as leadership, morale, geography, doctrine, strategic and tactical warning, mobilization rates, command and control, and quality of weapons. Nevertheless, it is clear and has been clear since the formation of the two opposing coalitions that the Warsaw Pact enjoys superiority in conventional weapons.

In the face of this imbalance, the NATO alliance does not have the option of trading distance for time. Fully 30 percent of the population of West Germany and 25 percent of its industrial capacity are situated within 100 kilometers of the inter-German boundary. Because of the demographic situation, the alliance's defense must be very strong and as far forward as possible.

Over time the Western allies have sought to make major improvements to the conventional force posture of the alliance. Probably the most famous of these was the agreement reached in 1952 to attain a strength of ninety-six divisions by 1954. That goal was unrealistic when it was adopted, and other force objectives soon replaced it. Political impediments, which differ for each country of the alliance, have generally prevented full realization of the improvements that have been sought.

Concurrently, the Eastern Bloc has been improving its conventional warfare capability and altering its own doctrine. Whereas twenty years ago Soviet spokesmen were averring that any war that involved the two opposing coalitions must necessarily be a nuclear war, more recently they have been suggesting that that need not necessarily be so. A conventional phase, in fact a prolonged conventional phase, is now said to be possible. Even though the NATO strategy of flexible response does not require meeting the threat with comparable capability across the board, the large and growing shortfall in Western conventional strength must be redressed if deterrence is to continue to be effective, especially in view of the shift of Soviet warfighting emphasis.

Most distressing and frightening is the mounting Soviet capability to carry out a "lightning" thrust through NATO defenses, the momentum and impact of which could deal NATO a crippling blow before it could react; that is, before reinforcement plans could take effect. Conventional forces need toughness up front to give reinforcements a chance to attain full fighting potential.

The ground and air elements also need staying power—not just for days, but for weeks and months. Prepositioning of equipment for six U.S. divisions on the continent, and the airlift to bring the troops to marry up with that materiel must not be squandered by an ineffective forward defense. A sustained ability to fight will add greatly in *deterring* the *Blitzkrieg*. It is not sought out of an interest in waging a protracted conventional war in central Europe, but to ensure that such a war will never be fought.

In the face of such imbalances in conventional forces, the credibility of NATO strategy hinges on the threat by the allies to use nuclear weapons to offset conventional weaknesses relative to Soviet and Warsaw Pact strengths. This reliance on escalation to nuclear use has remained high over the years, but it has been devalued by a growing fear of nuclear weapon use, which itself has been accelerated by the fact of strategic nuclear parity between the United States and the Soviet Union. Moreover, the quantitative edge in nuclear and chemical weapons is also held by the Eastern Bloc. In brief, erosion of the credibility of first nuclear use to compensate for conventional force weakness undermines in a very serious way the very foundation of NATO strategy. All signposts point to the only sensible corrective to this very dangerous and worsening situation: conventional fighting force must be improved, and conventional doctrines must be adopted to take maximum advantage of new capabilities acquired and new technologies adopted.

A war between the two blocs that originates in Europe should be confined to Europe, in the continentalist view. Efforts to take the war elsewhere reduce the forces available to the Western allies for the war in the center, and thus incur high risks of failure to defend the principal object of the war. To suggest that pin pricks on his flanks or rear will distract an aggressor and keep him from pursuing his primary objective with determination is to misunderstand the situation—perhaps fatally. Moreover, even if military actions at places other than the point of attack might appear attractive, the West does not have sufficient forces—either on the land or seaborne—to attempt to pursue multiple actions simultaneously in geographically separate areas. In fact, with the advantages of interior lines, excess forces, and many targets from which to choose, the Kremlin enjoys a larger agenda of useful options for employing this strategic technique—sometimes called horizontal escalation—against the West than the other way around. Consequently, proponents of this school conclude, starting a campaign elsewhere to distract an aggressor or to keep him from shifting forces to the main arena of war would act to the net disadvantage of NATO. Sequential, rather than simultaneous, action is the best that can be hoped for by NATO. Thus, the West has no choice but to keep its attention and effort locked firmly on the center of Europe, the area where defeat would equate to disaster.

Of all the important countries in the world, the continentalists maintain, the Soviet Union is perhaps the most impervious and insensitive to attack from seaward. While, for example, no place in the United States is farther than 1,500 kilometers from the ocean, Soviet strategic depth is on the order of 3,300 km. No allied sea-based weapons, other than strategic ballistic missiles, can reach targets deep in the Soviet homeland. The Soviets maintain very powerful coastal defenses and forces capable of attacking sea-based adversaries in three dimensions. Thick Soviet air defenses would be formidable in thwarting any air-breathing attack.

Forty-five important U.S. cities, with a total population of 75 million people lie within 850 kilometers of the hundred-fathom curve at sea, while the comparable figure for the Soviet Union is but six important cities with a population of 2.2 million. Thus, vulnerability from the sea is asymmetrical, and to the Soviet advantage. Economically, the Soviet Union stands as one of the most self-sufficient countries in the world; it has virtually no critical dependence on international trade, either for imports or exports.

In brief, by virtue of its geographic gifts—strategic depth and natural resources—the Soviet Union is relatively immune to the kind of pressure maritime forces can bring to bear. For these reasons, and because the Soviet Union maintains exceptionally powerful military capability to negate the effect of attacks from the sea, the continentalist school argues that power projection from the sea other than by strategic submarines is potentially very expensive in terms of high-cost military hardware that might be lost, excessively risky, and cannot deliver strategically significant blows to the adversary.

Even if the Soviet fleet and all the ships of its allies could be decisively defeated—literally swept from the seas—that fact could not guarantee that allied forces would prevail ashore. The West could be supreme at sea and still lose the war. Therefore, in continentalist logic, a maritime emphasis to Western strategy conveys to its allies a deep-seated desire on the part of the United States to reduce its commitment to support land war on the continent, which is a retrograde movement toward isolationism and an implicit unwillingness to bear the burdens of alliance. This is frequently referred to as the "sin of unilateralism."

While few voices are raised to appeal for greater U.S. military force presence in central Europe, all continentalists agree that much more can be done qualitatively and in terms of operational doctrine to improve the effectiveness of forward defenses. At the same time they urge resistance to force *reductions* in Europe in the strongest terms. Such reductions, first proposed by Senator Mike Mansfield in 1966, reappear from time to time, as Americans become impatient with the apparent foot-dragging of allies. More recently, legislation was introduced by Senators Nunn and Roth to withdraw up to 90,000 U.S. troops over three years if the allies did not improve their conventional force capability. Continentalists rebut such efforts both by arguing the merits of the case, and by drawing attention to the fact that if forces were to be withdrawn it would be at greater, not lesser, cost to the U.S. taxpayer. This is so because, according to the U.S. Secretary of Defense:

> A withdrawal of 100,000 U.S. personnel from Europe would incur one-time costs of $500 million for transporting the forces home. Renovating or constructing new facilities for them in the United States would cost another $4.7 billion. . . .
>
> If we were to withdraw a force of 100,000 from Europe, we would, under our current rapid-reinforcement policy, need the capability to return it there in ten days or less. The least expensive way to do this would be to buy a second set of equipment for prepositioning and enough airlift to move residual equipment. This would cost about $20 to $25 billion. . . .

Alternatively, returning the entire force and its equipment by air would require over 1,000 additional aircraft at a cost of around $100 billion. But, we probably could not operate such a large number of additional aircraft on already overcrowded European airfields.[5]

The program of those who argue for emphasis on land-based forces in Europe involves increased defense outlays on conventional forces by *all* allies, improved rationalized burden-sharing, closer alliance co-operation, and more host-nation support for allied forces. Much of this, continentalists are not reluctant to suggest, might be supported by reductions in the allocations provided to maritime forces.

THE MARITIME SCHOOL

The logic of the maritime school pivots on a conviction that to deter a Soviet attack in Europe one must do more than threaten to halt the advance of Warsaw Pact armies on the ground in West Germany. Put another way, why should Soviet leaders be persuaded not to attack merely by the prospect that their army might be stalemated on West German, French, Belgian, Dutch, or Danish territory? If that were the only deterrent, aggressors might well judge the risks to be acceptable, especially if they calculate that they have a confident advantage in military power, and stand a reasonable chance of success. Which is to say, would the Soviets be deterred if there was reasonable prospect for gain, and little possibility of losing?

Rather, asserts the maritime school, to deter adequately one is obliged to threaten Soviet core values. Offering a stout defense at the point of attack constitutes only one of the elements of which the deterrent fabric is made. The whole cloth has several more threads: namely, the prospect to the attacker that the conflict he ignites might not turn out to be what he planned for in terms of *intensity, geographic scope,* or *length.* Deterrence depends not merely on maintaining strength where attacks might occur, but threatening to alter the war in its various dimensions: violence, breadth, and time. Stable, confident deterrence requires that an aggressor be faced with either probable outcomes or risks that are clearly unacceptable to him. This, the maritime school maintains, a continental emphasis cannot achieve.

An appropriate historical example lends concreteness to the abstraction: the origins of the Second World War. In 1940 Hitler was not deterred from attacking westward by the large and capable allied ground and air forces opposing him on the continent. What then of the other threads in the fabric of deterrence? With regard to the *intensity* of the war, Hitler believed that dimension was his to modulate. Even though he made blunders that eventually caused his defeat, at the initiation of war he alone controlled the magnitude of combat. His expectations were that England could be neutralized by diplomatic means, that he could subdue the Soviet Union, and that the United States would not provide support in sufficient time or amount to make a difference.

As far as *geographic scope*, Hitler's assessment prior to invading France was that his rear was secured by the conquest of Poland and Czechoslovakia, and by treaty with the Russians. His strategic left flank was fortified by a combination of geography, weakness, and alliance with Italy, and he took the precaution of invading and gaining control of Norway on his right flank before attacking in the center. His demonstrated appreciation for the importance of secure flanks and rear illustrates that if there is a perception that they might *not* be secure, the decision to attack must be much more problematical.

The *time dimension* was also, Hitler felt, both in his favor and under his sway. The swiftness and success of *Wehrmacht* attacks right to the English Channel did nothing to disabuse him of that conviction. Whether the conflict should be prolonged or quick in its termination was to be entirely under his control. It should be understood that if he did not believe that he could control the time lines of war, deterrence against attack in the first place would have been buttressed.

Maritime strategists suggest that whatever allied forces on the ground and in the air over Central Europe can accomplish forms but the first of the threads of deterrence: meeting force with force at the point of attack. Yet, there is no disagreement that NATO's conventional forces are weaker than those of the WTO, and the long-standing option to raise the ante by the first use of nuclear weapons *while necessary* has become more and more unattractive over time. Even the continental school admits that parity has eroded the credibility of U.S. action at the strategic level—that is, a response to a ground attack in Europe by employing strategic nuclear weapons against the Soviet homeland. In the face of current Soviet dominance at every level of nuclear and chemical warfare, threatened escalation to the use of nuclear weapons to offset conventional force deficiencies offers important benefits by increasing Soviet risks and uncertainties. Accordingly, the deterrent effect of tactical nuclear weapons is important and should be retained. But if deterrence were to fail nonetheless, the prospect of actually using nuclear weapons in West Germany would be very daunting. In addition, nuclear phobia on the part of European populations, which has been present since the very beginning of the alliance, has intensified in recent years. This undercuts the credibility of the threat of nuclear use to compensate for conventional force deficiencies.

One is forced to conclude, therefore, that even the deterrent leverage in the threat of escalation no longer carries the weight it once did. Neither conventional force weakness nor nuclear escalation are compelling deterrents, asserts the maritime school. Therefore, establishing and maintaining concerns on the part of Soviet planners that they could not control the course or the duration of a war have taken on fresh importance as important pillars of deterrence. Prospects to alter the geographic scope and duration of war lie largely within the province of maritime forces.

NATO defense policy, in maritime perspective, must recognize that weakness on the flanks might well precipitate collapse in the center. Norway, Iceland, the Danish Straits, and NATO's Mediterranean states prevent Soviet forces from outflanking NATO defenses. This is important since, to offer a single example, if the Soviets were to secure control of Iceland they could bring severe pressure to bear on the Atlantic sea lanes. Soviet submarines would be offered significantly easier access to allied shipping; Soviet attack aviation could range deep into oceanic areas to which it has only very restricted access without forward basing. An additional complication resides in the fact that about a third of all supporting air strikes into the NATO central region are planned to originate in Britain. If Iceland, or if airfields in Norway or North Africa for that matter, became available for use by Soviet tactical air power, or if Soviet submarines were accorded free exit to the Atlantic, it would be extremely difficult to carry out the transoceanic operations crucial to successful allied defense on the continent.

While it is true that the United States has prepositioned equipment for six divisions in Europe (the troops would arrive by airlift in the early days of a war), subsequent re-supply for the ten (four in-place and six reinforcing) divisions of U.S. forces in Europe must come by sea. Millions of tons of supplies and millions of gallons of petroleum products will be needed to support the war effort, even if the conflict lasts only a few months. Nearly all of this re-supply, 95 percent or more, must be transported in ships. There are no other possibilities.

No one *desires* a long war, no doubt including the aggressor. The central argument, therefore, is that to deter war the alliance must be prepared, among other things, to prolong it. Demonstrating sensitivity to the security of the flanks, and making preparations to secure them in time of war sends a signal to aggressors that the price of attempts to wrest the flanks from their defenders will be high.

Looked at from the offensive, rather than the defensive, point of view, the flanks offer options to take advantage of the strength of the offensive form of warfare at sea. If the WTO attacks NATO in Central Europe, it would be because that is where the Soviets and their allies prefer to fight. Obviously, the initiator of conflict will not choose to open the fighting in an arena unfavorable to him. It makes strategic sense, therefore, to force aggressors to deal with military actions that are not in times or places of their own choosing, once they have started the war. Taking the fight to the Soviet fleet by keeping it bottled up in its own home waters, raising the prospect of power-projection operations from seaward against the Russian homeland, sinking out-of-area Soviet warships and merchantmen, and raising the prospect of destruction of elements of Soviet sea-based strategic nuclear forces—all these provide ways to improve deterrence, compared to the continentalist promise only to stalemate invading armies on allied territory. All these possibilities, moreover, stem from Western preponderance in maritime forces.

Proponents of maritime emphasis in U.S. and NATO strategy contend that conditions today are significantly different than at the onset of World War II, and that that must be taken into account. By the time the United States entered that war, German submarines were operating freely in the Atlantic. The U.S. Navy was unprepared to deal with the submarine threat, and took a long time to obtain the forces and develop the strategy necessary to combat it. As a consequence, early in the war Allied forces at sea were able only to follow defensive courses. Conditions today, on the other hand, favor strong, early offensive action by maritime forces.

NATO seapower, led by the U.S. Navy, must seek to exploit the advantage it has at sea. No one suggests that NATO can or should attempt to match WTO ground and air capability on the continent. Some inferiority in force levels is expected to persist, and there are no plans to alter that fact in the future. It would seem to be the height of folly, therefore, to fritter away the one area of relative strength the alliance enjoys, while not establishing any other area through which leverage might be gained.

In the end analysis, the maritime school maintains, continental defense should rest more squarely on the shoulders of the European allies. Not only has the strategic situation changed markedly since the time the alliance was forged, but the economic situation has also altered in ways not fully appreciated. When NATO was formed in 1949, the gross national product (GNP) of the United States was on the order of that of the rest of the world combined. Now, *not counting the United States*, the other fifteen countries of NATO have a greater gross national product than the entire Warsaw Pact, *including* the Soviet Union. Today the United States spends over 6 percent of its GNP on defense; its NATO allies average about half that.

Over 350,000 United States servicemen and women in Europe—along with over 300,000 military dependents—provide more than a token U.S. involvement and commitment. We have either lost sight of or forgotten that the original military plan for NATO, the "unified defense plan" of 1949–50, was constructed so that individual special capabilities of the allies could be emphasized, not duplicated. Thus, the primary U.S. contribution was to be in the form of strategic air power and seapower, the continental states would emphasize land forces, and Britain and France would specialize in tactical air power. Later, the 1967 "flexible response" concept was predicated on maintaining a minimum force on the continent and a large reserve of conventional forces that could be used wherever they were needed in the world. Marginal dollars for conventional defense in Europe should be contributed by the allies, and the United States should concentrate on and emphasize the area in which it has both a *survival* interest, and a current and inherent advantage—seapower.

The argument with the ring of finality employed by the maritime school is this: Certainly the United States intends to assist with and provide significant forces for a vigorous defense in Central Europe, including options for the first use of nuclear weapons: *to lose in Europe would be a calamity.* But for the United States, and as demonstrated in the past, losing on the continent need not be the end of the war. If, however, the United States were to lose at sea as the allies were losing ashore, that would be the ultimate disaster short of a strategic nuclear exchange. Remember, exhorts the maritime school:

- Defending West Germany is more than defending Bavaria and Hesse;
- Defending Central Europe is more than defending West Germany;
- Defending Western Europe is more than defending Central Europe;
- Defending NATO is more than defending Western Europe;
- Defending the free world is more than defending Western Europe;
- U.S. national strategy involves more than just defending the free world.

SYNTHESIS

As is the usual case in arguments with only two poles or nodes, arguments tend to be oversimple, overheated, and overdrawn. Frequently, in the rush to score debating points, the schools—or those who attribute certain positions to the two schools—approach caricature. Thus, the continental school would appear to devalue Soviet strategy, ignore the essential elements of deterrence, focus myopically on NATO's center, elevate NATO defense above more narrow vital U.S. defense interests, and be unwilling to provide adequately either for at-sea dimensions for defense of the continent or for defense of the territory of the United States itself. The maritime persuasion would seem almost willing to lose on the ground in Germany or even farther westward; to be rash in its insistence on risky, low-payoff forward operations early in a war; indifferent to the threat of the use of nuclear weapons at sea and to the asymmetry between the two sides regarding nuclear employment; and reliant on strategic maritime depth as a cushion for U.S. security, narrowly defined.

Each should acknowledge, instead, that maritime and continental forces in the context of NATO defense must be thought about and planned for as complementary, not competing. The question truly at issue for debate is the proper mix of conventional forces at the margin, not a simplistic binary choice between the two. Neither could succeed without the other. Indeed, the maritime school acknowledges that maritime power is necessary but not sufficient for victory, which must be earned on the ground, while the continental school recognizes the importance of controlling the seas to success on the continental European battlefield.

To be sure, the arguments are never open and shut. While both recognize that the preponderance of strength on the ground lies with the Warsaw Pact forces, in fact, there is genuine disagreement among reasonable men as to whether NATO's conventional capability is or is not currently adequate. There is ample room for debate on how conventional forces might be improved, or even whether important improvement is possible or needed. Some analysts are convinced that the alliance today, because of the defender's advantage and the superior morale of its forces, could win a conventional war in Europe.

Those who insist that rejuvenating U.S. maritime strength in the form of the 600-ship navy has been undertaken at the expense of the ground and air forces are hard-pressed to demonstrate their case in terms of how defense funds have been allocated and spent. Over the past decade service budget shares have been noteworthy in their lack of large fluctuations. As the accompanying figure shows, the army's share of the defense budget has remained between 24 percent and 25.8 percent; for the navy the respective figures are 31.7 percent to 34.1 percent; for the air force, 27.9 percent to 35.8 percent.

More surprising, perhaps, is the fact that the navy was relatively better off in the Carter administration than in the Reagan administra-

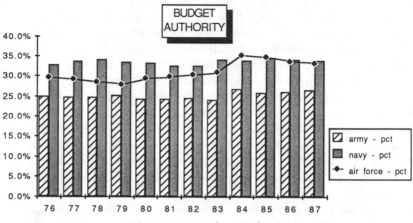

Figure 14-1. Budget Authority.

tion. Additionally, possibilities for major change do not loom large in the immediate future. The debate will be inflated again before too long, however, by the very important issue of aircraft-carrier replacement, because nine large-deck U.S. aircraft carriers will reach the end of their forty-five-year service life by the year 2006.

In point of fact, both NATO and the WTO have demonstrated greater understanding and desire for employing combined arms, and interest and activity have waxed on both sides for unity in strategic doctrine and operational command. The chief of naval operations and his Soviet counterpart mirror one another's thinking in this regard.

Given improved Soviet capabilities and interest in adventures outside the NATO area, there may be little choice for the alliance but to seek a different burden-sharing arrangement. Although frequently one hears arguments about the importance and value of out-of-area operations for NATO forces, except when disaster strikes, such as the Iraqi attack on the USS *Stark* in the Persian Gulf, few voices are raised that the NATO countries (or Japan, for that matter) ought to assume a much larger burden of countering Soviet thrusts elsewhere in the world. That responsibility devolves primarily on the United States, and essentially on the navy. Likewise, the allies are quick to point out that they provide the lion's share of the manpower, the tanks, the artillery, and the combat aircraft for the defense of NATO. The overwhelming predominance of naval power comes from the United States, however. It is as natural and necessary that the allies should look first toward continental defense, as it is understandable and inarguable that they will not increase their maritime forces substantially—especially in peacetime. Of course, this means not at all, for highly capable naval forces can be acquired only in peacetime. Therefore, the primary responsibility for countering burgeoning Soviet maritime capability will fall on the United States.

The NATO allies appear content to tolerate the occasional carping of the U.S. government—and the disconcerting but only marginally credible threats within the Congress to reduce the number of U.S. fighting men in Europe—rather than increase significantly their allocations for European defense. Yet, the U.S. military commitment to the European Command (EUCOM) area has fluctuated widely over the years in ways difficult to reconcile with the prevailing strategy. Record high troop levels were recorded in 1953, when 427,000 U.S. military personnel were stationed in EUCOM. Since the buildup began in 1951, the low level was 291,000 (because of the Vietnam War) in 1970. The total costs of U.S. involvement in NATO have been very difficult even for the government to estimate, but respectable estimates range from about $120 billion to $150 billion per year, or roughly half the U.S. defense budget. The argument, and the congressional focus as a consequence, centers not on the need for a continental commitment, but on its size and function, on opportunity costs, and on alternative investment for the funds. Indeed, the uniqueness of the U.S. forward commitment to NATO lies in its longevity—it has never been rationalized as a permanent commitment, but a temporary one until the allies could undertake their own defense against a very powerful Soviet presence in Eastern Europe—and in its large size as a peacetime force.

The continental allies are also genuinely torn between their sincere concern over the possible use of nuclear weapons in the event of war and the unattractive prospect of a prolonged conventional war should NATO's conventional warfighting capability be substantially improved. It is also unusual that the contention is made, in the United States or abroad, that either the Europeans or the United States intend to alter their contributions to the common defense in a way that will substantially improve conventional defense on the central front or on the flanks. There have been no suggestions that NATO seeks to match Warsaw Pact capability there; such a goal is invariably labeled "unattainable."

In fact, the prospects of even modest increases in the contributions of allies for conventional defense are generally considered to be poor, which provides fuel to the debate over the question of the disproportionately modest contribution of the allies and their willingness to remain in a dependency status so long as "Uncle Sugar" is content to foot the bill. As a consequence, arguments that suggest that reduced naval spending by the United States will somehow transform itself into tanks for the defense of West Germany and stimulate the allies into greater efforts for their own defense have a hollow ring.

Unattainable also are a set of defense options for NATO that have been ruled out on political grounds. The geographic maldeployment of allied forces in West Germany has long been recognized as a major deficiency in defense against invasion, but redeployment to more defensible lines and positions has been politically unacceptable to West Germany. Forward barriers and fortifications offer the prospect of absorbing much of the shock of invasion with passive means, and thereby improving deterrence. They are also not possible for political reasons. The West German government does not wish to erect physical or psychological barriers to German reunification. Enhanced radiation weapons carry the promise of blunting an armored blitz, and thereby shoring up considerably the forward defenses by innovative use of technology. Such weapons also have the advantage of causing very little collateral damage: it would not be necessary to destroy Germany in order to save it. While enhanced radiation weapons would be militarily very effective, their deployment was the subject of great political unrest in the late 1970s, and the option was dropped. Once again politics intervened to thwart a promising military option. Finally, the concept of a retaliatory conventional ground-forces offensive into WTO territory in an effort to break Soviet control over East Germany has also met with strong objection.[6]

The competition between the opposing blocs, one led by the United States and the other by the Soviet Union, is systemic and enduring. The question for the United States is not whether it should resist Soviet power but where and how. If the United States accepts the necessity to think and fight better than its adversaries, rather than relying on overpowering them, then it must be willing to spend its defense dollars where they promise the greatest return. Should the options listed in the preceding paragraph all be truly unattainable for political reasons, the navy, with its maritime strategy, has some very convincing arguments to bring to the debate and some very powerful stakes to drive in claiming budget dollars at the margin. The allies must be counted on to understand and to act in their own interests by making the necessary sacrifices to provide for adequate deterrence, and if necessary the defense of their homelands. For in the final analysis it is true that: "The preservation of a free Europe is vital to American security, but American power is vital to European survival."[7]

NOTES

1. Mahan, *The Influence of Sea Power Upon History*, 1660–1783 (London: Methuen, 1965), p. 67.

2. Quoted in Michael Howard, *The Continental Commitment* (London: Temple Smith, 1972), p. 49.

3. Quoted in Harold W. Rood, *Kingdoms of the Blind: How the Great Democracies Have Resumed the Follies that So Nearly Cost Them Their Life* (Durham: Carolina Academic Press, 1980), p. 42.

4. Article 5 reads, in its entirety: "The Parties agree that an armed attack against one or more of them in Europe or North America shall be considered an attack against them all, and consequently they agree that, if such an armed attack occurs, each of them, in exercise of the right of individual or collective self-defence recognized by Article 51 of the Charter of the United Nations, will assist the Party or Parties so attacked by taking forthwith, individually, and in concert with the other Parties, such action as it deems necessary, including the use of armed force, to restore and maintain the security of the North Atlantic area.

"Any such armed attack and all measures taken as a result thereof shall immediately be reported to the Security Council. Such measures shall be terminated when the Security Council has taken the measures necessary to restore and maintain international peace and security."

5. Caspar Weinberger, Secretary of Defense, *Remarks before the Denver Rotary Club*, 22 January 1987, mimeo., p. 8.

6. The concept was most lucidly set forth by Samuel P. Huntington in his "Conventional Deterrence and Conventional Retaliation in Europe," *International Security* (Winter 1983/84), pp. 32–56.

7. Eliot A. Cohen, "The Long-Term Crisis of the Alliance," *Foreign Affairs* (Winter 1982/3), p. 328.

BIBLIOGRAPHIC NOTE

Factoring out authors into two "schools," such as those described in this chapter, is fundamentally an arbitrary undertaking. It is far safer to indicate "leanings." Those works that "lean" toward the "continentalist" school include Robert Komer, *Maritime Strategy or Coalition Defense?* (Cambridge, MA: Abt Books, 1984); Keith A. Dunn and Colonel William O. Staudenmaier, USA, *Strategic Implications of the Continental-Maritime Debate*, Washington Paper #107 (Washington: Center for Strategic and International Studies, 1984); Senator Gary Hart and William S. Lind, *America Can Win: The Case for Military Reform* (Bethesda, MD: Adler & Adler, 1986, pp. 77–81); John Mearshimer, "A Strategic Misstep: The Maritime Strategy and Deterrence in Europe," *International Security* (Fall 1986), pp. 3–57; and Barry Posen, "Inadvertent Nuclear War?: Escalation and NATO's Northern Flank," *International Security* (Fall, 1982), pp. 158–66.

The maritime school is amply represented in: testimony by the secretary of the navy and the chief of naval operations, U.S. House of Representatives,

Committee on Armed Services, Seapower, and Strategic and Critical Materials Subcommittee, 99th. Congress, 1st. session, *Hearings: The 600-Ship Navy and the Maritime Strategy* (Washington: Government Printing Office, 1986); Admiral James D. Watkins, USN, "The Maritime Strategy," and Secretary of the Navy John F. Lehman, Jr., "The 600-Ship Navy," both in U.S. Naval Institute *Proceedings* (January 1986 supplement). Francis J. West, Jr., *Naval Forces and Western Security* (Washington: Pergamon-Brassey's, 1986); Colin S. Gray, "Maritime Strategy," U.S. Naval Institute *Proceedings* (February, 1986), pp. 34–42; Captain Linton Brooks, USN, "Naval Power and National Security: The Case for the Maritime Strategy," *International Security* (Fall, 1986), pp. 58–87; and Seth Cropsey, "Forward Defense or Maginot Line? The Maritime Strategy and its Alternatives," *Policy Review* (Fall, 1986), pp. 40–46.

ADDITIONAL SOURCES

Arkin, William M. and David Chappell. "Forward Offensive Strategy: Raising the Stakes in the Pacific." *World Policy Journal* (Summer 1985), pp. 481–500.

Cohen, Eliot A. "Do We Still Need Europe?" *Commentary* (January 1986), pp. 28–35.

Connell, John. *The New Maginot Line.* New York: Arbor House, 1986.

Friedman, Norman, "U.S. Maritime Strategy." *International Defense Review*, 7/1985, pp. 15–25.

Epstein, Joshua M. *The 1987 Defense Budget.* Washington: The Brookings Institution, 1986.

George, James L., ed. *The U.S. Navy: The View from the Mid-1980s.* Boulder, CO: Westview Press, 1985.

Gray, Colin S. "Keeping the Soviets Landlocked: Geostrategy for a Maritime America." *The National Interest* (Summer 1986), pp. 24–36.

———. *Maritime Strategy, Geopolitics, and the Defense of the West.* New York: National Strategy Information Center, 1986.

Kaufmann, William W. *The 1986 Defense Budget.* Washington: The Brookings Institution, 1985.

Lehman, John F., Jr. *Maritime Strategy in the Defense of NATO.* Washington: Center for Strategic and International Studies, 1986.

Oliver, James K., and James A. Nathan. "Concepts, Continuity, and Change." In Stephen Cimbala, ed., *The Reagan Defense Program: An Interim Assessment.* Wilmington, DE: Scholarly Resources, 1986, pp. 1–22.

Stefanick, Tom A. "America's Maritime Strategy—The Arms Control Implications." *Arms Control Today* (December 1986), pp. 10–17.

Turner, Admiral Stansfield, USN (Ret.). "U.S. Naval Policy," *Naval Forces* (III/85), pp. 15–25.

Wettern, Desmond. "Maritime Strategy: Change or Decay." *Navy International* (May 1986), pp. 304–8.

Reflections

BY COLIN S. GRAY AND ROGER W. BARNETT

THEORY AND PRACTICE ACROSS THE CENTURIES

With the important exceptions of the introduction and the chapters in Part I on "The Basics," this book has been designed to present the entire fabric of maritime strategy rather than just the theory of maritime strategy. In the center section, an historical approach was adopted in order to root important ideas in the actual experience of war. Theory, however, is important. In the words of a famous passage by Karl von Clausewitz:

> A specialist who has spent half his life trying to master every aspect of some obscure subject is surely more likely to make headway [in understanding that subject] than a man who is trying to master it in a short time. Theory exists so that one need not start afresh each time sorting out the material and plowing through it, but will find it ready to hand and in good order. It is meant to educate the mind of the future commander, or, more accurately, to guide him in his self-education, not to accompany him to the battlefield.[1]

A little earlier in his masterwork, Clausewitz claims that:

> Theory . . . becomes a guide to anyone who wants to learn about war from books; it will light his way, ensure his progress, train his judgment, and help him to avoid pitfalls.[2]

Nevertheless, war is a truly unique activity. Maritime strategy can be studied usefully across many historical periods, notwithstanding the obvious changes in technology and identity of the leading participants. The reason for this assertion has been well expressed by Michael Howard.

> If there are no wars in the present in which the professional soldier, sailor, or airman can learn his trade, he is almost compelled to study the wars of the past. For after all allowances have been made for historical differences, wars still resemble each other more than they resemble any other human activity. All are fought, as Clausewitz insisted, in a special element of danger and fear and confusion. In all, larger bodies of men are trying to impose their will on one another by violence; and in all, events occur which are inconceivable in any other field of experience.[3]

Maritime strategy must be approached vicariously through books because:

- As Howard observed, there is a benign shortage of contemporary war on a major scale of a kind most relevant to naval professionals;
- The practice of war at sea is the realm of tactics. First-hand experience with genuinely strategic responsibilities for, and problems bearing upon, the conduct of maritime conflict is always confined to a relatively small number of staff officers and an even smaller number of senior admirals, and;
- The direct experience of any one person with strategic issues is infinitesimal in comparison to the historical record of maritime strategy accessible through the written word.

Still, in two key senses one cannot learn maritime strategy from books. First, studies of maritime strategy, whether they be theoretical or historical in form, cannot function as *"manual*[s] for action," or cookbooks.[4] Changing technologies alter tactics which, in their turn, affect the range of practicable options in strategy. This is not to say that today's naval officer cannot learn from Francis Drake, Horatio Nelson, or Chester Nimitz. But it is to say that he is not going to learn the proper operational way to fight his ship, his squadron, or his fleet. Second, even if maritime strategy could be taught as a "manual for action," human and material considerations function as critical modifiers. A navy can train as realistically as it is able for prospective excellence in war, but the "friction" unique to war can be comprehended fully only by the actual experience of war.[5] As Wayne Hughes emphasizes in his chapter, a superior maritime strategy will be of little avail if the men who must fight, and their ships, cannot generate superior fighting power. Furthermore, it is no criticism of strategic theory to recognize that strategy is a pragmatic art practiced by fallible human beings.

To some extent, judgment can be taught—certainly the basis upon which it is founded can be educated. To an important degree, however, strategic judgment is a matter of personal character, which cannot be taught. A thorough education in the theory and historical application of maritime strategy can be helpful to those navy professionals who need to understand the purposes to which their ships and aircraft may be put. The successful practice of maritime strategy, however, cannot be guaranteed to follow from careful study. There is no known correlation in history between mastery of the theory of war and mastery on the battlefield, success in campaigns, or victory in war as a whole. Military theory is not so much a body of knowledge to be taught and learned as it is a set of living questions with assorted answers. Strategic theory, for the sea as for the land and the air, is empirical, founded more upon the record of what has worked in action than upon logic and the application of some alleged "first principles."

The ten themes identified in the introduction were specified because the editors believe that they each would appear, on the historical evidence, to have enduring merit. These themes say important things about the utility of seapower and of navies, and about the nature of war at sea. They help make sense of what otherwise can be a mere historical narrative, although without any obvious distortion of the meaning of events. Lack of understanding at the very general level of analysis of these ten themes promotes inadvertent abuse of historical evidence for the advancement of arguments on contemporary defense issues.

Here, in summary form, are the ten unifying themes presented in the introduction:

1. There are enduring differences between the operational objectives of conflict at sea and conflict on land.
2. The purpose of seapower in war is to influence the course of events on land.
3. In historical reality, seapower and landpower are not abstractions, imbued with the certain essential qualities for combat; instead, they are different forms of power specific to the capabilities of particular states.
4. Military method is different for war at sea as contrasted with war on land.
5. The offense is the stronger form of war at sea.
6. Political and physical geography provide less "friction" in sea war than in war on land.

7. Seapower and landpower have great difficulty reaching each other for the purpose of forcing a clean-cut decision.
8. States tend to rest the military support for their grand strategies upon expectations of the efficacy of their traditional military instrument of excellence—either the army or the navy (with their airpower adjuncts).
9. No state in history has been equally competent in the conduct of sea warfare and land warfare.
10. The United States is a continental-sized maritime power, but it is not a natural sea power.

Strategic theory must never lose touch with its historical, empirical base. Flights of theoretical fancy can always be supported by some historical illustration. The historical record is a very rich storehouse for raiding by the unscrupulous. The case studies in this book have been presented with a determination to avoid a danger outlined by historian John Horsfield.

> . . . a sense of period, chronology, and cultural background must be kept to the forefront in considering naval and military leadership, otherwise we are here with Caesar, there with Napoleon, and somewhere else with Marshal Zhukov, slipping effortlessly, but in a not very informative way, on a historical magic carpet or random package tour.[6]

Time, place, technology, strategic circumstances, and the respective fighting qualities of the tactical instruments all serve to shape the ways in which strategic theory should be applied. A classic example of the relevance of immediate historical detail to the passing of judgment on the conduct of war at sea, is the contrast between Nelson's behavior at Trafalgar and Jellicoe's behavior 111 years later at Jutland. There is only so much that an understanding of the strategic relationship between seapower and landpower, or about the character of maritime strategies best suited to an insular sea power and a continental power, can provide.

At Trafalgar on 21 October 1805, what really mattered was that the Royal Navy had a crushing superiority in gunnery over the Franco-Spanish Combined Fleet (Nelson's ships could fire broadsides in the favorable ratios of between 3:2 and 2:1); the Royal Navy enjoyed a critical advantage in seamanship (as a result of spending years on blockade duty in all weather conditions); and the Royal Navy had a fleet commander who believed in himself, in his ships, in his men, in his plan of attack, and in the ability of his subordinate admirals and captains to improvise in real time in a sound fashion as circumstances might require.

Tactically speaking, according to any general criteria, Trafalgar was a mess. Under pressure of time, weather, and faulty assumptions about the enemy's intentions, plans of attack had to be amended from an endeavor to break the enemy's line in three places, to an assault in two places. The attack with two, rather than three columns (very roughly speaking), meant that some of Nelson's ships came late into the battle. The tactical conception of breaking the enemy's line meant running a gauntlet of fire and was a recipe for disaster against a competent opponent.

Trafalgar illustrates vividly that the validity of particular axioms or principles concerning war at sea depend strongly upon the specific historical context. Nelson's tactics at Trafalgar exploited a well-judged disdain for the competence of the French and Spanish fleets as tactical fighting instruments. Nelson was no great strategist, but he had sufficient vision to see the strategic consequences of destroying the enemy's fleet. He favored any tactic that would maximize the prospect of his being able to wage a battle of annihilation. (This was not a problem at the Nile or at Copenhagen, given that on both of those occasions the enemy fleet was at anchor in very shallow water!)

The Royal Navy functioned strategically in the First World War much as it had in the wars of the French Revolution and Empire. The Grand Fleet at Jutland on 31 May 1916, however, was led by a man who, with some good reason, did not trust his ships or his admirals and captains in what Nelson termed a "pell-mell Battle."[7] More particularly, Jellicoe did not trust his ships and his men in a fleet battle in any save the most advantageous of circumstances against the German High Sea Fleet. Jellicoe proved to be superbly competent as a fleet-handler—twice he crossed the German "T" at Jutland—but he was far more concerned not to lose the battle than he was to find a way of gripping the German fleet for a struggle to annihilation once it was located.

When considering maritime strategy in action across different periods, it is well to remember the most important difference between the twentieth and all past centuries—the lack of realistic experience with the naval tactical instrument in combat. In the apt words of Winston Churchill, comparing Jellicoe at Jutland with Nelson at Trafalgar:

> . . . nothing like this particular event [Jutland] had ever happened before, and nothing like it was ever to happen again. The "Nelson touch" arose from years of fighting between the strongest ships of the time. Nelson's genius enabled him to measure truly the consequences of any decision. But that genius worked upon precise practical data. He had seen the same

sort of thing happen on a less grand scale many times over before the Battle of Trafalgar. Nelson did not have to worry about underwater damage. He felt he knew what would happen in a fleet action. Jellicoe did not know. Nobody knew.[8]

SEAPOWER AND THE HISTORY OF WAR:
SOME POINTERS FOR THE FUTURE

The editors will not risk doing violence to the complexities of the historical cases treated in this book by attempting to summarize a few simple lessons from the history as presented. Instead, we will provide some terse "pointers" on important subjects that have been pervasive throughout many of the chapters, but that could bear being brought more sharply into focus. These "pointers" are complementary to the ten themes of the introduction and, as discussed briefly above, in this concluding chapter.

The character of war. If history teaches anything about armed conflict, it is that war is a unity; when great coalitions collide in combat, they do so in every environment in which it is possible to fight. Should deterrence fail, a future East-West conflict will see war on land, at sea, in the air, and in space. The four environments for contemporary conflict are interdependent. If NATO were to lose the war at sea, that outcome would surely condemn the alliance to defeat on land. Moreover, even limited Soviet success on land on the flanks—as adjuncts to a principal continental campaign that might be stalemated—could contribute massively to the likelihood that NATO would lose the war at sea, and hence ultimately the main campaign for Western Europe.

The wartime activities of the U.S. Navy can make strategic sense only with reference to national, and to coalition, military strategy as a whole.

Grand strategy. Grand strategy is the selection among, and orchestration of, the many instruments of state power for the goals set by high policy. If the principal operational goal of U.S. national security policy is to contain, and preferably to shrink, the geostrategic bounds of the Soviet empire, it is the task of U.S. grand strategy to direct national assets of all kinds to the achievement of that goal. A great offshore (off the Eurasian-continental shore, that is) sea power like the United States, as with Britain before her, wisely has elected to pursue a coalition policy for the encouragement of continental opposition to the continental threat. Like the Royal Navy, the U.S. Navy requires a decisive advantage in military effectiveness at sea over the naval strength of the continental enemy. Such an advantage is essential in order to:

- Deny to the enemy the ability to attack the offshore center of strategic gravity of the Western coalition;
- Safeguard the (sea) lines of communication of the mixed maritime-continental coalition and;
- Grant leverage through the ability to exploit the global flexibility of sea-based power for agile force projection.

The U.S. Navy is one element in the multi-faceted military instrument that is but one of the assets of U.S. statecraft. U.S. military assistance and a modest scale of regional ground-force commitment, set within the diplomatic architecture of a functioning anti-hegemonic coalition, serve importantly to contain the ability of a continental enemy to "put to sea." With ease of geostrategic access to the open ocean, the continental rival could launch a challenge of a severity unparalleled in U.S. history.

National military strategy. A poor fit among plans for the wartime use of the army, the navy, and the air force is not only a theoretical danger—such a condition approximates the norm of the actual historical behavior of states. Very few of the more competent generals and admirals of modern times have been well educated in the proper use of sister services. Nelson's feel for land warfare, on the considerable evidence available, was at least as poor as was Wellington's feel for war at sea. The only practicable solution to the ever-present problems posed by separate, environmentally specific, service military "cultures" was that effected very successfully by Britain and the United States in World War II—namely, coordination. The idea that the inarguable need for a national, overall perspective upon military strategy might be met by creating (through cross-appointment and higher education) a superior, non-service-oriented American Military Person, is romantic nonsense. Experience and common sense suggest overwhelmingly that the unexciting, even prosaic, solution to the difficulties of creating *coherent national military strategy* can lie only through the coordination of the environmental-specific elements of U.S. military power.

In theory, one or two superheroes could emerge who would be able to direct joint strategic planning and execute joint operations with a competence pertaining evenly to all kinds of military power. A country, however, should not design a military organization that can be fought competently only if military genius is in command of the enterprise. Genius always is in short supply, its presence is not reliably identifiable in peacetime, and there are no means to guarantee that it will spring to the forefront in time of war.

Maritime strategy and naval strategy. Such distinguished contemporary theorists as Edward N. Luttwak and Samuel P. Huntington have argued that strategy is about ways of using force; it is not about the kinds of force that are used.[9] Hence, on this algorithm, one can refer to offensive or defensive strategies, but not to conventional or nuclear strategies, or to naval or airpower strategies. This view, leaning upon the universality of strategy as contrasted with the partial focus—and indeed focus upon particular means (as contrasted with methods)— of nuclear, naval, and so forth strategies, is certainly defensible. However, the argument is neither self-evidently persuasive nor useful. Given that strategy is about the purposeful relation of military power to political goals, "maritime strategy" and "naval strategy" stand as terms: hallowed by long usage and, hence, familiarity; blessed with clear meaning; and not at all contradictory to the spirit and content of the concept of strategy in general.

Maritime strategy refers to the purposeful exercise of the sea-using national assets of all kinds for the political goals set by government. *Naval strategy* refers more narrowly to the purposeful exercise of naval forces, again for the political goals set by government.

By this very late stage in the book, readers must have been sensitized to the fact that references to maritime or to naval strategy invite attention to the maritime or the naval *component* in national and coalition military strategy as a whole.

Operational art and regional warfare. In recent years the U.S. and British armies have rediscovered the concept of "operational art." This concept refers to the skills and methods with which a theater campaign is waged. Battles are orchestrated into campaign design by operational art. The concept is valid and important for armed forces operating in a geographically naturally constricted environment, although there are pitfalls for the unwary even with respect to operational-level thinking, planning, and execution for land warfare.

Whether or not operational art for the operational (theater) level of war has validity for naval forces remains to be resolved. The inherent mobility for maneuver of sea-borne platforms, the continuity of the oceans, and the most typically indirect manner in which seapower influences the course of events on land—all sit uneasily with the rather distinctively continentalist notion of a theater-focused, operational level of war.[10] Again, the question in need of answer is not whether it is in some sense "right" to conceive of an operational level of war at sea, but rather, whether it is useful.

Tactics. In chapter 3 tactical competence is described as the engine of strategic possibilities. If a navy cannot win battles, the strategic ends that it can serve are very confined—as the leaders of continental powers with strong navies have discovered over the centuries. A maritime power must be able to win naval battles; nonetheless, as Julian Corbett advised:

> There is no clearer lesson in history how unwise it is to despise and ridicule a naval defensive. Of all strategical attitudes it is the most difficult to meet and the most deeply fraught with danger for the opposing belligerent if he is weak ashore and his enemy strong.[11]

The strategic purpose of a continental coalition most typically has not been to secure a working control of sea lines of communication for the exercise of some variant of "command." Instead, continental powers have been content to inhibit or to deny maritime-dependent coalitions the freedom in use of the sea and diminish critically their sea-based war effort as a consequence. The tactical instrument suitable for such sea harassment (or denial) is radically different in kind from that necessary to challenge the sea power's fighting fleet for command. As naval warfare became three-dimensional in the first half of the twentieth century, command of the surface of the sea conferred less and less direct benefit for the protection of sea lines of communication against the modern tactical offensive instruments of the *guerre de course*—the submarine and the aircraft.

If a country needs to use the seas for positive military purposes, then it has no choice other than to attempt to acquire a battle fleet that, through combat, can win the right to freedom of navigation. Thus far in modern times, no continental power or coalition has succeeded (for long) either in wresting maritime command from offshore seapower (which is not surprising, for the reasons developed in chapter 1), or in prosecuting a war on trade to the point where logistical or financial damage has obliged the sea power to abandon the war on very unfavorable terms. It is not so much that sea harassment or denial *inherently* is inferior as a strategic object to maritime control or command, as it is that no continental power to date has assembled a tactical instrument sufficient in quantity and quality to achieve strategic success.

Technology. In its very nature, naval warfare is high-technology warfare: Moreover, this has always been true. A great naval historian has observed that:

> An ocean-going ship, with her masts and sails, was incomparably the most elaborate mechanism which the mind of man had yet developed.[12]

It is an American cultural trait, flowing from ideas on material progress and from the exigencies of the labor shortage produced by continental expansion, to seek solutions to problems by means of technology. In and of itself, technological advantage over an enemy always is to be welcomed. It can be difficult, however, particularly in the United States with its long-standing love affair with technology, to assess properly, and to prioritize all of the factors that make for tactical effectiveness and hence, possibly, for strategic success. Suffice it to say that great powers in military competition almost invariably stay close enough in relative technological competence—although the complex balance of advantage will be dynamic within a modest range—that technological prowess itself hardly ever can qualify as a prospective war-winning factor.

One should not assert blindly that problems in the past must repeat themselves. Anyone attracted to the notion, however, that weapon systems can be developed that would yield a decisive tactical advantage—ultimately for strategic effect—at least should be aware that there is very little in the history of 2,500 years of naval history that persuasively lends support to such an idea. Ideas and techniques for potentially major technological sources of combat advantage are:

- Developed roughly in parallel by competing states;
- Stolen, copied, and adapted; and,
- Offset—to an ever-important degree—in their implications for tactical success by the opportunity costs attendant upon their acquisition, and by the fact that war supremely is a *combined*-arms and a *man*-machine enterprise.

The future may differ radically from the past, but readers should be alert to the fact that in none of the historical cases discussed in this book was superior seapower traceable to a very significant and lasting technological advantage. The pace of technological change today certainly increases the possibility that a necessarily transient technological edge might yield major combat advantage that could be exploited in action for lasting geopolitical gains. War, however, is a *political* phenomenon. Statesmen have no strong record of going to war because a window of military-technological opportunity appears briefly to have opened.

Logistics and trade. One of the reasons why there is merit in referring to maritime, as contrasted with naval, power or strategy is that the excitement of professional and public interest over issues of prospective combat has a tendency to drive from view an appreciation of the principal purpose of that combat. Justly it has been said that naval power without merchant shipping is like a locomotive without freight or passenger cars. At least that maxim holds true for a maritime-dependent country or coalition. It is not valid for a continental naval power whose strategic ambitions in war at sea are confined to harassment and denial.

Preponderant seapower must both provide logistically for its own sustenance in sea areas often very far removed from home ports, and ensure a flow of mercantile shipping that permits sea-dependent economies to function. That obvious point pertains to the strategic influence of seapower on war. Combat superiority at sea—resting crucially upon battle fleet command—enables a maritime-continental coalition to exploit its economic strengths and function as a combined enterprise. But, to say that war at sea most critically is *about* the protection of maritime transportation through sea control, is not to say anything specific about the methods by which that war should be waged.

Changing technologies, tactics, the balance of material strength, and the specific geographical referents of conflict must influence critically the choice of naval methods by which a working measure of sea control best can be safeguarded. It does not follow as a necessary truth that because the primary wartime duty of the U.S. Navy would be the protection of the North Atlantic and North Pacific sea lines of communication, passive protection measures must be the most appropriate operational activities—e.g., convoy escort, or barrier defenses across geographical choke points.

Convoying has a very long and very distinguished history of practical success. Its necessity, however, has been a function of the anticipated or demonstrated intensity of the raiding threat. If the raiders could be burned out in their bases, bombed in their pens, or reliably intercepted before they were loose on, under, or over the high seas, then there would be scant necessity for the local and immediate naval protection of seaborne logistics and trade. There are no eternal truths of sea warfare on this subject.

Professionalism and tradition. Chapter 12 made the point that great fighting navies, as contrasted with mere collections of ships, are founded upon the achievements of generations of sailors. Admiral Andrew B. Cunningham, the most distinguished "fighting admiral" of the Royal Navy in World War II, is reported to have said of the commitment of the navy to evacuate British soldiers from Crete in 1941:

> Stick it out, we must never let the Army down. . . [then he proceeded to observe that] although it took the Navy three years to build a new ship it would take three hundred years to build a new tradition.[13]

Fighting forces that lack confidence in themselves tend not to fare well in combat. Expectations of defeat function as a self-fulfilling prophecy. A tradition of excellence in war, on land or at sea, is neither the accidental product of a single inspired combat performance, nor can it be fabricated convincingly by the rewriting of history. Inevitably, and for the most pressing of reasons, continental powers are obliged to be proficient in land warfare, whereas sea powers are obliged to excel in maritime conflict. Particular circumstances can enable a great continental power to assemble a large and even a very proficient fleet—as Germany demonstrated in the period from 1900 to 1918, and as the Soviet Union may achieve—while sea powers have been known to have competent and highly capable armies. Yet, a sea power does not develop its national landward fighting instrument with a view to its being charged, unaided, with the defeat of a continental enemy in the field. Similarly, a continental power, so long as it remains confronted by major landward security problems, does not require of its naval forces that they be capable of challenging the main battle fleet of a sea-power enemy to stand-up combat.

Although traditions of excellence and reputations for success can be lost, they are not necessarily lost simply as a consequence of military defeat. As an obvious example, Germany lost both the world wars of this century, but the reputation for superior fighting power enjoyed by the German Army has not been diminished notably as a consequence of that repeated fact. The reason, of course, is that observers agree that the German Army turned in superior performances in the field—in contexts that its political superiors had so crafted as to render victory impossible.

The all-time peak of professional competence in the Royal Navy probably was achieved in the middle years of the wars of the French Revolution and Empire. Incomparable sea-time, shared doctrine, understanding of the tactical possibilities accorded by existing technologies, and a century of success in war at sea (against the same enemy), yielded a tradition of victory that tended to feed positively on itself, just as frank recognition of these facts tended to demoralize the enemy.

Chapter authors have emphasized the fact that the offensive is the stronger form of war at sea. Whatever may be said on behalf of defensive strategies for war at sea—and a great deal can be said on their behalf for disadvantaged navies—it is exceedingly difficult to turn around a navy habituated to the fearful, if prudent, avoidance of fleet-scale engagements and require that it take the offensive and succeed. Apart from the superior seamanship and advantages in tactical fleet-handling enjoyed by the U.S. Navy over its typically port-bound Soviet adversary, that U.S. Navy is imbued with an offensive spirit that rests solidly on a tradition of successful conduct of offensive war at sea. If Moscow ever should ask of its navy that it serve as the cutting edge of a Soviet Union determined no longer to be continentally confined in its grand strategy, that navy would have no historical resources of important achievement upon which to draw for its radical reorientation.

Finally, one should never forget the importance of moral factors in war. Other things being about equal, the will to win is a reliably critical quality. A tradition of success in the offensive conduct of war at sea fosters that will to win. A tradition of failure, or even simply of relative inactivity in the defensive conduct of war at sea, is not the foundation upon which a navy second-to-none in tactical fighting power for strategic purposes can be built.

SEAPOWER AND STRATEGY:
FIGHTING POWER AND STRATEGIC EFFECTIVENESS

Many defense professionals, although firm in the sound opinion that maritime, land, air, and missile (and space), power must be applied in concert, according to a *joint* framework of military planning, still have difficulty identifying a common currency that makes sense, say, of the maritime contribution to the national security. That common currency should be thought of as *strategic effectiveness*—a value that can be produced by military power of all kinds. Again and again in this book authors have emphasized the fact that as a matter of politics and strategy war is one, it is a unity. War is waged by different tactical means and methods, for different kinds of military objectives, in the four different geographical environments. Ultimately, however, a state requires strategic effectiveness of its military instruments, be they maritime, land, or whatever. Policymakers do not wish to win a war at sea as an end in itself. Instead, they wish to use victory at sea (for example), in a wide variety of ways, for the purpose of influencing the will and the ability of the enemy to continue his war-making efforts.

Superior fighting power, or tactical effectiveness, is a quality essential if the military means are to be capable of bearing ambitious traffic in the realm of policy ends. Yet, fighting power bears a quantitative as well as a qualitative figure of relative merit, and its utility for the national security easily can be vitiated if policy and strategy ask too much of it. Ship for ship, the capital units of the German High Sea Fleet of 1916 almost certainly generated more fighting power than did their British counterparts. The German problem was that they had too few of such superior capital ships. To continue with this example, in principle the potential strategic effectiveness of the German High Sea Fleet, and indeed of the U-boats, was far greater than was the potential strategic effectiveness of the Royal Navy's Grand Fleet. Germany, fighting against an increasingly sea-dependent enemy coalition, could have won the war on a whole through victorious seapower. For its part, the Allies could only use victory at sea to enable the war as a whole to be won by eventual success on land.

Strategic questions are means-ends questions. The concept of strategic effectiveness provides the common denominator by which contributions to national security made by armed services specialized for combat in particular geographical environments can be weighed.

ENVOI

The "themes" and the "pointers for the future" on important topics have been developed to help readers interrogate what otherwise may be formless raw material as they delve into naval history. A considerable cumulative wisdom is available for understanding the subjects of the effective uses of seapower, broadly, and of naval forces, narrowly. The beginning of wisdom has to be with the formulation of useful questions. Those questions provide the framework upon which education can proceed. The historical and theoretical analyses in this book have been designed to provide insight upon the nature, and particularly upon the purposes, of war at sea.

In the spirit of scholarly enquiry, although of scholarly enquiry with practical relevance, this work will conclude with a brief listing illustrative of the more important questions that pertain to maritime strategy.

- What is the strategic utility of a navy: (a) to a sea power or a maritime coalition; (b) to a continental power or coalition?
- By what "system of war" do preponderant land powers and preponderant sea powers endeavor to engage each other to achieve a favorable decision—given the difficulty that each has in reaching the strategic center of gravity of the other?
- How robust are the national advantages of continental powers in land warfare, and of sea powers in war at sea?
- How should the different characters of national or coalition geopolitical circumstance manifest themselves in alternative kinds of maritime strategy?
- What are the relationships of mutual dependence among technology, tactics, strategy, and grand strategy? Is any one of these levels of analysis truly in the driver's seat?
- What elements, in what relationship, make for excellence in a navy?

Readers should now be well equipped to address these questions in the particular contexts of immediate concern to them.

NOTES

1. Carl von Clausewitz, *On War*, Michael Howard and Peter Paret, eds. (Princeton, NJ: Princeton University Press, 1976; first pub. 1832), p. 141.

2. Ibid.

3. Michael Howard, *The Causes of Wars and Other Essays* (London: Counterpoint, 1984; first pub. 1983), pp. 214–15.

4. Clausewitz, *On War*, p. 141. Emphasis in the original.

5. *Ibid.*, pp. 119–21.

6. John Horsfield, *The Art of Leadership in War: The Royal Navy from the Age of Nelson to the End of World War II* (Westport, CT: Greenwood Press, 1980), p. 10.

7. John Terraine, *Trafalgar* (New York: Mason/Charter, 1976; first pub. 1975), p. 132.

8. Winston S. Churchill, *The World Crisis* (New York: Charles Scribner's, 1931), p. 631. In fact, Jellicoe had grave suspicions that, ship-for-ship, his fleet probably was at a technical disadvantage in battle with the Germans—hence the rigidity of his Grand Fleet Battle Orders, designed to enable him to fight his fleet as a truly united force, lest it be beaten in detail.

9. Edward N. Luttwak, *Strategy: The Logic of War and Peace* (Cambridge, MA: Harvard University Press, 1987), chap. 11; and Samuel P. Huntington, "U.S. Defense Strategy: The Strategic Innovations of the Reagan Years," in Joseph Kruzel, ed., *American Defense Annual, 1987–1988* (Lexington, MA: Lexington Books, 1987), pp. 35–39.

10. See Luttwak, *Strategy*, chap. 7.

11. Julian S. Corbett, *England in the Seven Years' War: A Study in Combined Strategy*, vol. 2 (New York: AMS Press, 1973; first pub. 1907), pp. 373–74.

12. Laird G. Clowes, quoted in Geoffrey J. Marcus, *Heart of Oak: A Survey of British Seapower in the Georgian Era* (New York: Oxford University Press, 1975), p. 10.

13. Quoted in Peter Kemp, "Cunningham," in Sir Michael Carver, *The War Lords: Military Commanders of the Twentieth Century* (Boston: Little, Brown & Co., 1976), p. 467.

BIBLIOGRAPHIC NOTE

Just as there are very many more people who think about ships than about seapower, so there is much more written about seapower than there is about how seapower contributes to national or coalition military strategy. General works of strategic theory are rarer still. The following is a very short, annotated list of works that endeavor, with differing degrees of success, to provide "big picture" understanding of the subjects relevant to seapower and strategy.

ADDITIONAL SOURCES

Booth, Ken. *Navies and Foreign Policy.* New York: Crane Russak, 1977. A rare book that delivers most of what its title promises.

Clausewitz, Karl Von. *On War*. Incomparable penetration on the character of war in general and particularly on the relationship between war and politics. But Clausewitz has nothing to say about the connections between the land and the sea in the conduct of war.

Corbett, Sir Julian S. *Some Principles of Maritime Strategy*. Annapolis, MD: Naval Institute Press, 1988; first pub. 1911. Less dogmatic and reductionist than Mahan, and a fund of practical, history-based wisdom on the utility of maritime power.

Gray, Colin S. *Theories of Victory: Strategy, Statecraft, and War*. New York: Simon and Schuster, 1989. A wide-ranging study that emphasizes the unity of conflict.

Huntington, Samuel P. *American Military Strategy*. Policy Papers in International Affairs No. 28. Berkeley, CA: Institute of International Studies, University of California, Berkeley, 1986. A controversial, but always insightful, examination of the content and making of U.S. strategy "in the round."

Kennedy, Paul. *The Rise and Fall of the Great Powers: Economic Change and Military Conflict from 1500 to 2000*. New York: Random House, 1987. Kennedy's discussion of the contemporary United States makes an easy mark for criticism, but the book is very valuable as a sustained exercise in empirically rooted strategic thinking.

Luttwak, Edward N. *Strategy*. Unduly reductionist in its general thesis about the paradoxical nature of conflict and superficial in its treatment of maritime matters. Nonetheless, the book is a major theoretical achievement and will probably, in time, be considered a classic.

Millett, Allan R., and Williamson Murray, eds. *Military Effectiveness*, 3 vols. London: George Allen and Unwin, 1988. Covering the performance of the major participants in the First World War, the interwar period, and the Second World War, these three volumes comprise the outstanding military historical enterprise of recent years.

Paret, Peter, ed. *Makers of Modern Strategy: From Machiavelli to the Nuclear Age*. Princeton, NJ: Princeton University Press, 1986. Suffers from a lack of directing vision and "grip," and painfully weak on maritime subjects, but still a rich treasure house for selective enrichment.

Wylie, J. C. *Military Strategy: A General Theory of Power Control*. Westport, CT: Greenwood Press, 1980; first pub. 1967. An under-recognized classic that takes a truly joint, or combined-arms, view of its subject.

Index

The **Naval Institute Press** is the book-publishing arm of the U.S. Naval Institute, a private, nonprofit professional society for members of the sea services and civilians who share an interest in naval and maritime affairs. Established in 1873 at the U.S. Naval Academy in Annapolis, Maryland, where its offices remain today, the Naval Institute has more than 100,000 members worldwide.

Members of the Naval Institute receive the influential monthy naval magazine *Proceedings* and substantial discounts on fine nautical prints, ship and aircraft photos, and subscriptions to the Institute's recently inaugurated quarterly, *Naval History*. They also have access to the transcripts of the Institute's Oral History Program and may attend any of the Institute-sponsored seminars regularly offered around the country.

The book-publishing program, begun in 1898 with basic guides to naval practices, has broadened its scope in recent years to include books of more general interest. Now the Naval Institute Press publishes more than forty new titles each year, ranging from how-to books on boating and navigation to battle histories, biographies, ship guides, and novels. Institute members receive discounts on the Press's more than 300 books.

For a free catalog describing books currently available and for further information about U.S. Naval Institute membership, please write to:

Membership Department
U.S. Naval Institute
Annapolis, Maryland 21402

or call, toll-free, 800–233–USNI.